HANDBOOK FOR SCOUTMASTERS

A Manual of Troop Leadership

FOURTH EDITION

Ninth Printing, 1955

COPYRIGHT 1947 BY

BOY SCOUTS OF AMERICA

NATIONAL COUNCIL   NEW BRUNSWICK, N. J.

No. 3500 -- $1.00   Printed in U.S.A.   40M1255

THE SCOUT OATH

On my honor I will do my best—

1. To do my duty to God and my Country, and to obey the Scout Law;
2. To help other people at all times;
3. To keep myself physically strong, mentally awake, and morally straight.

THE SCOUT LAW

1. A Scout is TRUSTWORTHY.

A Scout's honor is to be trusted. If he were to violate his honor by telling a lie, or by cheating, or by not doing exactly a given task, when trusted on his honor, he may be directed to hand over his Scout Badge.

2. A Scout is LOYAL.

He is loyal to all to whom loyalty is due—his Scout leader, his home, and parents and country.

3. A Scout is HELPFUL.

He must be prepared at any time to save life, help injured persons, and share the home duties. He must do at least one "Good Turn" to somebody every day.

4. A Scout is FRIENDLY.

He is a friend to all and a brother to every other Scout.

5. A Scout is COURTEOUS.

He is polite to all, especially to women, children, old people, and the weak and helpless. He must not take pay for being helpful or courteous.

6. A Scout is KIND.

He is a friend to animals. He will not kill nor hurt any living creature needlessly, but will strive to save and protect all harmless life.

7. A Scout is OBEDIENT.

He obeys his parents, Scoutmaster, Patrol Leader, and all other duly constituted authorities.

8. A Scout is CHEERFUL.

He smiles whenever he can. His obedience to orders is prompt and cheery. He never shirks nor grumbles at hardships.

9. A Scout is THRIFTY.

He does not wantonly destroy property. He works faithfully, wastes nothing, and makes the best use of his opportunities. He saves his money so that he may pay his own way, be generous to those in need and helpful to worthy objects.

He may work for pay, but must not receive tips for courtesies or "Good Turns."

10. A Scout is BRAVE.

He has the courage to face danger in spite of fear, and to stand up for the right against the coaxings of friends or the jeers or threats of enemies, and defeat does not down him.

11. A Scout is CLEAN.

He keeps clean in body and thought, stands for clean speech, clean sports, clean habits, and travels with a clean crowd.

12. A Scout is REVERENT.

He is reverent toward God. He is faithful in his religious duties, and respects the convictions of others in matters of custom and religion.

FOREWORD

We take great satisfaction in presenting this edition of the *Handbook for Scoutmasters,* a practical manual of Troop leadership. It was developed from the experiences of thousands of Scouters, and to the many in the Field and to others who have contributed suggestions and criticism we give thanks.

The manuscript was written by WILLIAM HILL-COURT, National Director of Scoutcraft—himself a long active Scoutmaster.

The well-known Scout artist, REMINGTON SCHUY-LER, contributed the drawings for this book. Most of the photographs were taken by MARSHALL SPAAN, NEIL MACDONALD and CLINTON MARTIN, and to the Scouts of TROOP 1, MENDHAM, N. J., is due a special vote of thanks for unflinching service as subjects for the camera.

We are indebted especially to WILLIAM E. LAW-RENCE, FRED C. MILLS and WES H. KLUSMANN for technical criticism and advice. Format of the book is the work of DON ROSS. Others, particularly JOHN TED-FORD and A. HEMLER, gave much editorial assistance.

To the Scoutmasters of our many thousands of Troops and to their teammates, the Assistant Scoutmasters, we dedicate this handbook. We sincerely trust that it will prove a valuable tool in their service to boyhood.

C O N T E N T S

PART TWO

The Scoutmaster's SECOND Job:
Helping each individual BOY to grow

Introduction

SCOUTING AND
SCOUTMASTERSHIP

THE AIM OF SCOUTING

SCOUTING trains for CITIZENSHIP

by inculcating in the boy, from within instead of from without, the qualities of

Character
Health and Strength
Handcraft and Skill
Service to Others

THE METHODS OF SCOUTING

SCOUTING is a game

The Scout Way
(1) A Game, NOT a Science

played by boys in boy gangs

Patrol Method
(2) The Scout Patrol

under boy leaders chosen by the gang,

(3) Boy Leadership

guided by a man

Men in Scouting
(4) The Scoutmaster

backed by other men of the community.

(5) Troop Committee and Local Council Scouters

SCOUTING provides the boy with an active outdoor life,

Activities
(6) Adventure in the Out-of-Doors

grants him recognition for mastering various skills, and

(7) Scout Advancement

gives him a chance to wear an attractive Uniform.

Uniform
(8) The Scout Uniform

It holds before him the ideals of a true Scout, and

Ideals and Service
(9) The Scout Law

encourages him to "help other people at all times."

(10) The Scout Oath or Promise—Service: Good Turns

WHAT SCOUTING IS

WHY DO BOYS by the millions flock into the world-wide brotherhood of Scouting?

Because they **want** Scouting!

Because the founder of the Scout Movement had the genius to give youth a picture of the ideal boy—a picture which appealed to the imagination and captured the hearts of boyhood around the world.

If it were only possible to swing the gates of Scouting wide open, and show you in one immense view, the full panorama of the Scout Movement! Under the open sky you would see a milling mass of wide-awake boys, busily occupied with a multitude of self-appointed tasks—all of them living, breathing, absorbing Scouting.

The boys swarm around you, and as one of them runs by, you ask him: "Tell me, what **is** Scouting?"

As the boy passes, his smile and his answer come back: "Scouting is **fun!**"

You bend over a boy who seems to have forgotten his surroundings, completely absorbed in preparing a simple outdoor meal, and ask him the same question.

And the boy answers as he looks up wonderingly: "Scouting is **adventure!**"

A gang of Scouts, led by one of their number, comes running, and as they draw near their answer sings out: "Scouting is **comradeship!**"

Thus the boys define their activity, their game.

And **GAME**—that's the word!

SCOUTING IS A GAME

Yes, to a boy **Scouting is a game**—a wonderful game, full of play and full of laughter, keeping him busy, keeping him happy. Scouting is "learning by doing" things that are enjoyable, exciting things!

That's the strength of Scouting! A boy becomes a Scout for the sheer joy there is in it.

To you and me Scouting is a game, too—but it is more than a game of fun. To us, it is **a game with a purpose**—the purpose of helping boys to become men, training them for citizenship. **Training for citizenship—that's the aim of Scouting.**

CITIZENSHIP—well, what **is** citizenship? Instead of seeking a definition in the cold words of a dictionary, perhaps you'd better do some defining yourself. Close your eyes a moment and think of the people you know whom you consider "good citizens." What makes them that, in your estimation? Isn't it a matter of fine character, of ability, of the way they go about helping other people?

Now think of the boys in the Troop—think of them as Bob and John and Joe. Then consider citizenship in terms of **things to do** which will help Bob and John and Joe become the kind of men you would want sons of yours to be.

Then see to it that the boys get those values by giving them Scouting. See to it that each boy, through the give-and-take of group living and doing things that appeal to him, has the chance to develop himself into a MAN — **fine in character, healthy in body, skillful with his hands and keen of mind, ready to be of help to other people.**

To reach your aim of training boys for citizenship, boys must stay in Scouting long enough for Scout **ideals** to become a part of their everyday thinking and living. And the way to make them stay is to give them what they want.

So, in everything you do with those boys of yours, keep in mind that they joined Scouting for fun and fellowship. They expect to have a grand time with a lot of good friends.

Make Scouting the happy game it is! Keep it simple—keep it enjoyable.

SCOUTING IS A GAME WITH A PURPOSE

Character

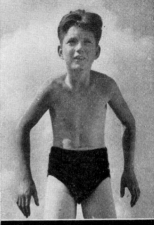

Health and Strength

Handcraft and Skill

Service to Others

THE PATROL METHOD

THE SCOUT PATROL

Boys want companionship. They want to have fun with other fellows. They want to feel that they "belong." And so they travel in gangs—their own gangs, under their own leadership.

This boys' gang becomes the Scout **PATROL—a small group of boys working together under the leadership of one of their own number.** The Patrol is the unit of Scouting, whether for work or for play, for duty or for discipline.

In the Scout Patrol you have democracy at work on a small scale. The boys choose the leader they want to follow. They plan their own activities and carry them out together. They learn Scoutcraft according to their individual abilities and desires.

In the good Patrol, gang spirit—Patrol Spirit—is steadily at work producing a whole-hearted participation of all the members. The life in the Patrol creates in its Scouts a strong feeling of comradeship, of obedience to a common cause, and the willingness to help and share so necessary in life.

BOY LEADERSHIP

The **PATROL LEADER,** elected by the boys themselves, encourages and assists his Scouts to train themselves in Scoutcraft. Besides, he helps to plan and carry out the program of the **TROOP,** which is simply a group of Patrols—two, three, four or more—working, playing, hiking and camping together.

The leadership involved sounds like quite a responsibility for a boy. But he can carry it, provided he feels that his Scoutmaster stands behind him, ready to guide and train him, and just as ready to trust and depend on him to carry through.

This guidance and training of the boy leader is given in the **PATROL LEADERS' COUNCIL** where the Patrol Leaders meet with the Scoutmaster and the other leaders of the Troop. **The Patrol Leaders' Council is the heart of the Patrol Method** which, as Baden-Powell says, "is not so much to save trouble for the Scoutmaster as to give responsibility to the boy — since this is the very best of all means of developing character."

THE PATROL METHOD

The Scout Patrol

Boy Leadership

THE MEN IN SCOUTING

THE SCOUTMASTER

The **SCOUTMASTER** is the KEY MAN in Scouting. The effectiveness of the program depends upon this volunteer—on his understanding of Scouting, on his enthusiasm and energy, and on the quality of his efforts. He shows the Patrols the road ahead, and as the boys work toward the goal, each Patrol grows strong, and through the Patrols the Troop prospers.

The Scoutmaster's job is not an easy one. However, it isn't nearly as difficult as it may appear on the surface, particularly if he has efficient **ASSISTANT SCOUTMASTERS** and cooperation of an **EXPLORER ADVISOR** working with the Explorers—those members of the Troop who are fourteen and older.

To be a successful Scoutmaster, you are not expected to spend weary hours on the details of running the Troop. **A Scoutmaster's job is to train and guide boy leaders to run THEIR Troop, NOT to run HIS Troop HIMSELF.** By placing the leadership where it belongs—with the boys—you will have time to plan ahead for the Troop and the chance to get close to the heart and mind of each boy.

Furthermore, you don't have to be an expert in every Scoutcraft subject. **A Scoutmaster's job is to help boys grow by encouraging them to learn for themselves, NOT to instruct individual boys in Scoutcraft.**

TROOP COMMITTEE AND COMMISSIONER

You have the backing of a group of men who are pledged to help you. They are the **TROOP COMMITTEE**—three or more men picked by the institution or group of citizens that sponsors the Troop. The Troop Committee handles mostly those Troop matters which do not require direct boy contact, so that you may concentrate all your efforts on working with the boys. An **INSTITUTIONAL REPRESENTATIVE** is the head of Scouting in the institution and a member of the **DISTRICT COMMITTEE** and **LOCAL COUNCIL.**

In your District you will find a Commissioner who is ready to help you at any time. Like yourself, he is a volunteer, interested in your success as a Scoutmaster. The Commissioners in your District conduct monthly Roundtables to give you program ideas and skills.

THE MEN IN SCOUTING

The Scoutmaster

Troop Committee and Commissioner

THE ACTIVITIES OF BOY SCOUTING

ADVENTURE IN THE OUT-OF-DOORS

"By the term **SCOUTING**," says Baden-Powell, "is meant the work and attributes of backwoodsmen, explorers, hunters, seamen, airmen, pioneers and frontiersmen." The word "Scout" opens up to the boy the picture of open spaces, woods, rivers, lakes, mountains which are to be his playground and where he will have his fun.

It is this promise of adventure, of camping and life in the outdoors that lures the boy into Scouting. We **must** keep faith with him by giving him that adventure—not just to satisfy him, but because it is the best way we have of holding him.

So, get the Patrols away from the meeting room and into the out-of-doors. Send the boys hiking through the woods and over the mountains. Take them camping in the wilderness. Have fun with them around the camp fire.

SCOUT ADVANCEMENT

As a boy learns the hiking and camping skills that a Scout is supposed to know, he receives recognition for his efforts by advancing in the first three **SCOUT RANKS**—Tenderfoot, Second Class, then First Class.

The **MERIT BADGE** subjects give the boy further opportunities. They encourage him to learn crafts and hobbies and outdoor skills. By earning Merit Badges, the boy continues his upward climb in Scouting towards the ranks of Star, Life and Eagle Scout.

"BE PREPARED" is the **SCOUT MOTTO.** By meeting the Scout requirements, a boy prepares himself to stand on his own feet and to be helpful to others—to render service as a Scout.

THE SCOUT UNIFORM

The **SCOUT UNIFORM** is part of the romance of Scouting. It is a symbol of the ideals and outdoor activities of our Movement.

A boy likes to have a uniform to wear, with badges to show his rank—it gives him pride in his appearance. Besides, a uniform helps him to feel that he belongs, that he is truly a member of the Patrol and the Troop and our great World Brotherhood, on the same level with all other Scouts. In this way, the Scout Uniform helps to foster true democracy within the Troop

THE ACTIVITIES OF SCOUTING

Adventure in the Outdoors • Advancement

THE SCOUT UNIFORM

THE IDEALS OF SCOUTING

THE SCOUT LAW

The **SCOUT LAW** is the foundation of the Scout Movement It expresses the ideal toward which we guide the boy in making himself a man of high character.

The Scout Law is based upon the codes of old, but it transforms them into a positive, living ideal for the modern boy. Most laws start with a "Do" or a "Don't," with a "You must" or "You musn't"—they either command or prohibit. The Scout Law does neither. It is a simple statement of fact, of what is expected of a Scout: "A Scout **IS** Trustworthy, Loyal, Helpful. . . " The Law, then, serves as a guide by which the boy can measure his everyday actions.

By keeping this guide before each boy from the minute you receive him into Scouting, and by inspiring him to show his loyalty to his Scout ideals, you slowly develop in the boy a desire to prove himself a true Scout. Your own personal example is of tremendous importance here. If you live the Law yourself, your boys are more likely to live it.

THE SCOUT OATH—SERVICE: GOOD TURNS

The Scout Law expresses what a boy IS, but it is what he DOES that proves how much the Law has become a part of his life.

The day he becomes a Scout, a boy takes the **SCOUT OATH or PROMISE** and makes the pledge: "On my honor, I will DO my best . . . to help other people at all times . . ." He accepts the Scout obligation to "DO A GOOD TURN DAILY."

These small **GOOD TURNS** are the boy's first steps toward service to others. They lead him naturally on, as Baden-Powell says, "to learn first aid and help to the injured. Then, in the natural sequence of learning how to save life in the case of accident, he develops a sense of duty to others and a readiness to sacrifice himself in danger."

By encouraging the boy to replace Self with Service to Others, you aid him in fulfilling his promise "to do my duty to God and my country," and help him to become an active citizen, ready to do his part for the good of his fellow man.

THE IDEALS OF SCOUTING

The Scout Law

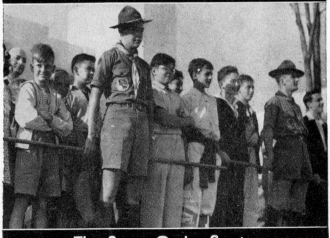

The Scout Oath • Service

THE SCOUTMASTER

by

Edgar A. Guest

There isn't any pay for you, you serve without reward,
The boys who tramp the fields with you but little
    could afford,
And yet your pay is richer far than those who toil
    for gold,
For in a dozen different ways your service shall be
    told.

You'll read it in the faces of a Troop of growing boys,
You'll read it in the pleasure of a dozen manly joys,
And down the distant future—you will surely read
    it then,
Emblazoned thru the service of a band of loyal men.

Five years of willing labor and of brothering a Troop,
Five years of trudging highways, with the Indian cry
    and whoop,
Five years of camp fires burning, not alone for pleas-
    ure's sake,
But the future generation which the boys are soon to
    make.

They have no gold to give you, but when age comes
    on to you
They'll give you back the splendid things you taught
    them how to do,
They'll give you rich contentment and a thrill of hon-
    est pride
And you'll see your nation prosper, and you'll all be
    satisfied.

The Boy,
the man, and
the job

HONESTLY NOW: Why did you become a Scoutmaster—a job that involves thought, effort and
time?

Can it be that you are a Scoutmaster because you
realize that, through Scouting, you can help these boys
of ours—these wild Indians, mischievous youngsters,
studious bookworms—grow into better men than they
would otherwise be? Can it be that the outdoors is a
great hobby of yours? Can it be that being with boys
gives you a lift in your own existence? Or is it a

combination of these things that made you agree to become a Scoutmaster?

Whatever the reason, you must have seen in Scoutmastership the challenge to do a worth-while job. Somehow or other, there must be in your mind—however vague—a picture of values to be accomplished, something to help boys as they grow into men.

Boys growing into men . . . that's it, isn't it? Not just growing up, but growing into citizens the community can be proud of.

THE BOY

Who is this boy we're talking about?

He is a human being, an *individual* — never forget *that!* He is eleven years old or older. He is no longer a child, nor yet a man. He has reached that turbulent stage between childhood and manhood where physical changes, urges and instincts within him sometimes tear and pull and leave him no peace.

Most of the time he doesn't even understand himself. He has his ups and downs of enthusiasm and despair. One moment he is rarin' to go out to conquer the world. The next moment he wishes only to be left alone, to lie on his back and watch the clouds overhead. One minute he is full of unbounded energy and determina-

"A Boy Scout is a boy 11, 12 or 13 years of age who has met the requirements and accepted the obligations of a Tenderfoot Scout and has been enrolled with the consent of his parent, guardian or other responsible adult in the Boy Scouts of America"—*From the By-Laws of the Boy Scouts of America.*

The BOY is the reason for Scouting. Our aim is to help him become the best kind of MAN he aspires to be.

tion. The next he is listless and ill at ease and tired—"lazy," the adults call it. One hour he is bubbling over with happiness, full of high spirits as he goes tearing down the street. The next he is grouchy, depressed, irritable.

He is a creature of a hundred contradictions.

And yet, there are certain tendencies, wishes and wants in him that drive him on. They are parts of his nature as a boy. We can serve him best if we try to understand them, so that we may satisfy them, mold and direct them toward Scouting's aim: good citizenship.

What Makes Him Tick?

First of all, the boy wants to be in with the gang, to feel that he is an important part of it, that he "belongs," that he is accepted. He wants to share in the work and the play of the gang—to give the gang his loyalty.

He wants to stand on his own feet, to make decisions, to show his independence and initiative. He dreams of being a leader.

He wants action and fun. He wants to be in the thick of things, to run and play and fight, to be on the move.

He craves adventure, a change of surroundings. He wants to experience new things in new ways, to feel the wind in his hair, the sun in his eyes. He wants to escape, to get away from his everyday life.

He wants to find out about things. He experiments. He makes things, takes things apart and puts them together again. He wants to see "what makes them work."

He wants to assert himself, to do things he considers worth-while, to show his pals how good he is. He wants to have his efforts recognized, approved and appreciated.

He wants to look up to somebody. His idealism is slowly awakening. He wants a hero to admire and follow and imitate.

But also, when this boy comes to us, he is in the midst of a period of rapid growth and great physical

"A Scoutmaster shall be at least twenty-one years of age and shall be chosen because of good moral character and his interest in work for boys. . . . He, with the cooperation of the Troop Committee, is responsible for the general program and supervision of the work of the Troop." *By-Laws, BSA.* Badge: silver, green.

change. He is clumsy and awkward. His bones are growing so fast that his untrained muscles have trouble handling them. "What will crash now?" is the standing question people ask when he enters a room. His heart is increasing in size—it skips a beat from time to time. His sex organs are maturing. He has new feelings of wonder and fear. His voice is changing—the same old vocal cords give off unfamiliar sounds that often embarrass him. He is a mixture of strength and weakness, energy and inertia, aggression and submission. In short, he is that puzzling individual known as a BOY!

Helping the Boy Grow

We must take him as we find him and help him grow into the man he hopes to be, by using what he has and what skill we have to help him grow into his best possible self.

We must remember that Scouting does not have the sole responsibility for helping the boy become a man. Much of the responsibility—most of it—rests with his home, his church, his school. They have their special functions. We can help the boy by helping them.

Then, in our work with the boy, let us stress the values that Scouting experiences can help him get.

Our best ally in working with him is the boy himself.

He comes to us because he wants to, not because he has to—often with his interest at white heat. He wants to join; he wants to become a Scout—he wants to scout!

The boy's interest—that's our key to helping him. Interest in what? Certainly not primarily in our aim of citizenship training. It would be an abnormal boy who would come around to Troop meetings week after week to get himself trained in citizenship. No, the boy's interest is in the GANG he is going to join, in the FUN he is going to have, the outdoor thrills of hikes and camp. Those values are what he comes for. And they are what we must help him get. The Scouting adventures he expects!

By making sure that he gets pure, unadulterated Scouting, we come closest to reaching our goal. By helping him "learn by doing," we give him a chance to acquire Scouting skills that will make him self-reliant, strong and helpful. We encourage him to practice good citizenship in his Patrol and in the Troop, to get along with others, to play fair.

THE MAN

The kind of Scouting a boy receives depends greatly upon his Scoutmaster. The Scoutmaster is the greatest single force affecting all of Scouting. As the Scoutmaster succeeds, our whole Movement succeeds. His enthusiasm and energy and personal example are the driving powers.

As a Scoutmaster, you have a great responsibility— but it is a responsibility that is easy to carry, if you go about it the simple way, with joy in your heart.

Stradivari, the great violin builder, is quoted as having said:

"If my hands slack, I would rob God—for God cannot make Stradivarian violins without Stradivari."

So a Scoutmaster gives his best—for otherwise he would rob his boys of opportunities to grow. He thinks Scouting every day, figures out ways and means of improving the Troop influence. He enjoys the out-of-doors. He hikes with his boys, camps with them. He is enthusiastic with his Scouts about all that Scouting has to offer and is therefore accepted as one of them instead of as a leader on a pedestal.

This enthusiasm for Scouting should bubble up in all your contacts with boys. "Scouting is a game"—

The Scoutmaster holds the key. The kind of Scouting a boy receives depends on this leader's enthusiasm and ability.

and it should be just as enjoyable to you as to your boys.

So, approach Scouting with a smile. Laugh with your boys and live Scouting with them. Be like an older brother, setting out with them on an exciting journey. And pick up Scouting skills with them as you travel along.

A Leader of Boys

To one who doesn't know, the qualifications for Scoutmastership may seem appalling. But to be successful, a Scoutmaster doesn't have to be a "know-it-all." His job is not to teach the whole subject matter of Scouting to a group of youngsters, but to lead boys —which is something entirely different.

He leads by helping his boys to help each other—

TEN ESSENTIALS OF
SCOUTMASTERSHIP

•

A belief in boys that will make you want to invest yourself and your time on their behalf.

A zeal focused upon one point—the boy's happiness through his formative years—"A happy boy is a good boy, a good boy is a good citizen."

An immense faith in Scouting as *the* program that will best serve to mould our youth into fine men.

A realization that to the boys Scouting is a game— to you, a game with a purpose: Character building, citizenship training and physical fitness.

A knowledge that to your boys *you* are Scouting. "What you are speaks so loud that I cannot hear what you say!"

A steadfastness of purpose to carry out a planned program with energy and perseverance, patience and good humor.

A willingness to submerge yourself and make boy leaders lead and grow through an effective application of the Patrol Method.

A desire to advance in Scoutmastership by making use of training offered and material available on the subject.

A readiness to work hand in hand with home, church, sponsoring institution, school, Local Council, National Council for the good of the individual boy and the community as a whole.

A love of the outdoors in all its phases and a vision of the hand that created it.

by encouraging cooperation and teamwork, by strengthening the hand of his Patrol Leaders, so that each boy may have the best possible Scouting experience as a member of a strong and active Patrol, an ambitious Troop.

He leads by helping each boy to help himself. A Scoutmaster has a buoyant interest in boys—in their happiness, in their future. He searches out each boy's characteristics and habits in order to understand him. He makes each boy feel that he has his welfare at heart. He encourages each boy in his Scout activities. He leads through his own example—by living the same Scout Oath and Law he expects his boys to live.

THE JOB

And there, in the last two paragraphs, you have the simple approach to Scoutmastership: First, helping the boy, *as a member of the group,* to a joyful Patrol and Troop experience; and, second, helping the boy, *as an individual,* in his "pursuit of happiness" in Scouting.

Or, in other words:

A SCOUTMASTER'S JOB IS TO TRAIN AND GUIDE BOY LEADERS TO RUN THEIR TROOP—for the purpose of building strong Patrols in which each boy can have a happy and satisfying group experience.

And:

A SCOUTMASTER'S JOB IS TO HELP BOYS GROW—BY ENCOURAGING THEM TO LEARN FOR THEMSELVES.

Training boy leaders and *helping boys grow*—those are your main tasks as a Scoutmaster.

By concentrating on those two objectives and delegating routine details to your helpers, you will accomplish most effectively the task you have set for yourself.

GOOD LUCK to you—and lots of HAPPY DAYS!

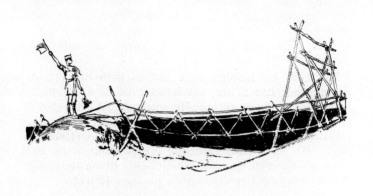

Part I

THE SCOUTMASTER'S FIRST JOB: HELPING BOY LEADERS TO MAKE THE PATROL METHOD WORK

CONTENTS OF PART ONE:

THE PATROL METHOD I
How the Patrol Method Works

Why the Patrol Method?

CHAPTER 1

"**A** SCOUTMASTER'S JOB is to train and guide boy leaders to run THEIR Troop. . . ." That's one way of stating one of your important tasks as a Scoutmaster.

"MAKE THE PATROL METHOD WORK," is another way of saying the same thing.

Well, what is the Patrol Method?

"And why insist upon it?" you may ask. "Aren't there many other ways of working with boys?"

There are—ranging the whole way from the schoolroom method of past generations with a schoolmaster trying to force a bit of knowledge into the brains of his pupils, to the method of dividing a group of boys into teams and keeping them happily occupied for hours banging a basketball about.

But none of these methods will give you the results which you can get through the Patrol Method—the method by which boys in boy gangs with boy leaders train themselves in Scoutcraft.

The Patrol Method is the one thing that makes Scouting different from other programs for boys. It is as much a part of Scouting as the Scout Oath (or Promise) and Law.

In other words: The Patrol Method is not ONE way of running a Troop—it is the RIGHT way!

And it is RIGHT for these reasons: it is the boys' own way of organizing; it is the best way of accomplishing the aim of Scouting; it is the most effective way of running a Troop; and boys grow most through this process.

The Boys' Own Way

Take a large group of boys. Turn them loose—and you know what happens. There will be plenty of noise and argument—and out of the large group, you'll soon have a number of smaller gangs ready for action.

Boys are that way. The instinct for forming gangs is natural to them. They can't help themselves.

In its simplest form the gang is merely a group of boys who play with each other after school or after work. They come together in a casual way—because of neighborhood, similarity of interests, age—and immediately begin to react on one another. A leader comes to the fore. He takes his position naturally, with little form or ceremony.

This gang begins to do things. Usually it has some

Boys pal around together in gangs. To belong to a gang is an important part of the business of being a boy.

particular interest, such as baseball, football, going on hikes, or—in bad gangs—stealing. Gang spirit starts to develop, gang honor and gang loyalty thrive. The gang becomes a little social organism with a life of its own.

The gang, this natural unit of boys for boy activities, is the all important unit in Scouting. It changes its name from gang to *Patrol,* but it is a gang just the same—a small group of boys joined by common interests, working together under the responsible leadership of one of their own number, a Patrol Leader, who is chosen by the boys themselves and trained for the job by his Scoutmaster.

The Scout Patrol is far more than the casual gang of the street corner—here today and gone tomorrow. It is made permanent and effective through the guidance of an understanding adult. Its activities are full of variety and boy-interest—the activities of Scouting. It is strengthened by following a special code of honor—the Scout Law. It is stimulated by working with other similar gangs.

One, two, three, four, or even more Patrols, each under its own boy leader, form the Troop. The Patrols are the working units in Scouting, while the Troop organization provides incentive and supervision.

The Scoutmaster shows the Patrols the road, and as the Scouts work toward the goal, each Patrol grows strong—and through the Patrols the Troop prospers.

Accomplishing the Aim of Scouting

As Scoutmaster, your aim is to train your boys for citizenship.

Boys learn what they practice. If you want them to become good citizens, you must encourage them to practice citizenship. If you want them to learn to play fair, to take responsibility, to get along with other people, to be self-reliant, you must give them the chance to practice all of these things.

They get that chance as members of good Patrols.

Character is high on the list of qualities of a good citizen. And one of the best means of building character in boys is to place responsibility on their young shoulders.

The boy Patrol Leader has such a responsibility—what happens in his Patrol depends upon his initiative and ambition for the gang. But right along with the boy leader, each member has his own responsibility to the Patrol. Each boy has his part in making the Patrol a well-knit team. Slowly but surely, doing things together in the Patrol creates in each of the members a strong sense of loyalty and affection—Patrol Spirit is born and grows.

In Scouting, the gang becomes the Patrol. The Scoutmaster teaches the boys the skills that will make them Scouts.

The Patrol Method is Scouting's great chance to help boys govern themselves.

The way in which a Patrol is formed, and its leader elected by the boys themselves, makes for a harmonious unit—a "happy family." Each boy gets a feeling from the very start of belonging, of sharing. He learns to get along with other boys and other Patrols in work and play. He helps to plan the activities of his gang, to carry out the plans in a cooperative manner. He learns to adjust himself to the wishes of the majority.

The Patrol Method is self-government in action— democratic living on a level which a boy can understand and appreciate.

The Most Effective Way

The wholehearted use of the Patrol Method makes

your work as a Scoutmaster far more effective, yet much simpler than any other way, because it places the responsibility for the success of the Troop where it belongs:

With the boys themselves.

By letting your boy leaders run THEIR Troop under your guidance, you are not tied down to the details of instructing John and Joe, and Mac and Bill, in first aid and signaling—the boys train each other in the Patrol.

You do not have to worry about making up next Friday's meeting program—the boy leaders have planned it at the last get-together of the leaders.

You do not have to bother about Bob's dues and Pete's attendance or lack of it—that's the job of one of the boys.

You have time to think up new ideas, to keep the Troop moving ahead, and above all, you have time to help each individual boy in the Troop through frequent personal contacts.

And besides, the Patrol Method is your best insurance that the Troop will live on.

The Troop that is run as a club, with the Scoutmaster as boss, dies when the boss leaves. But where Patrol Leaders are trained to lead, they will keep their Patrols active, and thus carry on the Troop in case you have to be away for a time, or should find it necessary to give up the Troop.

The Patrol Method is Simple

The Patrol Method is simple. It is merely a matter of letting the boys form their own gangs under the leadership of one of their own number, and of giving these boy leaders the guidance and training, and free-handed responsibility for doing their job.

Scouting succeeds where the Patrol Method is used. It succeeds where the wise Scoutmaster has faith in

The Scout Patrol—a gang of boys who stick together through thick and thin, learning and living Scouting.

boys and in their ability to govern themselves, and the patience to help the boy leaders carry on.

Why Some Troops Fail

But in spite of the fact that the Patrol Method is simple and that success follows the Troop that uses it, why do some Troops attempt to go on without it? Why do some Scoutmasters cast aside the most effective tool that Scouting provides? They may have grouped their boys in Patrols, but beyond that, nothing very much happens.

We may as well face some of the reasons for failure:

Some men don't grasp the possibilities of the Patrol Method, and so do not see the importance of using it.

Some men lack faith in boys' ability to carry out responsibilities. These men may have made a half-hearted stab at using the Patrol Method, giving it up because it didn't function perfectly right off the bat.

Others do not like to part with authority. They have found, in taking over a Troop, a chance to play boss and show off their specialties, and don't realize they are stifling their boys' chances for character development.

Still others have the old idea of training by mass instruction too ingrained in their systems to change it.

Also, a few men, by temperament, are not suited to the Scout way of training, and would be happier in work which does not involve using the Patrol Method.

Sooner or later, most of these men lose their boys *because they don't give them Scouting.*

The Key to Success

To succeed with a Troop, the Patrol Method is an absolute necessity!

"The formation of the boys into Patrols of from six to eight, and training them as separate units each under its own responsible leader, is the key to a good Troop. . . . Where this system is applied, it is absolutely bound to bring success. It cannot help itself!" says Baden-Powell.

The thing, then, is to get the Patrol Method firmly established in your Troop and to stick to it throughout. That's the way of making Scouting grip the lives of your boys.

Setting up the Patrol Method

CHAPTER 2

THE FIRST STEP in setting up the Patrol Method is to help the boys form Patrols that are as close to the boys' natural gang as possible. The method varies somewhat, depending upon whether you are starting a new Troop or reorganizing an old one.

Forming Patrols in a New Troop

Let's say you are starting a new Troop and have asked in a few boys to get the Troop under way. From that very first meeting, get the boys to think in terms of Patrols. Tell them what Patrols are. Explain to them that eventually it will be up to them to decide how the Patrols will be made up.

Then show them what a good Patrol does by running that meeting of the new Troop and a couple more after it as Patrol meetings, with you as the "Patrol Leader" of a single Patrol. (For programs for starting a new Troop, see Tool 1, back of book).

Start off with a simple ceremony. Then work on the Tenderfoot requirements and on plans for the future.

But most important—include a couple of fun games requiring two teams. Let the boys form teams for the first of these games without any suggestions from you. Play the game, then try another—after suggesting to the boys that they may want to change around a bit. In this way they begin to find out which fellows they like.

At the next meeting, try a few Scoutcraft games— such as a knot relay or a Flag quiz—again with teams the boys have formed themselves.

When you feel that the boys know each other quite well, announce that the Troop is ready to form its Patrols. Then simply ask the boys to make up their gangs, as they would for a game. And there you have your Patrols.

However, if you have any reason to think that this easy method won't work in your Troop, try another: After the boys have played their team games, give them pencil and paper, and ask each fellow to write down the names of those he would like to team up with in a Patrol.

Before the following meeting, work over the sheets and arrange the boys in Patrols according to their wishes, using your best judgment in case of doubt, or if a boy is left out.

At this stage of the Troop, don't worry about the smallness of the Patrols. You will have quicker success by having the boys work in two small Patrols instead of in a single larger Troop group. The Patrols will grow naturally, as more boys join.

Forming Patrols in the Old Troop

In an old Troop it is not so much a matter of *forming* Patrols, as of *re-forming* them, if necessary.

At some time or other most Troops find that their Patrols aren't what they should be. Some of the older Scouts have left, new recruits have come in; or one Patrol has become weak, another too large; or one Patrol Leader has left town; another is due to become Senior Patrol Leader.

The first thing to do is to bring up the matter of re-forming the Patrols, at a meeting of the leaders of the Troop. Explain the situation, and get the Patrol Leaders to agree to surrender their office, with the understanding that they are eligible for re-election.

At the next Troop meeting announce that the leaders have decided that the Patrols should be re-formed. Then ask the boys to write down the names of the five, six or seven fellows—as the case may be—they would like to have in their Patrol.

Take the sheets home with you, and, before next Troop meeting, arrange the Scouts in Patrols according to their preferences.

Composition of the Patrols

It is a good idea to tell the boys, before they vote, something about the way to form strong Patrols.

A good Patrol is likely to come out of a *natural gang* of three or four good friends. However, the gang should be encouraged to take in a few more boys to form a full Patrol. Otherwise, you may find you have a clique on your hands, that will have little sense of cooperation and little regard for the other Patrols. Usually a bit of guidance given at the right time will keep such a gang straight and help to develop Patrol Spirit rather than clique spirit.

A group of boys who know each other because they live in the *same neighborhood,* or go to the *same school,* makes a good foundation for a Patrol. It will be easy for them to get together regularly for Patrol activities.

On the other hand, boys who did not know each other before they joined the Troop may have struck up a strong friendship on a hike or an overnight camp. They may want to be together although they live some distance apart and go to different schools. *Friends,* whether new or old, should be encouraged to join the same Patrol.

The question of *age* needs to be considered. On the surface, it might seem well to have all the boys in a Patrol of the same age. But age alone means little, unless the boys have other common bonds. Simply being thirteen does not necessarily mean that a boy has the same maturity and interests as all other thirteen-year-olds in the Troop.

Another point is that a Patrol made up of boys of different ages is more likely to be permanent, because not all of the boys will leave the Patrol at the same time. In such a Patrol, the older Scouts can help train the younger ones, and the younger Scouts have a better chance for leadership, as the old-timers grow out of the Patrol.

Size of the Patrol

Another important factor in the "ganginess" of the Scout Patrol is its size.

The size depends a lot on the boys' own choice of Patrol mates and should pretty much be left up to the boys themselves.

Generally speaking, six or seven boys in a Patrol seems to be about right. A four- or five-man group may

The Patrol will eagerly follow a Patrol Leader who is a good Scout—a boy with ability, initiative, and a sense of humor.

work efficiently, but is often handicapped when it comes to inter-Patrol activities. Eight should usually be the maximum, since few boy leaders can handle more.

THE PATROL LEADER

The Patrol Leader is elected by the boys in his Patrol.

But the Scoutmaster plays an important part in this selection: When a Patrol Leader is to be chosen, you should discuss with the boys what to look for in a Patrol Leader, and outline his duties. Certainly they will want a leader who is an all-around good Scout, with a fair amount of Scoutcraft knowledge, with initiative and energy, with a spirit of helpfulness to each fellow of his Patrol, and with a sense of humor and a good supply of common sense.

If you think the boys may be about to elect a leader who may be popular, but whose popularity is of a cheap "Smart Aleck" type not in line with the Scout ideals, it may be especially important to explain the high standards that are expected of a Patrol Leader, so that the boys will further consider their choice.

It may be worth-while also to suggest that the boys put their heads together to plan a Patrol hike, or some other outdoor activity, before they get down to the business of electing a leader. Leave the boys to themselves to work out such a plan. In doing this, they'll come to discover for themselves some of the duties and abilities involved in the job of Patrol Leader.

Most of the time you can depend on boys to choose the right boy for their leader—and in doing so, they are exercising one of the precious rights of citizens in a democracy. Do all you can to dignify this process.

The leader chosen may not always be the one you would have preferred, but the wise Scoutmaster will not use his right to veto a Patrol's decision except in a serious emergency. If the wrong leader has been picked, the process of finding out that the leader they elected is *not* the right one is in itself a valuable experience that will serve the Scouts well later on.

The Patrol Leader has his own manual to help him in his work—the *Handbook for Patrol Leaders.*

Patrol Leaders and Assistant Patrol Leaders are sometimes referred to as "Green Bar Men"—from the color of the bars they wear to indicate their offices. The Patrol Leader's badge consists of two green bars, the Assistant's of one. These are presented to the boy leaders at their installation.

The Patrol Leader's Appointment

Announce the Patrol Leader's appointment before the whole Troop with an appropriate ceremony. Here is one that has been used successfully:

PATROL LEADER INSTALLATION

1. The Troop forms a circle of its Patrols.

2. The Scoutmaster speaks a few words about the importance of good Patrol Leadership and announces the appointment of Scout .... as the new Patrol Leader of the .... Patrol.

3. Scout .... is called forward. He places his left hand on the pole of the Troop flag, above that of the Scoutmaster, salutes, and gives the *Patrol Leader's Promise:* "I promise to do my best to be worthy of my office as Patrol Leader, for the sake of my fellow Scouts, my Patrol and my Troop."

4. The Scoutmaster pins the Patrol Leader's badge on the boy's left sleeve, presents him with a copy of the *Handbook for Patrol Leaders,* and the youngest member of the Patrol steps forward and gives him the Patrol flag.

5. The Troop gives a cheer for the new Patrol Leader, who then steps back into his Patrol, where he is congratulated by his fellow Scouts.

Selecting the Assistant Patrol Leader

The Patrol Leader may select his Assistant, or he may decide to have him elected by the whole Patrol.

Since the two boys are to work closely together, it is important that the Assistant be a Scout with whom the Patrol Leader gets along well. On the other hand, the Scoutmaster should try to make clear that the choice should be governed by "Who will make the best Assistant for the Patrol?" and not "Which fellow do I like best?"

After the selection, the Assistant Patrol Leader is appointed by the Scoutmaster before the Troop, with a ceremony similar to the Patrol Leader Installation.

Term of Office

As a general rule, a Patrol Leader stays in office as long as he gets results, or until he moves into another leadership position in the Troop.

In some cases, it is well to agree on a term of office —say, six months or a year—with the Patrol Leader eligible for re-election. This may simplify matters where a boy proves a poor Patrol Leader and may have to give up his job to a better leader.

The Duties of the Patrol Leader

The Patrol Leader serves in two capacities—as the leader of his Patrol, and as a leader in the Troop:

1. HE IS THE LEADER OF HIS PATROL.

He leads his Patrol by his initiative and his personal example, in Scoutcraft knowledge as well as in Scout Spirit.

He plans, *with his Scouts,* the Patrol's activities— meetings, hikes, Good Turns, special projects—and carries them out to the best of his ability.

He trains his Assistant Patrol Leader to lead the Patrol in his absence, and gives each of the other Scouts a chance to do some leading in the Patrol.

He keeps well ahead of his Patrol in advancement, and helps his Scouts to advance by training them and examining them in Scout Requirements.

He sets an example for his Patrol by wearing his Scout uniform at all Scout activities, and urges his Scouts to do the same.

He is responsible for the routine business of the Patrol —attendance, dues and the like—but gets some other Patrol member to keep the records.

He makes a special effort to be a friend to each Scout of the Patrol, and to know his home, his parents, his school or work, so that he may be able to help each one individually.

In picking his Assistant, the Patrol Leader must put the good of the Patrol ahead of his own personal preferences.

He keeps handy a list of his Patrol members and their telephone numbers, so that he can gather them quickly for emergency or some unexpected assignment.

2. HE IS A LEADER IN THE TROOP.

He faithfully attends all sessions of the Patrol Leaders' Council to receive training for his job, and to do his part in planning the program of the Troop.

He represents his Patrol at Troop Leaders' Council. He brings the wishes of his Patrol to its meetings, and takes back to his Patrol the decisions made by the Leaders' Council.

He promotes the wholehearted, punctual and well-disciplined participation of his Patrol in all Troop events.

This may look like quite a list, but you will be happily surprised to see the way boys measure up when you trust them to carry through on their responsibilities.

THE PATROL METHOD II
Leadership

The Patrol Leaders' Council

CHAPTER 3

A S SOON AS THE PATROLS are formed and the Patrol Leaders are elected, the next step is to establish the Patrol Leaders' Council—or "Green Bar Council," as it is sometimes called because of the green bars in the boy leaders' insignia.

The Patrol Leaders' Council is the heart of the Patrol Method.

It is through this Council that the Scoutmaster carries out one of his two jobs: Helping boy leaders to make the Patrol method work. It is here that your

Patrol Leaders, under your guidance, plan the activities of the Troop and learn to run their Patrols.

These boy leaders are the same boys, whether they get together for business-like planning sessions, or whether you take them out as a special group on a hiking or camping trip to give them ideas they can use in running their Patrols.

Everything you do with them is training of some sort. And your enthusiasm is an essential part in all this training. When you get eagerly behind an idea, your boy leaders will do the same. When you are enthusiastic about a project—whether it is fixing up the meeting room or making camp equipment—the boy leaders will be in there pitching, too.

1. TRAINING BOY LEADERS TO RUN THE **TROOP**

One of your greatest satisfactions as a Scoutmaster comes to you when you see your boy leaders developing into a smooth-running Patrol Leaders' Council, learning to run the Troop.

Few youngsters when they join Scouting have had any experience running their own affairs. Many of them come from homes where all decisions were made by the parents. Such simple things as deciding on the best day for a hike or a good place to go camping may seem hard for them when they have had little previous opportunity to decide anything. The first few times you call on your boy leaders to suggest things to do, their suggestions may be far-fetched or impractical—or almost non-existent.

But gradually, with practice, the suggestions get better. The boys take hold—they get to know what is involved and what to do about it.

It takes ingenuity on your part—and sometimes in-

The Patrol Leaders' Council has assembled. The Senior Patrol Leader takes the chair. The meeting will now come to order!

finite patience—to get youngsters into the habit of making suggestions, then voting on them and assuming their share of the responsibility for carrying out whatever the majority decides.

But that in essence is the Patrol Method—a first step in self-government.

Who Belongs to the Patrol Leaders' Council?

The Council is basically composed of all Patrol Leaders, the Senior Patrol Leader and the Scoutmaster. The boy leaders have a voting privilege and the Scoutmaster serves as advisor. If a Patrol Leader is unable to participate, his Assistant Patrol Leader may represent the Patrol with full voting powers.

There must be some flexibility in providing for greater participation when circumstances require it. For purposes of coordinating Troop program, Junior Assistant

Scoutmasters, Assistant Scoutmasters, Explorer Crew Leaders and Den Chiefs may be invited to the Patrol Leaders' Council, but without vote and, under the same condition, the Troop Scribe may act as Secretary.

The Chairman

In a young Troop, where inexperienced Patrol Leaders are just starting out, the Scoutmaster may act for awhile as the chairman—but only for awhile.

As soon as the Patrol Method is well established, a *boy chairman*—the Senior Patrol Leader—takes over and conducts the meetings of the Council.

The boy chairman at first naturally looks to you for help in conducting the meeting. Be ready to give that help, but do it from the side lines.

The boy will soon gain confidence and make a good job of it.

What the Patrol Leaders' Council Does

Quite simply, the Patrol Leaders' Council plans the activities of the Troop—its meetings, hikes, camps, Good Turns, entertainments, parents' nights, special projects—and assigns the responsibility for carrying out the plans to Patrol and Troop Leaders.

As in any other governing body, decisions are no good unless they result in action. If the leaders decide in March to have a Commando Hike in May and assign the job of working out the details to a couple of Patrol Leaders, the Leaders' Council will expect to hear reports of progress by April and to have the final plans worked out in time.

The Patrol Leaders' Council is also the "clearing house" for special problems that arise and need to be straightened out: Advancement is slow—well, what can we do about it? Getting meetings started on time isn't up to scratch—what'll we do to improve?

Suggested Order of Business for
PATROL LEADERS' COUNCIL MEETING

CALL TO ORDER by the Chairman.

RECORD OF DECISIONS made at last meeting read by the Scribe.

UNFINISHED BUSINESS, such as reports on various jobs that had been assigned: Getting a nature expert for a bird hike, finding out about first aid course, and so on.

PATROL LEADERS' REPORTS — Each Patrol Leader reports on the activities of his Patrol since the last meeting, including advancement progress of his boys. Tells of his Patrol's plans for the following month.

CHECK ON SEASON'S PROGRAM — This is a comparison of the things that have been accomplished with the program that was planned for the season, to find out how well the program is being followed, and what needs to be done.

PLANNING NEXT MONTH'S TROOP PROGRAM — Troop meetings, hikes, camps, community service, advancement. Patrol work to fit into the Troop work. Assignment of duties and leadership responsibilities for games, projects and other activities.

OTHER BUSINESS, such items as thank-you letter for use of camp site, call for volunteers to repair camp equipment, or ushers for church supper, etc.

SCOUTMASTER'S MINUTE — Pats on the back for work well done in the Patrols, congratulations on the way the Troop meeting room looks, suggestions on better uniforming, information on changes in Requirements announced in SCOUTING Magazine and so on.

ADJOURNMENT by the Chairman.

Approval of Candidates for Advancement

The records of Scouts ready for advancement are reviewed in the Patrol Leaders' Council. Each Scout's record is here checked and approved before he appears before the Board of Review.

Short Monthly Meetings

In addition to monthly meetings, in many Troops the leaders gather for a short meeting right after the regular Troop meeting to talk over the strong and weak spots of the meeting while they are still fresh in mind and to check on details for the next Troop meeting.

Conducting the Meetings

The meetings of the Patrol Leaders' Council should be businesslike. Boys like it that way, the experience is valuable to them later on, and things stand a far better chance of getting done.

The chairman—the Senior Patrol Leader—should have a written outline before him of the order of business. He should learn the gentle art of bringing the talkers of the group back to the subject under discussion and of encouraging those who are slow of speech to express

Base the training of your boy leaders on the book which was written especially for them—the *HANDBOOK FOR PATROL LEADERS.* Get them into the habit of consulting this handbook whenever they need program ideas or suggestions for handling Patrol problems. They will find numerous valuable suggestions in it.

their ideas. In a general way the meeting should follow parliamentary procedure, with everyone accepting the decisions of the majority.

Although the Scoutmaster does not have a vote, since he expects his boy leaders to decide what is going to happen in their Troop, you do reserve the right to veto. On you rests, after all, the final decision on matters in which there are differences of opinion that cannot be ironed out in discussion.

If, however, it is understood that you have the right of veto, you will probably never have to use it.

Don't expect meetings to run without a hitch the first few times the boy leaders get together. You will have to guide them into knowing what is expected of them.

When they know that, you can take the coach's seat on the sidelines and let the boy chairman carry on. He can do it—don't worry—if you let him.

2. TRAINING BOY LEADERS TO RUN THEIR **PATROLS**

The kind of Scout a boy will become is determined to a great extent by what happens in his Patrol. If a boy's Patrol is ambitious, there's a good chance he will catch some of that ambition. If his Patrol is energetic, he'll probably make a try at keeping up with the gang. If steady advancement in Scoutcraft is a Patrol tradition, the natural thing for a boy is to want to be in there with the rest.

But a Patrol is not ambitious or energetic unless its leader is. A Patrol doesn't move forward unless the Patrol Leader knows how to get it moving and keep it moving.

It is the Scoutmaster who gives the Patrol Leaders the steam for the job and the know-how for doing it.

The Steam for the Job

Many Scoutmasters set aside an evening a week for "open house," when Scouts can drop in for a chat, or to get something off their chests. Or if you feel that a Patrol Leader is having trouble solving a problem for himself, you may say, "Why don't you drop around to the house tomorrow night and let's see what we can do about it?"

More than once a Patrol Leader has revealed the real reasons for his Patrol difficulties during a friendly talk on the way home from Troop meetings, and the Scoutmaster has been able to give the boy confidence to get things moving right again. Often a few words of encouragement or a little sound advice is all that is needed.

These informal friendly contacts are training of the finest kind.

The relationship between you and your boy leaders is the biggest single factor in the success of your Troop. How well the boy does his job depends on how well you are able to get him to see where he is going, and how to get there with his gang.

Patrol Leadership Training

The more specific kind of training in Patrol leadership has to be carefully planned. It takes place at

Provide each Patrol with a copy of the PATROL RECORD book. It is the basis for a business-like handling of the Patrol records. It contains pages for individual records, attendance and dues, addresses and advancement. Make the Troop Scribe responsible for checking the Patrol records regularly.

Patrol Leaders trained in outdoor skills ensure good hiking and camping Patrols. The training takes place in the Leaders' Patrol.

monthly meetings or out on a hike or camping trip where your four—or three or five—Patrol Leaders form a natural Patrol gang. You are the Patrol Leader of this "Leaders' Patrol"—or "Green Bar Patrol." The Senior Patrol Leader is your Assistant PL, and Assistant and Junior Assistant Scoutmasters are special helpers.

A setting like this is practically a duplication of the conditions these boys have in their own Patrols. The result is that the boys can put the training you give them to immediate use in running their weekly Patrol meetings, taking their Patrols on hikes, and doing Patrol camping. In all of this, encourage your boy leaders to make full use of their *Handbook for Patrol Leaders.*

An important responsibility of your Patrol Leaders is to help their boys to advance. Therefore, sufficient time should be given to make the boy leaders understand the standards which the Troop expects of its Scouts.

Give Them Things They Can Use

The important thing is to fill your "Green Bar" activities with so many ideas of putting Scouting across that each Patrol Leader will have a pack full of them to take home for use in his own Patrol.

To give them enough to work with, games and projects may have to be taught in condensed form. Start a game, for example, by explaining it in a few words, then run it. As soon as the Patrol Leaders have caught on to the rules, cut the game off short. Repeat it several times, each time with a different boy leader in charge. You can't expect a Patrol Leader to run a game in his Patrol, unless he has had a try at running it beforehand.

The same goes for various Scout skills. In teaching axemanship, for instance, on a hike of the Leaders' Patrol, demonstrate the sharpening of an axe and its proper use (or bring along an expert to do it), then have each Patrol Leader practice under guidance until he knows enough about axemanship to show *you* how it should be done. He will then be able to teach it to his Patrol with real confidence. Use the *Scout Field Book* with its hundreds of photographic illustrations as your basic text for teaching your leaders Scoutcraft.

Sample "Green Bar" Meetings

In the program section in the back of this book you will find some sample "Green Bar" meetings to help you get started on your Patrol Leaders' training. They are not intended to be used "as is," but rather as an outline you can adapt to your own use.

After a number of such meetings your boy leaders will get an understanding of what it means to be a good

Teach new Scouting skills first to your Patrol Leaders. They, in turn, will teach them to the members of their Patrols.

Patrol Leader, and you will begin to see the results in the way they get their Patrols working as close-knit groups.

MAKING THE PATROL METHOD WORK

An old experienced Scoutmaster said once: *"The test of the Patrol Method is in the easy chair!"*

His audience looked puzzled, so he elaborated:

"Get an easy chair and place it in a corner of the Troop meeting room. If you can sink into it just after the opening ceremony and just *sit* throughout the meeting, without a worry for its success, until time comes for the closing—well, then your Troop is using the Patrol Method—your boy leaders are actually leading."

It will take time and earnest effort before you reach

this point, but it is the goal you are working toward.

It requires humility—to sit back and let others run the show.

It requires patience—to train boy leaders to do the job, to help them, guide them, and inspire them.

It requires faith—faith in boys to the extent of considering them responsible individuals who can be taught to handle their own affairs.

It requires a firm belief in the democratic way of life, and a willingness to let democratic processes take their course.

It requires a strict adherence to the one important point that will ensure the success of the Patrol Method:

Keep the Patrol the unit always, through thick and thin, in victory and defeat, in games and projects, at meetings, on hikes and in camp.

If you stick to these convictions and give the Patrol Method its chance, you will get your compensation as you see your boys take on responsibilities, go ahead on their own initiative, pick up new skills, learn to live and work together.

In other words, you will see them step forward to take their place as intelligent citizens in a democracy.

That is the aim of Scouting.

That is the purpose of the Scoutmaster.

Other Leaders and Helpers

CHAPTER 4

THERE'S A SIMPLE ILLUSTRATION of the way leadership works in the theory of magnetism which you probably learned in high school: A bar of ordinary iron is supposed to be made up of particles, each with a north and a south pole, all of them lying at cross purposes to each other. When you hold a magnet close to the iron, all its particles turn their poles in the same direction, and the iron becomes "magnetized." Another thing happens: The iron you have magnetized gets the power to magnetize other iron.

In much the same way, a Scoutmaster's personality and enthusiasm "magnetize" his Patrol Leaders, and they in turn have a similar effect on the boys in their Patrols. When you get the boy "atoms" in the Troop all turning their energy in the same direction, then you have Patrols that get somewhere when they have a job to do.

Besides having this "magnetism," a Scoutmaster needs to be something of an executive. As someone put it, "A good executive is not the person who does the work of ten men, but who gets ten men to do the work."

You are not alone in your work with Patrol Leaders and boys. You have your "ten men" ready to help you—or you can develop as many of them as you need.

Each well-trained helper lightens your load, and makes a better Troop. Decide on the leaders who will be most useful. Then set out to get them.

Senior Patrol Leader

The office of Senior Patrol Leader is one of the most important positions of leadership in the Troop. It is open to a First Class Scout or an Explorer with equivalent rank or higher who has a strong character, is proficient in Scouting, and has marked ability as a leader. Since the Senior Patrol Leader is expected to work with the Patrol

The Senior Patrol Leader is another Green Bar Man. This office is open to First Class Scouts who are of strong character, proficient in Scouting and of marked ability as leaders. The Senior Patrol Leader performs such Troop administrative and executive duties as are assigned to him by his Scoutmaster.

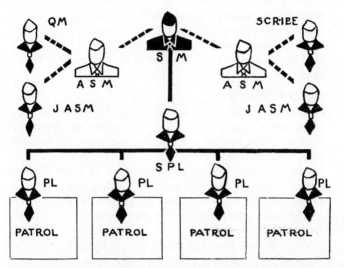

A simple chart of the Troop leadership shows effectively the relationship between the various Troop leaders.

Leaders and assist them in their jobs, he should know what it means to run a Patrol. Generally speaking, a Boy Scout or Explorer with an outstanding record as Patrol Leader makes the best Senior Patrol Leader.

The Senior Patrol Leader is elected by the Patrol Leaders' Council. His appointment is authorized by the Troop Committee on the Scoutmaster's recommendation.

His main duty is to be responsible for the Troop program. He is the chairman of the Patrol Leaders' Council which does the planning. Because he is a boy himself, you can depend on him to see that the program is planned the way the boys want it.

He is in charge of Troop meetings, keeping the program moving. He is also responsible for the activities of Troop hikes and camps.

He encourages and helps the Patrol Leaders with their Patrol meetings and hikes, and knows pretty well what goes on in every Patrol.

Make good use of your Senior Patrol Leader. You will be amazed to see how well he can handle his job if you trust him to do it.

Assistant Scoutmasters

For the running of a successful Scout Troop you need adequate assistance—the kind of assistance which can best be given you by one or more well-trained Assistant Scoutmasters.

An Assistant Scoutmaster must be at least eighteen years of age. He is commissioned by the National Council of the Boy Scouts of America on the same conditions as the Scoutmaster, on the recommendation of the Troop Committee.

Four points are important for getting the greatest amount of help from your Assistant Scoutmasters:

1. *Know your Assistants.* Determine what makes them "tick." Are they activity-minded? Or are they detail men who like to dabble in records? Are they production men who create ideas?

2. *Give your Assistants jobs that suit their abilities,* and which gear in with the work of other Troop staff members within the organization plan of the Troop.

In the average Troop, assignments for Assistant

"Assistant Scoutmasters shall be at least eighteen years of age and may be elected and promoted because of their experience as members in a Troop and efficiency in Scouting. An Assistant Scoutmaster performs such duties as may be assigned by the Scoutmaster." *By-Laws, B.S.A.* Badge: gold and green.

Scoutmasters might be developed in two categories: one man might work in the area of physical arrangements, the other in the area of activities.

The physical-arrangements Assistant could be in charge of equipment and the maintenance of the meeting facilities. He could be responsible for the physical arrangements for hiking and camping, including transportation, equipment, menu, campsite, parental permission. He could be the "overseer" for the uniforming of the Troop, and the liaison man with Troop Committee members relative to Boards of Review and Courts of Honor.

The activities Assistant may cooperate with the Senior Patrol Leader in working out details of Troop and Patrol program activities. He would be responsible for Scoutcraft instruction, including the follow-through with junior leaders, who will be doing the actual instructing, and would take charge of certain Troop meeting and Troop camp activities.

3. *Once the responsibilities are fixed, let your Assistants share in all planning.* Ask their advice and make them feel a part of the team. Let them make decisions in light of the responsibilities which they carry.

4. Finally: *Praise your Assistants for jobs well done.* "Credit where credit is due" enhances prestige and builds up dedication and loyalty to the Troop.

A most important duty of an Assistant Scoutmaster is the running of the Troop in the temporary absence of the Scoutmaster. But more important is the fact that one of the Assistants is going to have to be selected and trained with the idea that he will some day take over permanently the position of Scoutmaster when the current leader, for one reason or another, is no longer able to carry on.

So choose your Assistants well! And remember: the way to keep them—and keep them happy—is to make them work.

OTHER TROOP LEADERS

Older Boy Scouts and Explorers staying on in the Troop should be given their chance at leadership. To help them in their growth and to help the Troop, you will place special responsibilities on their shoulders—provided, of course, that they have the necessary qualifications of leadership ability and knowledge.

Junior Assistant Scoutmaster

When an Explorer becomes fifteen years of age, of strong character, proficient in Scouting, with marked ability as a leader and at least a First Class Scout, he may be appointed Junior Assistant Scoutmaster upon the recommendation of the Scoutmaster and the approval of the Troop Committee. This office may be utilized to provide for Assistant Scoutmaster service in cases where there are no men eligible for commissions or where there are not enough Assistant Scoutmasters. It may also serve to hold the interest of Explorers—as expert instructors or for other service to the Troop.

A Junior Assistant Scoutmaster may act as the leader of games and as judge of Patrol projects. He may handle Troop formations and be in charge of a Troop Good Turn or a service project. He may be responsible for decorating the meeting room.

Warrants may be issued as Junior Assistant Scoutmaster to an Explorer fifteen years of age or over, as instructor or for other service. This rank may be utilized to provide for Assistant Scoutmaster service to the Troop in cases where there are not sufficient Assistant Scoutmasters. Badge: bronze, green.

If he has special knowledge, such as first aid, pioneering, lifesaving, he can be a valuable helper to the Patrol Leaders in training their Patrols.

Troop Scribe

The Troop Scribe keeps a record of all Troop activities in the Troop "Log Book," and an attendance record of all Troop undertakings.

He keeps a record of the decisions made by the Troop Leaders' Council and the things planned.

He keeps the individual record of each member of the Troop—name, age, rank, office, length of service, advancement, attendance, etc. (See Tool 8, "Troop Records.")

He collects dues from the Patrols, records payments, and turns over all money received to the Troop Treasurer—a member of the Troop Committee. (See Tool 5, "Financing the Troop.")

He writes any letters the Scoutmaster asks him to write—to Scouts, parents, new boys, and so on.

He furnishes the Local Council with publicity material about the Troop, for use in bulletins or in local newspapers.

Troop Quartermaster

The Troop Quartermaster takes charge of all Troop equipment, including camping equipment—tents, cooking gear and tools. He keeps an inventory of it, checks it in and out as it is used by the Patrols, and sees to it that it is kept in good repair.

He gets the Scouts and the Patrols to make their own camp equipment.

He is responsible for the upkeep of the Troop meeting room.

In camp he works with the Assistant Scoutmaster in charge of supplies and food buying.

Troop Bugler

The Troop Bugler sounds the necessary calls at Troop activities.

Troop Librarian

The Troop Librarian is in charge of Scout handbooks, Merit Badge pamphlets and other books belonging to the Troop. He keeps a list of them and a record of books lent and returned.

Special Instructors

Explorers, particularly from the Troop itself or an Explorer Unit under the same sponsorship as the Troop, may be on tap to help Patrol Leaders train their Scouts in such subjects as nature, camping, swimming, etc.

Den Chief

If your Troop is cooperating with a Cub Scout Pack, the opportunity is open for some of your Scouts to give leadership as Den Chiefs. Warrants to serve as Den Chiefs are issued by the Troop Committee upon recommendation of the Cubmaster, with the approval of the Scoutmaster of the Troop with which the Den Chiefs are connected.

The Den Chief works with the Den Mother in giving the boys in his Den the best possible Cub Scouting experience according to the program laid down in the Cub Scout handbooks.

THE EXPLORER ADVISOR

As soon as one Scout reaches his fourteenth birthday and elects to stay on in the Troop as an Explorer (instead of joining a separate Explorer Unit), a mature adult Explorer Advisor should be recruited. He will be the advisor of all Explorers in the Troop in those activities which relate to the Explorer program alone.

Since you will have to work in close cooperation with the Explorer Advisor, you should have a voice in his selection by the Troop Committee. He must be at least twenty-one years of age, but preferably about the age of the fathers of the Explorers. In fact he may very well be an Explorer's father. He should have a background of experience and standing in the community which will lend purpose, dignity and distinction to Exploring in the eyes of all young people.

If an Explorer Unit is sponsored by the same institution as the Troop, the Unit Advisor should serve also as Advisor to the Explorers in the Troop.

Whenever Explorers participate in activities for the whole Troop, they will be directly under your guidance, as Scoutmaster. You should reach an understanding with the Advisor in regard to these separate functions as soon as possible. Build a foundation for harmony, understanding and mutual help.

THE TROOP COMMITTEE

Behind the Troop is the Troop Committee—the representatives of the institution or group of citizens that sponsors the Troop. These men have been picked because of their high caliber. Some of them may be fathers of Scouts in the Troop.

This Committee stands ready to help you at any time in your work, provided you request their help.

You, as Scoutmaster, deal directly with the boys. The Troop Committee, on the other hand, seldom has such direct boy-contact. Its members do everything possible to help the Scoutmaster and to make Scouting a joyous experience for the Scoutmaster and the Troop.

An Institutional Representative helps to coordinate the work of the Troop with that of the Institution and the Local Council (see page 84).

Responsibilities of the Troop Committee

Briefly these are the duties of a Troop Committee:

Selection of Scoutmaster, Assistant Scoutmasters and Explorer Advisor.

Providing facilities for meetings.

Advising with Scoutmaster on policies affecting Scouting and requirements of the institution.

Helping in the observance of the rules and regulations of the Boy Scouts of America.

Encouraging the Scoutmaster to carry out the Scout program and helping him get the boys uniformed.

Aiding in the operation of the Troop in such a way as to insure its permanency.

Taking care of finances.

Helping to secure needed equipment.

Assuring every Scout the opportunity to have a year-round outdoor program totaling at least ten days and nights of hike, overnight camp, camporee, and summer camp experiences.

Assuming active direction of the Troop in case the Scoutmaster leaves, until a successor is found.

In a nutshell: *The Troop Committee keeps a good Scoutmaster at the head of the Troop and helps him where he needs help so that Scouts get the utmost benefit, as well as fun, out of Scouting.*

A Committeeman who regularly offers to help *without* waiting to be asked is a joy to any Scoutmaster. He's the type of man who can see with his own eyes, for example, that the Troop meeting place is inade-

The Troop is supervised by a Troop Committee, "of three or more male citizens of the United States, twenty-one years of age or over, selected by the institution with which the unit is connected, or, in the case of a community unit, of those who make application for unit charter. . . ," By-Laws, Boy Scouts of America.

The Troop Committee that understands its responsibilities and "commits" is the Scoutmaster's greatest help.

quate and says to the Scoutmaster, "Wouldn't it be a good idea if I tried to get you the use of a good-sized room instead of this basement you're meeting in now?"

That has been known to happen—although more often it is up to the Scoutmaster to make his needs known to the Troop Committee before they can help him.

An active Troop Committee is good "insurance" for the permanency of the Troop. This is particularly true if the Scoutmaster must resign his post or is suddenly incapacitated. Members of the Committee are there to pitch in and give the necessary adult supervision, if there is no Assistant Scoutmaster, and to go about selecting a new Scoutmaster if needed.

There are a great number of things Committeemen can do for the Troop. Here are some of them:

Policies and Institutional Contact: Attend special training sessions for Troop Committeemen put on by the Local Council or the District, to get a better insight into what Scouting does for boys.

Keep the Chartered Institution informed about what the Troop is doing.

Meeting Room: Secure paint, lumber or other materials needed for decorating the Troop meeting room.
Do special jobs which the boys themselves cannot handle, such as wiring, plumbing, installation of heat, and so on.

If meeting room is inadequate, get a better one.

Uniforming: Help boys to secure their Scout Uniforms by finding jobs for them to earn money.
Establish a uniform fund or a uniform exchange of used uniforms.

Troop Funds: Assist the Scoutmaster in adopting the Troop Budget Plan and establish the necessary Revolving Fund.

Secure finances as needed for special projects, and help the Scoutmaster work out ways for the Troop to earn money.

Assign a Committeeman as Treasurer to handle Troop funds, paying bills on authorization of the Scoutmaster. Audit the financial records from time to time.

Troop Property: Assist the Troop Quartermaster in checking the inventory of Troop equipment and devise means of taking care of needed repairs, replacements and additions.

Get prices before new equipment is bought, to secure best value for money spent.

Activities: Get speakers or experts in various Scoutcraft skills for special occasions, as requested by the Scoutmaster. A Troop Committeeman himself may be the speaker or expert if he has a specialty.

Secure movies on Scouting and other subjects of interest to boys. Check with the Local Council Office for list of movies that are available.

Make arrangements with the necessary authorities for visits to local industrial plants or places of unusual interest.

Provide transportation when needed.

Act as judges for Inter-Patrol competitions.

Because of his connection with the institution, a Troop Committeeman often knows of community affairs arranged by the institution, the local church, school or other organization in which the Troop can take part as a Good Turn.

Arrange for Parents' Meetings, handle attendance, reception and other details, leaving Troop leaders free to carry out the program.

Help build up a Troop Library of Scouting literature and suitable boy's books.

Camping: Help boys to pay their way to summer camp by securing work for them to do. At the request of the Scoutmaster, call on parents to get them to send their boys to camp.

Arrange for transportation to camp if necessary.

Offer services in filling leadership positions in camp.

Advancement: Arrange for regular Boards of Review.

Preside at Troop Courts of Honor for presentation of badges earned.

Accept position as Merit Badge Counselors in subjects with which the members are familiar.

Exploring: Help the Explorer Advisor to offer a suitable special program for the young men fourteen and older.

Troop Reregistration: The Troop charter is renewed each year. It is the Troop Committee which fills out the application forms, complete with all information necessary for review and action by the Local Council. The Scoutmaster is best able to fill out the Troop roster part of the application, but the reregistration process itself is the responsibility of the sponsoring institution and the Troop Committee. It is not the Scoutmaster, but the institution which is applying for a renewal of charter for the Troop. (See Tool 2, back of the book.)

The Troop Committee also meets with representatives of the District and Local Council for a Charter Review, and makes sure that there is a yearly Charter Presentation ceremony in the presence of parents and friends.

Opportunities for Service

This gives an idea of the things there are for Com-

SUGGESTED ORDER OF BUSINESS FOR TROOP COMMITTEE MEETING

ROLL CALL of Committeemen, Scoutmaster, Explorer Advisor and Assistant Scoutmasters.

READING of and action on minutes of previous meeting.

REPORTS

    a. Scoutmaster:

        (1) Troop progress as revealed by : (a) Record of attendance. (b) Record of advancement. (c) Record of recruiting and tenure.

        (2) Coming month's program proposed by Troop Leaders' Council.

        (3) Financial problems of: (a) Scouts; (b) Troop.

        (4) Disciplinary problems; individual situations needing home contact.

        (5) Irregular attendance—Why?—Follow-up.

        (6) Camping and hiking plans—equipment, places to go, etc.

        (7) Other needs of the Troop.

    b. Status of Institution—Troop relations, Council plans.

    c. Finances and thrift training projects.

    d. Good Turns.

    e. Publicity.

    f. District and Council activities including dates and plans for Camporees, Courts of Honor, circuses, Merit Badge Shows, etc.

    g. Advancement procedure — arrangements for Boards of Review, Courts of Honor.

    h. Explorer activities.

OLD AND NEW BUSINESS including plans for recruiting, visiting parents of boys, problem boys, service to sponsor and neighborhood, etc.

MESSAGE from Commissioner or Local Council staff member (if present).

CHARTER RENEWAL (when due).

FIX TIME, place and date for next month's Committee meetings.

ADJOURNMENT.

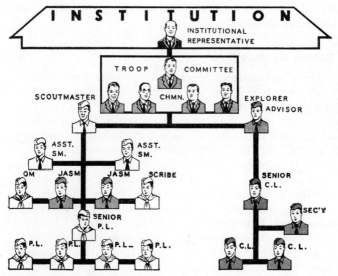

When the relationship between Scoutmaster and other Unit Leaders is clearly understood, the work is made easier.

mitteemen to do, if you will be specific when you request their services.

"We need transportation for thirty-six for Jockey Hollow on Washington's Birthday" is to the point and will result in action. "Do you think you can provide the whole Troop with transportation some time?" means nothing and will result in nothing.

The Troop Committeemen are ready and willing to help you. That's what they are there for.

But they cannot do their share unless you let them know what things need to be done.

Meetings of the Troop Committee

The place to present your needs is at the regular monthly—or bi-monthly—Troop Committee meeting.

The Chairman and the Scoutmaster together prepare

the order of business for these meetings, along the lines
suggested on page 78.

Getting the Work Done

Troop Committees around the country have discovered various methods of handling their responsibilities
and getting the work done.

In some cases, the Committee may prefer to deal with
all matters that come up as a full Committee, without
assigning specific jobs to individual members.

In other cases the Committee may find that it works
more effectively by distributing among its members,
specific responsibilities related to Troop finances and
property, recruiting, uniforming, outdoor program, advancement, Exploring, etc.

In some church Troops a Troop chaplain is added.

But whichever way the Troop Committee is organized, the important thing is the feeling of common
responsibility which much exist between the Committee
and the Scoutmaster.

The spirit of cooperation that comes from planning for
the welfare of the Scouts and carrying out the things
decided upon has a great influence on the succes of any
Troop.

PARENTS' COOPERATION

Thoughtful parents are interested in finding out what
the Troop expects of their sons and what, in turn, their
sons have a right to expect from the Troop.

They want to know the Scoutmaster.

They want to do their share to make Scouting benefit
their boys.

Many of the problems of individual Scouts—the boy
who is not taking part in activities; the boy who is be-

No one is more interested in Johnny's welfare than Johnny's father and mother. Get them interested in helping the Troop.

hind in dues; the boy who has no uniform—can be solved by a brief private chat with one or both of the parents. Other problems are best solved cooperatively.

That is why many Troops organize their Scout parents—sometimes into a single group, "Parents' Auxiliary"—sometimes into separate groups of mothers and fathers, the "Scout Mothers' Auxiliary," the "Scout Dads' Club" or, simply, "The Scout Mothers (or Fathers) of Troop One"—or whatever the Troop number happens to be.

A Parents' Auxiliary is established with the approval of the Sponsoring Institution, the Troop Committee and the Scoutmaster. It is a definite part of the Troop, not a separate organization, and is subject to the regulations of the Troop. It usually has a chairman, a vice-chairman, a secretary and a treasurer.

Activities of the Parents' Auxiliary

Here are some of the things that may be undertaken by an active Parents' Auxiliary—some of them best by the mothers, others best by the dads:

Money Earning: Arrange pancake suppers, spaghetti suppers, chicken and turkey dinners, covered-dish suppers, strawberry festivals. Scouts and fathers sell tickets, the mothers cook and serve the food.

Food Sales—Make and sell cakes, doughnuts, baked beans, potato salad, homemade candy and numerous other things. One Troop took orders for clam chowder, which was then cooked by the mothers.

Rummage Sales—Collect and sell discarded clothing, furniture, knick-knacks, kitchen utensils. The fathers provide transportation, if necessary.

Game Parties—Run bridge and pinochle parties, possibly with refreshments served at the end of the party.

Fun Evening—Sponsor and run a community game evening, or a community dance.

Show—Help with a Troop play, minstrel show or circus, including the making of costumes and decorations. Penny carnival with 1c admission to side shows.

NOTE: In this connection, the Scout parents should be fully informed about the policies of the Boy Scouts of America concerning commercialism (see Financing, page 396), so that all money-earning activities will be organized in strict accord with these policies. Also, the Auxiliary should understand that all funds raised by it are for the use of the Troop and are, therefore, to be deposited in the Troop Treasury. Funds earned by the Auxiliary are to be expended with the joint consent of the Auxiliary and the Troop Committee. The Auxiliary itself does not maintain a separate treasury, except for a petty cash fund of a few dollars, to cover postage and incidentals.

Equipment Making: Make special camp emblems and flags.

Assist in making hike tents, packs, signal gadgets and various camping equipment.

Troop Events: Prepare Fathers' and Sons' Banquet. Family Picnic, Troop Birthday Party, Anniversary Dinner during Boy Scout Week in February.

Arrange for refreshments for the Troop for its last meeting before Christmas, or for Troop Hallowe'en **Party** or other occasion.

Serve refreshments at Parents' Nights.

Special Service: Help to look after sick Scouts.

Send candy, fruit or books to Scouts sick at home **or** at hospital.

Where the Parents' Auxiliary is properly organized and its members kept informed about what is going on, it can accomplish a great deal of good by keeping the Troop Committee alive to its responsibilities, by helping the Scoutmaster to realize some of his aspirations for the Troop, and by encouraging and aiding the individual boys in their efforts to become good Scouts.

Some good ways to stir up parent interest and activity in the Troop are described in greater detail in Chapter 12. See "Family Get-Togethers," page 286.

DISTRICT and LOCAL COUNCIL SCOUTERS

Many of the things that go to make up a successful Boy Scout Program are in the hands of the Sponsoring Institution, the Troop Committee, the Scoutmaster, his Assistant Scoutmasters and his junior leaders. But there are a number of services vital to the success of your program which your Troop cannot provide for itself.

For one thing, there is training — of Committeemen and, especially, yourself. Doing a good job takes a lot of know-how. Activities like camporees, circuses and community service projects, in which many Troops get together, and which stimulate the Troop's own program, form a second item. Providing camping sites and facilities is another. A fourth is establishment of standards of performance to inspire quality Scouting in all Troops.

Add to these the maintenance of a nearby "service station" office and providing of expert guidance by experienced Scouters, and you have at least the principal services which the Troop cannot provide for itself. Providing such indispensable services as these is the purpose and job of your *Local Council*.

Your Local Council

Your Council is one of more than five hundred such associations chartered by the National Council of the Boy Scouts of America reaching every nook and cranny of the United States and its territories. Membership of the Local Council consists of *Institutional Representatives,* one from each of the institutions or groups which sponsors a Scout Unit, including your own, together with representatives at large of the civic, educational, social, religious, business and labor interests of the Council area. This body representing the community is responsible for the overhead leadership, supervision, operation and extension of Scouting in your area. It appoints a well-trained, professional *Scout Executive,* experienced in program and administration, and such Assistant and Field Scout Executives as may be needed to give general guidance to this work. You can count on this executive staff to give you sincere and well-informed advice. The Local Council Office is a *service station* to help you.

Your District

Large Councils create Districts for efficiency in carrying out the Council program. A District Committee, composed of Institutional Representatives and Members at Large, works through operating committees on Training, Camping and Activities, Advancement, Organization and Extension, Finance, Health and Safety.

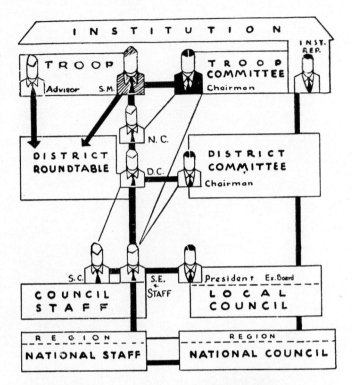

S.M.—Scoutmaster
N.C.—Neighborhood Commissioner
D.C.—District Commissioner

Inst. Rep.—Institutional Representative
S.C.—Scout Commissioner
S.E.—Scout Executive

The organization of the Boy Scouts of America is developed to give the best possible Scouting to the greatest number of boys.

The District Commissioner heads a group of Neighborhood Commissioners, each of whom is assigned to help three or four Units with their Unit program. The Commissioners also put on monthly District Roundtables which provide program helps for Unit leaders and Committeemen.

THE PATROL METHOD   III
Planning the Work

Planning for the Year

CHAPTER 5

A N OCEAN LINER lies in New York harbor, ready for its journey.

The captain steps out on the bridge and gives his orders: "Full steam ahead! We don't know where we're going, but we're on our way!"

Crazy? Certainly! The captain of a liner knows exactly where he is going—his men know it. The journey is charted in complete detail from home port on one side of the ocean to ship's destination on the other.

Apply the same idea to a Troop.

Your Troop could, of course, start out with no goal and no plans—but it wouldn't get very far.

The way to set about this task is to know your goal and develop the steps for getting there.

Generally speaking, the Troop's journey is best planned with a starting point in September, when school vacation is over; through July-August, when you arrive at the climax of the year's journey—summer camp.

Obviously, the best time to do this planning is August. But if it happens that this is not August, don't let that bother you. Consider where you are today, then plan ahead through next summer's camp.

Fortunately, there is no standard way of planning the program of a Troop. A group of robots using a standard pattern in exactly the same fashion would pretty soon kill Scouting. Each Troop works out its own way of giving its boy a rousing good program of Scout activities.

But through planning the job there runs a thread. If you pick it up by one end and follow it, you'll get there. And that's what this chapter is about.

A SESSION WITH YOURSELF

First you need to have a serious session with yourself: "What do I want to accomplish as a Scoutmaster?" You want to do your level best to give your boys the

The Troop Advancement Chart is highlighted by full color reproductions of Scouting scenes, insignia and badges; has space for records of 44 boys from Tenderfoot to Eagle. This chart makes a handsome wall decoration as well as being a record of advancement.

best possible Scouting experience and in that way help them become better citizens of their country.

"Better citizens" takes in a lot of territory. So we should settle for the qualities of citizenship that we know from experience Scouting can bring out. Scouting can help a boy develop in himself the traits of good character. It can help him realize the responsibility he has for keeping his body physically fit and can encourage him to do something about this responsibility. It can interest him in learning a number of skills of hand and mind that will benefit him in later life. It can sow in him the seed of thinking of other people and wanting to help them.

Character—Health—Skill in working with hands and mind—Doing things for other people—there's the fourfold object of your efforts.

Let's look at these points one by one:

CHARACTER—Here your best tools are the *Scout Oath and Law* and your own example. Not just knowing the Law, but practicing it. Not just reciting "A Scout is Clean," but making it a Troop tradition to leave a camp site spotlessly clean, to talk clean. The life the boy leads in a good *Patrol* helps to shape his character. He learns to get along with other boys, to do his share, to plan with his gang, to accept responsibility, to take part in team games and to show the proper spirit whether he wins or loses. The hours he spends in the *outdoors* will open his eyes to the beauty of nature, and his thoughts can be turned subtly to a realization of God through His handiwork.

HEALTH—You give the boy his finest opportunity for developing good health and a strong body by the *outdoor activities* of Patrol and Troop. There's hiking and camping, tramping and climbing, cross-country games, swimming and rowing, sleeping under canvas, and all the other things that go with an active life in the open. At Troop meetings, *vigorous games* help toward the same purpose.

SKILL IN WORKING WITH HANDS AND MIND—*Camping* is tops for giving a boy a chance to do things with his hands. Equipment needs to be made, tent pegs need to be cut. There's a fireplace to put up, gadgets to make, a shelter to build. Numerous *Merit Badges*—Pioneering, Wood Work, Home Repairs and a dozen others—encourage handiness. So does the decorating of Patrol dens and Troop meeting room. *"Learning by Doing"* is the Scout way, whether for training the hands in manual skills, or the mind in initiative and resourcefulness.

DOING THINGS FOR OTHER PEOPLE—*"Do a Good Turn Daily"* is a steady reminder to the boy of what is expected of him as a Scout. You can promote the Good Turn habit indirectly by encouraging the boy to learn the *skills* that will prepare him to help others—such as first aid, life saving, firemanship—and directly by including in the Troop program a certain amount of service to the community. But possibly the best way is by making a boy feel, in the many subtle ways of personal contact, that you expect him to live up to the *Scout ideals* of helping others, and by building up in the Troop a spirit of *mutual helpfulness* that will carry over into the boy's everyday life. Again, your own example is all-important.

Now, coming right down to brass tacks:

What does all this add up to? To something like this:

Full use of the PATROL for group work and gang living.

MEETINGS, with team games for fun and fitness and training, preparation for outdoor experience, moments of inspiration, and just the fun of being together as a group.

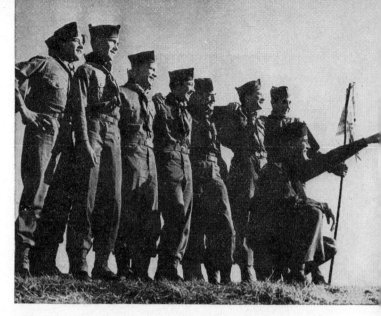

A boy joins your Troop for fun, fellowship and adventure. Will you meet the challenge he gives you?

HIKES, with vigorous games, nature lore, training in Scouting skills.

CAMPS, with real camp life, pioneering, swimming, practicing Scoutcraft, self-government in running the day's program.

SERVICE PROJECTS for the whole Troop from time to time, and encouragement of individual GOOD TURNS.

Opportunity for ADVANCEMENT—training in Scout skills and general handiness.

Here you have the first general outline of the program to which you must give guidance and inspiration. You are ready for the next step.

A SESSION WITH THE COMMISSIONER

If you are a new Scoutmaster, this is the time to have a good heart-to-heart talk with your Neighborhood Commissioner. You will find that your Commissioner, like yourself, is a volunteer and his Scouting job is to help you succeed. He won't know all the answers but he will be anxious to do everything he can to help you get started on the right foot and to keep going with the kind of Troop program that boys want. This Commissioner maintains a helpful cooperative relationship like that of a *coach,* with the leaders of Troops, Cub Packs and Explorer Units of two or more sponsoring groups in your neighborhood or District.

Get his advice and help in thinking of the Troop and specifically in fitting the special District and Council activities into the Troop program. Make use of this Commissioner of yours. That's what he wants.

If you are an old-timer, you will already have had many contacts with your Commissioner. Also, you will have taken part in Scoutmasters' Roundtables or other get-togethers, where programs are discussed and plans made for activities involving cooperation of all the Troops of the community.

These events are often held on a District or Council basis. In *October:* Scout Circus or Exposition. In *February:* Boy Scout Week Celebration. In *June:* Camporee. In *July* and *August:* Council Summer Camp is in full swing.

You make notes of them and bring these notes with the notes from your own personal planning session to a meeting of the Troop Committee.

A SESSION WITH THE TROOP COMMITTEE

So far, you have lined up activities that *might* be done. The next step is to find out which *can* be done.

So you have the chairman of your Troop Committee call a special meeting—unless it is about time for the next regular meeting anyway.

There is the matter of Troop meetings. Is your present meeting room satisfactory, or do you need better facilities? If you need another meeting room, put it up to the Troop Committee to find it. That's one of the responsibilities the Committee agreed to accept.

Can the Troop give the boys all the overnight camping they should have the year around? Possibly this means more tents, new cooking equipment, which, in turn, means money. Another job for the Troop Committee. What's to be done about it?

The District Camporee comes up next. That pretty well determines the date when the new camping equipment should be available. How will the Troop get to the Camporee? Can the Troop Committee provide transportation?

The Scouts want to advance. Members of the Troop Committee form the Board of Review which reviews the work of boys who appear after they are recommended for such advancement by the Scoutmaster and the Patrol Leaders' Council. The Committee will also want to review reasons for lack of accomplishment on the part of other Scouts.

Summer camp! What arrangements can be made now to make sure the Scouts have a chance to go? What about camp savings, Mr. Troop Treasurer?

There may be other things that need to be determined at the Troop Committee meeting, but the items mentioned are among the important considerations. Every decision made by your Troop Committee will affect the way in which the boys get Scouting.

A SESSION WITH THE TROOP

You now know what *can* be done. The next step is to determine what *will* be done.

Well, what is Scouting? "Scouting is a game for boys . . ."

A game for boys . . . so, of course, the boys should be in on the planning.

You hope to hold these boys in the Troop long enough for Scouting to have a chance to help them grow. The only way you can do it is by holding their interest. What interests them? The simplest way to find out is to ask them.

So, you have a session with the Troop—with those live-wire boys you are trying to guide. In this session, remember that where you as an adult may be thinking of the deeper values of Scouting, the boys will be thinking of the *fun* they are going to have.

You bring up the subject during your next Troop meeting or hike, starting off something like this:

"It is up to you fellows to get together in your Patrols and make up your minds about the program you want, so that your Patrol Leaders can place your ideas before the Patrol Leaders' Council where the final plans will be made.

"Here are some of the things you'll have to decide:

"First, about Patrol meetings and hikes: When and how often should they be held?

"About Troop meetings: We have been meeting on Wednesday night. O.K.? Or will another night be better? Any special types of meeting you want?

"About Troop hikes and camp: We should have at least one hike or camp every month. Should we set a definite date each month, for example the third Saturday? What about our part in the District Camporee?

"About summer camp: Should it be early or late in the summer?

Dream ahead with your Troop. Give your boys a chance to express their hopes and desires for a rich Scout life.

"About Good Turns: Think up one or two good ones we can do for our church—or our town.

"About Advancement: How often do we need to have a Troop Board of Review?

"Now, go to it at your next Patrol meeting. What the Troop does this year depends on what you decide and on the suggestions your Patrol Leader brings to the Patrol Leaders' Council."

A SESSION OF THE PATROL LEADERS' COUNCIL

And so we come to the final step: The planning session of the Patrol Leaders' Council.

Since boy leaders are responsible for carrying out the program, they need to have a great deal to say in determining the details. You do the guiding, but you keep

THE ACTIVITIES

PATROL ACTIVITIES—*The Patrol on Its Own*

   Year-round Regular Activities:
     Patrol meetings—weekly
     Patrol hikes or camps—monthly
     Steady Advancement training
   Year-round Special Activities:
     Projects: Den, equipment, etc.
     Visit or hike with other Troop

TROOP ACTIVITIES—*The Patrols Together*

   Year-round Regular Activities:
     Troop meetings—fortnightly (or weekly)
     Troop hikes or camps—monthly
   Year-round Special Activities:
     Inter-Patrol contests—occasionally
     Investituture nights—when required
     Troop Courts of Honor—every two or three months
     Drive for 100% uniforming
     Money earning projects
     Improvement of Troop meeting room
     Visit or hike with other Troop
   Seasonal Activities:
     Summer camp—one week, ten days or more

the game the boys' own. You assist the boy leaders to run THEIR Troop.

It takes thought and time for the leaders to plan a year's program, based upon what the boys say they want, but it is the best investment we know of because it makes certain that you get into the program all the things that should be there, and it simplifies the work for the whole year.

The main thing to keep in mind in this final planning is to keep looking toward summer camp as the climax of the Troop year, and to point every meeting, hike and overnight camp during the year toward that climax.

In some Troops the planning session is held at Troop headquarters or at the Scoutmaster's home. Other

OF THE YEAR

Winter camp—two to four days
Boy Scout Week celebration—in February
Troop Birthday celebration (Family Night)
Father and Son Dinner or Hike
Reunion of old Scouts
Entertainment for Troop funds
Memorial Day and Fourth of July activities
Service Projects: Thanksgiving and Christmas
    Good Turns, Gardening, Tree Planting, Scrap
    Collecting, Bird Feeding, etc.
District or Council Rally or Camporee
Other District and Council activities

LEADERS' ACTIVITIES
Patrol Leaders' Council meetings—monthly
Troop Leaders' Patrol hikes—every two or three
    months
Troop Leaders' Patrol camp—occasionally

TROOP COMMITTEE ACTIVITIES
Troop Committee meetings—monthly or every
    other month
Service projects to the Troop
Troop Boards of Review—every two or three
    months

Troops have established the tradition of doing the planning around the camp fire during an overnight camp of the "Leaders' Patrol."

Planning for the Whole Year

Well, the Troop leaders have gathered—"All present." The Senior Patrol Leader is in the chair. He has an outline of some of the possible activities to help him keep things moving. He has the *Boy Scout Leader's Program Notebook* and the Troop Program Planning Chart. Each Patrol Leader is ready to speak up and present the recommendations of his Patrol.

The meeting gets under way.

The first part of the planning is to list the activities

SEASONAL EVENTS

(Add special holidays of your own State)

SEPTEMBER   Labor Day, First Monday
                School Year begins
                Constitution Day, Sept. 17
                County and State Fairs

OCTOBER   Fire Prevention Week
                Community Chest Campaign
                Rosh Hashanah; Yom Kippur[1]
                Columbus Day, Oct. 12
                Navy Day, Oct. 27; Hallowe'en, Oct. 31

NOVEMBER   Election Day, Tues. after first Mon.
                Armistice Day, Nov. 11; Book Week
                Thanksgiving, last Thursday

DECEMBER   School Christmas Vacation
                Christmas Day, December 25

JANUARY   New Year's Day, January 1
                Thrift Week

FEBRUARY   Boy Scout Week (includes Feb. 8 to 12)
                Boy Scout Day, February 8
                Lincoln's Birthday, February 12
                St. Valentine's Day, February 14
                Washington's Birthday, February 22
                Baden-Powell's Birthday, Feb. 22

MARCH   Arbor Day
                Red Cross Drive
                St. Patrick's Day, March 17

APRIL   Kind-to-Animals Week
                Army Day, April 6
                Easter[2]; Passover
                Pan American Day, April 14
                Forestry Week
                St. George's Day (Scout World
                    Brotherhood Day), April 23

MAY   Child Health Day, May 1
                Boys' Week
                Mother's Day, second Sunday
                Memorial Day, May 30[3]

JUNE   Flag Day, June 14
                Father's Day, third Sunday
                School Year ends

JULY   Vacation; Independence Day, July 4

AUGUST   School Vacation

---

[1] Occasionally in September.
[2] Occasionally in March.
[3] Observed in Alabama, Florida, Georgia, Mississippi, April 26th; Kentucky, North Carolina, May 10th; Tennessee, June 3rd.

Planning for the year is important business. Time and effort spent in planning means smooth sailing toward your destination.

that all agree should be carried out. A successful Troop will include many of the items listed above in such a list. Your Patrol Leaders' Council will subtract or add until the list fits your particular Troop.

Next comes the job of arranging these activities on a monthly basis.

You will know, for example, that there is a school holiday on February 22nd, Washington's Birthday. Here's a date for which a hike can be planned. Religious devotions at various times during the year may require changing the dates of a few Troop meetings. Special flavor may be given to a Troop activity around March 17th, St. Patrick's Day, or to one around October 31st, Hallowe'en. Troops in Massachusetts or Maine may want to schedule a hike for April 19th, Patriot's Day, Troops in Virginia on January 19th, Lee-Jackson Day; in California on September 9th, Admission Day.

So look over the list of seasonal events on page 98, and include among them the special holidays of your own state and the information you have on local school vacations.

Your skeleton outline soon begins to look like the schedule on page 101. Notice that on this skeleton special activities which may become Troop traditions are shown in capital letters. A Troop Birthday Picnic and Family Campfire is planned for May. That, of course, should be changed to your own date.

So much for lining up meetings and hikes and camps.

Now, what "meat" will we put on the skeleton?

Laying Out the Steps

Remember you are planning toward summer camp. At the same time you should aim to make it possible for your boys to realize their ambition to become First Class Scouts. The two go hand in hand—preparing and training boys in outdoor camping skills automatically brings all the Scout Requirements into the picture.

The Chinese have a saying for it: "A journey of a thousand miles starts with a single step." A step at a time, and eventually you reach your goal.

So, one month you concentrate on special hiking skills, the next on first aid, and then on signaling, pioneering, observation, campcraft, concealment, pathfinding, water skills, or what other subjects the boys want or need.

Or, instead of spending one month on a subject, you may plan to use two months or three on it—possibly concentrating on hiking skills for the fall, on skills the boys can train in at Troop meetings for the winter, on camp preparation for the spring—and then on summer camp!

You will find that this method of centering the year's activities around themes will keep the program full of variety and action.

PLANNING THE YEAR
("Skeleton")

SEPTEMBER	Meetings
	Hike or camp
OCTOBER	Meetings
	COLUMBUS DAY HIKE OR CAMP
	Troop Board of Review
NOVEMBER	Meetings
	Hike or camp
DECEMBER	Meetings
	CHRISTMAS GOOD TURN
	CHRISTMAS VACATION CAMP
JANUARY	REUNION
	Meetings
	Hike or camp
	Prepare for Boy Scout Week
	Troop Board of Review
FEBRUARY	BOY SCOUT WEEK
	DISTRICT RALLY
	FAMILY DINNER
	Meetings
	WASHINGTON BIRTHDAY HIKE
	OR CAMP
MARCH	Meetings
	Hike or camp
	Troop Board of Review
APRIL	Meetings
	EASTER VACATION HIKE OR
	CAMP
MAY	Meetings
	MEMORIAL DAY CAMP
	TROOP BIRTHDAY PICNIC AND
	CAMP FIRE
	Troop Board of Review
JUNE	Meetings
	DISTRICT CAMPOREE
JULY	FOURTH OF JULY PARADE
	TROOP SUMMER CAMP
AUGUST	Troop outdoors

Your "Three Assistants"

You have three silent assistants ready to help you and your boy leaders pick the themes for the year:

1. *Boy Scout Leader's Program Notebook* is a booklet published every year by the Boy Scouts of America and presented to you through your Local Council. This notebook combines a number of seasonal monthly themes into a suggested program for the year, with blank pages for your own notes. The Troop Program Planning Chart contains the same material in convenient shape for posting. Each theme is treated in detail from month to month by your other two silent assistants.

2. The BOY SCOUT PROGRAM QUARTERLY picks up the theme suggested for each month in the program notebook and gives a large number of program suggestions on the subject, from the Troop leaders' angle.

3. BOYS' LIFE Magazine, to which your boys may be subscribing under the Troop Concession Plan (Tool 5), puts program material for the theme of the month in the hands of every Patrol Leader through its Green Bar Bill pages, and gives each boy, through its Scoutcraft photo features and special articles, the technical information he needs for practicing and mastering the month's subject.

Your three "Silent Assistants". BOY SCOUT LEADERS' PROGRAM NOTEBOOK, published every year and made available to you free; BOY SCOUT PROGRAM QUARTERLY, which you receive as a Scoutmaster; and BOYS' LIFE, a most valuable help for you and for your Scouts.

PLANNING THE YEAR

("Meat")

SEPTEMBER
Get-Together Party
Theme 1: Concealment
HIGH-SPOT of Theme 1: Wide Game (hike)

OCTOBER
Theme 1: Concealment (continued from Sept.)
HIGH-SPOT of Theme 1: 24-Hours Commando Raid, Columbus Day (camp)
Theme 2: Emergencies

NOVEMBER
Theme 2: Emergencies (continued from Oct.)
HIGH-SPOT of Theme 2: Disaster Mobilization (hike)
Prepare for Christmas Good Turn

DECEMBER
Theme 3: Observation
Christmas Good Turn
HIGH-SPOT of Theme 3: Treasure Hunt during Christmas Vacation (camp)

JANUARY
Troop Reunion
Theme 4: Boy Scout Week Preparation
HIGH-SPOT of Theme 3: Man Hunt (hike)

FEBRUARY
Theme 4: Boy Scout Week Preparation (continued from Jan.)
HIGH-SPOT of Theme 4: Boy Scout Week— Rally, Family Night
Theme 5: Communications
Washington Birthday Pilgrimage (hike)

MARCH
Theme 5: Communications (continued from Feb.)
HIGH-SPOT of Theme 5: Night Fire Signal Relay (hike)
Theme 6: Orientation

APRIL
Theme 6: Orientation (continued from Mar.)
HIGH-SPOT of Theme 6: Cross-Country Game during Easter Vacation (camp)
World Brotherhood Day, April 23rd

MAY
Theme 7: Campcraft
HIGH-SPOT of Theme 7: Troop Camporee
Troop Birthday and Family Picnic

JUNE
Theme 7: Campcraft (continued from May)
HIGH-SPOT of Theme 7: District Camporee

JULY
HIGH-SPOT OF YEAR: Troop Summer Camp

ANGUST
Theme 8: Water Skills
HIGH-SPOT of Theme 8: Waterfront Carnival

Pick the Themes to Fit the Troop

It is not the object of the *Boy Scout Leader's Program Notebook* and the two magazines to provide you with a series of "canned" programs for your Troop.

The idea is, rather, that these silent assistants can suggest to you a number of themes from which you can pick those that best suit your Troop—either because your Scouts will get a special thrill out of them, or because a particular subject is a weak point with the Scouts.

If you are starting a new Troop, you'll naturally have one main theme for quite some time: Training your boys in the Tenderfoot Requirements. But, at the same time, you can start the boys on hikecraft—by giving them pointers and inspiration at meetings, and taking them out on simple hikes.

In an old Troop, you may already have certain themes laid out without recognizing them as themes. Training for a Council Camporee is certainly theme enough for a month or two. Special watersport events during August is another theme used in many Troops. The annual Christmas Good Turn is a tradition that is a theme in itself, requiring planning, preparation and work. Add a few more themes, and your year is complete.

The themes chosen are incorporated into your skeleton outline. What eventually emerges as the year's program for the Troop may look something like the set-up on page 103.

How does it strike you? Looks pretty good?

Well, it *IS* good—

Because it was planned in a democratic manner to suit your particular Troop, by the boys who are going to enjoy it and by the boy leaders who are to administer it.

Planning for the Month

CHAPTER 6

THE PROGRAM DETAILS for any particular month are plotted out about the middle of the preceding month at the meeting of your Patrol Leaders' Council.

At this get-together, the Troop leaders decide upon the specific items that will make up the Troop meetings and the hike or camp for the following month, and determine which leader will be responsible for each.

But not only that: Here also each Patrol Leader, while helping to plan for the whole Troop, gets to see the complete picture of what is ahead, and picks up ideas for Patrol activities that will make the whole month's work a success. Whenever one of your Patrol Leaders, at this planning meeting, volunteers his Patrol for putting on a demonstration or a game or a stunt, he accepts, at the same time, the responsibility for training his Patrol for it in advance—his boys will have to get busy at Patrol meetings and on Patrol hikes.

And that's exactly as it should be: Each Troop activity should inspire every Patrol and every individual boy to do Scouting in the intervals between the times the whole Troop meets.

Using the Monthly Theme

You have already determined the "big idea," the theme for the month. That was done when you planned the program for the year. What now needs to be done is to put life and action into the theme.

You'll soon discover that building the activities of the month around a theme, with an exciting high spot to cap it off, greatly simplifies the planning job of the Patrol Leaders' Council.

It is ten times easier to sit down and make plans for "Signaling Month" or "First Aid Month" or even "Indian Month" or "Robinson Crusoe Month," than it is to plan for the month of September. "May" suggests very little, but "Pioneering Month" immediately brings up thoughts of rope and knots and axemanship, rafts, and bridges and towers—rugged adventure in the out-of-doors.

How a Theme Works Out

Now, let's see how the theme can be turned into the Troop program for the month.

Let's say that you're planning for May. It is now the middle of April, and the regular planning meeting of the Patrol Leaders' Council is in session.

The Senior Patrol Leader has the floor:

The Leaders' Council discusses the program for May and studies models for the "radio tower" planned for the Commando Raid.

"Well, fellows, we have Pioneering on the program for May. What'll we do about it? What suggestions have you?"

"What about building a couple of bridges over Mac-Vicar Creek so we don't always have to take the long way to camp?" suggests a Patrol Leader.

"Aw, do we have to go through that again?" counters another. "We did something like that last year."

"Yeah, my gang wouldn't go for it either," says a third PL. "They want Commando stuff."

"That would fit in all right," says the Senior Patrol Leader. "Commandos had to be pretty slick at going places. They had to cross rivers and swamps and scale cliffs and set up communications. They had to knock a bridge together in a hurry or get across a stream on a rope or put up an emergency radio tower . . ."

	INDOORS	
MIDDLE OF PRECEDING MONTH	**LEADERS' COUNCIL MEETING** Laying out programs, scheduling details of theme over four weeks Determining responsibility for leadership	
END OF PRECEDING MONTH	**LEADERS' PATROL HIKE** Training in Patrol Leadership and in: *Axe:* Sharpening and handling of axe; chopping, lopping and logging	
	PATROL MEETINGS	**TROOP MEETING**
FIRST WEEK	Whip Patrol Lashing ropes Review knots especially clove hitch, timber hitch, sheet bend Speed knot tying Blindfold knot tying Learn use of axe	Inspection: Each Scout a lashing rope Demonstration of model bridges Game: Knot Relay Project: Logging
SECOND WEEK	Learn lashings Design Bridge Axe sharpening Plan Patrol hike	Inspection: Each Scout with bowline tied in lashing rope Demonstration of model signal tower Game: Knot Hoop Relay Project: Get the Message
MIDDLE OF MONTH	LEADERS' COUNCIL MEETING	
THIRD WEEK	Review Lashings Practice trestle building Make bridge models	Inspection: Another knot in rope Display of Patrol Bridge Models Game: Chain Gang Race Project: Trestle Making
FOURTH WEEK	Knot games Two man knotting Champ-nit Knotting Make signal tower Models Plan for HIGH SPOT	Inspection: Another knot in rope Display of Patrol signal tower models Game: Knot Champ-Nit Project: Hang the Pot
END OF MONTH	LEADERS' PATROL MEETING	

and for securing needed material Patrols volunteering for demonstrations, display or equipment projects	
Knots: Types of rope, whipping; knots, lashings *Project:* Make trestle, small signal tower	

OUTDOORS		OTHER ACTIVITIES
PATROL HIKE OR CAMP	TROOP HIKE OR CAMP	
		Usual features of
		Patrol and Troop
		Meetings, hikes
Collect material for model making Cut Scout staves (saplings) with permission, for trestle poles Make simple bridge		and Camps
		woven into
		Program
Planning next month's program		
		SEASONAL ACTIVITIES:
		Good Turns
		Boards of Review
	HIGH-SPOT: Commando Raid involving construction of "radio" signal tower	Etc.
Training in Patrol Leadership and for next month's theme.		

"That sounds OK!"

"Yeah, let's do something like that!"

"That's what we want. Tough, and fun, too!"

The High Spot of the Theme

"All right, then: The high spot of the month will be some kind of Commando Raid that will involve some pioneering trick, such as . . . well, what'll we say . . . ?"

"Make it that radio tower you talked about!"

"O.K.—it'll involve putting up a radio tower per Patrol."

"Now you're talking!"

"We'll have the Junior Assistants work out the rules for the raid. But you Patrol Leaders better get busy right away to decide what you need to do in your Patrols to get the thing across."

There's a quick consultation. "What do we need to do? What do the fellows need to know?"

It finally comes down to this: All of the Scouts have to know certain knots and lashings, and all of them require more training in axemanship.

"We'd better plan a hike of the Leaders' Patrol before the end of this month. We Patrol Leaders need a bit of practice before we attempt to get the fellows going with ropes and axes."

"When'll we have that hike? O.K., let's put that down. And now let's decide what we'll do in the Troop so that you can get busy for it in your Patrols."

Details of the Month

And so the leaders settle down to detail planning. It may work out somewhat like this:

During the first week of the month, the Patrols will get some lashing ropes, about twelve feet long, for each boy of the Patrol. The Patrol Leaders will teach their boys to whip the rope ends, and to tie a couple of

"The real thing!" The **"radio tower"** models of your planning meeting (page 107) have come to life and the raid is on!

important pioneering knots—clove hitch and timber hitch. The boys will start practice in the use of the axe. The Troop meeting for that week will feature a couple of knotting games, making use of the lashing rope, and a demonstration of model bridges.

During the second week, the Patrols will go in for lashings and sharpening of axes. The Troop meeting will include knotting games, demonstration of signal towers, and a Patrol project involving use of lashings, such as "Spear that Message." During that week, each Patrol will have to get a hike in, for there's material to be collected for model making, and each Scout needs a Scout staff for the trestle building project coming up at the next Troop meeting. That, in turn, means getting permission to cut saplings which may be turned into Scout staves.

Third week coming, with practice in trestle building and making bridge models at the Patrol meeting. Then comes the Troop meeting with display of the Patrol models, with a couple of fun games based on knots, and with the Patrol contest in trestle building.

The fourth week means final Patrol preparations for the Commando Raid, getting axemanship and lashings down pat. The Troop meeting features display of models of the "radio" towers that will be built during the Raid, and may wind up with a couple of games in knotting.

And finally, the high spot of the month: The Commando Raid—a Troop hike with all the trimmings of fun, excitement, pioneering, stalking, fighting—a whale of a good time for all.

"O.K., fellows? Are we all set?" asks the Senior Patrol Leader.

"Bet we are!" The Patrol Leaders voice their unanimous approval.

Turn to pages 108-109. Here you will find the suggestions we've just discussed developed in the form of a diagram showing the over-all picture. Notice how the theme is broken down into a schedule for Leaders, Patrols and Troop —into things to be done in advance and from week to week—into indoor and outdoor activities.

In making up the program, keep in mind that the

HANDBOOK FOR BOYS and the SCOUT FIELD BOOK are your boys' guides to a successful Scouting experience. *Handbook for Boys* describes the steps in advancement. The *Scout Field Book* is a supplementary book of Scoutcraft which will provide you and your boys with technical material and helps you need.

activities based upon the theme do not make up the whole program for the month. To those activities must be added special seasonal events, Troop's birthday, Troop and Patrol Good Turns, Boards of Review and other things that will make the program complete.

Helps for Planning

In the planning of program details, make use of every available help you can lay your hands on.

For your convenience, a series of themes, worked out in detail, is included in the program material section in the back of this *Handbook for Scoutmasters*. The section contains a wide variety of games and ideas (page 409).

The *Handbook for Patrol Leaders* gives each of your Patrol Leaders the basis for running a good Patrol, with description of numerous Patrol projects that will go into the program of the Troop as a whole.

The *Handbook for Boys* is the basic Boy Scout handbook. It describes the steps in advancement and tells how to do the things Scouts want to know about. The *Scout Field Book* is a supplementary book of Scout-craft which will provide you and your boys with all of the necessary technical material.

And if you follow the themes in the *Boy Scout Leader's Program Notebook,* as suggested in the previous chapter, your leaders will receive additional help from the quarterly program supplements to SCOUTING Magazine, and your boys from each month's issue of BOYS' LIFE.

Your Part

You have the program material at your fingertips, and you have the boy leadership for developing a successful monthly program for the whole Troop.

To make that program a reality, only one thing further is needed—the thing to which we must return again and again: The training and guidance that only *you* can give your boy leaders in running THEIR Troop.

THE PATROL METHOD   IV

The Life of the Patrol

The Patrol Carries On

CHAPTER 7

THE TRAINING YOU GIVE your Patrol Leaders through the Leaders' Patrol is intended to teach them to turn their gangs into real Scout Patrols.

And a *real* Scout Patrol is a group of boys who enjoy being together, doing Scouting together, learning from each other, helping each other in the spirit of the Three Musketeers: "All for one, one for all!"

The spirit of such a gang is not built overnight. It is

nursed along in a lot of ways—some small, like winning or losing a game—some large, like working hard on a Patrol Good Turn—some obvious, like giving an ear-splitting Patrol yell—some hidden, like the voice that whispers: "Keep on! Don't let the gang down!"

A true Patrol spirit will do much to shape the character of the boys in the gang.

Developing Patrol Spirit

A good Patrol Leader and the right make-up of the gang are the two biggest factors in developing Patrol spirit.

Once a boy becomes a member of a Patrol he ordinarily remains in that Patrol until he leaves the Troop or becomes a leader. A boy needs this feeling of knowing that he is "there to stay." That is why there is little chance for Patrol spirit in a Troop where the Scoutmaster shuffles the boys together at frequent intervals and deals them out into new Patrols. Under such a system they have no sense of belonging anywhere.

The *Patrol Name* is important. Instead of being merely a boy, the new Scout on entering his Patrol becomes a Buffalo, a Beaver, or a Falcon. He learns to give his *Patrol Call* and sets out to learn the habits of his Patrol animal or bird. He uses the *Patrol Signature* whenever he signs his name. He wears the Patrol's totem in the *Patrol Medallion* on his sleeve. His *Patrol*

Encourage your Patrol Leader to develop Patrol Spirit by all means available. Challenge each Patrol to produce the best possible homemade Patrol Flag, then, call for its use at all Troop and Patrol functions. Make certain that a boy secures his Patrol Medallion as soon as he joins a Patrol.

Flag, carried on the hike and planted in front of the Patrol tents in camp, comes to mean something to him (see *Handbook for Patrol Leaders,* Chapter Two).

Use these features of a good Patrol whenever you can. At Troop meetings, let Patrol leaders report "Beavers all present, sir" instead of "All present, sir." Have a Patrol indicate that it has finished in relay game by giving its call. Ask for the Patrol signature on the hike report. Give the Patrol flag a prominent place at Troop meetings and in camp.

Each Patrol should, as far as possible, have a corner of the Troop meeting room to call its own. Let the boys decorate the *Patrol Corners* themselves with knot boards, nature exhibits, pictures, hike souvenirs and the like. If the Troop does not have its own quarters but meets in a church or school room, *Patrol Screens* that can be folded up and put away between meetings will do the trick. Besides, encourage the Patrols to find *Patrol Dens* of their own for their Patrol meetings, and to make their own *Patrol Equipment.*

All these things help to build Patrol spirit. But when everything is said and done, it is DOING THINGS TO-GETHER that counts the most. It is the Patrol's own meetings, hikes and camps and special activities that make up the life of the Patrol.

Patrol Meetings

When we speak of Patrol meetings, we mean meetings of the Patrol with no adult present; where the Patrol Leader gets his chance to use leadership ability and the training you have given him.

A Patrol meeting once a week seems to get the best results. Many up-and-coming Patrols with boys of the same neighborhood or school get together almost daily to train in Scoutcraft.

A new Patrol often meets at the home of one of the members—usually a different home each week. While some mothers may like to serve refreshments, others will welcome Patrol meetings more readily if it is made clear that "eats" are not expected. As a Patrol grows older, it should aim to have its own regular meeting place.

The ingredients of good Patrol meetings are the 3 C's—short and impressive *ceremonies, checking* on attendance, dues and advancement, *coaching* in Scoutcraft requirements; and the 3 P's—*planning* future activities, working on service, money-earning and other *projects,* and *play*—games, songs and stunts. (See Chapter 5 of the *Handbook for Patrol Leaders.*)

How will you know that your Patrols have successful meetings? Certainly not by a formal inspection. Certainly not by sitting in the corner listening while an embarrassed Patrol Leader tries to carry on.

A better way is to watch what happens.

If a Patrol has a rousing good stunt ready for Troop meeting, you can be pretty sure that it had a busy Patrol meeting.

If a Patrol brings a carefully made knot board or a number of exhibits for its corner, you know it has been working. Also, the spirit of the Patrol is reflected in the way the boys react—whether they volunteer when there's a job to be done—whether they are full of ideas of things to do when you ask for suggestions.

Patrol Hikes and Camps

When the weather is good, a Patrol meeting can take the form of a hike.

Patrols are ready to go hiking and camping on their own just as soon as the Patrol Leader has been trained, and the Scouts have learned to take care of themselves, have learned to respect growing crops and live trees, to avoid unnecessary danger, and in all ways conduct themselves as Scouts. Until they arrive at this point, a responsible Troop leader should accompany the Patrol.

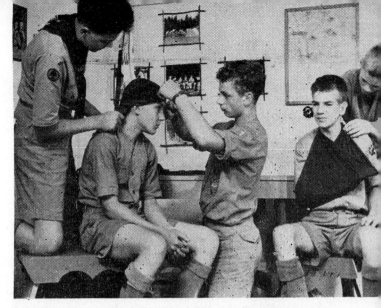
Trained Patrol Leaders mean profitable Patrol meetings. The time you spend in training your boy leaders bears rich fruit.

Or a Patrol dad may go along to provide the maturity of judgment the Patrol Leader may lack.

It should be your goal to get your Patrol Leaders qualified for hike and camp leadership at an early stage. So let's see what should be expected of a Patrol Leader before he can be considered ready to take his Patrol hiking or camping. Something along these lines serves as a good basis for judgment:

PATROL HIKE LEADERSHIP—The Patrol Leader should be a First Class Scout. He should have experienced at least three Troop hikes and one hike of the Leaders' Patrol. He should have the written consent of the parents of each boy (some Troops arrange to get a written consent which does for a whole season). He must be reasonably familiar with the country to be covered on the hike, and he must have permission of the property owner to build fires and cook.

PATROL CAMP LEADERSHIP—The Patrol Leader should, in addition to the above, have taken part in at least two Troop overnight camps and one Leaders' Patrol overnight camp. He must be familiar with the camp site and must have secured the necessary permission to make camp.

These are not hard and fast "requirements," but rather a measuring stick for the Scoutmaster's use. One of your Patrol Leaders, not yet a First Class Scout, may have enough judgment to be trusted to make a Patrol hike a success, while another needs still stricter requirements before he is allowed to take his Scouts out alone. Use these "requirements" with a grain of salt for the good of the Troop—and the boy leaders themselves.

You should be the one to approve all plans for Patrol hikes and camps, since, in the last analysis, parents look to you for the safety of their boys.

Patrol hikes are built around such Scout activities as orientation, mapping, exploring, use of knife and hatchet, fire building, cooking, signaling, tracking, nature lore, pioneering.

On Patrol overnight camps the Scouts have the opportunity to practice what they have learned on hikes and to become good all-round campers.

It's when hiking and camping that the Patrol Leader has his best chance to train his boys in Scoutcraft and to help them advance in Scout Rank. The details of Patrol hikes and camps are described in the *Handbook for Patrol Leaders*, Chapters Six and Seven.

Patrol Advancement

The good Patrol Leader will strive to have his boys step ahead through the Second Class and First Class

Scout Ranks as fast as is consistent with thoroughness. This naturally means that he must be stepping, too!

It is customary to have the Patrol Leader examine his boys toward a rank which he has already reached himself.

Patrol Good Turns

Many Patrols have become a closer knit team by taking on a continuous job of helpfulness—such as caring for an elderly cripple or a blind person, directing traffic at a school corner, running games in a children's playground, helping to train the boys in a newly organized Troop.

Patrols that meet in churches and schools can give very practical help to these institutions. Keeping the church lawn cut, painting the basement, distributing posters for church affairs, are only a few of the many useful services that Scouts can render.

Patrol Specialization

Sometimes a Patrol decides to concentrate on a particular specialty.

First aid, pioneering and signaling are popular—but there are a number of other activities:

A group of good swimmers may train themselves as a life savings corps. A Patrol interested in nature may work together to make a nature collection. Or a Patrol may specialize in long-distance hikes, primitive camping or some similar outdoor hobby. All your Patrols may work for Standard Patrol rating (*HPL*, p. 362).

The Patrol and the Troop

In placing so much emphasis on Patrols, the idea is not that each Patrol should run off in a different direction, independent of the others. On the contrary. A Patrol is a gang living its own life and at the same time the life of a larger group, the Troop—just as a family lives its own life and also the life of the community. If boys understand this there will be little chance of Patrols developing into cliques.

It is only natural for each Patrol to want to be top Patrol in the Troop, but the best relation between Patrols seems to be the result of mixing cooperation and competition in about equal parts.

There is nothing contradictory in this.

The sound of one lone tuba, cornet, saxophone, or bass drum may not in itself be very pleasing, yet in an orchestra, the combined result is good music—which certainly doesn't prevent the cornet player, for example, from trying to become the best musician in the outfit. In the Troop orchestra the aim is to make each Patrol player as nearly perfect as possible.

At *Troop meetings* let each Patrol have its regular place in the Troop line-up, each Patrol its own sessions during the meeting in its own corner. Games and contests are conducted on a Patrol basis, with the Patrol the team. Each Patrol has a chance to bring in a new game and lead the others in playing it, or put on a demonstration of its specialty, or challenge the others in a competition.

On *Troop hikes* each Patrol takes care of its own commissary. The Patrols outdo each other in hunts for hidden "treasures," they compete with each other in cross-country games, test each other's ability in signaling, axemanship, cooking and other Scout accomplishments.

In *Troop camp* each Patrol has its share of the work. Tents are grouped by Patrols, cooking is done by Patrols, games and activities are run by Patrol teams.

Let Them Lead!

Again and again we come back to the important point

Less work and more fun for the Scoutmaster who qualifies his Patrol Leaders for hike and camp leadership at an early stage.

that you can't expect a gang of boys to build a good Patrol without a boy leader who has been trained to lead. And, as Baden-Powell says, "To get the best results, you must give the leader real freehanded responsibility. If you only give partial responsibility, you will only get partial results."

Let Patrol Leaders take over in practically everything. Let them work out their own problems, with the boys in their Patrols. Interfere as little as possible—but always be there to give guidance when they ask for it. Mistakes are bound to be made—therefore, be ready in a friendly spirit to urge the boy leader and his gang to try again.

"Train'em, trust'em, and let'em lead!" That is the formula for success in using Patrol Leaders and for building strong Patrols.

THE PATROL METHOD   V

The Life of the Troop

Troop Meeting Tonight

CHAPTER 8

IDEALLY, NO TROOP should have a single indoor meeting—all its activities should be in the outdoors!

Ideally, we say—for Scouting is a Movement of the out-of-doors, teaching boys citizenship through woodcraft. Boys join Scouting to have fun under the open sky, not to be cooped up in a Troop room.

But because of climate and the set-up of modern life, we have to confine some of the activities of the Troop to the surroundings of a meeting room—or even within its four walls.

When we do take the boys indoors, let's be positive that they don't get the impression that the indoor meeting *is* Scouting, but that it is simply a necessary step to outdoor Scouting.

Purposes of the Troop Meeting

A good Troop meeting can serve three main purposes:

1. The Troop meeting can help each Patrol to become a stronger team by keeping it on its toes preparing for the meeting. If, for instance, a Patrol project in first aid or lashing or fire-by-friction is scheduled for the Troop meeting, the Patrols will have to do something about it before the meeting comes around. If a signaling or knotting game is on the program, a Patrol will have a better chance of making a good showing if the boys have practiced before the meeting.

2. The Troop meeting can give each Scout a chance to learn something new that will make the outdoor experience that follows more enjoyable. A demonstration or dramatization of some outdoor skill can give the boy pointers he can use as soon as he gets outdoors.

3. The Troop meeting can have great value by simply bringing the boys together for a common experience. It can make them feel that they belong together, as parts of the whole big Scouting Brotherhood.

How Often Does the Troop Meet?

Although many Troops meet every week, this is by no means a requirement for running a good Troop. Patrol work is the important thing. Troop hikes and camps come next. Troop meetings are only necessary to hold the gang together and help the boys to steer the right course.

The idea, then, is to have just enough Troop meetings to round out the Troop's program of hikes and camps and Patrol activities.

The Patrol Leaders' Council meets for a short session after the Troop meeting to smooth out details for the next Troop event.

If you have smoothly working Patrols and a Patrol Leaders' Council that's running in high gear, *one meeting a month* may be just enough to supplement your outdoor activities.

Or you may find that your schedule of hikes, Patrol meetings, and leaders' meetings, will suggest a *Troop meeting every two weeks*. The monthly arrangement for the whole gang might then be somewhat along this line: Patrol meetings every week . . . Troop meetings, first and third week . . . planning meeting of Patrol Leaders' Council, second week . . . training get-together of Leaders' Patrol, fourth week . . . Troop hike or camp, third Saturday. This arrangement has proved satisfactory to numerous Troops.

Some Troops may come to the conclusion that they can manage *weekly Troop meetings,* besides the weekly

Patrol meetings, regular leaders' meetings and Troop hikes. Fine—but only if such a schedule strengthens the Patrols. If weekly Troop meetings crowd weekly Patrol meetings off the calendar, then you'd better take stock and reconsider—the tail may be wagging the dog, the Patrols may be losing out.

In all events, let the Patrol Leaders' Council make the final decision. The boy leaders know how much time their Scouts can give to Scout activities without impairing their school work and home life.

Setting Your Dates

When the frequency of Troop meetings has been determined, consult the whole Troop, if yours is a new gang, to find out what days suit the majority of the boys. Then set specific dates for the future. In an old Troop, you'll already have your meeting nights set.

If you meet twice a month, a rhyme may keep your boys reminded: "Every Scout in the Troop has heard: We meet on *Wednesdays—first* and *third!*" If you have weekly meetings, have a slogan of *"Friday Night* is *Scout Night* in Troop Five!"

Keep these dates as permanent as anything in this world can be, so that if something else comes up, your Scouts will automatically say: "Sorry, can't make it. It's Troop meeting night!"

The policy of the Boy Scouts of America is opposed to the erection of buildings for Scout headquarters, except in very rare cases. The National Council holds that the best interests of the boy are conserved by organizing Troops in institutions which will provide the Troops with the proper facilities.

The Meeting Place

OUTDOORS—The outdoor program of the Troop begins just outside the meeting room door. Get those youngsters outdoors for every meeting you can—if not for the whole meeting, then at least for part of it.

City Troops may meet in a park or vacant lot or schoolyard for the complete meeting. Or the meeting may start and end indoors, with the main feature an outdoor treasure or scavenger hunt.

If your Troop is located in a small town, you can plan to get entirely out of town for evenings of outdoor work and fun. Patrol suppers can be part of the program, and you can wind up with a camp fire, a commando game in the dark, or orientation by the stars.

The chapter on Hiking will give you numerous program suggestions that are applicable to the outdoor type of meeting.

INDOORS—A number of Troops are lucky enough to have their own Troop room, decorated in a Scouty manner, with a corner for each Patrol.

Other Troops have to meet in rooms used by other groups during the week—church halls, Sunday school rooms, club rooms. With very little effort you can give that kind of a room a Scout atmosphere, by hanging charts, pictures, banners, maps on the walls, to be taken down and stored between meetings. Patrol screens can here take the place of permanent Patrol corners.

Whether you have your own room or not, you need some place to keep Troop records and equipment used for the meetings, such as flags, ropes, staves, signal devices and so on. An artificial camp fire will prove a great asset.

The activities of the meeting will be influenced to a great extent by the type of place you have. If the meeting room is large, vigorous games are in order. If it is

small, activities will have to be comparatively quiet—
games and Scoutcraft projects that need plenty of elbow-
room are out.

What Goes Into the Troop Meeting?

In determining the activities of your Troop meetings,
keep in mind that they must not only fit the facilities
you have, but, what is even more important: They
must fit your Troop—your Patrols and your boys.

So, early in the game, have a session with your Troop
Leaders' Council for the express purpose of lining up
your Troop meetings. Go over the great variety of possible activities listed below. Pick those that best suit
your Troop. Then arrange them into a skeleton outline
on which you can base your future meetings:

THE INGREDIENTS OF THE TROOP MEETING

SCOUTCRAFT INSTRUCTION—By this we mean the introduction of some Scoutcraft that will help each Scout
to become better prepared. If you use the idea of planning
the program of your Troop around a monthly theme,
this presentation will, of course, cover the skill you are
concentrating on at the time. This part of the meeting
may be put on in several ways:

Talk—a SHORT and snappy one, by a qualified
speaker on the theme of the month.

Pictures—A talk will be greatly strengthened by the
use of a blackboard, charts or large-sized pictures.
Filmstrips or slides are even better. Occasionally,
use one of the special Scoutcraft training films that
are available through your Local Council.

Demonstration—Many subjects are best treated in the
form of a demonstration with the actual materials
at hand: "Packing Your Pack," "Making a Camp
Bed," and so on.

The activities of the Troop should motivate the Patrol. Smart Patrols practice at Patrol meetings for the next Troop meeting.

Dramatization—A number of skills adapt themselves easily to dramatization—axe safety and first aid, among others.

SCOUTCRAFT PRACTICE — The actual use during the Troop meeting of some Scouting knowledge, for practice in the subject, or for testing. This, too, will be based on the "theme of the month."

Scoutcraft Games—involving Scout skills, quickness of action or thought, observation and deduction, use of the senses—with the Patrols the teams.

Scoutcraft Projects—each Patrol showing its ability in a skill by completing a project in it. Such projects lend themselves especially well to contests between the Patrols.

Scout Formations—Just enough practice in the use of silent Scout hand signals to keep the boys alert, and to move the Patrols quickly into various formations for games and other activities.

FUN—Different program features that will add variety to the meeting and will help to build Troop spirit and enthusiasm:

Recreational Games—with emphasis on physical action and fun.

Songs—serious or humorous, old and new.

Yells—to "blow off steam," for unity and morale.

Story-Telling—by Scouts, leaders, outsiders.

INSPIRATION—Various means of keeping the ideals of Scouting before the boys in a natural manner:

Ceremonies—opening and closing ceremonies, investitures and advancement ceremonies.

Scout Oath and Law—occasional recitation of the Law, and re-dedication to the Scout Oath at special, outstanding events in the year's program.

Scoutmaster's Three Minutes—a *short,* inspirational talk by the leader.

ADMINISTRATION—Business matters will have to be looked after, but keep the time spent on them at a minimum.

Reports—by Patrols on attendance, advancement, uniforming. Reading of the Troop log by the Troop Scribe.

Dues—Payment of the Troop dues.

Inspection—of Uniform for neatness and correctness and proper wearing of Badges and Insignia.

Announcements—of forthcoming meetings, hikes, camps, and so on.

Skeleton
TROOP MEETING PROGRAM

Period	Activity
Before Meeting	Service Patrol arranges room. Patrol meetings. Games for arrivals to join. Personal conferences. Business (dues, attendance, library). Final check with leaders.
Opening Period	Patrol Reports. Opening ceremony. Scribe's Report. Inspection. Announcements relative to meeting.
Formations	Patrol Formations—silent signals.
Scoutcraft Presentation	Short talks on Scoutcraft. Instruction movie. Demonstration—Dramatization.
Patrol Corners	Patrol projects. Preparing for Patrol's participation in later contests, stunts, etc.
Scoutcraft Games	Scout skill games. Sense games.
Scoutcraft Projects	Contests between Patrols or between Patrol representatives.
Recreational Games	Strength games. Fun games.
Council Fire	Songs. Yells. Story-telling. Stunts. Scoutmaster's Minute.
Closing Period	Announcements of future events. Closing ceremony.
After Meeting	Personal interviews. Service Patrol cleans up. Short Leaders' Council meeting.

Planning the Details

When the skeleton of the Troop's meetings is once determined, it becomes comparatively simple to lay out the details of each individual meeting. While the program for the month as a whole is planned at the monthly meeting of the Patrol Leaders' Council, the plans for the Troop meeting immediately ahead are best checked at the short get-together of the leaders after each meeting is adjourned.

This short meeting has several advantages:

1. The leaders have the meeting just finished freshly in mind.

2. There may have been weak spots in the meeting that need to be corrected in the future, or good points worth following up.

3. All the leaders are present so that responsibilities for the next meeting may be assigned or volunteered for, and arrangements made for having necessary equipment on hand.

4. Patrol Leaders may get further suggestions for tying the activities of their Patrols in with the Troop activities.

The Senior Patrol Leader, as usual, is in the chair for this planning get-together. He has before him the Troop meeting skeleton, and the general program for the month. Now the specific meeting details are decided.

What ceremonies for the next meeting? What business do we have to cover? Is everything in readiness for the Scoutcraft presentation? What Scoutcraft games and projects? What Patrol corner activities? What fun games? What songs for the camp fire session? (Specific suggestions, see back of book). *Put the details down on paper, in a suitable arrangement* (See page 135).

Who will lead what? Some responsibilities are routine,

Troop One

Troop Meeting Program, Jan. 15th

7:25	Dues Collection and Attendance.	John
7:30	Line up. Opening: Flag Ceremony	Ralph
7:40	Scribe's Report.	Bill
	Patrol Contest Report.	Art
7:50	Game: Noises in the Night.	Marshall
8:00	Game: Who am I?	Ralph
8:10	Morse Signal Demonstration	Chief
8:20	To Patrol Corners. Make Signaller	
8:30	Morse game	Marshall
8:45	Newspaper Calisthenics	Art
8:55	Campfire – Songs	Sam
	Stunts	Patrols
	S.M.'s minute	Chief
9:20	Taps. Candle Ceremony	Ralph

such as: The Senior Patrol Leader in general charge of the meeting; the Scribe reading the accounts of the last hike from the Troop log book, handling dues and attendance, and so on. Other leaders and Explorers may receive special jobs for the meeting: One Assistant Scoutmaster will make the inspection and check on the month's advancement; the other will see how the decoration of the Patrol corners is coming along; the Beaver Patrol will put on the traction splint first aid demonstration; one Junior Assistant will handle the Bandage Relay and the Tourniquet Race, another will take Horse and Rider and British Bulldog. And so it goes. *Put the leaders' names down on paper next to their subject.* (See page 135).

Many Troops rotate special duties among the Patrols: The Patrol which is the *Service Patrol* arrives early; puts room in shape; starts the fire, if necessary; has material ready for games; is the last Patrol to leave after tidying up the room. The Patrol that has the job of being the *Program Patrol* is in charge of opening and closing ceremonies; of the "council fire" period with its songs and stunts, and of the Scoutcraft demonstration of the evening. These duties may be assigned on a monthly basis or from one meeting to the next. *Put the names of the duty Patrols down and make sure the Patrols know what is expected of them.*

Keep your old Troop meeting programs on file. In this way you will have on hand a list of good things which have been tried in the past and which have worked —games and projects requiring little preparation. They may come in handy some evening in a dull spot, when the program planned seems to slip.

With everything planned in advance, the Troop meeting should run off without a hitch.

The Scoutmaster's Part

What's your responsibility at the Troop meeting?

Your job will be on the side lines mostly.

You may get a questioning glance from the Senior Patrol Leader, that plainly says "Is the game dragging?", which you may answer with a slight nod: "Better shift, Joe."

A Junior Assistant may come to you: "Bob couldn't be here tonight. Will you be one of the judges in the relay?"

You may spend some of the time examining a new boy in his Tenderfoot requirements.

You may have occasion to say at the close of the meeting: "You did a swell job tonight, fellows!"

And you may catch yourself feeling good all over for the way in which the boy leaders run the Troop!

The Ideal Troop Meeting

The ideal Troop meeting—like the ideal after-dinner speech—is one that runs smoothly and is truly informal. But just as the successful "improvised" speech is the one that has been carefully planned, so the really informal Troop meeting is one in which the informality has been carefully thought out.

Don't be discouraged because every detail doesn't click as was expected. A meeting that looks perfect on paper may not quite work out that way, because boys are, at times, something less than predictable. But, just as often, a meeting will turn out to be infinitely better than it looked on paper—so it more than evens up.

Just keep working and hoping. Some day your Patrol Leaders' Council will devise a program for the Troop meeting that will work 100 per cent . . . maybe!

A FEW MEETING HINTS

Begin on time—close on time.

— — —

ACTION—VARIETY—PURPOSE—The Three Musketeers of all Troop activities.

— — —

Recipe for a good meeting:

Something old (a couple of the old favorite games)

Something new (a brand-new game; a new song; a new Scoutcraft trick)

Something surprising (a special visitor; a treat; a Scout movie)

Something true (a story based on the Scout Law; a story of a hero)

— — —

Boys have a thousand muscles to wiggle with and only one dozen to sit still with. That dozen gets mighty tired mighty quickly.

— — —

Keep every moment busy. Crowd things along, and you will have no discipline problems, no uncontrolled rough-housing.

— — —

As a general rule, allow no more than twenty minutes to any one activity.

— — —

Plan for more than can be accomplished rather than too little. Better leave some good things undone than to have the meeting "peter out" a half hour early.

— — —

Shift to something else before the boys tire of what they are doing.

— — —

If the planned program doesn't work, be resourceful. Throw some out, if necessary, to suit conditions.

— — —

Encourage members of the Troop Committee to attend regularly. When they come, have something definite for them to do.

— — —

Keep visitors on the side lines. Most of the time visitors come to see what is happening. Don't let them interrupt the meeting.

THE PROGRESS OF THE TROOP MEETING

Now that we have discussed the general idea behind the Troop meeting and the planning of it, let's follow the progress of a full and well-rounded meeting.

In the following pages you will find a great variety of suggestions from which your Patrol Leaders' Council can select the features that will best suit your Troop.

Well, let's say it's Troop meeting night tonight, and let's see what may happen:

Before the Meeting Opens

The Patrol assigned the duties of *Service Patrol* arrives about half an hour before the meeting starts to arrange the room and lay out needed equipment. During the winter, the Service Patrol may also have the responsibility for starting the stove in time for the room to be properly heated—unless heat is provided from a central source in the building.

As the boys arrive, they gather in their *Patrol corners*. The Patrol Leaders get busy with their boys to make sure that the Patrol is fully prepared for its part in the evening's program. The Patrol Scribes are busy, too, making up the attendance record and collecting dues.

PATROL CHECK-UP—In some Troops, a fifteen minute period is set aside for the Patrol check-up. The Patrols meet, say, at 7:30 P.M., and the Troop meeting begins at 7:45 P.M. SHARP.

PATROL RECORDS—Provide the Patrols with the "Patrol Record" books, and encourage them to keep their records in this helpful ten cent pamphlet.

DUES-ATTENDANCE ENVELOPES — A simple Troop record of attendance and dues is made possible by the use of the Dues-Attendance Envelopes advocated in the "Troop Budget" pamphlet. Dues are placed in the envelope and attendance marked on the outside (see page 140).

If the Troop has a *library,* this is the time for the Troop Librarian to go into action. He exchanges books and Merit Badge pamphlets until the meeting is called.

This is also a good time for the Scoutmaster to have *personal talks* with individual boys about particular questions or problems they may have. If you have these talks *before* rather than after the meeting the boys can return home promptly at the closing hour.

There will also be opportunity for early arrivals to get some *personal coaching* in Scoutcraft within their own Patrols.

Games? Possibly. There are differences of opinion on this subject. Some Scoutmasters feel that it's a good idea to have a few simple games in which the boys can enter as they arrive, to occupy the time before the meeting. Other Scoutmasters hold that the Patrols will be busy and should not be interfered with, and that no Troop activity should be undertaken previous to the exact moment for which the meeting is called—and least of all a vigorous game that might detract from the effect of a later regular game period.

PRE-OPENING TROOP GAMES—In case your Troop decides to use games before the actual start of the meeting, pick simple recreational games that can be started with two or three boys and which others can join upon arrival, such as: Skunk Tag, Spud, Jump the Shot, Dodge Ball, Poison (see Tool 11).

Make use of the Dues-Attendance Envelopes advocated in the Troop Budget Plan (see Tool No. 5 in back of the book). They are your simplest means for keeping correct records of dues and attendance. Dues are placed inside the envelope, the records marked on the outside. The Scribe is responsible for their use.

PRE-OPENING PATROL GAMES — Several games are suitable for occupying the Patrols as their boys arrive, such as Scout Law Hunt, Stamp Hunt, Letter Observation, Art Gallery (see Tool 11).

PRE-OPENING SING-SONG—Have a song leader present ahead of time. Start singing as soon as the boys begin to arrive and continue until time for meeting to start. Wind up with some vigorous songs sung wth body movements, such as "Down by the Old Mill Stream," "Under the Spreading Chestnut Tree," "One Finger, One Thumb."

Opening Period

At exactly the appointed hour the "curtain goes up" and the Troop meeting begins. If it is meant to start at 7:30 P.M., start at 7:30 P.M. If a Scout comes in late one week he will hurry a little more next week to be on time.

Patrol Line-Up

At the start of the meeting the Patrol Leaders line up their boys in their Patrol corners. The Patrol Scribe makes a final check of the boys present and the dues paid, and turns the record and the money over to the Troop Scribe.

Troop Formation

The Senior Patrol Leader brings everybody to attention with the silent attention signal, then gives the hand signal for Troop assembly.

The Patrol Leaders lead their boys into their proper position, and stand their Patrols "at ease."

Each Patrol Leader in turn may now give his Patrol's attendance record for the evening ("Beavers all present, sir" or "Six Foxes present, sir; John absent, sick; Charlie absent, out of town with his family"). It is also worthwhile to have each Patrol Leader report on the activities of his Patrol during the time since last Troop meeting, Calling for reports helps to encourage doing something to report.

The Troop then comes to attention. The Senior Patrol Leader turns to the Scoutmaster, salutes and reports: "The Troop is formed." The Scoutmaster salutes and tells the leader to proceed.

Opening Ceremony

The opening ceremony is handled by the Senior Patrol Leader or by the Program Patrol.

Make this formal opening dignified and impressive.

You may make it Scouty, by incorporating the *Scout Law* into the ceremony. There should be no special objection to using the Law regularly in Troop ceremonies, but refrain from using the Scout Oath too often in this manner. Use the Oath for special occasions, such as investitures and rededication during Boy Scout Week in February.

> SCOUT LAW CEREMONIES— (1) The Scout Law is recited by Tenderfoot Scouts only.
>
> (2) The newest Tenderfoot and the oldest Eagle Scout lead the Troop in reciting the Scout Law.
>
> (3) One point of the Scout Law is recited in full by the whole Troop.
>
> (4) One point of the Scout Law is assigned to each of twelve boys. Each boy in turn, takes a step forward, salutes, gives his point of the Law, steps back in line.

The opening ceremony may be given a patriotic atmosphere, by centering it around *The Flag of the United States.*

> FLAG CEREMONIES— (1) Troop in single rank formation. The Flag is carried to the front, whereupon the Patrol Leader of the Honor Guard Patrol leads whole Troop in Pledge of Allegiance: "I pledge allegiance to The Flag of the United States of America and to the republic for which it stands, one nation, under God, indivisible, with liberty and justice for all."

The opening ceremony of the Troop meeting should be short and Scout-like. It sets the tone for the rest of the meeting.

(2) Troop formed by Patrols in two lines facing each other. The Flag is marched up between lines with Scouts saluting. It is halted at the head of the lines and turned about face, whereupon whole Troop gives the Pledge of Allegiance.

(3) Troop in horseshoe formation, The Flag in center. Each Scout in turn steps forward one step, salutes and steps back.

(4) Troop in single rank. Bring Scouts to attention, turn out all lights with the exception of a single spot (or flashlight) focused on The Flag. A Scout from the Color Guard Patrol recites—doesn't sing—first verse of the "Star-Spangled Banner." The Troop then sings the verse, whereupon lights are turned on.

(5) Troop in line faces end of room where at the top of the wall a small pulley with a flag line is fastened. Troop comes to attention. The Flag is slowly hoisted while the bugler plays "To the Colors" or the Troop

sings one verse of the National Anthem, "My Country, 'Tis of Thee," "God Bless America," or "America the Beautiful."

In some Troops, the opening ceremony is tied in with the *Troop Flag* and with the traditions and history it represents.

TROOP FLAG CEREMONIES—(1) Salute the Troop flag. Give the Troop yell or sing the special Troop song.

(2) The Scouts salute the Troop flag and repeat after the Senior Patrol Leader the Troop's special pledge, along this line: "As a member of Troop One, I pledge that I shall always strive: To be a good member of my Patrol—To take part in all Troop activities—To advance in Scoutcraft—To act as a Scout at all times."

(3) Form the Patrols as spokes in a wheel, with the Troop flag in the center. Patrol Leaders hold on to the flagpole with the left hand. Behind them, their Scouts place their hands on the shoulder of the boy in front of them. The Troop sings an appropriate Scout song, such as "Hail, Hail, Scouting Spirit" or "Trail the Eagle."

The opening ceremony may have a *religious touch,* with a half-minute silence for silent, personal prayers, or, in a church-sponsored Troop, with the recitation aloud of a prayer approved by the church.

Develop a ceremony that fits your particular Troop and may become a Troop tradition. Or develop several and vary the opening from time to time.

The Troop Log Book contains the history and traditions of your Troop. It should be a vivid account of the doings of Troop, Patrols and individuals — reported with tact, humor, impartiality and good judgment. Keep it well illustrated with photographs and sketches, even if a primitive type.

Historian's Report

The Troop Scribe reads aloud from the Troop log book the minutes of the previous meeting and the report of Troop activities that have taken place since. Someone makes the motion that the report be accepted as read or as corrected. The motion is properly seconded and voted upon.

Having the log publicly read at each Troop meeting is one of the best ways of assuring that it is good and up-to-date. The Troop Scribe will do a much better job on the "glorious history of the good, old Troop" if his work is considered important enough to be a feature of every Troop meeting instead of being "one-of-those-things" that has to be done.

Inspection

The formal opening may be followed occasionally by an inspection of the Patrols for correct uniforming. While the Troop stands at ease, the Scoutmaster and other Troop leaders make their rounds. As they approach each Patrol, the Patrol Leader brings his Patrol to attention. Or the Patrol Leaders themselves form the inspecting party, the Assistant Patrol Leaders bringing the Patrols to attention.

During the first few weeks of a new Troop, correct uniform may consist of the Troop neckerchief only. When it is known that a boy has a uniform, he should be made to feel that he has failed in his obligations if he does not wear it.

GENERAL INSPECTION takes in tidy appearance, clean face, hands, shoes, and correct Uniform, including Badges and Insignia.

SURPRISE INSPECTIONS may be sprung from time to time. Such combinations as "left ear—right shoe" or "neckerchief—hair combed" or "Patrol medallion—stockings" and others add fun to the inspection.

In the course of inspection, give praise where praise is due, and make any criticism impersonally and with care. Better no criticism than some that might embarrass a boy before his friends.

You will never get good uniforming in your Troop unless you insist upon good uniforming. And you can't very well insist upon it unless *you* are correctly uniformed. Again, your example is one of the most important factors—as in everything else connected with the Troop.

Announcements

At this stage, there may be a few announcements that need to be made concerning the program of the meeting. Make them short and sweet and to the point. They can be in the form of "Orders of the Day" written out in advance and now read aloud before the Troop by the Scribe.

Formations

Simple Troop formations are necessary for orderliness and smartness, and for getting the Patrols lined up quickly for games and projects.

These formations call for a certain amount of drill —the Scout type of drill, using silent hand signals, and not the military drill with its barked commands.

Scout Drill is described in Tool 15 in the back of this book.

The most useful Troop formations are these:

TROOP FORMATIONS—*Single Rank and Double Rank Formation* for general Troop line-up, inspection, and line games.

Parallel File Formation (Indian file by Patrols) for relay games.

Council or "U" Formation — for investitures and other ceremonies.

Simple Troop formations are necessary for orderliness and smartness. Scout drill, using silent signals, is most suitable type.

Circle Formation—for circle games, for watching demonstrations and for camp fire.

Open Columns and Closed Columns by Patrols — for marching, for special reviews and parades.

Since Scout drill treats drill as a game, to be enjoyed just as much as any other game, the point is to drill just enough to take care of possible needs. Never overdo it to the point where the boys tire of it.

When Scout drill is first introduced, a couple of minutes' practice in it may be included in the program for a few meetings.

When the boys have become familiar with the silent signals and the formations that go with them, no further special practice is necessary.

They will then fall naturally into formation when a signal is given.

Scoutcraft Presentation

*Scout*craft, obviously, is one of the most important parts of a *Scout* meeting. A boy should go home from every Troop meeting feeling that he has learned something new in Scouting, something he wants to practice at home and in his Patrol.

In all probability your Troop bases its program on themes, concentrating a month's work around a certain Scouting skill. The Scoutcraft presentation will logically feature some phase of this skill. It will not attempt to teach it, but will try to give the Patrols the incentive to follow up on the subject at Patrol meetings and on Patrol hikes.

The Scoutcraft presentation at the Troop meeting is not meant to be a formal instruction, dividing the subject into so many lessons, with an "expert" putting his stuff across. Scouting is not interested in mass instruction. Scouting is not regimented learning. Our efforts are directed toward giving each boy an opportunity to grow according to his own abilities and interests, to learn at his own speed. We want to see Scouts train themselves and each other right in their own Patrols.

This is one factor which makes Scouting distinctive as an educational movement. As Baden-Powell says: "If once we make Scouting into a formal scheme of serious instruction in efficiency, we miss the whole point and value of Scout training, and we encroach on the work of the schools without the trained experts for carrying it out. We want to get ALL our boys along through cheerful self-development from within and not through the imposition of formal instruction from without."

Besides being against Scouting principles, mass instruction in the Troop is impractical: The average Troop consists of a mixture of Tenderfoot, Second and First Class Scouts. Any mass instruction at Troop meeting would be too advanced for some and too elementary for others. And furthermore—no Scoutcraft subject can be thoroughly taught and learned in weekly twenty-minute periods.

Ways of Presenting Scoutcraft

The main purpose of the Scoutcraft presentation is to show some of the aspects of a Scouting skill in such a fashion, that the boys will be inspired to get deeper into the subject and master as much of it as possible.

If your theme for the month is "Communications," for instance, several types of presentations may be made during a series of Troop meetings: At one meeting, a good speaker may tell an exciting "camp fire" story of life saving through signaling. At the following meeting, an Explorer may show how to make a simple blinker or buzzer from scrap metal. Next time one of the Patrols may demonstrate signaling methods during the ages. And finally, the leader in charge of the commando game scheduled for the Troop hike of the month will explain the signaling project planned for the climax of the game.

If properly presented, the result should be: A vivid interest in the subject, a desire to learn more about it, tricks to be tried out in the Patrol, a way of using the knowledge in the out-of-doors which will require Patrol practice.

You have a wide choice of methods for presenting Scoutcraft at the Troop meeting:

TALK—A talk is probably the least effective method. Yet, if well done, by a person who knows his stuff and how to present it to boys, a talk may provide a good starting point. A general treatment is better than one going into too many details. True-life incidents add color. A first aider, for instance, may tell of "Accidents I Have Dealt With,"; a forest ranger of "Forest Fires we Have Fought," combining information and drama.

BLACKBOARD TALK—A blackboard provides the chance to illustrate a talk with simple sketches and diagrams. The principles of building a pioneer bridge or a signal tower can be shown more easily in a diagram than by demonstrating with full-length timbers. A blackboard presentation also makes boy participation possible: The speaker can draw out the boys and write down their ideas on such a subject, for example, as: "What Equipment Do I Need for an Overnight?"

LARGE-SIZE PICTURES, SLIDES AND FILMSTRIPS — make a talk even more effective. The BOYS' LIFE photo features on Scoutcraft may be used here. A number of series of slides and filmstrips are available; many more are under preparation.

MOTION PICTURES—Our special Scout films are excellent for interesting the boys in a Scoutcraft subject. They range from "Axemanship" and "Life Saving" to "Conservation" and "Forestry" ("The Scout in the Forest"). Your Scout Executive has a list of Scout films and can get them for you.

DEMONSTRATIONS—are your best bets for the Scoutcraft presentation. They can be put on by individuals or by Patrols. A leader may demonstrate fire-by-friction; how to pack a pack; how to sharpen an axe. A Patrol may show how to lash a bridge trestle; how to improvise emergency stretchers; how to make a fire rescue. Take time off after the demonstration to answer all questions the Scouts may raise.

DRAMATIZATIONS—work well for a number of subjects. Axe safety, for example, may be shown in a Patrol skit of "Tenderfoot Willie Brings His Axe to Camp"—Willie, of course, being shown by his Patrol pals how to use his axe correctly after having handled it in the most dangerous manner. Any number of first aid "dramas" are possible.

Of the various methods of Scoutcraft presentation, demonstrations and dramatizations *put on by Patrols,* are the most beneficial all-round. They kill three birds with one stone: They present the subject in an interesting way to the whole Troop; they give the Patrol putting on the presentation the incentive to get to-

The Scoutcraft theme of the month should be brought into each Troop meeting program. A game or a demonstration will do it.

gether at Patrol meetings for practice; and they encourage friendly rivalry between the Patrols to give the best performance.

Suggestions for projects for demonstrations and dramatizations may be found in Tools 10 and 11.

Patrol Corners

The Scoutcraft presentation becomes especially effective if it is followed immediately by Patrol practice in Patrol Corners.

"Patrol Corners" is the name usually given the periods during Troop meeting when the Patrols meet by themselves in their respective corners. Patrol Corners are primarily meant as breaks between activities—opportunities for the Patrols to check up on plans and to prepare for the things that follow.

If, for instance, a special game or project based upon the Scoutcraft presentation of the evening has been announced for later in the meeting, this is the time when the Patrol picks its team. If volunteers are needed for a Troop Good Turn, the Patrol finds out which boys are available. If the camp fire period calls for a stunt from each Patrol, this is when the Patrol develops its skit.

Patrol Corners are not, of course, a substitute for the Patrols' weekly meetings. They are an *extra chance* for the Patrols to get together by themselves. With scheduled things to do, Patrol Corners can be among the most profitable parts of the Troop meeting.

PATROL CORNERS IDEAS—(1) Each Patrol develops a dramatization based upon the Scoutcraft skill presented earlier in the meeting, to be put on as a contest between the Patrols.

(2) Prepare pantomime or charade of assigned point of Scout Law, for the council fire period.

(3) Develop a new Troop yell, to be demonstrated later. The best yell will be taught to the whole Troop under the leadership of the Patrol that invented it.

(4) Make up a couple of new verses for the Troop's favorite stunt song.

(5) Run an elimination contest in knotting, signaling, fire-by-friction, Scout Quiz, talk fest or the like—the winner to enter in the contest period which follows.

(6) Discuss the Scout Law for the purpose of having each Patrol present a one-minute speech: "Why our Patrol considers the . . . . point of the Scout Law of greatest importance."

(7) Similar one-minute speech on "The most important Scout Requirement for First Class" or "The most important Merit Badge."

(8) Spring surprise games while the Patrols are in their corners, such as Famous Visitors, Newspaper Search (see index: Games).

Scoutcraft Games and Projects

Baden-Powell says: "The training of Boy Scouts is done mainly by means of games, practices and competitions such as interest them . . . "

"Patrol corners" during the Troop meeting give the Patrols a chance to train for a contest or work on a project by themselves.

At the Troop meeting this training takes the form of Scoutcraft games and competitions in Scoutcraft projects, *with the Patrols the teams throughout.*

The distinction between a Scoutcraft game and a project is this: A Scoutcraft game may be considered *playing at a skill* for further practice, while a project is *doing the real thing,* or a reasonable facsimile, for the sake of determining the Patrols' ability.

If, for instance, the Scouts of each Patrol run up, one after the other, to tie eight clove hitches around a post in Knot Relay, they are playing a game. If the same Scouts use the same clove hitches for making a trestle for a bridge, they are carrying out a project. If the Scouts run up, relay style, to put bandages on a victim, they are playing a game. If they use the bandages to solve a first aid problem, they are working out a project. The project becomes a competition when all the Patrols take part at the same time, each Patrol trying to do a quicker and better job than the others.

SCOUTCRAFT GAME IDEAS—(1) Announce in advance a Scoutcraft game, giving each Patrol a chance at a couple of Patrol meetings to train in the skill involved; such as Signaling Relay, using the whole Morse alphabet; Knot Relay using a couple of new knots; Bandaging Relay calling for use of the triangular bandage.

(2) Follow a Scoutcraft presentation with a game based upon the new knowledge required, maybe in the form of a Scout Quiz, or an "Information, Please" panel.

(3) Scoutcraft games may be arranged to lead the Patrol outdoors: A Treasure Hunt may start in the meeting room, then continue with outdoor clues. A nature talk may be followed by a Nature Scavenger Hunt. An indoor memory game like The Peddler may be followed by The Leaking Packsack outdoors.

(4) Scoutcraft games based on the same subject may be varied by choosing games calling for a variety of formations: Relay, circle, line games.

Tool 11 in the back of this handbook contains numerous Scoutcraft games.

SCOUTCRAFT PROJECT IDEAS.

(1) Immediately after a demonstration or dramatization by one Patrol, have each of the other Patrols try its hand at the same presentation, with the original Patrol the judge of their efforts. Give the Patrols a chance for practice in Patrol Corners.

The Scout Movement has a full program of its own. It does not depend on activities borrowed from gymnasium or ball field. Boys join the Troop to get Scouting. Give it to them. Boys can get their interest in ball playing satisfied by belonging to a ball club, while keeping up their Scout membership.

(2) From time to time spring a surprise competition in some Scoutcraft project, not recently presented.

(3) Try "Challenge": A Patrol with a Scoutcraft specialty challenges the other Patrols to a contest in that subject. Rules are prepared by junior leaders and sufficient time is allowed for training.

For description of a large variety of Scoutcraft projects, see Tool 11.

Recreational Games

Some of the games at the Troop meeting should be for fun, to provide physical exercise, and to give an outlet for the boys' boundless energy.

An inexperienced Scoutmaster may try to hold the Troop together by giving the boys "plenty of games" of the fun type. As the games grow stale, the leakage starts. He may make a desperate effort to keep the boys by providing "games he knows they want"—basketball, softball and the like. The leakage stops for a moment, then accelerates: Boys don't come to Scout meetings week after week for games they play daily on playgrounds or in school gymnasium.

The important thing is to strike a proper balance between games of physical action and general fun with games related to the Scoutcraft theme of the month. Scouts want both. They tire as readily of a game menu that is all one thing as of one that is all the other.

As a general rule, the recreational games of the Troop meeting should *not* be the same games the boys play in the playground. They should be "different"—more scouty and with rules changed to fit the set-up of the Troop.

The Patrols are the game teams. If two teams are needed, make them as even as possible without breaking up the Patrols. Most relay games can be run by natural Patrols, even if they are of different size: If a Patrol has five members, three of its Scouts run twice, to make up for the full number of the Patrol that has eight members.

RECREATIONAL GAME IDEAS—(1) Occasionally have a "Hit Parade" of games. At the beginning of the meeting, give out ballot sheets for the boys to vote for their most popular game. During game period, run the four most popular games, beginning with No. 4, ending with No. 1.

(2) During Patrol Corners have each Patrol choose its two favorite games. Each Patrol then leads its favorite during the game period. (The reason for picking two is to provide second choices if two Patrols pick the same game as their favorite.)

(3) Run the Troop's favorite games *in the dark* as a new thrill.

See Tool 11 in the back of the book for many types of recreational games.

Council Fire Period

After the physical activities of games and projects, the Troop settles down for the council fire period. A few Troops are able to squat down in front of a real log fire in the fireplace of their meeting room, others form a circle around an artificial camp fire built of logs illuminated by a red electric bulb. Still others are fortunate enough to have a council fire outdoors.

Now starts a period of fun, fellowship and inspiration as song follows song, interspersed with yells, stories and stunts.

Possibly the council fire period is the most important part of the Troop meeting for bringing in the more serious side of Scouting. Be sure, therefore, that the program of this period is as good as possible.

Singing

Boys like to sing. The council fire—even an artificial fire—provides a good chance. So get them singing!

Some of the games of the Troop meeting give practice in Scout skills, others are for fun and physical exercise.

In any Troop there is apt to be at least one natural song leader.

Find him and let him lead.

Encourage the Patrols to build a selection of their own favorite songs and to develop their own song leaders. Have the Troop song leader work them into the program.

Start the council fire with peppy solo-and-chorus songs such as "Old MacDonald Had a Farm," "Three Wood Pigeons," "Australia," "Climbing up the Ladder." Shift into lively hiking songs, such as "We're Happy While We're Hiking," "As We Swing Down the Trail," "Trail the Eagle," and proceed from those to the old, soft, familiar songs like "Old Black Joe," "Home on the Range," "By the Blazing Council Fire's Light."

You will find songs and hints on song leading in the

Scout book, *Songs Scouts Sing,* and in Tool 16 of this handbook.

Yells

Yells—by Patrols or by the whole Troop—belong in the early part of the period. They are good as applause for stunts.

See *Handbook for Patrol Leaders* for suggestions.

Stunts

Stunts by Patrols or by individuals should form a part of every council fire period. These stunts may be short skits, improvised dramatics rehearsed during Patrol Corners, Scoutcraft demonstrations, Indian ceremonies, and camp fire challenge games.

Keep them short, wholesome, and lively.

See *Handbook for Patrol Leaders* for ideas.

Story Telling

Stories, by all means!—*told,* not read, by the Scoutmaster, a member of the Troop or an outsider.

These, too, should be short and to the point, preferably focusing upon one "hero," one idea. Toward the end of the council fire the boys will be receptive to the suggestion of a hero tale, simply, briefly told. Only, be careful to select "live" subjects that appeal to boys. Don't make it "goody-goody" and naturally DON'T POINT OUT THE MORAL.

Further story telling suggestions will be found in Tool 17.

The Scoutmaster's Three Minutes

Closing the council fire period, the Scoutmaster should leave with the Scouts a "thought for the week," so to speak—impressing upon them the fact that they are Scouts and therefore are expected to act like Scouts.

The council fire provides inspiration and fellowship. Even the artificial fire of the meeting room serves the purpose.

This may be done in story form—which can take the place of any other story telling in the council fire period —or it may be in the form of a short talk based upon some point of the Scout Law or Oath.

Make it brief, stop short when the idea has been expressed (remember the rule of a good speaker: "Stand up, speak up, shut up!"), and proceed quickly to the closing of the meeting.

COUNCIL FIRE IDEAS

(1) Announce winners of Troop competitions. Yells for and by the lucky Patrol.

(2) Which Patrol knows and can sing most songs? Have a "Sing-Song" contest.

(3) Try debates on everyday problems involving the Scout Law. Examples: "In a rally your Patrol is all set to win when one of the fellows muffs a knot in the

knot tying event. Your Patrol loses. What would you say to him after the event?"

"At camp a Scout in your tent has to go to church very early and leaves his bed unmade, asking you to attend to it for him. This you refuse to do. What mistake have each of you made? What points of the Scout Law are involved?"

(4) Start a round-robin story, the Scoutmaster telling the first chapter, leaving the hero facing an "insurmountable" obstacle, the next boy to get him out of it, the following boy to get him into another difficulty, etc.

(5) Scouts to tell: "My Most Exciting Scout Experience."

(6) Call for reports of nature study, camp site exploration and the like.

(7) Which Patrol can tell the tallest tall story? Contest between Patrol representatives. The winner receives the "Silver Cup of Oratory"—an old tin can.

(8) Reading of the week's "Mystery Letter." Interest a Scout, a leader or a member of the Troop Committee with writing ability to send the Troop a weekly letter, commenting upon the activities, jokingly, seriously, or even critically, signed "The Mystery Man of Troop Five." This opens up a means of straightening out many small difficulties in an interesting and exciting manner. Naturally, the identity of the writer must always remain a deep secret.

(9) Use the council fire period for investiture of new boys.

The Council Fire period of the Troop meeting is greatly enhanced if the boys can gather around a camp fire—although an artificial one. Such a "fire" may be made by nailing together pieces of wood into a council fire "lay" and lining it with red paper. The base is plywood, with an electric bulb.

Closing Period

And so we get to the final period of the meeting: the closing exercises.

Have each meeting end on a high note. The last things the Scouts do, the last impressions, are the ones they carry away with them from the meeting.

Announcements First

In closing, announcements may be necessary, but do not present a fine closing ceremony, then spoil it by winding up with some commonplace reminders.

Make all statements definite and clear-cut, so that no mistake is possible. Follow all important announcements with a snappy: "Any questions?" If questions arise, repeat the announcement and clarify vague points.

And by the way, if announcements of future events were made at the opening, repeat them at closing, but always *before* the ceremony. The memory of boys is not very long.

Closing Ceremony

Make the closing ceremony itself brief and dignified, and time it in such a way that it ends the meeting as close to the appointed hour as possible.

The Flag of the United States has a place in many closing ceremonies. Several of the ceremonies on page 142, suggested for openings, may be used equally well in closing.

Many Troops use "Taps" or a similar soft evening song.

Often the Scoutmaster brings the meeting to its close with the Scout Benediction, whereupon the boys are dismissed by Troop, by Patrols, or occasionally by rank— the Eagle Scouts first, then Life, Star, First Class, and so on.

CLOSING IDEAS—(1) Close meeting with Troop singing of "Taps" (words in *Songs Scouts Sing*), unaccompanied or led by a muffled bugle, the lights dimmed (or use two bugles, one giving the call, the other the echo effect). Each boy slowly raises his outstreched hands in front of him during first two lines (to ". . . from the sky . . ."), then lowers them again during the rest of the song.

(2) Troop formation. Scout Benediction: "May the Great Master (all make gesture toward heavens) of all Scouts (inclusive gesture from right to left at height of shoulder) be with you till we meet again (right hands being brought to hearts and heads bowed)."

(3) Form a circle. Have each boy make the Scout Sign and with the left hand grasp the lifted right wrist of his left neighbor. Recite the Scout Law or a Troop Pledge.

(4) Bring all Scouts to attention. Give the order, "Fall in alphabetically within the Patrols." Upon which the Scouts scramble into line as nearly as they can make it in the alphabetical order of their surnames. This will merge the game period into the closing.

(5) Finish with America yell ("A-M-E-R-I-C-A, Boy SCOUTS, BOY Scouts, U-S-A"), followed by Sky Rocket ("Ssss," the hiss of the rising rocket; "Boom," the bursting; and then the soft exclamation as it spreads, "Ah-h," and the terrific boy-satisfying yell, "Scout.")

(6) Retire The Flag with proper camp ceremony, using bugle. If no bugle, whistle "To the Colors" and "Retreat."

(7) One round of Patrol calls. Troop yell. Scoutmaster: "Good night to you." Scouts: "Good night to you, sir."

(8) Form brotherhood circle, arms around each other's shoulders. Song leader leads Troop in Scout Vesper song, or similar good-night song. When the song is ended, Scouts leave room in silence.

(9) Form circle. Each Scout crosses arms in front of himself, grasps his neighbors' hands. Sing "Auld Lang Syne," swaying bodies softly in rhythm.

Close the meeting with a short ceremony, and send the boys home with the ideals of Scouting uppermost in their minds.

(10) Troop in line. The Scoutmaster says, "Be Prepared." To which all Scouts respond in unison, "We are prepared!"

After the Meeting

See that Scouts leave immediately after the meeting is over so that they get home at the hour their parents expect them. Unless you insist on this, a number of them will "hang around."

Many Troops build up traditions of prompt dismissal and Scout-like conduct on the trip home. Such traditions prevent unfortunate complaints from a Troop's neighbors about yelling and rough-house disturbing them on Scout meeting nights.

The "closing" should mean exactly that and no Scout other than members of the Patrol Leaders' Council, should be permitted to stay beyond a few minutes unless he has an extra duty to perform or an important personal problem. As far as possible, personal problems should be discussed with the Scoutmaster *before* rather than after the meeting—but, of course, the Scouts should feel at liberty to approach you with their problems at any time.

The Work of the Service Patrol

As soon as the meeting is over, the Service Patrol for the evening gets to work cleaning up the room, putting away equipment used, and finally turning off the lights. If anything has been damaged during the meeting, arrangements are made to repair or replace it.

Patrol Leaders' Council

The Patrol Leaders' Council gathers for a short get-together to discuss the meeting just finished and check the plans for the coming week (see page 58).

With the leaders' meeting another Troop meeting comes to a close.

The Troop Goes Hiking

CHAPTER 9

ADVENTURE IN THE OUTDOORS — that, more than anything else, makes a boy want to be a Scout.

When a boy joins your Troop, does he feel the out-of-doors sweeping through all the activities, even those between the four walls of the meeting room? Is there always the promise of a hike or camping trip ahead— and still another one ahead of that?

If the answer is "Yes," you will hold him. You won't be able to keep him away.

What is a Hike?

One way to define a hike in Scouting is to call it "a tramping trip for training." Short or long, unless there's a reason for going on a hike, with plenty to do along the way, you'll have only a bunch of bored youngsters on your hands.

In a young Troop, the purpose of the first few hikes will be to train the boys in the simple handy knowledge of how to get along in the open. The hike will be easy, with observation games on the outward trek, fire building and the preparing of a simple meal upon arrival at a suitable spot, a bit of practice in first aid or signaling, and a return trip possibly with nature study along the route—all of the skills required of a Second Class Scout.

As the Troop grows older, the purpose of its hikes broadens. There will be more difficult things to do—a bridge to be built to get across a stream, a shelter to be constructed, an unexpected, staged "disaster accident" which requires immediate action to save the *victim's* life.

How Often?

In addition to the hiking and camping the Patrols do on their own, have *at least one outdoor Troop activity each month*—either a hike or a camp.

The simplest way to put enough hikes into your pro-

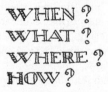

WHEN?
WHAT?
WHERE?
HOW?

There are four important points to a Hike: *When?* — Saturday, Sunday or a holiday. *What?*— Scoutcraft, exploration, nature lore, mapping, and so on. *Where?* Along an interesting route, ending up at a spot suitable for hike cookery. *How?* What equipment to take along and how to carry it.

The Patrol Leaders' Council discusses hike routes on a map of your territory and determines the details of the hike.

gram is to decide, for example, at the beginning of the year: "A Troop Hike every third Saturday of the month"—and then stick to it. Knowing what is ahead, the boys can plan for it, their parents know about it, and most of the Troop will show up.

On the other hand, "What about a hike this Saturday?" won't get out many Scouts. And the Troop that says: "Let's see if we can't manage a hike next month," will get nowhere in an outdoor program.

Planning the Troop Hike

When?

When will it be?

Usually, *Saturday* is the best day for hikes. The boys are out of school, leaders are apt to have the day off.

Certain *holidays,* such as Washington's Birthday, Memorial Day, Columbus Day, are also good days.

As far as *Sunday* is concerned, you are asked to conform to the resolution of the National Council of the Boy Scouts of America:

"WHEREAS, the Boy Scouts of America is specifically pledged to encourage reverence and faithfulness to religious obligations; and WHEREAS, the attention of the National Council has been called to the fact that in some cases Scouts have been permitted to neglect church attendance while at week-end camps or on week-end hikes,

"BE IT RESOLVED, that the National Council records its disapproval of programs for week-end hikes or camps which preclude the attendance of Scouts from religious services, or which cause loss of credits for the individual or Patrol or Troop, if the Scout elects to remain at home to attend church."

This does not mean that Sunday hikes are out, but they should be planned with the approval of the parents and the clergy involved and should not interfere with the boys' religious obligations.

What?

With the day set, the Patrol Leaders' Council works out the details of the hike a month ahead, and assigns leadership for each game and project.

The hike program follows the theme the Troop is working on for that month. If the theme is Observation, have a Treasure Hunt. If it's Concealment, a Commando Raid might be the thing. If it's Orientation, try a Bee-Line Hike. See chart page 169.

Have the Patrol Leaders' Council look over and discuss the list of possible ingredients for the hike, and develop a *skeleton outline* of suitable activities (page 170).

HIKES WITH A PURPOSE

Detailed suggestions about each of these hikes are found in Tool 12 in back of book.

PURPOSE	TYPE OF HIKE
KNOWLEDGE OF COMMUNITY	Historical Hike
NATURE	Nature Hike Star Hike
OBSERVATION	Explorers Treasure Hunt Industrial or Institutional Hike
PHYSICAL FITNESS	Long Distance Hike Swimming Hike Mountain Climb
SELF-RELIANCE	Primitive Cookery Hike Survival Hike
SCOUT SPIRIT	Rovering Knights Conservation Hike "Lost Child" Hike
PLUCK	Commando Hike (Wide Game) North Pole Race Bee-Line Hike
SCOUTCRAFT	Map Hike Signal Hike First Aid ("S.O.S.") Hike Scoutcraft Obstacle Hike Sealed Orders Hike Advancement Hike
FRIENDSHIP	Visiting Troop Hike Father-and-Son Hike Reunion (Old Timers') Hike

Some of the hikes mentioned above fall under various classifications but appear under the heading of the main emphasis. Several of them may be combined into one hike.

Skeleton

TROOP HIKE PROGRAM

PERIOD	ACTIVITY
BEFORE THE HIKE	Each Patrol meets in dens or at separate meeting points. Travel to Troop gathering place. Check by Patrol Leaders.
TROOP ASSEMBLY	Patrols Report. Inspection. Announcements and final instructions.
OUT-TRIP	Formations. Games along the trail. Competitions. Singing.
AT DESTINATION	Scoutcraft demonstration. Outdoor Living. Games—Scoutcraft. Games—Recreational. Competitions in Scoutcraft projects. Examination in Scout Requirements. Outdoor Ceremonies. Camp Fire. Clean-up of site.
TROOP DISMISSAL	Announcements. Dismissal.
RETURN TRIP	By Patrols.

Have a definite theme for each hike. A "Survival Hike," looking for edible plants, is more exciting than "just another hike."

THE INGREDIENTS OF THE TROOP HIKE

SCOUTCRAFT INSTRUCTION — The introduction of some phase of the Scoutcraft skill that forms the monthly theme, or some other skill related to hiking. *Demonstration*—is the best method for such an outdoor presentation and is especially effective if it is followed immediately by practice.

SCOUTCRAFT PRACTICE—Using new skills just learned and other skills that make a hike a success:

Outdoor Living—Learning to become a self-reliant hiker, showing efficiency in applying outdoor knowledge: Firemaking and cooking for preparing a meal; axemanship and knotting for building a rustic bridge, orientation and map reading for finding the way.

Scoutcraft Games and Projects—with Patrol teams.

FUN—Program features that provide variety, team spirit, and a chance for vigorous activity:

Recreational Games—for physical fitness and fun.

Songs and Yells—to build morale and shorten the way while on the road.

INSPIRATION—Different activities that will help to remind the boys of their Scouting ideals:

Camp Fire—with a balanced program of songs, yells, story-telling, inspirational talk by the Scoutmaster. (This provides recreation as well).

Ceremonies—investitures and advancement ceremonies in an outdoor setting.

Natural Occurrences—may give real inspiration: A colorful sunset, a rainbow, a distant storm, and so on. They can, of course, not be planned for, but if they do happen and are subtly brought to the boys' attention, they may affect them deeply.

ADMINISTRATION — Business matters directly related to the hike. Keep them down to brass tacks:

Reports—on Patrol attendance, before the start of the hike.

Inspection—check on uniforming and equipment before the hike, for appearance at time of dismissal.

Announcements — whatever is necessary to explain the activities of the hike.

When an outline is developed, add a simple *time schedule* giving the approximate time to get to the hike destination, the time involved in a game or a project, the time the Patrols will get their cooking under way, the time the clean-up should be completed, the time to start on the return journey to get back to town as planned. A schedule fairly well kept helps to establish standards of promptness and good management in the Patrols.

The outline and time schedule may look something like this:

Troop One

Scoutcraft Hike
May 31st

9:00   Troop meets.
Patrol Leaders check on their Patrols.
Check up. (Jack and Bill in charge)

9:15   Start of out-journey.
Scout's Pace. (Clocked by Bill and John)
Game: Hares and Hounds. Eagle Patrol responsible.

10:45   Tracks of "Hares" end at Gilwell Camp.
Signaling Relay. (Jack in charge)
First Aid "Accident". (Marshall)

11:45   Building of Patrol Fires.
Lunch: Kabob, baked potatoes, sandwiches
brought from home.

1:15   Clean-up. Check-up by Troop Leaders'
Council.

1:30   Game: Capture the Flag. (Bill in charge)

2:30   Dismiss Troop.
Start home journey by Patrols.

4:00   Back in Town.

Where?

Where will we go?

At the Patrol Leaders' Council suggestions will come up about the hike route. You may pick an old familiar one or determine to strike out over new ground.

If you decide to try something new, a topographic map in the scale of one-inch-to-one-mile is particularly good for hike planning. For a new route, it is always best to have a couple of leaders investigate it in advance, to find out whether it is suitable, and to get permission from landowners for lighting fires, or cutting dead wood, or simply for trespassing. The leaders also make it a point to learn things of local interest along the way. Indian and pioneer facts always make the country more interesting to a group of young hikers.

How?

The *How?* takes in *transportation, equipment,* and *food.*

TRANSPORTATION—It's usually a good idea to start the hike by having each Patrol meet by itself and join the other Patrols at the time decided upon. This puts promptness squarely up to each Patrol, and gives the Patrol Leader a chance to use his leadership. Another advantage is that smaller groups can get to the Troop starting point more easily than a large group, which may overload or even spill out of a bus or trolley if all try to get on at the same time.

EQUIPMENT—The equipment depends upon the hike.

For a Bee-Line Hike you need compasses; for a Pioneering Hike, rope.

If there is cooking to be done, utensils must be brought —unless you have decided to cook without utensils.

If the weather is cold, bring sweaters. If it looks like rain, ponchos or raincoats had better come along. Uniform should be insisted upon, with suitable shoes.

HIKE EQUIPMENT

PERSONAL EQUIPMENT

Necessary:

Scout Uniform
Raincoat or Poncho, Sweater (when needed)
Suitable Stockings and Hike Shoes
Eats   Matches (waterproofed)
Cup   String
Notebook and Pencil   Toiletpaper
Canteen (if you aren't sure of drinking water)

If wanted:

Haversack   Extra Socks
Eating Utensils or Individual Cook Kit
Camera   Compass
Watch   Flashlight
HANDBOOK or FIELD BOOK Knife
Halazone tablets for water purification

PATROL EQUIPMENT

Necessary:

Belt First Aid Kit

As Needed:

Maps   Trench Shovel (for fire
Axe   building and latrine)
Rope   Cooking Utensils
Soap—Paper Towels   Signal Flags

TROOP EQUIPMENT

Necessary:

Troop First Aid Kit

As Needed:

Tracking Irons or Trail Making Material
And so on, according to the theme of the hike.

No hike should be undertaken without adequate first aid supplies. Each Patrol should have a completely outfitted first aid belt kit.

FOOD—Sandwiches are best for a hike that is mostly tramping and active games.

If the hike destination provides a good chance for some of the boys to meet their cooking requirements, suggest that they bring food for individual cooking. Patrol cooking of a complete meal for the whole gang should be strongly encouraged on hikes—it gives needed training for the camping that's ahead.

Announcing the Hike

The boys get most of the details about the hike from their Patrol Leaders, but it adds interest if final announcements are saved for the last Troop meeting before the hike.

Make the announcements short and to the point. Take a leaf from radio mystery announcers, and put some suspense in it. A little imagination will go a long way. A "Commando Hike," "Survival Hike," "Buckskin Hike," has an appeal that lifts it out of the ordinary hike class.

Tell exactly where and when the *Troop* will meet. Let each Patrol Leader arrange with his boys where and when the *Patrol* will gather to get to the Troop meeting place at the appointed hour.

Finally, announce the approximate time for the return. Of course, unforeseen things may happen that may delay the return. That's why many Troops have an "information center," at the home of the Troop Committee Chairman, to which the Scoutmaster can telephone if the Troop is delayed, and where mothers may be reassured about their boys. If you use this arrangement, all parents should be informed of it.

To make doubly sure that the boys have everything straight—when to meet, where to meet, what to bring,

Each Patrol meets at a regular spot to make its own preparations before joining the rest of the Troop.

take the time to ask "Has anybody any questions?" Repeat what is not clearly understood.

THE PROGRESS OF THE TROOP HIKE

It is almost time for the Troop hike to start. The Patrols are arriving, and one of the adult leaders is at the Troop gathering point to receive them.

Troop Assembly

At the exact starting time, the Senior Patrol Leader gives the signal for Troop assembly, and the Patrol Leaders line up their Patrols. While the boys stand at ease, Patrol Leaders report on attendance. The Senior Patrol Leader gives final instruction, and the whole gang is off.

You may feel like dispensing with this rather formal start to a Troop hike. But don't. Any Troop activity started in a casual manner with a "Well, I guess we won't wait any longer—let's get going," quickly results in the boys themselves being casual about their attendance. If the boys know that punctuality is expected, the Patrols will deliver every time.

Some Do's and Dont's on the Way

You want your boys to become good hikers, and a good hiker is one who observes the hiking rules of health, safety and courtesy. They are described in the *Handbook for Boys* and at greater length in the *Scout Field Book,* Pow-wow 3. Here is a short resume:

Safety on the Road

Moving a group of boys safely on a highway takes constant care to avoid accidents. Leave nothing to chance.

Walk on the left side of the road, *facing the oncoming traffic.* This is the rule throughout the country, and the law in many States.

When the Troop follows a highway, insist upon Patrols walking single file. The Patrol Leader should be 25 feet ahead of the first Scout, the Assistant Patrol Leader 25 feet behind the last. Patrols keep 100 feet apart.

Safety on the hike involves not only proper walking techniques, but also such details as safe water. On the road, permit the boys to drink only water that is known to be pure, or water they have brought along in a canteen. If you are not certain of the water, purify it as suggested on page 180.

If part of the hike is along a highway at night, each Scout should wear a white handkerchief tied flat around his lower right leg. Each Patrol is in single file, the leader 50 feet in advance and carrying a light. The rear guard walks 50 feet in the rear of the column also with a light.

Hitch Hiking Taboo

Hitch hiking has no place in Scouting.

No Scout should ever resort to hitch hiking, except in a case of real necessity. Nor should any Scout leader allow it. This applies also to riding on running boards of vehicles.

Hike Health

The health of your hikers should be checked in advance, especially before a long hike.

A sore throat or a cold should automatically rule out any Scout—for the boy's own protection and for the sake of his companions.

Even with healthy Scouts, precaution should be taken to make certain that no boy overdoes it. Let the boy return home tired, but not worn out. Scouts whose medical examination has shown that they have organic defects should do only as much as permitted by their doctor.

FOOTWEAR—Check the footwear. Old shoes with strong soles are best. When canvas-topped rubber shoes are worn, they should be of the heavy soled type. Do not permit thin-soled, sneaker-type canvas shoes. They give little support, cause hot feet, blisters and fatigue. If blister or cut appears on heel, apply antiseptic and protect with sterile dressing. *Do not open a blister.*

CLOTHING should be loose-fitting around knees, waist, shoulders and neck.

DRINKING WATER—If there is any doubt about safe

drinking water, bring along canteens with water from home. On the road, permit the boys to drink water only that is known to be pure. Even "clean" water may be dangerous. Water you are not sure about may be purified by dissolving two Halazone tablets from your official First Aid Kit in one quart of water. LET STAND THIRTY MINUTES BEFORE USING.

RESTS—A hike is not a race. Keep a good steady pace throughout, and make the rests short and frequent— five minutes every half hour or so. Let the slowest boys set the pace, but don't drag.

Hike Courtesy

Get your Scouts to see that they can have just as much fun and still behave in a way that will make them welcome over the same trail again. The example of the leader plays a decisive part here.

SIGNS—Obey all "Keep Off," "Private," and "No Trespassing" signs. If you expect to build fires and cook, get permission, and leave the place cleaner than you found it.

FENCES are put up to keep somebody out or something in—not for climbing over. If you have permission to trespass at all, use the gates and leave them as you found them.

PROTECT FIELDS—Nothing in the world makes it right for a Scout to cross a *planted* field or a meadow before mowing. To do so is to destroy a farmer's crop.

ANIMALS are property also. Horses and cows should never be disturbed. Besides, there may be real danger in passing through fields where farm animals are grazing.

WOODLANDS are crops. Scouts are interested in conserving them, not in marring or destroying them. Do

Teach your boys correct safety practices for the highway. The Troop moves by Patrols, single file, facing oncoming traffic.

not tolerate the hacking urge that seems to enter the mind of a boy who has had an axe presented to him.

RAILROADS—Crossing railroad trestles or walking on railroad tracks is dangerous and unlawful. Keep off!

Activities on the Out-Trip

Scoutcraft Training

As soon as you are well off the highway your Scouts are out where Scouts belong—in the out-of-doors. Now they have a chance to try out the things they have been practicing at Troop meetings.

Now it is no longer *talking* about what to do in the open—it's *doing* it.

It is no longer games involving the compass points. Instead, Patrols take turns leading the rest of the Troop cross-country with the help of an honest-to-goodness compass, the hike leader calling out from time to time a change in the course.

Now mapping becomes a matter of each Patrol in turn studying a route on a genuine map and then leading the Troop to its destination.

The Patrols may stop from time to time to measure widths of rivers, distances to prominent landmarks, heights of trees.

During it all, the Patrol Leaders have the chance to train their own boys.

SCOUTCRAFT IDEAS—(1) Send a Patrol ahead to stage an "accident." When the rest catch up with it, demonstrate proper way of holding back imaginary crowd, of treating "wounded." Then send another Patrol forward to stage another "accident."

(2) Send a junior assistant ahead to signal simple hike directions, using signal flags. First Patrol to decipher will lead the whole Troop, until it is stopped for further signal instructions.

(3) Have Patrols look for especially clear animal or bird tracks. Make plaster casts to be picked up on the return trip when they have hardened.

(4) Have each Patrol make simple map sketch of hike route—pacing distances, taking bearings, measuring distances.

(5) Practice finding compass directions without a compass, using watch and the sun.

Games Along the Way

Numerous games with the Patrols as teams provide good practice in Scoutcraft on the out-trip.

If signaling is the theme of the hike, for instance, a game of Signaling Touch may start the Patrols off, in the general direction of the hike destination. First Aid races are easy to arrange. Nature lore may be in the form of collection and matching games. Tracking is particularly adapted to Patrol competitions. Training in observation may be in the form of variations of Kim's Game.

Give each Patrol a chance to lead the Troop. Here one of the Patrol Leaders determines the azimuth the Troop will follow.

Keep the rules simple—simpler than those used in a meeting room, since it is harder to call the boys back to explain rules once they have started out. If a game involves the scattering of the Patrols, a definite time should be announced at which the Troop will meet for a roll call and further activities.

HIKE GAME IDEAS—(1) *Apache Relay Race.* Each Patrol is a band of Apache warriors attempting to carry a message by means of a relay of runners over a stretch of approximately one mile. Each band is taken out by its chief (the Patrol Leader) who places Scouts at convenient points along the one-mile route. When all are in position, a written message is handed to the first runner of each Patrol and the race is on. The first runner brings the message to the second, the second to the third, and so on, until the last Scout in each Patrol delivers the message at its destination. The race may be varied by using a short verbal message.

(2) *Shadowing.* One Patrol is to shadow a party of "desperadoes" (another Patrol or the rest of the Troop) advancing through the country. The shadowing Patrol must follow the others as closely as possible without being seen, with one or two Scouts ahead to signal when it is safe for the rest to advance. If the "desperadoes" see a Scout shadowing them, they may give chase, and if the Scout is caught, he becomes a prisoner and must march with the "desperadoes." If the "desperadoes" cannot throw the shadowers off their tracks within 1½-2 miles, or do not capture more than half of the shadowers, the shadowers win. Then another Patrol becomes shadowers.

(3) *Ambushing.* A group of pioneers (two Patrols) advance along the trail, with Scouts walking in front of and behind them to prevent a surprise attack. The Indians (also two Patrols) follow them. They shadow the pioneers as they advance, until suitable territory is reached for one of the Indian Patrols to try to get ahead of the pioneers by flanking them. If the Indian Patrol succeeds, it hides in ambush and attacks the pioneers when they arrive. For the ambush to be a success the other Indian Patrol should be ready to attack at the same time. If the Patrol making the flanking movement is seen, all of the Indians in both Patrols may be captured by being pursued and touched by the pioneers.

Additional games for the out-trip will be found in the game section, Tool 11, in the back of the book.

See also the special hikes in Tool 12, especially Explorers, Sealed Orders, First Aid Hikes, and Treasure Hunts.

At the Hike Destination

Immediately upon arrival at the hike destination the Patrol Leaders, with the Senior Patrol Leader, make a quick survey and choose their Patrol sites for fire making and cooking.

A leader should inspect the sites from time to time to see to it that the Patrols keep them free from paper, equipment and chips. If a rigid check is made the first couple of times the Troop goes hiking, the Patrols will get into the habit of keeping their spots clean without further reminders. A good slogan is—"No mess made, no mess to clean up."

Scoutcraft Demonstrations

On a first hike, fire building and cooking will probably be the main activities of the day. If the Patrol Leaders have been trained, they are able to show their Scouts how to build a fire for cooking. Otherwise, let someone who knows how — perhaps a couple of junior assistants —make the demonstration, which should include clearing the ground, preparing tinder and fire wood, constructing a simple fire place, laying the fire and lighting it, burning refuse, extinguishing fire and cleaning the site.

Boys are impatient to show what they can do, therefore a demonstration should be snappy and to the point, and should be followed immediately by a chance to get the job under way.

When the hike is tied in with the theme of a special Scoutcraft skill, a quick demonstration will prove valuable before the Patrols set out for the day's climax in that skill:

DEMONSTRATION IDEAS—(1) Get a good axeman to demonstrate axemanship: Sharpening, safety precautions and correct techniques.

(2) If pioneering is the theme, have the junior leaders

or one of the Patrols demonstrate lashings, laying out timbers and making a trestle.

(3) Show how smudge fires are made for signaling with smoke, or how to construct a rolling curtain for signaling with fire.

(4) Demonstrate track casting with plaster-of-paris.

(5) Show the making of a fire-by-friction set from native material and how to make fire with it.

(6) Collect and show the Scouts five to ten native wild edible plants.

(7) On a smooth piece of soft ground, demonstrate a variety of tracks: Of person walking, running, carrying a burden, walking backward, and point out the difference in appearance.

Scoutcraft Practice

On a hike each Scout has a chance to practice things that will prepare him for camping—preparing a meal, making a shelter, cleanliness and sanitation, living happily with the other fellows.

On the early hikes of the Troop, each boy cooks his own meal or works with a buddy. But after most of the boys have met their Second and First Class cooking requirements, the meals should be prepared by Patrols, using the Patrol's own cooking utensils.

It is an easy matter for a Patrol to make a perfectly adequate cooking outfit from gallon-size No. 10 tin cans and frying pans bought at a ten cent store. Later the

On the first few hikes of a new Troop, the boys will cook individually. Encourage Patrol cooking as early as possible. Simple Patrol-size pots may be made from No. 10 cans. Polish them up with steel wool, then attach bail handle, made from heavy wire, with two copper rivets. Get frying pans from ten cent store.

Games and practice in Scoutcraft form the program of the hike. Silent walking can be taught in a game of "Sleeping Indian."

Patrol can get better utensils as it earns the money for them.

Simple Patrol menus should be discussed in advance at meetings of the Leaders' Patrol, and tried out on a Leaders' Hike. See *Handbook for Patrol Leaders* for suggestions.

Games and Projects

After a good hike meal, the whole gang is ready for a few games and for the projects that are the feature of the day. As always, the Patrols form the teams.

Some of these activities will be based on the Scoutcraft theme of the month, others will be for fun and recreation. Some of them will take place right on the spot, others will take in the surrounding territory. In all of them the Patrols, as always, are the teams.

Project Suggestions — String Burning, Water Boiling, Fire-by-Friction, Fire-by-Flint-and-Steel, Scene of the Crime, Trestle Making, Raft Making, Compass Stalking, Problem of Wounded Scouts, etc. See Tool 11 in back of the book.

Scoutcraft Games — The Leaking Packsack, The Robbed Camp, Leaf Matching, Tree Spotting, Signal Relay, Signal Tower Race, Deer Stalking, Visibly Hidden, Sleeping Pirate, Grandmother's Footsteps, Compass Relay, etc. See Tool 11.

Recreational Games — Skin the Snake, Antelope Race, various Tags, Crows and Cranes, British Bulldog, Capture the Flag, Border Scouting. See Tool 11.

Wide Games — See Tool 13.

Scout Advancement

Your Scouts will know that hikes will give them a chance to meet a great number of the Second and First Class Requirements.

The "examining" should be arranged so that it will not break up the main activities of the hike. Very often it is as simple as watching a youngster while he cooks and eats a hike meal, having a boy leading his Patrol with a compass, making a map sketch of the hike route.

Make advancement a matter of doing things in the natural sequence of events rather than a formal examination for the sake of "passing a test."

Camp Fire and Ceremonies

If the hike is held in the late afternoon and evening, it may conclude with a short camp fire, with a program as suggested on page 275.

A Tenderfoot received into his Patrol and Troop at an Investiture Ceremony, around an evening camp fire down at the water's edge, is likely to carry the memory of it with him for many years. Such a setting gives extra meaning to the presentation of badges to Scouts who have advanced to higher ranks.

Clean-Up

Before starting on the return trip, the Patrols should have time to do a good clean-up job. As each Patrol finishes, the Patrol Leader reports to the Senior Patrol Leader. When all reports are in, the Leaders' Council makes an inspection, the Scoutmaster commenting on the findings.

The rule is simple—a good camper leaves a camp site in the same condition in which he found it or, preferably, better.

A piece of soap and a few paper towels work miracles in getting your hikers back to town looking well-groomed Scouts instead of hobos. Also, each Patrol Leader should give his fellows a quick inspection before dismissal, so that neckerchiefs can be straightened and drooping stockings pulled up. A slicked-up return makes a good impression on the public in general, and on parents in particular.

Home Again

Possibly the best method is to dismiss the Troop following the inspection of the hike site. Make it formal, just as you did at the start of the hike, even if dismissal consists only of lining up the Troop by Patrols, having the Patrol Leaders report the presence of all their boys, and declaring Troop dismissed.

For the return trip, it is perhaps just as well to leave the Patrols to their own devices. Any activity undertaken on a Troop basis is apt to prove an anticlimax. Now the boys are as eager to get back home as they were to get going a few hours before.

Do everything you can to see that the Patrol Leaders get their boys home as close as possible to the time set for the return. It is poor Scouting to have Joe's mother wait for Joe for hours after he was supposed to be back from the hike.

Singing

Good, lusty singing at any time creates enthusiasm and pep and team spirit. On a hike, particularly on the return, it makes the distance shorter. Get one of the Patrols to start singing. Soon they'll all be singing and the last couple of miles of the home stretch will be covered easily.

After the Hike

After the hike, the leader in charge should prepare a short report, including advance plans and preparations and how they worked out, with suggestions for improvement. Don't just file it—use it to plan the next month's hike.

Also, the Troop Scribe, with such help as he can get from the Patrols, will prepare a story of the hike to be read at the next Troop meeting. This adds to each Scout's recollections of the hike, creates a laugh or two and makes the Scouts who didn't go, want to go the next time.

Camping Overnight

CHAPTER 10

TROOP MEETINGS ARE FUN and Troop hikes exciting—but one of their main purposes is to get the boy ready for his biggest thrill in Scouting—CAMP.

A Scout counts the days until he can go camping. The thought of camping gives him incentive to pick up the skills he knows he will need for having a good time —fire building, cooking, tent pitching, pioneering. Then comes the planning in the Patrol, and the work to get the equipment in shape. When he finally gets to camp, he pitches in with a will, eager to do his share.

And while the boy is enjoying his camping, you, as his Scoutmaster, know that Scouting is having its best opportunity for influencing the boy's life—making him grasp the ideals of Scouting while living the life of a Scout.

The Troop's Camping Program

The biggest camping event of the year is, of course, the summer camp when the whole Troop goes camping for a week or ten days or more.

But that is only part of the Troop's camping—sometimes even the smaller part.

The overnight camps during the fall and winter and spring may seem less important—but they add up! A good camping Troop may have as many as a dozen weekend and holiday camps during the year, and may take part in the District or Council camporee. These overnights often add up to twelve nights and twenty-four days in camp—without counting the overnight camps that individual Patrols take on their own.

Obviously, the thing to do is to plan the yearly program of the Troop, so that the boys will spend the greatest possible number of days and nights camping.

This starts with *your* determination to make the Troop a camping Troop. You need not be an *expert* camper yourself, just so long as you enjoy life in the outdoors

---

PRactice

PRoperties

PRemises

PRovisions

PRogram

If you like "alliterations" (starting several words with the same letters), the FIVE PR's of Overnight Camping will be an easy reminder for you: PRactice stands for the training you need, PRoperties for your equipment, PRemises for your camp site, PRovisions for the food, and PRogram for your activities.

---

and know how to make yourself comfortable, and can help your boys to do the same.

PLANNING FOR CAMP

Whether overnight camp, or Camporee, or a summer camp, five things go into your planning:

Preliminary training for Leaders and Scouts
Adequate equipment   *Good meals*
Suitable camp site   *Full program*

Training for Camp

The preliminary camp training of every Scout in the Troop begins with *you*. To guide the Patrol Leaders and help them to train their boys, you must first yourself know what is involved.

If you are an old-timer in Scouting, you will have had plenty of camping experience.

If you are new at the game, this chapter will give you a few hints. But no man ever learned camping from a book. He can pick up ideas from reading, but they mean little unless he goes out and applies them. So, if at all possible, get yourself and your Assistant Scoutmasters in on a training course in Troop camping in your District or Local Council. Here you will learn Scout camping while camping with experienced Scouters. You will see how they do things, and the course gives you a chance to practice while you learn.

If no training course is on, get hold of your Commissioner and get his advice and help. Find out some of the things that others have discovered for making Troop camping simple and effective.

Training Your Patrol Leaders

The next step is to train your Patrol Leaders so that they are ahead of their boys in camping.

Encourage them to go over the camping chapter of

the *Handbook for Patrol Leaders* and the campcraft sections of the *Handbook for Boys* and *Scout Field Book*.

Then, at a meeting of the Patrol Leaders' Council, plan for an overnight camp of the Leaders' Patrol, along the lines suggested for a regular Patrol in the *Handbook for Patrol Leaders*.

Finally, get the equipment together and set out for the overnight. Include in the program the whole idea of good Patrol camping—from pitching tents in proper Patrol arrangement to a full schedule of Scoutcraft activities. Give the Patrol Leaders a chance to learn the things their Patrols will do when the whole Troop goes camping.

Training the Scouts

The boy's own training for camp begins the day he enters Scouting.

At meetings he learns the camping traditions of the Troop, what equipment to take, how to make it, how to pack it. At hikes he picks up a number of camping skills. In his Patrol he participates in planning of meals and deciding things to do, and helps to determine what job each Scout will have to make a good camp.

He is ready for camp when the call comes.

The Troop Committee's Part

The members of your Troop Committee have pledged themselves to see that each Scout in your Troop has a chance for "a year-round outdoor program totalling at least ten days and nights of hikes, overnight camp, camporee, and summer camp experience, with adequate facilities and supervision."

This means that the Troop Committee will have to be in on the Troop's camp planning from the very beginning, helping to get equipment, secure camp sites, provide necessary transportation.

Study a variety of tent designs before you decide upon the type for the Troop. Let the Patrol Leaders' Council help.

Here again, if Troop Committee training is available in the Council, the members of your Committee ought to get it. Encourage them also to take the Troop camping course.

The Troop's Camping Equipment

Equipment is usually the thing that stands between a hiking Troop and a camping Troop. And even that is apt to simmer down to just one item: Tents.

Tents

A new Troop can often borrow or rent tents for its first few camping trips. But a Troop worth its salt will want to own its own. So start early to think of ways to get them.

Bring up the subject at a Troop Committee meeting.

Discuss it in the Patrol Leaders' Council and get the Patrol Leaders to take it up with their Scouts. If you have the mothers organized behind the Troop, get them interested. Decide upon a plan in which everyone can share in earning money for tents.

Think ahead when you are ready to buy your tents. Think of *all* the camping you want to do—not just of part of it.

One Troop rushed out and stocked up on pup tents—then found itself stuck. The pups were all right for overnight camping, but not for camping for a week or more. Another Troop bought large wall tents. They worked OK for summer camp, but the Troop was bogged down with cumbersome equipment every time it wanted to go overnight camping—therefore seldom went. Still another Troop purchased inexpensive army surplus, only to find that equipment suitable for army camping was of little use in Scout camping.

You want a tent that is good for one-night stands and also for a week or two of summer camping. There are a number of tents like that. They have these things in common: fairly light material, a ground surface of thirty square feet per camper, and sufficient headroom for the average boy to stand up without stooping uncomfortably.

Tents of this type are on the market. But you may

Before you decide on a tent type for your Troop, get all available information. Your Local Council will be glad to advise you. So will the Engineering Service of the Boy Scouts of America, New Brunswick, New Jersey. To develop your own design, follow the suggestions of the Scout Field Book.

SUGGESTED PATROL EQUIPMENT

Patrol equipment is grouped in two lists depending on their functions. Each Scout carries his fair share of these items. For details, see *HPL*, pgs. 157-162.

"Tenting" Crew

Two-boy Tents for all
Lantern with Candles
　for each Tent
First Aid Belt Kit
Spade
Axe

Tent Poles and Pegs (if
　they cannot be impro-
　vised at camp site)
2 Guard Ropes
Patrol Flag

Cleaning Bag containing: Polish, Brush, Rag

Repair Bag containing:
　Canvas Pieces
　Safety Pins
　Thin Wire
　File with handle, for
　　axe sharpening

　Sharpening Stone
　Needles and Thread
　String or Strong cord

"Cooking" Crew

2 Cooking Sets (each containing, for instance, one 6-quart pot and one 4-quart pot with lids, one frying pan, nesting in canvas bag), or 1 Trail Chef Cook Kit

2 Canvas Water Basins
2 Canvas Water Pails
Oilcloth or plastic table cover

First Aid Belt Kit
Axe
Spade
　(Dining Tarp)

Kitchen Bag containing:

Carving Knife	Can Opener	Dish Mop
Peeling Knives	Salt Shaker	Steel Wool
Ladle or Big Spoon	Pepper Shaker	Soap Flakes
Large Fork		(or detergent)

Bread Bags

Dustproof Provision Bags for flour, sugar, salt, oatmeal, cereal, dried fruits, beans, rice.

Waterproof and Fatproof Provision Bags for fresh meat, smoked meat, fish.

Screw-top containers for butter and jam.

want to make your own. The *Scout Field Book,* on page 137, has plans and working drawings for a tent that fills the bill—the Explorer Tent. If you prefer to develop your own type, the *Field Book,* in Pow-Wow 13, suggests how to do it.

Let the Scouts lay out the pattern and cut the material, but call upon mothers to do the sewing. You will find them willing to do it. After all, it is their Bill or Jack who will sleep in those tents. There is even the case of an 80-year-old grandmother insisting on sewing the tent her Jimmy was to use.

Tent making is simplest if you use material that is already waterproof. Otherwise, the finished tents must be treated—another job that can be handled by the Scouts.

Other Equipment

Cooking equipment comes next.

For the first few overnights, the Patrols will have no trouble borrowing pots and pans from home. But as soon as the Patrol Leaders have taken part in a Leaders' Patrol camp and have seen how easily Patrol cooking gear can be made from gallon pots and inexpensive frying pans, they will want to have their own.

From this point on, encourage the Patrols to make what equipment they can and earn money for equipment that must be bought, until they have what they need.

A Patrol equipment list appears on page 197. See also *Scout Field Book,* page 139. The camp equipment each Scout takes along is described on page 199; see also the *Field Book,* page 138. Stress the need of a waterproof ground cloth for each camper, and the use of change of clothing (pajamas) for night wear.

The Troop leaders have their own tents. An adult is in charge of the Troop first aid pouch, but each Patrol has its own first aid belt kit.

SUGGESTED PERSONAL EQUIPMENT

The following equipment list should be varied to meet specific conditions that exist during the varying seasons and in the different sections of the country, etc. On this page are listed the Scout's personal items. It is understood that each Scout will carry also his fair share of the "Patrol" equipment suggested on page 197.

Complete Scout Uniform
Blankets or Sleeping bag
Straw tick

Pack sack
Waterproof
    groundcloth
Raincoat or poncho

Clothes Bag containing:
    Change of underwear
    Sweater or lumberjack
    Extra pair of stockings

Pajamas
Swimming trunks
Handkerchiefs

Mess Kit containing:
    Plate   Knife
    Soup bowl   Fork
    Cup

Tablespoon
Teaspoon

Toilet Bag containing:
    Soap in container
    Toothbrush in container
    Toothpaste or powder

Metal mirror
Comb
Towel

Shoe Bag containing: Extra shoes or sneakers

Repair Bag containing:
    Needles
    Safety pins

Thread
Buttons

Carry in Outside Pocket of Packsack or in some Uniform Pocket:
    Pocket First Aid Kit or Sterile Bandage
    Matches in waterproof
        container
    Strong cord or thin wire

Notebook
Pencil
Scout knife

Other Equipment as Desired:
    Scoutcraft supplies
    Musical instruments
    HANDBOOK or FIELD BOOK
    Field glasses
    Blanket pins

Compass
Maps
Camera and Films
Canteen
Axe

The Overnight Camp Site

Many Local Councils own camp sites that are available to the Troops. Your Commissioner or your Scout Executive will tell you where they are, and on what conditions they may be used. But besides, your Troop will want to find a couple of sites of its own.

When you think you have found a place, go over it thoroughly. *Imagine the site under the worst possible weather conditions,* with a storm raging and rain pelting down. Will the Troop be blown out or washed out? Or will you be reasonably protected? If at all possible, spend a night on the site with the Leaders' Patrol before you OK it for Troop use. That is the only way to be sure the Troop won't be eaten alive by mosquitos, punkies or gnats, infected with poison ivy, trampled by roaming cattle, or disturbed by intruders.

Here are a few points to check:

LOCATION—Protection against prevailing winds. Exposed to the sun part of the day, preferably the morning hours. Not directly under trees. Grass-covered, light soil that affords easy drainage. Large enough to provide individual Patrol sites with a reasonable amount of privacy. Avoid rich vegetation that indicates damp ground, loose sand that gets into everything, and heavy clay soil that turns into mud in wet weather. Keep away from dead trees that may topple over and from trees with large dead branches.

WATER—Ample supply of pure water for drinking, cooking and washing. If you aren't positive it's pure, have it tested and certified by the County or State Board of Health. If this is not possible, bring chemicals for purifying it, or boil it for at least five minutes.

WOOD—Plenty of dead wood for fuel. Other wood for camp gadgets and pioneering.

FOOD—Stores located at a reasonable distance, includ-

Possible locations for overnight camps should be investigated by the Troop Leaders. Make a list of the most suitable spots.

ing pasteurized milk supply—unless you are bringing all supplies from home.

SURROUNDINGS — Adequate for Scoutcraft practices, games and exploring. If there is safe water for swimming nearby, fine! As far as possible, absence of hazards, such as cliffs, old mine shafts, swift streams, undertow, and so on.

If the camp site is suitable, speak to the owner and get his permission in writing for its use. If he specifies any restrictions, be sure that every Scout understands them and lives up to them.

Meals for the Overnight

For the Troop overnight camp, each Patrol plans its own menus, does its own buying and cooks its own meals. There are Patrol menu suggestions in the *Handbook for Patrol Leaders,* and recipes in the *Scout Field Book,* Pow-Wow 16. See also pages 238 and 239.

The Troop leaders may make arrangements to eat with the Patrols, paying their part of the cost.

Or, if you are good cooks, the leaders may want to do their own cooking and show off the kind of camp cooks they are!

Activities of the Overnight Camp

The overnight camp is, first of all, practice in camping. Here is the boy's chance to make use of the skills he has learned on hikes, to learn more about the tricks that mean comfort in camp, and to live with his gang for a day and a night in the outdoors.

But besides, there should be time for some activities in the month's Scoutcraft theme. If Observation is on the program, dig a tracking ground and stage some Sherlock Holmes problems for the Patrols to solve, or have a Treasure Hunt, or a Man Hunt out of camp. If the theme is Signaling, the Patrols will get a thrill out of fire signaling at night.

If the camp includes Sunday, be sure that the opportunity is provided for each Scout to fulfill his religious obligations. See page 168.

Whatever the program, better have the Patrol Leaders' Council work out an hour-by-hour schedule well ahead of camp, along the lines suggested on page 203. Have copies made for each Patrol. A schedule like this keeps the Patrols on their toes and helps to get everything done that you planned.

Announcing the Camp

The date for the camp is decided by the Patrol Leaders' Council. An overnight camp may run from Friday evening through Saturday, or from Saturday morning or

Troop One
Overnight Camp

Saturday, June 9th

2:00 PM Troop meets. Patrol Leaders check their Patrols. Inspection of Packs.

2:15 Start of trip to camp site.

3:15 Arrival at camp site. Choosing of Patrol sites and kitchens. Making camp.

4:00 Field Day. (Charlie in charge)

5:00 Start preparing evening meal.

6:00 Supper. Clean-up.

7:00 Capture the Flag. (Jack in charge)

8:30 Campfire. (Fox Patrol in charge)

9:30 Taps. Extinguish fire. Turn in. Lights out. Silence.

Sunday, June 10th

7:30 AM Get up. Start breakfast. Air blankets. Clean tents.

8:15 Breakfast. Clean-up.

8:45 Putting the tents in order.

9:15 Inspection of camp by Patrol Leaders' Council.

9:30 Nature Hike. (Bill in charge)

10:30 Church

12:30 PM Dinner. Clean-up.

1:30 Rest Period.

2:00 Start striking the camp.

3:00 Check up of camp site by Patrol Leaders' Council.

3:30 Start home trip

4:30 Dismissal

afternoon through Sunday afternoon, or from the day before a holiday to the holiday afternoon.

If you can start a week-end camp on Friday, so much the better.

As soon as the date is set, the Patrols get busy with their preparations. If yours is a new Troop, there'll be a hustle and bustle to get ready. If it's old, you will take an overnight camp in your stride—but even then there will be plenty to do.

At Troop meeting a couple of weeks before the overnight, find out how Patrol preparations are coming along. And at the meeting just before camp, have the Patrol Leaders report on the Scouts they expect to have in camp.

End the meeting with a "See you Saturday at headquarters!" And the whole gang is set for one of the thrills they joined Scouting to get.

THE PROGRESS OF THE TROOP OVERNIGHT CAMP

The day of the camp, each Patrol meets by itself. The Patrol Leader checks to see that every Scout has brought what is required of him. Patrol equipment is distributed among the boys to carry with their personal things. So is food stuff bought by the Patrol. When

For smartness and orderliness, get the Patrols into the habit of making a "duffle line" each time they make a halt and throw down their packs. The "duffle line" is simply the packs put down in a straight line, facing the same way, ready to be slung back on the shoulders at a moment's notice.

If the camp site is less than three miles from Troop Headquarters, hike to it! That's the way to learn proper packing for camp.

everything is ready, the Patrol sets off for the Troop meeting place.

Troop Assembly

The Patrols are gathering. As each of them arrives, the Scouts put down their packs in a Patrol duffel-line while waiting for the rest.

At the time set for starting, the Patrols line up, ready to go. The Patrol Leaders report on attendance, a quick inspection is made of the packs, the leader in charge gives final instructions—and the gang is off!

On the Road

If the distance to camp is not more than three miles, it should be easy enough for the boys to hike it in good shape, carrying their packs. On the other hand, if the distance is between three and five miles, it is better if the packs can be thrown on an automobile and taken to camp. If the distance is more than five miles, arrangements should have been made with the Troop Committee to furnish transportation. In many Troops, the Scouts all have bicycles. If that is the case in your Troop, the transportation problem solves itself.

Activities on the trip to camp naturally depend on how you are getting there. If the boys are carrying their packs, you can have a few observation games, but nothing much else. If the packs are sent ahead, you can use the activities suggested in Chapter 9, "The Troop Goes Hiking."

While hiking on the highway, the Patrols should, of course, follow the usual rules of hike safety, health and courtesy (page 178). If bicycles are used, insist upon proper bicycle conduct and safety.

Making Camp

On arrival at the camp site, the Scouts unsling their packs. Then you and the Patrol Leaders' Council look over the grounds. If you have had an overnight camp with your Leaders' Patrol before taking the whole Troop camping, the Patrol Leaders should know how to select the camping spots for their Patrols and go to work making camp—following a simple plan of

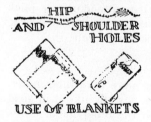

HIP AND SHOULDER HOLES

USE OF BLANKETS

Of all the camping tricks you may teach your boys, one of the most important is the method of making a comfortable ground bed from a waterproof ground sheet and a couple of blankets. As you probably know, the secret is in the hip and shoulder holes scooped in the ground where hip and shoulder will rest.

organization along the lines suggested in the *Handbook for Patrol Leaders.* Make it a point to offer your advice to any Patrol Leader who wants it; otherwise, don't interfere or go near the Patrol set-ups until the Patrol Leaders announce: "Camp completed, sir!"

Try to keep yourself an interested on-looker. In that way you'll have a chance to study your Patrol Leaders in action, to find out how well they distribute the work, to discover how willingly the boys follow their leaders. Seeing these things, you can later give the Patrol Leaders ideas on improving their leadership.

In the final checking-over of Patrol set-ups, notice the following points:

LATRINE. Is there a simple straddle latrine at some appropriate spot, and do all the boys know where it is?

TENTS AND BEDS. Are the tents carefully put up? If rain seems probable, have tents been ditched, with the dirt away from the tent walls? Is personal equipment neatly arranged? Are ground beds properly made, with ground sheet in place and blankets folded for greatest warmth? (Be sure your boys know of the importance of clearing bed site of all stray pebbles and twigs, and also of the value of a shallow hip hole and shoulder hole for comfortable sleeping).

KITCHEN. Is the fire site cleared of dry leaves and grass? Is the fire place adequate? Is the food supply kept cleanly and safely? Have arrangements been made for burning burnable garbage? Is there a hole for waste water disposal, covered with sticks with a layer of dry grass for catching the grease so that it may be burned? Are there proper fire safeguards?

SURROUNDINGS. Are the grounds kept clean? No paper, no candy wrappers, no chips, no equipment lying around?

Evening Activities

After supper prepared *by Patrols,* eaten *by Patrols,* and clean-up done *by Patrols,* the Troop gathers for the evening's activities.

Games

It is still light, so spend an hour or so playing a couple of favorite games, with plenty of physical action. There may not be much sleeping during the night for the fellows on their first camping trip. By sending them to bed healthily tired, but not exhausted, they stand a better chance of rest and sleep.

SUGGESTED RECREATIONAL GAMES — Capture the Flag, Border Scouting, British Bulldog, Various Tags. See Games Index.

Camp Fire

Before it gets dark, wood is gathered for the camp fire. Each Patrol can contribute some, or one of the Patrols may volunteer to build the fire.

The boys gather. The fire is lit, and you settle down for an hour of fun and fellowship.

Start with a simple ceremony, then have a junior leader take over and lead the gang in songs and yells. If told in advance, each Patrol can have a stunt ready to spring on the rest of the Troop.

Wind up with a few serious songs, and close with Taps, or the Troop's special good-night song.

For further camp fire suggestions, see page 275.

Sleeping in Camp

Before closing the camp fire, remind the boys that a real camper goes to bed to sleep and *permits others to sleep* from "Lights out" to Reveille. Ten hours of sleep is recommended. It is only thoughtless and inconsiderate "tenderfoots" who spoil the night for themselves and others, by gabbing and getting up before the break of dawn.

Have the boys agree that if anyone has to get up during the night, he will move quietly and get back to bed again immediately. Appeal to the boys' good sense,

Let the Patrols organize themselves for quick camp making with a Tenting Crew, and a Cooking Crew to prepare the meals.

and place the responsibility for silence directly with each Patrol.

If you make it a Troop tradition from your very first overnight, that the night is for sleeping, you will have little trouble on your future camping trips.

Tent Inspection

Have the Patrol Leaders check to see that the boys change into pajamas. Insist on this. Make it absolutely clear to the boys that no one sleeps in day clothes.

When the Patrols have turned in, make a quick round of inspection, specifically to see that boys on their first camping experience are properly bedded down for the night. Leave each tent with a soft "Good night."

Lights are going out. There's quiet in camp and it's your turn to retire.

SECOND DAY IN CAMP

When the signal to get up is sounded, life starts in camp. The boys wash and dress. The cooking crews get busy preparing breakfast, the others hang blankets out to air.

After breakfast, the Patrols have half an hour to get their camp sites spick and span. When the time is up, the Troop Leaders' Council makes a thorough inspection of the *whole* camp, not just the section immediately surrounding each tent.

Make this inspection stiff. The boys like it that way. Each Patrol site should be gone over with a "fine-tooth comb." Draw attention to chips, pieces of paper, scraps of food, carelessly made-up tents. Train the Patrol Leaders to be just as particular as you are. Don't pick up—that's the job of the Patrols—just make the fellows realize that you are "Eagle-Eye" himself as far as cleanliness around camp is concerned.

Habits formed in small things help form more important ones. And neatness in camp in the morning is the starting point for neatness throughout the day.

Forenoon Activities

If this is Sunday, each Scout should have an opportunity, in accordance with the policy stated on page 168, to fulfill his religious obligations. The most desirable practice is for Scouts to attend their own churches. If hiking to church is out of the question, arrangements should be made in advance for transportation.

Much of the morning will thus be taken up, but it should be possible to include a couple of projects or games among the morning's activities. Pick some that will help to carry along the Scoutcraft theme the Troop is working on at the time.

Cleanliness and orderliness are top requirements for camp. Have the Troop Leaders make an inspection that is really stiff.

SCOUTCRAFT PROJECTS — Trestle Making, Raft Making, Compass Stalking, Problem of Wounded Scouts, etc. See Tool 11.

SCOUTCRAFT GAMES — Leaf Matching, Tree Spotting, Signal Relay, Signal Tower Race, Deer Stalking, Sleeping Pirate, Grandmother's Footsteps, Compass Relay, etc. See Games Index.

WIDE GAMES — Some of the wide games may be planned to fill an hour or a two-hour period. See Tool 13.

SCOUT ADVANCEMENT — The regular activities of the camp will give the Scouts a natural opportunity to meet Second and First Class Requirements. That goes for such items as making camp, building fires, cooking, and so on. The remaining requirements can be brought into the program with very little imagination: First aid projects, nature (looking for animals, birds, trees, plants), signaling, map sketching, measuring.

SWIMMING—If swimming facilities are available, by all means give the boys a chance for a swim if the weather is good, *provided you use the "Eight Defense Method," which is the minimum standards for a Scout swim* (described on page 269). *Otherwise, make swimming absolutely TABOO.*

The Noon Meal

The noon meal of the overnight is best kept simple. It shouldn't take much more than an hour to cook and eat it. When it is over, pots and pans should be cleaned immediately and made ready for packing.

Afternoon Activities

If there is time before breaking camp for a few projects or games, arrange for them. Pick the activities from among the suggestions given for the forenoon game period.

BREAKING CAMP

Camp pitching was done by all the Patrols at the same time. Break camp the same way, and have a time set at which the packing should be completed. It is a good rule to start breaking camp a little earlier than you think absolutely necessary.

If you have had rain, the wet tents should be packed loosely, so that they can easily be unrolled for drying. If wet weather has been followed by dry, the tents

A Scout leaves a camp site in better shape than he found it, with hardly a trace to show that he camped there. Extinguishing the fires is especially important: sprinkle water from a pot onto the coals until the very last ember is out, then bury the dead coals, leaving a clean spot.

should be struck early and spread out so that bottom edges and sod cloths will have a chance to dry out.

Again, keep hands off until the Patrol Leaders report that the job is finished.

The Final Inspection

When all Patrols have been heard from, the Patrol Leaders' Council makes a final inspection.

You might feel that that's a job you could do yourself. You could! But don't! The boy leaders need to know what constitutes a clean camp, and the way for them to learn is for you to show them what standards you expect for the Troop.

A good camper leaves a camp site cleaner than he found it. Your Patrol Leaders and the Scouts in their Patrols will readily respond to such a tradition and they will think more of their Scoutmaster for being strict in regard to cleanliness than for letting them off easy.

When everything is satisfactory, the Patrols line up, the Troop is formally dismissed, and the boys return home.

AFTER THE OVERNIGHT CAMP

At the meeting of the Patrol Leaders' Council following camp, while the memories of it are fresh in mind, the camp should be discussed in detail from the angles of "What was good?" and "What wasn't so good?"

How was the site? The activities? Did the Patrols function properly? How were the menus? Was the cost too high? Were the meals easy to prepare? Were they well cooked?

Put the findings in writing. They will give you valuable pointers for future camping trips.

CAMPOREE

Some day you will wonder how good your Patrols really are at camping. The way to find out is to have a Troop "Camporee."

What Is a Camporee?

A Camporee is a demonstration of the camping skills of Patrols and Troops, which set up their own camps for one or more days and nights for fun and good fellowship, and for the opportunity to learn more about camping from each other.

Camporees are held annually in numerous Local Councils throughout the country. The Patrols and Troops taking part do not compete against each other, but against a standard with all having a chance to win.

The Council or District Camporee usually takes place in the spring, and you will certainly want your Troop to participate. But don't wait for a Council Camporee to come along. Try the Camporee idea in your own Troop with your Patrols. Such a Troop Camporee can be held any time during the year. It is one of the best ways you have of getting your Patrols excited about camp efficiency.

Preparing for the Troop Camporee

Bring up the suggestion for having a Troop Camporee at a meeting of the Patrol Leaders' Council and get the Patrol Leaders enthusiastic about it. Then settle down to decide the specific points that are to be covered. Suggestions for these points will be found in the scoring schedule on page 217.

Boiled down to simple terms, the Troop Camporee is just about the same thing as a good overnight camping trip—with a few special additions. The main features are honest-to-goodness Patrol camping, a couple of

Your Scouts will want to be proud of their Troop at the District Camporee. Prepare for it at a Troop Camporee.

Patrol Scoutcraft projects during the afternoon in camp, and a rating plan that will show the Patrols how well they camp.

You will need a number of observers to score the Patrols. The junior leaders of the Troop may be able to handle the scoring, but why not bring in some of your Troop Committee members? The Troop Camporee will give them a chance to do a real job, and they will get to know the Troop much better by watching it in camp.

During the following month or so, all the Patrols will be busy.

There's equipment to be lined up, menus to be developed, material to be gathered for camp gadgets, program stunts to be prepared. Training for a Camporee will have a profound influence on the Patrols and on the Troop as a whole.

Running the Troop Camporee

The day arrives. All the Patrols are ready. Every Scout is there, with equipment, packs and provisions, rarin' to go.

But not yet! Before the Patrols pitch camp, there's an inspection of each gang. How do the packs look? Are they correctly packed? Is Patrol equipment properly distributed? Is the personal equipment sufficient? And how is the appearance of each individual Scout?

Ready for camp making! How is the organization for effective camp construction? Is there a Tenting Crew busily engaged in putting up tents, and preparing the beds? Is there a Cooking Crew working full blast building fire place, getting water and wood, laying out pots and pans and starting cooking?

The Patrol camps are ready. How do they look? Are the tents properly located, trenched for the approaching shower, provided with well-constructed, comfortable camp beds, with blankets in place? Is the kitchen set-up satisfactory? Is there a definite place for tools, such as axes and spades, and are they kept there when not in use? Has provision been made for garbage disposal? And where, away from the camp site, is the latrine? How is it located and how constructed? Are there satisfactory fire safeguards?

And throughout the Camporee: Does every Scout have a definite duty? Does everyone carry through his responsibilities? Is the program schedule kept? How is the participation in special events? Are meals ready on time and served family style? Is everything done efficiently and promptly? Is the Scout Law truly the law of each Patrol's camp?

The observers study every Patrol and determine the scores.

The Rating Plan

Nearly every Council has a Camporee rating plan of some kind. Get a copy of this plan and use it. This is especially important, if you are holding your Troop Camporee in preparation for the Council Camporee.

If no such rating plan is available, make up one of your own. The plan suggested below has been used in a number of Troops. You may want to use it "as is," or add or substract to suit your Troop. A special pamphlet on Camporees, *The Scout Camporee Guide*, may be secured from the Supply Service. It contains a great many more ideas than can be included here.

CAMPOREE SCORE FOR THE ....*PATROL*

	Maximum Score	Score Earned
I. *Participation Sheets*		
1. Did the Patrol submit written sheets with the following information:		
Organization and work distribution	10	....
Equipment list	10	....
Food lists, menus, costs	30	....
Program	10	....
II. *Patrol Organization and Leadership*		
1. Did the Patrol Leader show effective leadership?	20	....
2. Did each Scout have definitely assigned duties in his Patrol?	15	....
3. Did all Scouts cooperate and demonstrate Scout-like conduct?	20	....
III. *Equipment*		
1. Did the Scouts bring in the equipment properly packed, with Patrol equipment and food stuff evenly distributed?	10	....

2. Was the equipment adequate? 20 . . . .

3. Did the Patrol have
   An axe and a shovel?
   (required in U. S. For-
   ests)   5 . . . .
   First Aid Kit   5 . . . .

IV. *Camp Site and Sleeping Arrangements*

1. Did the Patrol build a suit-
   able fire place?   10 . . . .

2. Did the Patrol improvise
   table on which to prepare
   food?   10 . . . .

3. Did the Patrol improvise
   table on which to eat?   10 . . . .

4. Was there evidence of
   imagination in making
   rustic camp gadgets?   10 . . . .

5. Did every Scout have adequate sleeping space under
   weatherproof shelter?   10 . . . .

6. Did each Scout have a warm,
   dry, comfortable bed?   10 . . . .

7. Was there a waterproof
   ground cloth under every
   bed?   10 . . . .

V. *Food Planning, Cooking and Serving*

1. Did the Patrol keep canned
   goods at a minimum in its
   menu planning?   10 . . . .

2. Did the Patrol follow its
   menu carefully?   15 . . . .

3. Was food protected from
   spilling, insects, dirt?   15 . . . .

4. Did the Patrol have some
   kind of refrigerator—des-
   ert cooler, pit?   15 . . . .

5. Were cooked dishes timed
   to be completed together?   10 . . . .

6. Did the Patrol sit down as a
   family for meals?   15 . . . .

VI. *Health, Safety and Sanitation*

1. Did all Scouts have at least 9 hours sleep? 15 ....
2. Were cooking fires small and safe? 10 ....
3. Were knives and hatchets used safely? 10 ....
4. Was all garbage and dish-water disposed of promptly and properly? 15 ....
5. Was the latrine well constructed and clean? 15 ....
6. Did the Patrol do a thorough job on cleaning the site when camp was broken? 30 ....

VII. *Appearance*

1. Did all Scouts who own Uniforms wear them during the Camporee? 15 ....
2. Did all Scouts keep neat and orderly during the Camporee? 20 ....

VIII. *Program*

1. Did the Patrol check in on time? 10 ....
2. Was everyone quiet between Taps and First Call? 20 ....
3. Were meals served and cleaned up according to the schedule? 15 ....
4. Did the Patrol take part in the Scoutcraft projects and camp fire activities? 20 ....

Remember that, in the scoring, it is not so much the intention to pick "the best camping Patrol," but rather to give every Patrol a chance to reach the Troop's camping standard. The maximum score in the suggested plan is 500 points. You may decide, for instance, that each

Patrol reaching 400 points or more is in Class A, that a Patrol scoring between 300 and 400 points is in Class B, and that a Patrol that participates but scores less than 300 points deserves a Class C rating.

Whatever scheme you use for rating your Troop Camporee—or even if you use no scoring at all, you will find your boys keenly eager to participate. You will provide them with an enjoyable experience. But you will do far more than that: You will lay the foundation for a successful Troop summer camp.

A Camporee is much more than just another overnight—*the Camporee is the perfect dress rehearsal for Troop summer camp.* The step from overnight camp to summer camp becomes comparatively simple after a successful Camporee experience.

The Summer Camp Adventure

CHAPTER 11

EVERY HIKE AND OVERNIGHT CAMP is a rehearsal for the biggest event in the Scouting year: the Troop's summer camp, when the whole gang sets out for a week or more of real honest-to-goodness, out-of-doors Scouting.

To a Scout, summer camp is the greatest adventure there is in Scouting.

To you, the Scoutmaster, summer camp is the greatest chance you have to get to know each of your boys, and by knowing him to help him grow—to help him become physically strong, mentally awake, and morally straight.

Take a boy to camp, and immediately you set to work a multitude of influences: The activities of each camp day harden the muscles of his body. The sun tans his skin. The fresh air sweeps through his lungs.

He picks up new Scoutcraft skills. He develops some of the resourcefulness and self-reliance of the pioneer. He learns teamwork and team play, learns to get along with other boys, to do his share in common duties.

Nature around him touches him deeply—the stillness of the forest, the calm of the lake, the freedom of the sky, the beauty of the sunset.

Life in camp has a way of bringing out the character traits of a boy, and the fact that you are there in camp with him, twenty-four hours a day, and can watch his reactions, gives you a clue to what you can do for him.

You can give the shy boy confidence by encouraging him to take on a job that will make it necessary for him to mix with others. You can give the tongue-tied boy a chance to entertain the gang with a stunt at the camp fire. You can put it up to the bully to lend a hand to the boy he bullied; make the shirker realize that working for the good of his Patrol he works for himself, too; make the braggard see himself as others see him.

You can strengthen the unity of each Patrol and bolster the leadership of each Patrol Leader by standing squarely behind him in his efforts.

The Scout Camping Method

The ideal method for Scout camping is the Troop camping under the Troop's own leadership—its own Scoutmaster, Assistants and Patrol Leaders.

And Troop camping is simply the Patrols camping together — just as a Troop meeting is simply Patrols meeting together, and the Troop hike Patrols hiking together.

Set the day early for summer camp. The boys can dream of the fun and the Patrols will have time to prepare for it.

The Patrol is the unit of operation in Troop camping as it is in all other Scout activities. Each Patrol puts up its own camp, looks after its own camp site, does its own cooking, has some of its own activities. But besides, the Patrols have the chance to do things together that are more exciting when done on a larger scale—to fight in wide games and commando raids, to have fun around a big camp fire, to compete with each other in Scoutcraft and woodcraft and watersports.

Two Types of Arrangements for Troop Camping

Generally speaking, there are two types of arrangements you can make for your Troop's summer camp:

1. THE INTER-TROOP CAMP. In this your Troop will camp on a site set apart for it in the Local Council camp.

The Troop will live its own life in charge of its own leaders, subject only to the Council regulations for use of the camp site.

In the Inter-Troop Camp, the Local Council often furnishes the Troop with tents, cooking gear and other equipment. Sanitary arrangements, a tested water supply and medical attention are there. Trained leaders are in charge of swimming and boating and health supervision. Other experts are available to help with Scoutcraft, nature lore and other activities. Besides, the Troop benefits from the association with other Troops, learning new tricks, enjoying occasional large camp fires together. The new Troop learns to stand on its own feet, to use its boy leaders, to train its own instructors in various skills that will help in building the program for the ensuing year.

2. THE INDEPENDENT TROOP CAMP. In this, the Troop camps on a suitable camp site procured by itself, and depends solely upon its own leadership to live up to Council regulations and National camping standards— except for such help as the Local Council may be able to give at long range.

For the Independent Troop Camp, the Troop provides its own camping gear, from tentage to waterfront equipment, and develops its own sanitary arrangements. It must test and treat its own water supply. It must develop safe swimming facilities and secure trained waterfront leaders. It must provide its own health supervision and medical examiner.

Whichever type you decide upon, you need to check with your District Commissioner or Scout Executive to find out what facilities are available in the Council's Inter-Troop Camp, and what arrangements must be made by the Troop itself if an Independent Troop Camp is your choice.

If you plan to take your Troop to Council Camp, meet early with your Commissioner to learn what facilities are available.

In either case, your Commissioner will be of great help to you, your leaders and your Troop Committee in your planning.

PLANNING FOR TROOP SUMMER CAMP

Your Troop Committee is responsible for ". . . assuring every Scout the opportunity to have a . . . summer camp experience . . ." while the Troop itself has the responsibility for providing the leadership. A joint meeting should therefore be called of all those involved.

Hold this meeting early in the year. Have a preliminary camp plan ready and get from the Troop Committee the cooperation in carrying out the details.

Where will we go? Decide whether you will go to the Council Camp or whether a separate site must be secured.

When do we go? Set a tentative date for the camp for late June, July or August. If you go to the Council Camp, make your reservations at the earliest possible moment. By setting the date early, Scouts who have work for the summer will have a better chance to arrange to get their vacation at the right time.

How will we go? Determine the way you'll get to camp so that you know what will be involved in transportation costs and can figure them into the camp fees.

What will we take? What new equipment do we need?

What will we eat? Start developing camp menus so that the Scouts can practice cooking camp meals.

What will we do? Think of the activities of the camp. If you are an old Troop, you may want to try some special type of adventure camping: Indian, Pioneer, Robinson Crusoe for which you need special equipment.

Who will be in charge of what? Determine at a meeting of the Patrol Leaders' Council who will be responsible for each of the things that needs to be done.

With a general idea of what needs to be done, you can begin to take care of the five things, mentioned in the previous chapter, that will make your camp a success:

> *Preliminary training for Leaders and Scouts*
> *Adequate equipment*   *Good meals*
> *Suitable camp site*   *Full program*

and the sixth thing also necessary: *Promotion*

PRactice
PRoperties
PRemises
PRovisions
PRogram
PRomotion

There were five PR's for overnight camping. There are six for summer camp: PRactice—the advance training; PRoperties—the equipment you need; PRemises—the camp site; PRovisions — the food; PRogram — the activities; and a final, sixth PR: PRomotion well ahead of time to get all boys registered for camp.

Training for Summer Camp

The training for summer camp is about the same as for overnight camping (page 193)—except more of it.

Probably the most important point is more emphasis on Patrol cooking. While individual cooking is all right on hikes, and, occasionally, on overnight camps, the closer you get to summer camp, the more the Patrols should be encouraged and helped to plan Patrol menus and to cook and serve food as complete Patrol meals.

Pitching and ditching of tents, making a comfortable bed and construction of camp gadgets are all mastered on overnights. Here, also, are demonstrated and practiced the proper handling and keeping of food, including cleanliness of kitchen and in food preparation, proper food storage. The Scouts should also learn safe dish washing methods, simplest way of cleaning pots, and correct disposal of garbage and waste water (see page 245). Be also certain that they get a fair amount of first aid training.

Besides the training of the Scouts their health condition needs to be ascertained. Arrangements should be made for each Scout to have a health examination before going to camp. A special form, Scout's Medical Record (Cat. No. 4126), is available for this purpose.

Equipment for Summer Camp

The equipment for summer camp is pretty much the same as for Troop overnight camps, except for a few additions. Since you go to a spot where you expect to stay put for ten days or more and, in all probability, require special transportation to get there, you can bring along some items that would be too bulky or heavy for an overnight experience.

The idea is not to drag everything with you, including the kitchen sink, but rather to choose those few things

SUGGESTED TROOP EQUIPMENT

This equipment is for the use of the whole Troop and supplements the equipment brought by each Patrol.

CAMP SET-UP

Flag of the United States   Troop flag
Pulleys and line for flag poles   Bulletin board (?)
Two ¾ Axes
Large shelter, if possible, under which whole Troop can assemble for rainy day activities
Store tent for supplies and commissary
Boxes for storage and shelves (carry supplies to camp in wooden boxes)
Hand saw   Mallet
Small tin snips   Assorted nails
100 feet light wire
Large ball of binder twine
(Straw for ticks to be secured locally)

SANITATION AND SAFETY

Troops first aid kits and refills for Patrol first aid kits
Clinical thermometer
Toilet paper
Screening for latrine, if necessary
Lantern for latrine
Can with kerosene. Mark plainly!
Chemical disinfectant for dishes, if scalding water is not used.
Food storage boxes
Thermometer for testing temperature of food storage
Scouring materials (steel wool, soap)
Water pails
100 feet of No. 5 sash cord for life guards (possibly also boat, ten-foot pole, and "Buddy Check" board for use in Independent Troop Camp)

SCOUTCRAFT AND GAME EQUIPMENT

Rope for pioneering
Maps
Gauze bandage for "lives" in Wide Games
Bugle or horn
Other equipment depending upon programmed activities.

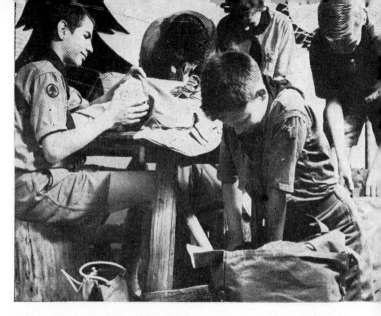

Summer camp begins in September! Start in the fall to encourage the Patrols to make equipment for their summer adventure.

which will add to your comfort without detracting from the scouty atmosphere of the camp or preventing the campers from using their ingenuity in developing camp gadgets from the material they find at the camp site.

The list of Additional Patrol Equipment on page 230 will supplement the list of basic Patrol Equipment on page 197. The needs of the Troop as a whole are covered on page 228. For yourself, you will want to bring along most of the items mentioned in the list of Scoutmaster's Materials, page 230.

Who Does the Job?

Give an Assistant Scoutmaster, a Junior Assistant Scoutmaster, or the Troop Quartermaster, if you have one, the complete responsibility for developing lists of

ADDITIONAL PATROL EQUIPMENT

Dining tarp

Table top for dining table

Patrol kitchen box, preferably with folding lid to provide kitchen table.

Refrigerator box (?)

2-3 Water pails

Individual water basins, one for each boy

Large plate, and bowls for serving

Dishwashing pots

Aprons for Cooks (?)

Patrol log book

Handbook for Patrol Leaders

SCOUTMASTER'S MATERIALS

In addition to equipment and tentage for your personal use, you may need or want some or all of the following:

Tent lantern

Alarm clock

Field glasses

Cash box

Song book: *Songs Scouts Sing*

Handbooks: *Handbook for Scoutmasters, Scout Field Book, Handbook for Boys*

Camera and films (possibly also movie camera)

Writing folder with paper, envelopes, postcards, stamps, etc.

Medical examination records of all Scouts

Home addresses and telephone numbers of all Scouts, including parents' vacation addresses if they are not home.

needed equipment and for getting the Patrols busy securing what they do not already have.

The same leader should be in charge of the final packing and should supervise the use of the equipment in camp and arrange for its return when camp is over.

The Summer Camp Site

The check list on page 200 in regard to a suitable site for an overnight camp holds true as well for the Troop's summer camp. Check it also against pages 232-233.

If you go to Council Camp, the site will already have been studied and laid out by camping experts, so you will have nothing to worry about.

On the other hand, before you decide upon the site for an independent Troop camp, investigate the spot thoroughly by camping overnight on it with the Patrol Leaders' Council. Also seek the advice of local people. They will know more about the spot than you can get from a short stay on it. If the site is found suitable, make the necessary arrangements with the proprietor for lending or renting it.

The Food in Summer Camp

No one ever heard of a successful camp without good eats. Boys want good tasty food. It does not need to be fancy, but it must be wholesome and substantial, enough to fortify the boys against the ravages of hunger during the hours between meals when they use up energy at a tremendous rate. But it is more than a question of satisfying hunger. It means meals that include the foods necessary for a boy's health and well-being.

Anybody can open a couple of cans and sling a stack of bread slices on the table. It takes imagination to plan well-balanced meals that contain all the necessary calories, proteins, carbohydrates, fats, vitamins and minerals. But it is relatively simple if you base your menus

SCORE	0	2
	BAD	POOR
LOCATION	In city	Edge city
DRAINAGE	Swamp	May flood
SOIL	Muck	Clay or gumbo
GROUND COVER	Bare	Weeds
TREE GROWTH	None	Shrubs and bushes
TOPOGRAPHY	Steep	Flat
WATER SUPPLY	None	Long carry
SWIMMING	SWIFT deep stream	Still deep stream
FUEL	None	Down soft wood
PUBLIC	Vandals	Curious
PESTS	Mosquitos	Other biting insects
TRANSPORTATION	Long hike by road	Long, hard hike

RATING SCALE

4	6	8	10
FAIR	GOOD	EXCELLENT	PERFECT
Suburban	Farms	Abandoned farms	Back woodland
Drains slowly	Drains two ways	Drains three ways	Drains all ways
Rocky or loose gravel	Gravelly	Packing sand gravel under	Firm loam gravel under
Grain Stubble	Hay crops	Leaf mold	Well grassed
Saplings	20-30 year 2nd growth	30-60 year 2nd growth	Forest primeval
12% slopes	5-8% slopes	Gentle slopes	Gentle slopes
Short steep carry	Medium carry safe well	Short carry safe well	Uncontaminated clear, cold spring— short carry
Safe depth stream	Lake, safe depth, clear and clean	Lake, safe depth, clear uncontaminated	Lake, clear, gradual slope, sand beach uncontam'd
Down soft wood	Standing, dead soft wood	Standing dead hard wood fat pine branches	Opportunity to cut and rick hardwoods. Fat pine stumps
Picnickers	Tolerant neighbors	Friendly natives	No one
Poisonous plants	Controllable flies	Few of anything	None
Long car ride and hike	Short car ride and hike	Low cost ride and hike	Low cost auto ride to site

on the *Basic Seven Food Groups* recommended by the United States Government for adequate nutrition.

THE BASIC SEVEN FOOD GROUPS

1. MILK AND MILK PRODUCTS—*Serve at least one quart of milk daily,* to drink plain or in flavored beverages, or use with cereals, and in cooked foods, such as soups, creamed vegetables, mashed potatoes, puddings, ice cream.

Milk is about the most nearly perfect of all foods. It is rich in vitamin B_2 or G, and is our best source of calcium. It also contains phosphorus and other minerals in considerable amounts.

Where possible, the milk for drinking should be bottled, *pasteurized* milk. If this is not obtainable, use evaporated or dried milk instead, diluted in the proper proportion. Seventeen ounces of evaporated milk (one tall can holds 14½ ounces) or four and one-half ounces of dried *whole* milk is equivalent to one quart of milk. (Five ounces American cheese has the same food value.)

2. ORANGES, GRAPEFRUIT, TOMATOES—*Serve at least one of these every day,* as is, as juice, or, in the case of tomatoes, canned, stewed. These three foods are our best source of vitamin C. Without them it would be almost impossible to get enough of this into the daily diet.

3. LEAFY, GREEN OR YELLOW VEGETABLES—*Serve one or more big helpings every day*—some raw, some cooked.

Green, leafy vegetables — cabbage, spinach, broccoli, lettuce, watercress — contain vitamin A and a good amount of iron. Other green vegetables, peas, stringbeans, lima beans—and deep yellow vegetables, such as carrots, yellow corn, sweet potatoes and yellow varieties of squash, also have vitamin A, and various minerals.

Vegetables should be cooked in as little water as possible, in a covered pot, to retain vitamins, flavor, color and texture.

4. POTATOES AND OTHER VEGETABLES AND FRUITS — *Serve two or more helpings of any of these:*

Fresh, canned, or quick-frozen vegetables: Potatoes, beets, cauliflower, eggplant, onions, celery.

The Patrol sitting down family-style to a meal it has itself prepared shows the highest degree of self-reliance.

Dried vegetables: Dried peas, dried beans, soybeans, lentils.

Fresh, canned, or quick-frozen fruits: Apples, pears, peaches, grapes, berries, melons.

Dried fruit: Apricots, dates, raisins, prunes, peaches, apples.

Several of these foods contain fair amounts of vitamins A, B_1 and C and are rich in minerals. They also give variety, flavor and color to the menu.

5. MEAT, POULTRY, FISH, OR EGGS — *Serve at least one helping of meat, poultry, or fish every day, and at least three eggs a week, or better, one egg a day.*

These foods are our main sources of protein. They contain many minerals and are rich in vitamins—lean meat and poultry especially in B_2 and G, eggs in practically all of them, liver in A, lean pork in thiamin. The main meal of the day is planned around meat or fish. Cook meat slowly to prevent excess shrinkage. Tender cuts of meat may be broiled or roasted; less tender cuts are better braised or stewed.

Eggs also should be cooked slowly, since fast cooking toughens the whites. They may be fried, boiled, poached or scrambled, and used in pancakes, custards and puddings.

6. BREAD, FLOUR AND CEREAL—*Serve at least two helpings of whole-grain products or enriched bread daily.*

Grain provides us with most of our carbohydrates; whole-grain also with large amounts of B vitamins and iron. In making white flour, most of the original vitamins and iron are lost. To offset this loss, flour mills now "enrich" their flour by putting back into it the vitamins and iron that were removed in the milling process. To give the boys all the benefits of bread and cereals, use either the enriched kind or serve whole-grain breads and cereals, such as whole-wheat bread, rolled oats, cracked wheat, whole-ground corn meal. Similarly, buy macaroni and spaghetti made from enriched flour and use brown rice instead of polished rice. Don't waste bread that has dried. Use it for toast, French toast, bread pudding, or as bread crumbs.

7. BUTTER, FORTIFIED MARGARINE, FATS—*Serve one-half to one pound of fat every week for each person.*

From these foods we get the fatty acids that are necessary to life. Butter contains the important vitamin A. Good brands of margarine are fortified with the same vitamin. Peanut butter, in addition to fat, contains proteins and some of the B vitamins.

Some of the fats are used for spreading on bread, others, such as shortening, lard and oils, for cooking.

The recipes for the menus on pages 238 and 239 will be found in the 16-page pamphlet, "Green Bar Bill's PATROL MENUS." This booklet is available free of charge from BOYS' LIFE Magazine, New Brunswick, New Jersey, in sufficient quantities for each of your Patrols to receive one or more copies.

In addition to the seven groups of food, certain other things are necessary in meal preparation. We may group them together as:

ACCESSORIES—*Use as needed or desired.*

Salt is necessary to make food tasty, and to replenish salt lost in perspiration.

Sugar, syrup, molasses, are used for sweetening; marmalade, jams and jellies for spreads. Use them with moderation so that they do not take the place of the more important foods.

Vinegar, mustard, pepper and other spices add flavor.

Cocoa is generally liked and is valuable for getting boys who do not care too much for milk to consume their daily quota.

Developing the Menus

In working out the menus, keep the following points in mind:

1. The menus should contain all the basic seven foods in adequate amounts.

2. They should be easy of preparation over a wood fire, even by unskilled cooks.

3. They should not take too long to prepare. A good schedule is: Breakfast, 30 minutes; lunch, 45 min.; dinner not more than 90 min., except on special occasions (stew, chicken fricassee!).

4. They should be moderately priced.

Sample menus that satisfy these requirements are found on page 238. The same menus, with food lists and complete recipes are available through BOYS' LIFE in the form of a free pamphlet, "Green Bar Bill's Patrol Menus."

In the suggested menus, the breakfast is large. It should be. There are often 14 to 15 hours between the evening meal and the next morning's breakfast. Therefore, have a big breakfast, of fruit, cereal, main dish and hot beverage.

SUGGESTED PATROL MENUS

Patrol Menu No. 1

BREAKFAST	LUNCH	DINNER
Fruit Juice (Prune, Pineapple, Apricot)	Salmon Salad Sandwiches	Smothered Hamburgers (with vegetables)
Corn Flakes	Sliced Tomatoes	Boiled Potatoes
Boiled Eggs	Bread, Butter, Jam	Cabbage Slaw
Bread, Butter, Jam	Apple Sauce	Bread, Butter
Milk, Cocoa	Milk	Chocolate Pudding, Milk
	Chocolate Milk	

Patrol Menu No. 2

BREAKFAST	LUNCH	DINNER
Bananas	Tomato Soup	Frankfurters
Wheaties	Egg & Lettuce Salad	Sauerkraut
French Toast, Syrup	Peanut Butter	Boiled Potatoes
Bread, Butter, Jam	Bread, Butter	Bread, Butter
Milk, Cocoa	Milk	Stewed Fresh Apples
		Milk

Patrol Menu No. 3

BREAKFAST	LUNCH	DINNER
Grapefruit Juice	Baked Bean Sandwiches	Lamb Stew (Potatoes, Onions, Tomatoes, Carrots)
Corn Flakes	Carrot & Cabbage Slaw	
Banana Pancakes Syrup, Jam	Bread, Butter, Jam	Sweet Pickles
Bread, Butter	Graham Crackers	Bread, Butter
Milk, Cocoa	Milk	Stewed Rhubarb
	Chocolate Milk	Milk

Patrol Menu No. 4

BREAKFAST	LUNCH	DINNER
Stewed Prunes	Stewed Tomatoes	Salmon Cakes
Wheaties	Cottage Cheese Salad	Buttered Beans
Scrambled Eggs	Bread, Butter, Jam	Boiled Potatoes
Bread, Butter, Jam	Fresh Peaches	Bread, Butter
Milk, Cocoa	Milk	Fresh Fruit Salad
		Milk
		Chocolate Milk

SUGGESTED PATROL MENUS

Patrol Menu No. 5

BREAKFAST
Sliced Oranges
Bran Flakes
French Toast,
  Syrup
Bread, Butter,
  Jam
Milk, Cocoa

LUNCH
Vegetable Soup
Cheese
  Sandwiches
Graham
  Crackers
Raisins, Jam
Bread, Butter
Milk
Chocolate Milk

DINNER
Chow Mein
  (Pork, Celery,
  Onions,
  Cabbage, Rice)
Bread, Butter
Prune Whip
Fruitade
Milk

Patrol Menu No. 6

BREAKFAST
Tomato Juice
Rice Crispies
Fried Eggs
Bread, Butter,
  Jam
Milk, Cocoa

DINNER
Fricassee
  Chicken (with
  Carrots, Onions,
  Potatoes)
Pickled Beets
Watermelon
Bread, Butter
Milk

PICNIC SUPPER
Toasted Weenies
Whole Tomatoes
Peanut Butter
  Sandwiches
Rolls, Bread,
  Butter
Crackers
Milk

Patrol Menu No. 7

BREAKFAST
Sliced Peaches
Wheaties
Pancake Syrup
Bread, Butter,
  Jam
Milk, Cocoa

LUNCH
Egg & Lettuce
  Sandwiches
Sliced Tomatoes
Peanut Butter
Bread, Butter
Raw Apples
Milk
Chocolate Milk

DINNER
Chili Con Carne
  (with Toma-
  toes, Onions,
  Kidney Beans
  and Lamb)
Bread, Butter
Magic Lemon Pie
Milk

Patrol Menu No. 8

BREAKFAST
Grapefruit Juice
Corn Flakes
Eggs
Bread, Butter,
  Jam
Milk, Cocoa

LUNCH
California Sar-
  dines (with
  Tomato Sauce)
Cucumber Salad
Peanut Butter,
  Jam
Bread, Butter
Crackers—Milk

DINNER
Italian Spaghetti
  (with Meat
  Balls, Tomatoes
  and Onions)
Pickled Beets
Bread, Butter
Apple Betty
Lemonade—Milk

Lunch is rather light. It is hot in the middle of the day, and a heavy meal does not set too well. Stick to sandwiches and salads and other light dishes, with a simple dessert, milk or fruit drink. Use hot soup if the day turns chilly.

The main meal of the day is best served in the evening. This is the time when it is most easily assimilated and put to best use. It should consist of meat or fish and vegetables, a satisfying dessert and a beverage.

In determining the amounts of food stuffs to be purchased, it should be kept in mind that a growing boy requires more food than a grown man. This was considered in developing the "Patrol Menus" pamphlet. It should be remembered if you develop your own menus from a regular cook book.

In developing menus, you will naturally take into consideration the conditions that will prevail in camp. If you have an independent camp, you need to do the whole job for yourself. If, on the other hand, your Troop plans to camp on its own site at the Council camp, several arrangements may be possible that will influence your menu development: You may want to bring in and prepare your own food; you may purchase the food at the camp trading post and prepare it on your own camp site; there may be provision in camp for one or more meals to be made in a central kitchen for distribution to the Troop camp; or one or more meals a day may be taken in a central dining hall.

Cooking Procedure

Cooking by Patrols is the easiest and most satisfactory way of preparing the meals in camp. The Patrols are already trained in Patrol cooking on hikes and in overnight camps, and have the necessary equipment. The camp schedule is more easily kept since all the Patrols are occupied at the same time and move along together.

The Patrol chest that did duty all winter in the meeting room becomes the Patrol kitchen box and work table in camp.

But what is possibly even more important, by having the Patrols cook for themselves you develop team work, strengthen Patrol unity, and give every boy a chance for practice by rotation of duties.

Remember that cooking is more than just preparing a meal, and think of Baden-Powell's words: "Patrol cooking is bound to be valuable—because I am not looking merely to the successful camp, but to the making of self-reliant resourceful men."

To simplify the work of the boys, the instructions that are given to the Patrols when they receive their food stuffs should give the step-by-step preparation of the *complete meal*, and not just consist of a list of unrelated recipes to be hunted for on various pages of a cook book.

The BOYS' LIFE pamphlet, "Patrol Menus," mentioned earlier, is developed on this basis.

It will add to the interest of the camp, if occasionally another cooking method is sprung on the boys, for a meal or a day, such as: Buddy cooking, individual cooking without utensils, one Patrol cooking a meal for the whole Troop, the leaders preparing a Troop feast of bean-hole beans or imu.

Food Buying and Delivery

After the menus have been completely developed and the amounts of food determined, a breakdown is made of the items.

Make a separate list of the staples involved, such as sugar, cocoa, salt, vinegar, flour, shortening, jams, canned goods. These may all be purchased at home and brought to camp, or arrangements may be made with a local grocery to have them ready on arrival.

The other foodstuffs are made up into daily purchase lists.

If you are going to the Local Council camp, check with the persons in charge of the camp trading post to see that provisions can be bought there. Otherwise, make arrangement with local tradesmen to have the items available on the dates scheduled.

One of the greatest problems in camp is keeping milk and meat fresh. Under certain conditions, a simple in-the-ground cooler will do the job for a short period. A better cooler is a double-walled, insulated box, provided with a wire-mesh bottom permitting draining of water from melting ice.

A simple arrangement for food deliveries in camp is to have two of them:

First Delivery—early in the morning, of milk only, which should, if possible, reach the Troop at a temperature not higher than 50 degrees, and be kept at that temperature until used.

Second Delivery—in late afternoon, as the Patrols come back from the swim period, so that dinner may be started immediately. This delivery will also include the next day's breakfast and lunch rations.

Keeping Food in Camp

To keep the food properly, each Patrol needs a box for staples and a simple refrigerator for perishables.

A Patrol kitchen box may be built so that it can be placed on legs, with the front hinged to fold down and provide a kitchen work table. (See illustration page 241). If no regular kitchen box is available, a cardboard box or a bag may be used for such staples as sugar, bread, flour and the like. Suspend it from the ridge pole of a tent or limb of a tree out of reach of animals.

When it comes to perishables, great care must be taken to keep them fresh.

Certain vegetables and fruits keep without refrigeration: potatoes, onions, cabbage, apples, bananas—while others should be kept cool: string beans, carrots, cucumbers, lettuce, berries, ripe peaches and pears. A simple cooler dug in the ground in a shaded spot and covered with a board cover will take care of these perishables. Better is a large wooden box with chicken wire bottom and hinged lid sunk in the ground.

Fresh meats and milk need even greater care. They will keep only at a temperature below 50° Fahrenheit—which means that ice will be needed.

If ice is not available, and you have to depend on spring houses, caves or pits for your cooling, do not attempt to keep perishables that spoil quickly, but buy your meats and milk fresh each day and use them up the day they are bought. Check the temperature of your cooling places regularly with a thermometer.

Don't keep left-over meat in an in-the-ground cooler. It requires greater refrigeration. And make it a rule *never* to keep cooked potatoes or dishes containing potatoes or eggs from one meal to the next. They spoil easily.

Kitchen Cleanliness

The way the cooks and their helpers go about keeping the kitchen clean depends much upon the training the boys have received on overnight camps. That's why it is of greatest importance to insist on cleanliness at all times.

Encourage each Patrol to bring aprons for its cooks. They add a touch to the proceedings that will develop pride in cleanliness.

Sanitary dish washing is important. To be safe, dishes and cutlery should be washed first in hot soapy water after thorough scraping, then rinsed in clear hot water, and finally submerged in a net bag or wire basket for two minutes in scalding water, at not less than 180° Fahrenheit. If the water boils, you are sure of your temperature—212°. When lifted out, the dishes will dry within a few minutes without the use of towels.

Another method is to wash in warm soapy water, then rinse in clear warm water, and finally submerge in a chemical disinfectant. Several such disinfectants are available through restaurant supply houses. Follow the directions on the containers for proper dilution. Remove the dishes from the solution to drain and to air dry.

Both these methods do away with the use of unsanitary dish towels.

Keep dishes between meals in a fly-proof box, bag or closet.

SCRAPE CLEAN . WASH CLEAN . DUNK IN BOILING WATER

GARBAGE

REMINGTON SCHUYLER

DRY GARBAGE . THEN BURN . DRY ON HOT STONES

Kitchen and dining table should be scrubbed thoroughly with soap and water after each meal.

Garbage should be disposed of by burning. If incineration is not possible, bury refuse in a refuse hole and cover it with at least twelve inches of dirt. Tin cans are burned out, crushed and buried.

Who Does the Job?

It is advisable to give an Assistant Scoutmaster, (or a responsible junior leader) the task of developing menus and food lists ahead of camp, and to keep the same person in charge of the commissary during camp— ordering, receiving and distributing the supplies to the Patrols and supervising their cooking, and keeping necessary accounts. The Patrol which is the Service Patrol for the day will be ready to help.

This is probably the toughest and most important of all jobs for the welfare of the campers and the success of the camp. So make certain that it is handled effectively.

The Program of Activities

You and your boys want summer camp to be the most magnificent experience in the Troop's life.

It is a mistaken idea to think that "the program will take care of itself." On the contrary, the program should, as far as possible, be mapped out in advance, with a daily schedule (see sample on page 247), and with planned activities for every day in camp (see suggestions on pages 248-249).

The program should provide for plenty of fun and fellowship, but it should also give each boy a chance to practice the things that make him an efficient and self-reliant camper.

Scouts want Scouting when they are in camp. They are not interested in just hanging around. Keep them busy with things they want to do, without running them ragged. Help them to enjoy nature. Teach them to live comfortably in the outdoors. Give them the opportunity to advance in rank and to become more physically fit.

Program details are found in the description of *The Day in Camp*, starting on page 261.

Be prepared for a couple of rainy days. Have special programs ready to spring when bad weather sets in.

Who Does the Job?

Discuss the program well ahead of camp at a meeting of the Patrol Leaders' Council. Give the Senior Patrol Leader, with an Assistant Scoutmaster, the responsibility for arranging the details and securing equipment that may be needed. He may arrange to have Junior Assistants take charge of demonstrations, games, contests and formations and special events.

The Patrol acting as Program Patrol for the day will be responsible, in camp, for getting materials in readiness for special events, and lining up many of the program features.

<u>Troop One</u>
Day in Summer Camp

7:30 AM Get up. Wash.
   Cooks prepare breakfast. (Cooks up one-
    half hour earlier)
   Others straighten up camp, clean tents,
    hang blankets up for airing.
8:15 Breakfast. Clean-up.
8:45 Sick Call.
9:00 Meeting of Patrol Leaders' Council.
9:15 Flag raised by color guard from the
    Service Patrol of the day.
   Inspection of Patrols and Patrol Camp
    sites.
9:30 Scoutcraft demonstration (Bill in charge)
10:00 Patrol training in Scoutcraft.
11:00 Waterfront period — Swimming and boating
    instruction. (Waterfront Director: John)
12:15 PM Lunch.
1:00 Rest Period. Diary writing. Letter
    writing.
2:00 Scout game or Inter-Patrol Contest
    (Bill responsible)
4:00 Waterfront period — free swimming and
    boating. (John again)
5:00 Cooks start preparation for dinner.
6:15 Flag Ceremony (Service Patrol of the day)
6:30 Dinner. Clean-up.
7:30 Free time or game. (Program Patrol)
8:30 Camp fire. (Program Patrol in charge)
9:30 Retire. Lights out. Silence in camp.

SUGGESTED
CAMP PROGRAM ACTIVITIES

FIRST DAY (Monday)	*Afternoon:* Arrival in camp. Camp set-up. *Evening:* Camp fire with discussion of camp, and announcements.
SECOND DAY (Tuesday)	*Morning:* Scoutcraft — Pioneering, axe and rope work, gadget instruction. Finish camp set-up. Swim. *Afternoon:* Review of Scout Requirements. Swim. *Evening:* Game. Camp fire.
THIRD DAY (Wednesday)	*Morning:* Scoutcraft—Fire making and cooking. Swim. *Afternoon:* Olympic Games. Swim. *Evening:* Game. Camp fires by Patrols on own sites.
FOURTH DAY (Thursday)	*Morning:* Scoutcraft — Compass, mapping. Swim. *Afternoon:* Treasure Hunt. Swim. *Evening:* Night game and camp fire.
FIFTH DAY (Friday)	*Morning:* Scoutcraft — Signaling. Swim. *Afternoon:* Scoutcraft Field Day. *Evening:* Game. Indian camp fire.
SIXTH DAY (Saturday)	*Morning:* Scoutcraft—Trailing and tracking. Swim. *Afternoon:* Trailing contest. Swim. *Evening:* Game. Stunt camp fire.

SUGGESTED
PROGRAM ACTIVITIES

SEVENTH DAY (Sunday)	*Morning:*	Church. Swim.
	Afternoon:	Nature Hike. Swim.
	Evening:	Camp fire — Tall Story contest. Star Study.
EIGHTH DAY (Monday)	*Morning:*	Scoutcraft — Woodcraft, nature lore. Swim. Story of Robinson Crusoe Expedition.
	Afternoon:	Survivalcraft. Swim.
	Evening:	Robinson Crusoe Dinner. Patrol camp fires. Arrival of "Rescue ship."
NINTH DAY (Tuesday)	*Morning:*	Scoutcraft — First aid. Swim.
	Afternoon:	First Aid Field Day. Swim.
	Evening:	Game. Surprise camp fire.
TENTH DAY (Wednesday)	*Morning:*	Scoutcraft—Observation. Swim.
	Afternoon:	Water Meet.
	Evening:	"Feature Camp Fire"— Announcement of Honor Patrol and Honor Camper.
ELEVENTH DAY (Thursday)	*Morning:*	Break camp. Swim.
	Afternoon:	Finish breaking camp. Swim. Goodbye.

Promoting the Camp

Tradition is your best camp promotion.

If your Troop is accustomed to go camping every summer, camp promotion practically takes care of itself. The old campers talk about what fun they had last year; they sing the same songs at the Troop meetings' "council fire" that they did at camp fires under the stars, and new boys soon pick up the excitement and anticipation.

If your Troop is new, promotion is a little harder, but your own enthusiasm for the coming adventure will transmit itself to the boys.

As soon as the dates have been set for camp, the first announcements are made. From then on, let no Troop meeting or hike pass without further announcements and suggestions for preparation.

A camp bank may be established to which the Scouts can bring their nickels, dimes and quarters as earned. Get the Treasurer of the Troop Committee interested in this idea.

Notices to Parents

The first notice to the parents should be sent out about two months before camp. This may be a mimeographed letter, arranged along the line suggested on page 251, containing the What?, Where?, When? of the camp, and announcing the camp fee.

Parents' Meeting

If at all possible, a Parents' Meeting should be called for about one month before the opening of camp.

At this meeting the Chairman of the Troop Committee will have an opportunity to describe to the parents the high standards under which the camp will be run and to reassure the more timid parents. The Scoutmaster will have a chance to talk about the activities planned,

TROOP ONE

OUR SUMMER CAMP 19

WHAT?	Summer is here and so is Summer Camp! Summer Camp means more in a Scout's life than all the meetings of the year put together. That's why we want every one of our Scouts to get to camp this Summer. Ten days in camp mean physical fitness, fellowship, and fun.
WHEN?	The Troop's Summer Camp will open on Monday, July 7th, and continue to Wednesday July 16th. The Patrols are expected to be on the camp site during the forenoon of July 7th, each Scout with his own lunch, with all personal equipment, ready to establish camp. First meal will be supper, July 7th; last meal lunch July 16th. (Family Day is Sunday July 13th, with picnic and campfire.)
WHERE?	The Troop Summer Camp will be established on the Gilwell Camp Site of the Schiff Scout Reservation.
CAMP FEE	The camp fee for the full period is only $10.00. This includes <u>all</u> expenses for the ten days, including three hearty meals a day. The camp fee should be paid on arrival in camp on July 7th, or it may be paid by check accompanying application coupon below.
HEALTH and SAFETY	The camp will be under efficient sanitary supervision throughout. Swimming and boating will take place only under the strictest supervision of experienced life guards. Our Troop has four Scout Life Guards who will be in charge of the waterfront.
IMPORTANT	(1) The SCOUT LAW is the law of the camp. Every Scout is expected to live up to it at all times. (2) No one is allowed to leave the camp site without the permission of the Scoutmaster or his representative. Campers will remain in camp for the entire camping period. (3) Every Scout is required to keep a diary of the camp. A special prize will be awarded for the best diary.

Please fill out the coupon below and return to the Scoutmaster in the enclosed envelope, as <u>soon as possible</u>, <u>AND NOT LATER THAN JULY 1st</u>.

For the success of our summer camp.

Lyall Merrill	Mrs.J.H.Hogan	Marshall Spaan
Chairman, Troop Committee	President, Scout Mothers	Scoutmaster

---

APPLICATION COUPON, SUMMER CAMP 19

<u>Hurry this coupon to the Scoutmaster.</u>

I desire to have my boy,.................(name of Scout), take part in the summer camp of Troop One, from Monday, July 7th, to Wednesday, July 16th, and agree to the rules of the camp.
I understand that the camp fee, $10.00 to cover all expenses for the ten days, is due the day camp opens.

Signed.....................................
(Parent or Guardian)

Send out your camp letters in plenty of time. Give the parents the main points of information on What? When? Where? How Much?

to get the mothers interested in training their sons in cooking, and to get the fathers interested in helping their boys secure needed equipment.

Final Notices

If it is impossible to have a Parents' Meeting, another notice should be sent out about a month before camp, containing information in regard to personal equipment, and time when camp fees are to be paid.

The Camp Fee

The camp fees should be budgeted to cover rental of camp site, rental of equipment (if you don't have your own), transportation of the boys (in public carriers, not in trucks), insurance while the boys are being transported (such insurance costs little and is worth the expense in the feeling of added security it gives those in charge), transportation of equipment if it cannot go with the Troop, provisions and miscellaneous supplies, straw for mattresses, plus a suitable amount to take care of emergencies.

Set the fee as low as possible. Even so, there may be parents who cannot afford to pay it. They may not say so, but their boys may indicate that they can't go. Try to visit the parents or arrange to have a member of the Troop Committee do so. If the boy isn't going because

Secure safe transportation to camp. If motor transportation is used, comply with these rules: Licensed driver, 21 years of age or older. Inspected and certified vehicles. Adequate property damage and public liability insurance carried. Driving done in daylight. Traffic and speed regulations obeyed.

the mother is worried about Johnnie's safety, such worries can be overcome. If there seems to be financial reasons, the Troop Committee member may frankly say that the Troop would like to have Johnnie in camp and may be able to help Johnnie earn his camp fees. A good Troop has a camp fund for just such cases.

Check Your Progress

To make sure that all points are covered, here's a list you can use for checking your progress:

At the Beginning of the Year

☐ Begin general promotion of camp. Get everybody enthusiastic.
☐ Focus Troop and Patrol activities toward camp.
☐ Have a joint meeting of Troop leaders and Troop Committee.
☐ Open a camp bank.
☐ Check equipment. Get the Patrols busy making what is missing.

Four Months Before Camp

☐ Contact your Commissioner and your Scout Executive and check with them about Local Council camp facilities.
☐ Determine place and dates.
☐ Announce the dates to the Patrols.

During Last Two Months Before Camp

☐ Send out first camp notice to parents.
☐ If possible, arrange for a parents' meeting to discuss camp.
☐ Make final overhauling of camp equipment.
☐ Develop camp menus.
☐ In case of an Independent Troop camp, have Patrol Leaders' Council camp overnight on site. Check swimming facilities. Have drinking water tested. Contact local grocer, butcher, dairy, farm selling vegetables. Locate nearest church. Get address of doctor and hospital.

☐ Send out second camp notice to parents.
☐ Have Troop Committee members visit parents of Scouts who have not signed up for camp.
☐ Finish camp menus, work out food lists.
☐ Develop program of activities.
☐ Have Troop Committee arrange for transportation.
☐ Send camp application to Local Council with list of boys and leaders, menus and program.

TEN DAYS BEFORE CAMP

☐ Send out final notice to parents.
☐ Collect camp fees. Draw out necessary camp funds from bank.
☐ Order staples and commissary for first days in camp.
☐ Finish program of activities.
☐ Have all Scouts and Scouters given health examination, using forms 4126 and 4250.

A COUPLE OF DAYS BEFORE CAMP

☐ Have inspection of personal packs and Patrol equipment.
☐ Have special Troop equipment ready for packing.
☐ Check transportation.

FINALLY: You're Off!

STARTING THE CAMP

The big day arrives! All preparations have been completed, all equipment is at hand. The Patrols have gathered, all packed, ready to be off. Into the cars or onto the buses or the trains, or off on the high road! And there you go, with high expectations for what is in store!

Try to arrive at the camp site around noon or in the early afternoon so that there are still several hours of daylight in which to set up camp.

At last you get there. And the busiest time of the whole experience is at hand: pitching camp.

Immediately upon arrival the Patrols establish their

The time has come! Up go the Patrol camps! The boys are all set for a couple of weeks of glorious days in camp.

duffel line. If the Patrol Leaders' Council has already inspected the camp site, the layout of the camp will have been decided, and the Patrols can go to work right away. Otherwise, the leaders go over the place, and decide on Patrol sites and location of various camp structures. After this quick survey, the Patrol Leaders call their Patrols and everybody gets busy.

Pitching the Camp

The Patrols sites should, if possible, be a hundred feet or more apart so that the Patrols get the feeling of being independent units in a cooperative camp. Each site should provide space for tents, with the Patrol kitchen and "dining room" in the background.

The process of setting up Patrol camp is described in full detail in the *Handbook for Patrol Leaders*.

Scouters and junior leaders put up their own tents. They should preferably be situated near the entrance to the camp or in a central location. The leaders also put up the supply tent and bring into it the supplies brought from home.

A group consisting of one volunteer from each Patrol —or the Service Patrol for the day—digs the latrine in a spot down stream and down slope from the entire camp, well below the drinking water supply. It should be at least one hundred feet from the cooking and eating places, but as nearly as possible the same distance from the different Patrols. Provide wash water at the latrine for washing immediately after elimination.

After the general camp set-up is finished, a flag pole with pulley and line is raised in the middle of the camp. The Flag of the United States and the Troop flag may be hoisted immediately—with or without ceremony.

Also lay out a camp fire circle about thirty feet in diameter and arrange log seats around it if you can get them.

If a large tent or tarp or tepee has been brought along to shelter the complete Troop for rainy day gatherings put that up. It may be advisable to build a Troop incinerator for burning rubbish, and make a covered pit for waste water disposal.

First Meal

As soon as the Patrols have built their fire places, the leaders in charge of the commissary distribute food for the first meal in camp, the evening meal, and cooking begins.

When refrigerators have been prepared and Patrol kitchen boxes put up, food stuffs for next day's breakfast and luncheon are distributed with sheets giving the menus and full instructions for the preparation of the meals. (See suggested menus earlier in this chapter.)

Make it a tradition in your Troop to start each meal in camp with the saying of Grace. The following Graces have the approval of the Protestant, Catholic, Jewish, and Mormon Committees on Scouting:

GRACES AT MEALS—*Morning Graces.* (1) "Gracious Giver-of-All-Good, Thee we thank for rest and food. Grant that all we do or say in Thy service be this day." (2) "Our Father, we thank Thee for this new day and for Thy loving care. Help us to be mindful of Thee in these happy, sunlit hours." (3) "Heavenly Father, we thank Thee for Thy care through the night and for this new day. Guide us by Thy spirit, and at the close of this day may we not be ashamed before Thee."

Noon Graces. (1) "Father, for this noonday meal, we would speak the praise we feel. Health and strength we have from Thee, help us, Lord, to faithful be." (2) "Our Father in Heaven, as this day leads on, let us not forget our obligations to honor and serve Thee. We thank Thee for these gifts of Thy bounty. Bless them to our use and our lives to Thy service." (3) "Heavenly Father, help us to see the beautiful things in earth and sky which are tokens of Thy love. Walk with us in the days we spend together here. May the food we eat and all Thy blessings help us to better serve Thee."

Evening Graces. (1) "Tireless Guardian of our way, Thou hast kept us well this day. While we thank Thee, we request care continued, pardon, rest." (2) "Heavenly Father, we thank Thee for this day and for Thy presence in it. Forgive us if we have not made it a better day and help us to be tomorrow what we have failed to be today." (3) "Our Father, God, we thank Thee for this evening meal. As Thou hast been mindful of us, so help us to be mindful of Thee, that we may know and do Thy will."

Graces Suitable for Any Meal. (1) "For health and strength and daily bread, we give Thee thanks, O Lord." (2) "For this and all Thy mercies, Lord, make us duly grateful." (3) "We thank Thee, Our Heavenly Father, for this food. Bless us as we partake of it that it may strengthen us to Thy service."

The First Camp Fire

After the evening meal is completed, wood is collected for the evening's camp fire. The program may contain a few familiar songs led by a junior leader, but the main feature will be your own *brief* talk about "Let's Make Camp a Success!"

This talk will remind the boys of the value in the days ahead of the things they have practiced on hikes and in overnight camps, and will explain what is expected of them:

The test of the *real* Scout camp is that everybody cooperates; that everyone lives up to the Scout Law; that the camp site is kept scrupulously clean; that all orders are obeyed cheerfully and immediately.

Tell your boys that it is up to them to act intelligently in matters of health and safety; to keep themselves clean and well; that swimming is only done during regular swimming hours; that axes must be handled so that no one will be hurt; that fires must be carefully watched and fire alarm given if any danger is apparent; that even the slightest scratch must have first aid attention; that anybody who does not feel well should immediately come to you.

Tell them that the general tidiness and special responsibilities will be in the hands of a Patrol working as a Service Patrol under the supervision of an Assistant Scoutmaster or a junior leader; that the program of the day will be handled by another Patrol acting as Program Patrol, under the Senior Patrol Leader and another Assistant Scoutmaster or junior leader. Describe the duties of these Patrols as given on the following page. Have the Patrols draw lots for their turns, so that the rotation between the Patrols may be decided. Place the schedule of this rotation on the bulletin board the next morning.

Responsibilities of
DUTY PATROLS

SERVICE PATROL

1. The period of service of the Service Patrol is from 9:00 a.m. until 9:00 a.m. the following day.
2. The Service Patrol is responsible for the general tidiness of the camp, and especially of the latrines (where water container must be kept filled), washing place, camp fire circle.
3. The Service Patrol will hoist The Flag in the morning and lower it at 7:15 p.m.
4. The Service Patrol will lay and light the camp fire on time.
5. The Service Patrol will immediately bring to the notice of the Scoutmaster or other leader in charge any unusual occurrence.

Scouter cooperating...

PROGRAM PATROL

1. The period of service of the Program Patrol is from 9:00 a.m. until 9:00 a.m. the following day.
2. The Program Patrol will see to it that the Troop is ready on time, with necessary equipment, for all scheduled periods.
3. The Program Patrol is responsible for getting ready necessary equipment for morning Scout-craft period and for afternoon game or contest period, and will carry out such responsibilities as may be given it in connection with these periods.
4. The Program Patrol will select and be ready to put on a few fun games for 7:30 p.m. game period.
5. The Program Patrol is responsible for arranging the program of the evening's camp fire, and leading it. It will contact the other Patrols and get from them lists of songs and stunts, to work into the program.

Scouter cooperating...

Rotation of Responsibilities of
DUTY PATROLS

Date	Service Patrol	Program Patrol
July 9th	Eagle	Lone Pine
July 10th	Beaver	Lenape
July 11th	Lone Pine	Eagle
July 12th	Lenape	Beaver
July 13th	Eagle	Lone Pine
July 14th	Beaver	Lenape
July 15th	Lone Pine	Eagle
July 16th	Lenape	Beaver
July 17th	Eagle	Lone Pine
July 18th	Beaver	Lenape
July 19th	Lone Pine	Eagle

Suggested Rotation of
DUTIES WITHIN THE PATROL

	July 9th	July 10th	July 11th	etc.
Head Cook	Jack	Joe	Tom	
Assistant Cook	Joe	Tom	Bill	
Fire Man	Tom	Bill	Fred	
Water Man	Bill	Fred	Jim	
Kitchen "Cleaner-Upper"	Fred	Jim	George	etc.
Assistant Kitchen "Cleaner-Upper"	Jim	George	Jack	
Camp Site "Cleaner-Upper"	George	Jack	Joe	

These duties are assigned by the Patrol Leader. They may be shifted in the evening, or better, in the morning, immediately after inspection.

See Chart, *Handbook for Patrol Leaders,* p. 205.

The Flag ceremony starts the day off right. Announcements about the day's program, and the whole camp gets into swing.

"Any questions?" There are apt to be several which should all be carefully answered.

Another couple of songs, of the quiet type, and the camp fire is closed with a short appropriate ceremony.

The boys have had a strenuous day, so it's off to bed early! And if they have had previous overnight camp training, they'll soon be asleep.

THE DAY IN CAMP

7:30 A.M. is an appropriate time for getting up in summer camp. The signal is sounded with a primitive horn, a gong, a bugle, or whatever else you can think of.

Immediately there is a bustle in the tents. The cooks get their fires lighted and breakfast prepared while the other members of the Patrol wash and perform their special jobs according to the rotation of duties within the Patrol, involving straightening up around camp, cleaning tents, hanging blankets out on lines for airing.

"Come and get it!" The boys dive into their breakfast. When it is over, dishes are washed and the kitchen put in shape.

Patrol Leaders' Council Meets

The Patrol Leaders' Council meets for a short session every morning to discuss the program of the day, to hear the reports of the Patrol Leaders in regard to special jobs undertaken. Personal problems that may have arisen are brought up and methods of solving them decided upon. The health of the boys is checked. The Patrol Leaders should be held responsible for reporting immediately any boy who is ill.

Flag Ceremony

If you have planned a *formal* Flag Ceremony in the morning, the Patrols with all Scouts completely uniformed, move into position, forming a horseshoe around the flag pole, and the Flag is hoisted. It may be followed to the top by a bugle playing "To the Colors" or with the boys singing "America," "America the Beautiful," "The Star Spangled Banner," "God Bless America," or other appropriate songs.

For an efficient camp, it sometimes pays to pit the Patrols against each other in a Patrol Recognition contest (See Tool No. 4 in back of book). No valuable prize is necessary. Make a special trophy from an old tin can around which Troop tradition can be built, or use a regular Honor Patrol banner.

After the Flag raising, you may have a full minute's silence for the boys' own silent prayers. Then announcements for the day are made.

If an *informal* ceremony is preferred in the morning, the Service Patrol should hoist the Flag while each Scout stands at attention wherever he may be.

Inspection

The Patrols, with the Assistant Patrol Leaders in charge, go back to their own camp sites while Patrol Leaders and Troop leaders set out on the morning inspection.

Make it thorough. It is the best opportunity you have for securing absolute cleanliness around camp. By making your inspections stiff and pitting the Patrols against each other for the cleanest camp, you may solve one of your major camp problems. By taking the Patrol Leaders around, you will make certain that not even the tiniest speck or scrap is overlooked. They will be severe with each other, knowing that they all have the same chance and the same responsibility.

TENTS—Are they properly straightened up? Are flaps tied up to provide thorough ventilation? Do tents contain only what should be there of personal and Patrol equipment? (Do not insist upon having the beds made up for this inspection. The blankets and straw ticks should rather be out in the sun for an airing of almost three hours' duration. But check beds later in the day.) Are the lanterns clean? Are clothes arranged neatly? Is the ground inside and outside the tents clean? Are ditches satisfactory? Is the fire pail in place and full of water? Are bathing suits and towels hung away from the tents?

DINING FLIES — Are the dining flies put up properly? Are tables and benches clean? Are plates, cups, cutlery clean and protected against flies? Are grounds clean?

KITCHEN—Are fire places in good shape? Are pots and pans clean? Are wood piles in order, with axes in chopping blocks and chips removed? Are kitchen boxes tidy and free from flies? Are the refrigerators in shape? Have covers of grease traps been replaced? Has garbage been burned or removed?

After the Patrol spots have been inspected, there follows the inspection of the places that are important to the whole camp.

LATRINE—Has the Service Patrol kept it in shape? Are seats clean? Are trenches properly covered? Is paper available? Is water for washing hands replenished? Is lantern for night use in place?

WASHING PLACES—Are the surroundings clean? Have individual basins been emptied, cleaned and turned up?

CAMP FIRE CIRCLE—Is ground clean? Are seats in position? Is wood piled up neatly?

GENERAL CAMP GROUNDS — Are the camp grounds cleared of all foreign matter?

All these details are quickly checked when everyone knows what to look for. The important thing is to have high standards and have all Scouts know what those standards are. Most boys will readily cooperate when they know the *reasons* for what is expected of them.

Forenoon Activities

After the inspection is over the forenoon's program begins.

Generally speaking, the forenoon seems to be the time best suited for improving the camp, for picking up new skills, and for practicing these new skills in the Patrols and individually.

Camp Improvements

Every effort should be made during the first few days of camp to develop the Patrol sites into really comfortable and efficient camps.

This is where ingenuity and imagination show themselves and where handiness can be encouraged.

Any number of things is possible:

Instead of continuing the use of the simple rock fire-

Demonstration, then practice, in a Scoutcraft skill is the most effective way you have of teaching it.

place a Patrol used for its first meal in camp, the Scouts may develop their own special type of raised fireplace that will make cooking easier for the rest of the camp. One Patrol may put up a rustic kitchen table and, immediately, the other Patrols will want to make even better ones for their kitchens.

Then follow in rapid succession other camp improvements: dining tables and seats, washstands, pot racks, clotheslines, rustic brooms and rakes, pot hangers of all descriptions, and many other things that show the difference between the Tenderfoot and the trained camper.

Demonstration Get-Togethers

A quick demonstration of special skills may prove a valuable morning activity, specifically if it is followed soon after by practice in the skill shown. Such a demonstration might be designed to help the Scouts to make the most out of camp, or to prepare them for an activity that is planned for a period later in the day. The demonstration will be a review and a refresher for the more advanced Scouts, and will aid the Patrol Leaders in training their new Patrol members.

It may be one of the duties of the Program Patrol for the day to put on the morning demonstration. Or it may be handled by the Scoutmaster, an Assistant or a junior leader, or, in an Inter-Troop Camp, by a member of the Council camp staff. It should be snappy and enjoyable and to the point.

The first full day in camp, for instance, the demonstration might be a dramatization of axemanship, along the lines of "Tenderfoot Willie and His Axe" suggested on page 150. This would, in an effective way, suggest to the boys the proper use of the axe throughout their stay in camp. Or the demonstration might be a display of improvised camp equipment or camp structures, involving the use of lashings.

During other days in camp, the demonstration might be a preview of skills that are required for making a scheduled activity a success.

On the morning of the First Aid Field Day, it would contain a quick review of proper first aid methods. The day of the Survival Hike, it would give the boys an idea of the useful wild plants that are found around camp and show their uses. If a Patrol feast of bean-hole beans is on the program, the demonstration would feature the proper way of preparing the hole and laying the fire. And so on.

Scout Advancement

A Scout cannot help but advance in camp! By taking part in the daily activities, he automatically advances

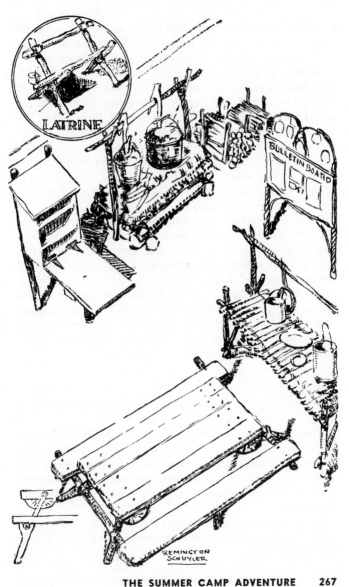

LATRINE

BULLETIN BOARD

REMINGTON
SCHUYLER

THE SUMMER CAMP ADVENTURE   267

in the best possible way. His advancement is a natural outcome of his life in Patrol and Troop—exactly the condition that should be encouraged at all times.

When a boy has cut fire wood, made a fire, cooked for his Patrol and cleaned up after the meal, he is certainly entitled to credit for the things he has done that are up to the standards of the Second and First Class Requirements in these subjects. When he has made a comfortable ground bed and has slept in it during camp, he has met a Camping Merit Badge Requirement and should receive credit for it.

The same goes for many other skills he will practice and demonstrate in camp.

There are certain Requirements for Second Class and First Class that may not be a natural part of the daily life in camp—such as first aid, signaling, measuring, and several others. Nevertheless, camp offers the boy the best possible chance for meeting them. It is a simple matter for the Patrol Leader to arrange for the boy to do the things that are involved. With a bit of imagination all the things that are necessary for meeting outdoor requirements can be put into practice in camp or on Patrol hikes out of camp.

Waterfront Period

The morning's Scoutcraft is usually followed by a swim.

This forenoon waterfront period should preferably be an instruction period—elementary swimming for non-swimmers, improving their strokes for beginners, life saving for advanced swimmers, with demonstration and practice in rescue methods using poles, life line, boat and canoe.

In the *Council Inter-Troop Camp*, a complete, expert waterfront staff will be in charge and will provide supervision and instruction.

The swim is enjoyed by all. But it is more than fun—it's learning to take care of yourself in the water and to help others.

In the *Independent Troop Camp,* the Eight Defense Plan must be strictly adhered to:

THE EIGHT DEFENSE PLAN:

1. *Medical Examination*—Each bather must have received a careful medical examination, using the special Form 4126, before coming to camp. A Scout whose health condition makes swimming dangerous for him must be kept ashore.

2. *Trained Supervisor*—A waterman who holds an up-to-date Life Saving Certificate of a Scout Aquatic School, Red Cross or Y.M.C.A., should be in charge. He must be at least 18 years of age. This may be the Scoutmaster or an Assistant.

3. *Safe Swimming Area*—The bottom of the swimming area should be carefully examined to discover deep holes, stumps, rocks and so on. The area is then marked off for the three classes of bathers: one not more than 3½ feet deep for non-swimmers, another from shallow

water to just over the head for beginners, deep water for swimmers. A Scout Life Guard or Patrol Leader is placed in charge of each section.

4. *Life Guards*—Two older Scouts who are able swimmers should be designated as Life Guards. They are stationed ashore and equipped with a life line. In case of emergency, one carries out the line, the other feeds it out and pulls in his partner and the bather in trouble.

5. *Lookout*—A lookout is placed at a point where he can see all swimmers at all times. If a boat can be secured, have it manned by two older Scouts, one to row and one, equipped with a ten-foot pole, to act as a guard.

6. *Ability Groups*—The Scouts are divided into three ability groups: non-swimmers who are learning to swim, beginners who have swum fifty feet, and swimmers who have met the test of a hundred-yard swim, floating and surface diving. Each group stays within its own area during the swim period.

7. *Buddy Plan*—The Buddy Plan check system is used. In this system every Scout is paired with another boy in his own ability group. They check in together, keep within ten feet of each other at all times, and, at the end of the period, check out together. A "Buddy Signal" is given approximately every ten minutes. Immediately each Scout grasps and holds up the hand of his buddy so that the lookout can make a check.

8. *Discipline*—Insist upon strict, but fair discipline, with no favoritism. A few intelligent rules which the Scouts understand, which they have a part in making and enforcing, will be readily obeyed.

You need a simple BUDDY BOARD for your Troop swims. It may be made from wood and screw hooks, or from plywood and canvas. Spaces are provided for Swimmers In and Swimmers Out, Beginners In and Beginners Out, Non-Swimmers In and Non-Swimmers Out. Shellac board and tags to withstand the weather.

The Waterfront is one place where it does not pay to be lenient. You do not want to be the person responsible for the loss of a human life. Therefore, take *full precautions*.

Noon

From the swim the Patrols return to a simple noon meal, followed by a rest period.

Rest Period

Encourage the boys to lie down for a good rest in the shade somewhere—not necessarily in their tents. They may talk quietly together, write letters home, bring the camp diary up-to-date. If anyone feels like taking a nap, by all means let him.

Afternoon Activities

The afternoon is the high point of the day as far as special activities are concerned.

It may be spent on a hike away from camp, or in a Wide Game suitable to the surrounding country.

SPECIAL HIKES—Hare and Hounds, Treasure Hunt, Lost Child Hunt, Signal Hike, Sealed Orders Hike, Nature Hike, Survival Hike, Bee Line Hike. For details, see Hikes in Tool 12 in back of book.

WIDE GAMES — See Tool 13.

Or the afternoon may be spent in camp on certain *Scoutcraft projects*—constructing a rustic bridge or signal tower, making fire-by-friction sets, developing a nature exhibit, building a nature trail, preparing a bean hole feast, finishing up on various advancement requirements.

Or there may be a specially planned *inter-Patrol feature* that will provide plenty of excitement, such as:

SPECIAL EVENTS—(1) *SCOUTCRAFT FIELD DAY.* Each Patrol is given a section of ground and told to place its flag in the center of it. Each Patrol leader is then given an envelope with the following instructions: "Directions to .... Patrol. Time limit to finish project: 60 minutes. Problems may be done in any order desired. No coaching permitted. (a) Have a Scout follow these directions: Start at Patrol flag, go 43 feet at 045 degrees, 40 feet at 270 degrees, 54 feet at 135 degrees, 20 feet at 180 degrees, 35 feet at 090 degrees, then 14 feet at 350 degrees, and drive a stake here. (b) Have a Scout collect, identify and list on paper ten different tree leaves. (c) Have a Scout build a fire, using only two matches furnished by judges, and keep burning while another Scout completes: (d) Make a twist on a stick from material furnished by the judges. (e) Have a Scout open the sealed envelope enclosed and send the message it contains. (f) Have the Scout who receives the message do what it directs. (g) Tie eight different knots around a stick four feet long, using a different rope for each knot. (h) Whittle a letter opener. (i) After finishing the problems, be ready to line up your Patrol and have your Scouts recite the Scout Oath and Law before the judges. (The envelope mentioned in (e) contains this message: "Find stone weighing four pounds." Have all the materials necessary on hand when the competition starts. Assign a judge for each part, making use of junior leaders.)

(2) *OLYMPIC GAMES*. Each Patrol draws lots from a hat for name of the country it will represent. Following this, the Patrol makes up an entry blank for its representatives in the scheduled events. The exact nature of the events, except their names, is kept secret until the events are actually run off: (a) *Discus Throw* (2 entries). Contestants are called out one by one by the starter and are given paper plates to throw for distance. All contestants and spectators must remain in their places until the judges have decided the places. (b) *100-Yard Dash* (2 entries). On starting signal, entry No. 1 walks from starting line to finish line and back to starting line, foot in front of foot, toe touching heel. At starting point he touches off No. 2 who completes the race, finishing at the starting line. (c) *Standing Broad Jump* (2 entries). On starting signal, entry No. 1 jumps to finish line and back using standing broad jump form. Returning to starting line he touches off No. 2 who completes the race. Finish at the starting line. (d) *Steeple Chase* (2 entries). No. 1 ties left leg at ankle

Camp is the place for your boys to do the advanced Scoutcraft they've dreamed about—making rafts, building bridges and towers.

to No. 2's right leg, with a neckerchief. They run up to finish line and return to starting line. (e) *Hurdle Race* (2 entries). No. 1 leaps over No. 2, leap frog style, No. 2 over No. 1, etc., to finish line and back.

Scoring: Team placing first in an event, 5 points; team placing second 3 points; team placing third, 1 point. Largest number of points decides the Olympic winner.

(3) *FUN FIELD DAY.* (a) *Potato Race.* Place, then pick up potatoes at even intervals. (b) *Candle Race.* Run with lighted candle. Whenever candle goes out, return to base, relight and continue race from place where it went out. (c) *Obstacle Race.* Have contestants creep through barrels, climb over fence, walk on logs, go hand over hand on stretched rope or sapling. (d) *Egg Race.* Run with an egg (hard-boiled) on a teaspoon. (e) *Bag Breaking Relay.* Run to goal, blow up bag, break it, return to touch off next man. (f) *Match Box Relay.* Place match box cover on nose of first con-

testant, to transfer from one nose to next without touching with hands. (g) *Izzy-Dizzy*. Run to goal, place finger on ground, turn while in this position six times and walk back to touch off next. (b) *Airplane Race*. Two men hold a plank, a third man stands on this plank and a fourth man runs in front to steady the third man.

(4) *WATER MEET*. (a) *25-yard Swim* (1 entry from each Patrol) and *50-yard Swim* (1 entry). (b) *Shirt Rescue* (2 entries). One boy swims out thirty feet, remains there to be rescued. Rescuer jumps in water, with shirt in mouth, swims out, throws end of shirt to victim, pulls him to shore. (c) *Boat Rescue* (2 entries). One Scout in water, 100 feet from shore. Second Scout runs to boat pulled up on shore, launches it, rows out to victim who catches hold in stern, is pulled to shore by rower. (d) *Two-Boy Boat Race* (2 entries). Over quarter-mile course. (e) *Four-Boy Canoe Race* (4 entries). Over measured course. (f) *Swim-Paddle-Run* (2 entries). Swim fifty yards to canoe, crawl in, paddle to shore, land properly, run fifty yards.

(5) *FIRST AID MEET*. Stage as many "accidents" as there are Patrols, such as the following, making "wounds," "shock" and other symptoms as realistic as possible with grease paint:

(a) Collapsed shack—dislocated shoulder.
(b) Arterial bleeding from cut in right wrist.
(c) Dummy under fallen tree-broken ribs.
(d) Pit—subject in bottom with broken leg.
(e) Dummy under cave-in, only legs showing.
(f) Gunshot wound through right arm.

Have a leader at each problem to "make up" the patient and tell him how to act, and to observe and judge the Patrols. In cases where dummies are used, "made up" Scouts take the place of the dummies when these have been moved away from the "danger" point. Each Patrol starts at a specific problem. When the problem has been solved, the Patrol moves to the next, until all Patrols have solved all problems.

(6) *SURVIVAL MEET*. Patrols are taken to suitable spot. The Scouts are equipped only with their Scout Uniforms, Scout knives and hand axes, and provided with raw food stuffs for one meal. They are to go

through a twelve-hour test (or, better, an overnight test) of Scout skills involving the following features:

  (a) Build a lean-to shelter to house Patrol.
  (b) Prepare beds of native materials.
  (c) Make a fire-by-friction set and produce fire.
  (d) Make four feet of fish line of native fibres.
  (e) Collect four wild edibles.
  (f) Cook meal in ground or on hot stones.

Afternoon Swim

The afternoon swim is just a good time for everybody. There is no formal instruction but plenty of opportunity to practice what was learned during the morning.

In camps where boats and canoes are available, a boating and canoeing period usually follows the afternoon swim.

Toward the end of the swim it may be necessary to let the Patrol cooks of the day know what time it is so they can get out and get dinner started.

Evening in Camp

At sunset, The Flag of the United States is lowered, with the boys either lining up for a formal "retreat" ceremony, or coming to attention wherever they happen to be, facing The Flag.

After the evening meal there are still a couple of hours of daylight. Play a few simple games, such as various Tags or Capture the Flag or Border Scouting over a small area. It should be a free and easy time.

During the early evening, the Service Patrol will be busy getting wood and laying the camp fire, while the Program Patrol lines up the program after arranging with each of the Patrols for special contributions in the form of stunts, songs or games.

Camp Fire

The camp fire is the heart beat of the camp. The memories of camp fire flames, songs and laughter, and silent gazing into dying embers will stay with the boys for many years to come.

The values of the good camp fire to the boy are far reaching. It relaxes him after his strenuous day in camp. It inspires him by the fire itself, the surroundings, stories, songs. It provides wholesome entertainment. It gives the boy a chance to give vent to his urge of self-expression.

As the group sits around the fire, there grows a bond of fellowship known only to the real outdoorsman who has experienced it. This comradeship breaks down individual selfishness and boastfulness, and tends to produce an understanding of the other fellow and his problems.

To the leader the camp fire offers a splendid opportunity. Here the man-to-man friendship, between leader and boy, grows stronger. Here the leader may discover a marvelous wealth of talent and ability in a lad who had previously struck him as being shy or awkward. Here the leader has the chance to inspire his boys with the Scouting ideals. Many a boy, around the camp fire, has come to look upon his leader with new admiration and respect, which have stayed with him into manhood, influencing his actions, his thoughts, his whole future.

What was said about leadership for the Troop Program in general holds especially true in regard to the camp fire program. Let the boys plan it and carry it out. Probably an adult leader will be able to put on a better "show" than an untrained boy leader. But that is not the point! Use the camp fire as a means of guiding your boys to leadership.

This is one of the big reasons for having a Program Patrol.

Make the Scouts of the Program Patrol realize that the full responsibility is theirs for a successful program of songs and stunts and other features, and that they are

The camp fire is the heartbeat of the camp. Memories of camp fire flames will stay with your boys for years to come.

to expect no helping hand after the curtain goes up—and you will see them rise to the occasion and deliver every time. But keep your standard high and let the Patrols aim for this standard always.

Occasionally have a camp fire without any formal program—where song follows song as the spirit moves, where the boys can talk of the day's adventures and the things that are ahead tomorrow.

CAMP FIRE SUGGESTIONS—*Lighting the Fire.* Make it a tradition to light the camp fire with either fire-by-friction or flint-and-steel, whether done in advance or in connection with a special ceremony. This is one of the small touches that makes the camp fire something special and makes the boys eager for their turn at lighting it.

Opening Ceremony. This may be an elaborate Indian style ceremony or a very simple opening said by the Scoutmaster.

(1) "From the North, from the South, from the East, from the West, may good luck come to us always. I now declare the camp fire open."

(2) "As the flames point upward so be our aim. As the red logs glow so be our sympathies. As the grey ash fades so be our errors. As the good fire warms the circle so may our ideals warm the world. I now declare the council open."

Songs. A proper mixture of rollicking songs, songs for a laugh, songs that create a mood. Start with the lighter type, then, toward the end, use more serious songs that will end the camp fire at a high level.

Stunts and Dramatics by Patrols or individuals. For suggestions, see *Handbook for Patrol Leaders.*

Reading of the single copy of the camp's not very serious newspaper.

Games suitable for the camp fire, such as Indian Hand Wrestling, Leg Wrestling, Dog Fight, and similar duel contests, with formal challenges: "I, Scout So-and-So of Blank Patrol challenge Scout This-and-That to Indian Hand Wrestling," and "I, Scout This-and-That of Such-and-Such Patrol accept the challenge," and with a champion of the evening finally announced when the game has been played long enough, or when one boy has stayed in three times in succession. See Tool 11.

Story Telling. See Tool 17.

Closing Ceremony. Singing of the Scout's Vesper Song, "By the Blazing Council Fire's Light," or Taps, with arms lifted high and slowly lowered as the song progresses. Followed by the Scoutmaster's Benediction or

If boats are available, a Nautical Camp Fire can become a highlight of your camp. Build a raft, about three feet square. Cover it with a one-inch layer of clay, and build the fire on this. Tow the raft to the middle of the lake. Have the Scouts, in boats, circle it slowly, singing songs of the sea.

the leader's traditional "Be Prepared!" with the boys answering in chorus: "We are Prepared!"

From the above suggestions, camp fires may be developed to fit many occasions. Be sure that a varied, yet balanced, mixture of these ingredients is used.

SPECIAL CAMP FIRES. (1) *First Camp Fire.* Ashes from the previous year's last camp fire have been kept and are used in a ceremony for new campers. The boys are called forward, and the Scoutmaster says, "Scouts, you have now been in camp one day and have attended part of our first camp fire. Earlier in the evening you listened to the traditions of our Troop and the responsibilities of every Scout. Will you help us keep these traditions as good campers should?" Answer: "I will." Scoutmaster: "I hold in this vessel some of the ashes of last year's camp fire. They stand for all that we enjoyed in our past. I now place some of these ashes on the right shoulder of each of you and pronounce you campers in good standing, entitled to the rights and obligations of our camp."

(2) *Tall-Story Camp Fire.* Paul Bunyan or John Henry tales. Have a Patrol contest to find the champion tall-story teller of the Troop. Announce the contest early in the day so that the boys can prepare for it.

(3) *Indian Camp Fire.* The boys arrive at the camp fire in Indian file, stripped to the waist, but covered with a blanket, and made up with war paint and feathers. Indian ceremonies, songs, and dances are featured.

(4) *Nautical Camp Fire.* A raft may be constructed of logs, or empty oil cans and board. On top of the raft is placed a one-inch layer of dirt on which the camp fire is lighted. The raft is anchored with a stone anchor in the middle of the lake. The Scouts circle around it in boats singing sea chanties.

(5) *Patrol Camp Fires.* One or more evenings in camp should be designated for Patrol camp fires for which the Patrols will make up their own programs entirely.

(6) *Inter-Troop Camp Fires.* If the Troop is camping in an Inter-Troop camp, the biggest evening events will undoubtedly be when the Troops gather for big camp fires together. For such events each Troop provides its best talent and best efforts for mutual enjoyment.

(7) *Camp Fires in the Rain.* Build the fire near the edge of a mess-fly, or as near the most compact group of several tents as possible, or near opening of the Troop's general assembly tent, leaving the Scouts under cover. Devote the program to songs and yells, tapering off as usual.

(8) *Camp Fire Snacks.* An appreciated pre-ending for a camp fire, if damp or chilly weather settles in, is to serve hot cocoa, cookies, crackers, or such.

(9) *Last Camp Fire.* At the last camp fire, honor campers and honor Patrols are announced. For this camp fire invite people who have helped you to make the camp a success and all special guests. Often the program for the last fire is made up of the features which have proved most popular the previous evenings. During the closing ceremony, some of the ashes may be lifted out to be kept for the opening of next year's camp fire.

Other Evening Activities

Occasionally during the camp a night hike for star study, or a night game may be put on instead of the camp fire.

NIGHT GAMES IN CAMP—(1) *Smugglers in the Square.* One half of the campers are guards, the other half smugglers. A white lantern is placed at each of the four corners of a large square, a red lantern is placed in the center. The guards are placed between the white lanterns, along the four sides of the square. Near the red lantern are placed a number of boxes. Some of these contain small quantities of cookies, candy, peanuts; others are filled with pebbles. The smugglers try to penetrate into the square, grab a box and get out of the square without being tagged.

(2) *The Night Attack.* Three-quarters of the Scouts guard the camp, one-quarter are the attackers. The attackers try to place cards with their names on them (bombs) on the tents, the flag pole, and so on. Each spot has a certain value in points according to its strategic location in camp. The guards attempt to capture the cards before they are placed. At the end of a

And so to bed! The boys turn in after an exciting day. Tomorrow will be another active day of fun and fellowship.

certain period, the attackers are called in and points are totaled for either side.

(3) Several types of Wide Games may also be adapted for night uses (see Tool 13).

After the game is over and the spoils of war have been disposed of, the Scouts gather around a fire and exchange their experiences in the game. This camp fire gathering is for the purpose of toning down the boys so that the excitement of the game will have worn off by the time they get to bed.

And So to Bed

At last the evening's activities are ended in time to provide for *ten hours' sleep.*

The Scouts turn in. One by one you see the lights go out.

You make your final round. Then you, too, turn in.
And tomorrow is another glorious camping day,
Make the most of it!

BREAKING THE CAMP

Start to break camp the day before you are scheduled
to leave. There are many things that can be done in
advance to insure a speedy get-away—such as cleaning
certain pots and pans no longer needed, packing away
Scoutcraft equipment, taking down some of the camp
gadgets.

One thing that *must* be done is to settle all bills with
the local trades people. Also, make the final check of
transportation back to town.

Breaking Camp

The order of breaking camp may follow this line:

1. Clean all kitchen gear and pack.

2. Pack all personal equipment and form duffle-line by
Patrols.

3. Take down all kitchen arrangements, including fire
places; fill in garbage pits and grease pits.

4. Clean out washing place, fill in latrine, and clean
camp fire circle.

5. Take down all tents and pack them up.

6. Clean all tent sites, filling in all ditches and replac-
ing sod.

7. Check your list of all equipment and supplies to
make sure that everything is there.

8. Form a line of all Scouts across the camp site and
have them move forward slowly, picking up every trace
of scrap found on the ground.

9. Have the owner of the place (or in an Inter-Troop
Camp, the Camp Director) make an inspection and declare the clean-up satisfactory. Then,

10. Gather around the flag pole for a short closing ceremony, while The Flag is slowly lowered, officially closing
camp. Take down flag pole and put it away.

It is sad to break camp. But the training gained will remain with the boys and will strengthen the Troop for the future.

Follow the advice of Baden-Powell in regard to the *only* two things which you are to leave behind you on breaking camp:

Nothing.

Your thanks to the owner of the ground.

AFTER CAMP

As soon as you have returned from camp, sit down and write letters of thanks to all those who helped make the camp a success. If possible, have these signed by the Patrol Leaders also on behalf of their boys.

Make a full report of your camping experience to your Local Council and to the Troop Committee, together with any recommendations you may have to make based on that experience.

Make sure that the equipment is stored away in good shape: Tents dry, iron utensils protected against rust.

Get the Camp Log completed with prints of photographs taken, copies of menus, programs, notices, camp newspaper, possible drawings, so that it may be a valuable memento of the past camp and a treasure trove from which to get ideas for future expeditions.

And use the increased Scoutcraft knowledge, the experiences shared, for the growth of the Troop and for its boys throughout the Scouting year ahead, until another Troop camping experience comes along.

REMINGTON
SCHUYLER

Other Things to Do

CHAPTER 12

THE ACTIVITIES we have discussed have been mostly those that take place directly in the Troop and in the individual Patrols. But then there is a specialized field of advanced Scouting activity, called Exploring, for the young men fourteen and older. And there are other activities that bring the Troop into contact with people beyond its own membership and with other Troops.

THE EXPLORER PROGRAM

The Scout Movement, through its Explorer program for Scouts fourteen and older, recognizes the fact that these young men have interests and capabilities definitely more advanced than they had when they became Boy Scouts. Older fellows may no longer find fun in doing the same kind of Scouting at fourteen and fifteen that they did at eleven and twelve. They may begin to resent the association with "kids." So, unless they are given a more challenging program as they grow older, they will tend to drop out of the Movement before they have absorbed all of the rich experiences that Scouting has to offer boys from the time they are eight until they are grown men.

Exploring is advanced Scouting—a program of training in self-reliance, leadership and good citizenship especially slanted toward young men of high school age.

The Explorer program emphasizes four fields of activity, fully described in the *Explorer Manual:*

Outdoor adventure—vigorous physical activity, including expeditions on land, on the sea and in the air.

Vocational exploration—strengthening the young man's growing concern with what he will undertake as a life's work.

Social companionship—guiding him in wholesome activities with young people of both sexes.

Citizenship responsibility—stimulating his interest and participation in the affairs of his local, state, national and world community, especially through civic service and emergency service training.

On reaching his fourteenth birthday, every Boy Scout automatically becomes an Explorer. He should then have every opportunity to decide for himself whether he will stay in the Troop as an Explorer, or transfer to a separate Explorer Post, Air Explorer Squadron or Sea Explorer Ship.

Your Explorers will have a chance for leadership in the Troop, and to take part in a special young men's program.

Those Explorers who stay in the Troop will continue to take part in all activities of the Troop as a whole. Many of them will be logical choices for positions of leadership. In addition to their participation in the whole Troop program, however, they will have an opportunity to carry out a special *young men's program* under the guidance of the Troop's Explorer Advisor.

A separate Explorer Unit may be organized in the same institution which sponsors the Troop. The Explorer Unit has its own Committee and adult Advisor.

Many Explorers who belong to Posts, Squadrons and Ships continue to serve their old Scout Troops as junior officers or as special instructors. Some help other Troops, or serve in special junior leader activities on a District or Council basis.

Explorers in the Troop

As a Scoutmaster, you will of course be most concerned with those Explorers who stay on as members of the Troop.

If you have only a few Explorers, all or most of them will naturally fit into positions of Troop leadership, because they are generally your most advanced and most mature members. An Explorer with a fine record of Boy Scout advancement and service as a Patrol Leader, for instance, is a logical choice for Senior Patrol Leader. Any who are fifteen or older may be given warrants as Junior Assistant Scoutmasters. Explorers may also serve as Patrol Leaders, Scribe or Quartermaster; however, before they are sixteen, they should train others to take their places so other Scouts and younger Explorers may have these leadership experiences.

Whether Explorers will remain in the Patrols they have belonged to as Boy Scouts, or automatically leave them on reaching fourteen, depends a great deal on the organization and experience of the Troop. In the situation mentioned above, where there are enough leadership and special responsibilities for all qualified Explorers, this is no problem.

But if Explorers make up a greater proportion of the Troop's total membership, there will not be enough top-level jobs to go around to keep all of them active and interested.

The diagram on page 289 shows some of the possibilities of meeting such a situation. Both the Scoutmaster and the Explorer Advisor have been appointed by the Troop Committee. The Scoutmaster has full responsibility for the Boy Scout program of the Troop, including guidance of the Explorers when they are participating in Troop activities as leaders, specialists, instructors or as members of Patrols. The Advisor is the adult to

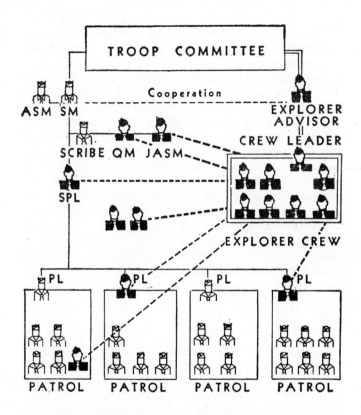

whom the Explorers look for counsel in their *Explorer* activities. (Read *Hints on Explorer Leadership.*)

In this situation most of the Troop's junior leaders, including two Patrol Leaders, are logically Explorers (although Boy Scouts may hold any of these jobs except that of Junior Assistant Scoutmaster). One Explorer, not even a Patrol Leader, is a member of a Patrol—probably because he has only recently passed his fourteenth birthday and prefers to stay in his old Patrol until he completes the Boy Scout rank he is working toward. Before he leaves the Patrol, he should be urged to recruit and train a new Tenderfoot Scout to take his place.

Now note that all of these Explorers, in addition to their Troop assignments, are members of the Explorer Crew. In this group, under the guidance of the Advisor, they will find the extra advantages of Exploring.

Also note that two of the Explorers have no leadership assignments, nor are they in Patrols. However, because of their particular experience and skills, they may be able to serve the Troop in special capacities, such as hikemaster, game director, nature instructor or emergency service instructor. Where there are many such Explorers in a Troop, without enough responsibilities to keep them happily occupied, they cannot be expected to attend all Troop meetings, only to stand around on the sidelines. They may be quite active as Explorer Crews, however, joining in the overall Troop program only on special occasions.

Explorer Crews in the Troop

As soon as there are as few as two Explorers in the Troop, they may form a *Crew* as the organization in which they will carry on the Explorer program, besides their normal Troop activities. An Explorer may hold an office in the Troop or retain his membership in a Patrol, in addition to his functions as an Explorer.

A Crew will elect a Crew Leader and, if there are enough members, an Assistant Crew Leader. If the Crew grows too large, two or more Crews may be formed. Then, in addition to the Crew Leaders, a Senior Crew Leader, a Deputy Senior Crew Leader and a Secretary should be elected.

All of these officers, together with the Explorer Advisor and the Troop Committee, make up the *Explorer Leaders' Council*. This group is to the Explorer Crews what the Patrol Leaders' Council is to the Troop as a whole. As it is likely that some Explorers will serve on both Councils, the Crews will be represented when the Patrol Leaders' Council is making plans for activities which will make up the program of the Troop as a whole.

Crews usually meet once a month. At these meetings the Explorers plan their expeditions, social affairs, service projects and other Explorer activities. The Crews should have the Troop's overall program before them when they sit down to plan their own activities, so that there will be no conflict between Troop and Explorer program. It would be impractical, for instance, for the Crews to plan an expedition on a week-end when the Troop is going camping and should have its full complement of junior leaders, some of whom are Explorers. In such cases, the Troop program takes precedence.

Unless the Crews are made up largely of Explorers who are also members of Patrols, it should be possible for them to meet frequently during the Patrol Corner periods of Troop meetings, and perhaps once a week separately, just as Patrols do.

Forming a Separate Unit

A Troop is primarily an organization for boys starting out or progressing on the Scouting trail as Boy Scouts. Therefore, a majority of Explorers over Boy Scouts in a Troop, especially a large Troop, may be the signal for the need of organizing a separate Explorer Unit under the same sponsorship as the Troop. Many Explorer Units have been born for just such a reason. If this situation exists in your Troop, talk to the Troop Committee and your Commissioner about getting a new Explorer Unit organized to accommodate the Explorers in excess of those you need as Troop junior leaders. Only five young men are required to form a new Unit.

TROOP-PACK COOPERATION

Den Chiefs

At the request of the Cubmaster of a Pack, one or more of your Scouts may be selected to serve as Den Chiefs of small groups, or *Dens,* of Cub Scouts. They are trained and coached for this job by the Cubmaster.

Cub Scouts look forward to the day they will be Boy Scouts. Hence, a Boy Scout is a natural leader for a Den. Ordinarily, but not always, younger Scouts who have recently been Cub Scouts make the best Den Chiefs. They know the program, are closer in spirit to the younger boys, and are less likely to have assumed Patrol or Troop leadership responsibilities.

It must be fully understood by the Scout, and his Pack and Troop leaders as well, that service as a Den Chief, although an important responsibility, will not be so demanding on his time and interest as to interfere with his Patrol and Troop activities. Dens usually meet one afternoon a week and Packs one afternoon or night a month, ordinarily at times that will not conflict with Troop activities.

Welcoming the Cub Scout Graduate

Several months before he will be eleven years old, the Cub Scout, with the help of his Den Chief or another Boy Scout, begins to prepare himself in the Tenderfoot Scout Requirements. If he is a Lion Cub Scout, he may earn the Webelos Badge, one requirement for which is that he prepare himself in the Tenderfoot requirements. The W, B and L of Webelos stand for Wolf, Bear and Lion, and the S stands for Scout; hence a Webelos Scout is one who has come up through the ranks of Cub Scouting and is ready to become a Boy Scout.

You can do a lot to make his graduation from the Pack into the Troop a great occasion in his life by taking part in the graduation ceremony which the Pack will arrange.

The Cub Scout becomes a Boy Scout! It is an important moment in the boy's life. Make it important to the Troop, too.

If you cannot take part yourself, you should be represented by an assistant or the Senior Patrol Leader and the Patrol Leader of the Patrol this new boy is to join when he becomes a Boy Scout.

THE WHOLE SCOUT FAMILY

As you will have discovered, Scouting is a game that takes in the boy of eight and carries him up to the threshold of manhood.

Cub Scouting, for boys *eight through ten,* is a program of home and neighborhood centered activities conducted in Packs, which are made up of Dens. *Boy Scouting,* for the same boys or new boys, *eleven through thirteen,* involves the activities of the Troop and its

Patrols as described in this handbook. *Exploring,* an advanced program, is for young men *fourteen and older,* whether they stay as members of a Scout Troop or join a separate Explorer Unit.

These three parts of the program together are known as the "Whole Scout Family."

Where there are a Pack, a Troop and an Explorer Unit in the same Chartered Institution, the Cubmaster, Scoutmaster and Explorer Advisor should get together from time to time with the several Unit Committees and the Institutional Representative to discuss common problems and plan for common activities. Matters for discussion might include the graduation of Cub Scouts into the Troop and of Boy Scouts into the Explorer Unit; and the appointment of Boy Scouts to serve as Den Chiefs in the Pack, and of Explorers as junior officers for the Troop (provided the Troop does not have adequate leadership material among its own Explorers and Boy Scouts). Plans may also be made for joint activities, such as an annual Father and Son Banquet for all three Units.

FAMILY GET-TOGETHERS

The aim and desire of the parents and the Scoutmaster for the boy are fundamentally the same. You can best achieve these aims when the parents have a real understanding of Scouting and are well-acquainted with the leader of their boys.

The Parents' Meeting

The best possible time to arouse the parents' interest is when an event of sufficient importance warrants it—such as the installation of the new Troop, or its anniversary.

The promotion of attendance for a parents' meeting is usually done by a personal letter signed by the Chair-

Suggested Program for
PARENTS' MEETING

OPENING. The opening should catch the interest of the parents, put the boys and guests at ease.

INTRODUCTIONS. Keep them short. The Head of the Sponsoring Institution may introduce the members of the Troop Committee. The Chairman then presents the Scoutmaster and the Assistants. The Scoutmaster introduces the Junior Leaders and the Patrol Leaders. The Scouts fall in behind their respective Patrol Leaders.

SINGING BY EVERYBODY. Have a good song leader who can get everybody to sing. Provide mimeographed song sheets.

DEMONSTRATION BY THE TROOP. Many parents will come to see their own Johnny or Jimmy perform. Arrange for a couple of Patrol stunts, or a few Scoutcraft demonstrations—first aid, fire-by-friction, signaling, and so on. Make them short.

PRESENTATION OF AWARDS. The awards should be handed out as snappily as possible. If there are many of them, suggest that applause be kept until the end. Suggestions for Troop Court of Honor ceremonies are found in Tool 14.

SPECIAL FEATURE. The most important part of the meeting is the presentation of the objective for which the meeting was called. In a new Troop, the big reason for a parents' meeting is to acquaint the parents with the Scout program in order to secure their whole-hearted cooperation. This may be accomplished by showing the film, "The Scout Trail to Citizenship." The same aim may be reached by a good speaker on the subject. In an old Troop, where most of the parents know their Scouting, the meeting may be to introduce new parents, to secure cooperation for the summer camp that is just around the corner, or to get the help of the parents in solving problems that may have arisen.

REFRESHMENTS may be desirable. They should be handled by a special mothers' committee.

FORMAL CLOSING. Taps or camp fire song.

man of the Troop Committee and the Scoutmaster, followed by a word-of-mouth appeal by each boy: "You'll have to come. All the other fellows will have their parents there!"

To keep the interest of the parents alive, many Troops include special family activities in the year's program:

FATHERS AND SONS HIKES are popular. The fathers hike with their boys to the Troop's favorite overnight camp site where special games and contests, from horse-shoe pitching to relay races, are held. A pot full of beans that have been "doing" overnight may be "unveiled."

ANNUAL FAMILY BANQUETS are held by a number of Troops in connection with Boy Scout Week in February, or to celebrate the Troop's anniversary. The mothers take care of the eats, the fathers of the decoration and the attendance, and the boys of the program.

ANNUAL CAMP FIRE. In still other Troops, the tradition is to gather the families for a camp fire and picnic supper on the Sunday during camp, or the last day of camp, or on a holiday evening.

COURTS OF HONOR. When Courts of Honor are held, either on a Troop, or a District or Council basis, the parents are, of course, invited to witness the success of their boys. It is becoming increasingly popular on these occasions, to present the Scout mother with a miniature badge of the same rank her son is receiving.

Activities of this kind will help to bring the boy, the parents and the Troop closer together and will greatly simplify your work as a Scoutmaster.

TROOP SERVICE PROJECTS

One of the things you want to develop in your Scouts is an unselfish spirit of service to others. A way of doing this is to include a number of service projects in the Troop's yearly program—Good Turns to your institution, your neighborhood or your whole community.

Scouts must be genuinely interested in the project, should be in on the selection of the project and should

The Troop that is ready for a Good Turn to its Institution can count on enthusiastic help from the Institution in return.

do the planning for it. Before you go ahead with a service project, be sure that it will gear in with the work that is being conducted by other agencies in the community and with the activities of the Local Council.

Scout participation in service projects must be in keeping with the dignity of the Scout Movement; it must be non-political and non-commercial; must involve no solicitation or handling of money by Scouts; must be carried out in Scouts' leisure time so that school duties are not interfered with, and must not deprive men of employment. Scouts shall not be placed in an environment dangerous to health, safety or moral development. The leadership must conform to the highest standards of Scouting.

Service Opportunities

Some of the service projects may be annually recurring opportunities for which plans can be made ahead, for adequate preparation and organization:

PERIODIC SERVICE— (1) Help welfare organizations in collection of old clothing.

(2) Collect old toys. Establish toy repair shop. Distribute reconditioned toys to needy families.

(3) Assist Institution sponsoring the Troop, whenever possible.

(4) Distribute posters for social and charitable organizations.

(5) Plan and carry out conservation projects, such as tree planting, bird and wild animal feeding, soil erosion.

Other opportunities for Scout service arise from the calls of institutions and organizations to meet specific needs, such as:

OCCASIONAL SERVICE— (1) Messengers, guides, or ushers for conventions and public meetings of various kinds.

(2) Distribution of literature for hospitals and other community organizations.

(3) Duty at parades, community gatherings, school athletic events.

(4) Assistance in safety drives, clean-up campaigns, and similar community projects.

(5) Safety patrols for small children at crossings.

To the people of our country Scouting has come to stand for SERVICE. It is the responsibility of every Troop to live up to this great tradition.

Emergency Service

In hundreds of disasters—fire and explosion, flood and earthquake, tornado and hurricane—Scouts have lived up to their Motto: "Be Prepared." Those who were prepared have served heroically under trying conditions, saving life and property and helping to care for the victims of disaster.

Every Troop should ready itself for service in case of any such emergency. This calls for intensive training in the basic skills of Scoutcraft, and for a well-rehearsed scheme of Troop mobilization as described in Tool 18. The nucleus of the Troop's plan of emergency service will be the Explorers, especially those who have met the rigid requirements for the rating of Emergency Service Explorer, as given in the *Explorer Manual*.

Any First Class Scout who declares his intention of working hard to become an Emergency Service Explorer, and who meets the physical fitness requirements, may be designated an *Emergency Service Apprentice*. He will be issued a special armband when called out for actual disaster service or for training.

DISTRICT AND LOCAL COUNCIL EVENTS

The special activities of your District or your Local Council are usually discussed and decided upon in the Scouters' Round-Table conferences.

Boy Scout Week

One of the high spots of the Scouting year is Boy Scout Week which is celebrated throughout the country during February. The week is planned each year to include February 8th, "Anniversary Day," the date of the original incorporation of the Boy Scouts of America. On that day the Scouts throughout the country rededicate themselves to the Scout Oath. The Sunday during Boy Scout Week is celebrated as Boy Scout Sunday.

In a small community, Boy Scout Week becomes an occasion for the single Troop to step out in public. In a large community, it consists of a series of Troop activities, possibly including a family dinner, and a number of Local Council doings carried out on a great and worthwhile scale.

Complete suggestions for Boy Scout Week activities are given every year in SCOUTING Magazine. Begin to plan and prepare for the celebration as soon as the announcements start to appear, usually in the November issue of the magazine. Make Boy Scout Week a good time for your Scouts and for their families.

Merit Badge Shows

A big annual event in many Local Councils is the Merit Badge Show or Scout Exhibit. The idea behind it is to present to the public the activities of Scouting.

The preparation for the show becomes an important part of the Troop's activities. All your Scouts may not be able to meet all the requirements of the Merit Badge your Troop will demonstrate, but they can take part in some feature connected with it, whether this be in the form of a related handicraft subject, making posters, designing the booth, or putting on a dramatization. The Merit Badge Library is a valuable help in procuring suggestions for dramatizing a Merit Badge subject.

Circuses and Pageants

Many Councils feature as a yearly event, a Scout Circus or Pageant, sometimes called a "Scout-O-Rama."

The program for this may include such Scouting skills as quick camp making, building of bridges and signal towers, large scale first aid demonstrations, cycle Patrols in action, signaling methods, and specialties such as Indian pageantry and ceremonies and early American pioneers on the westward trek.

Before the big night, there is plenty of work to be done in the Troop. The boys need training in pioneering, camp making, fire-by-friction, Indian dancing, or whatever the Troop's activity happens to be. Possibly costumes need to be designed and made.

Take part with your Troop in large Scouting events. Here your boys can mix with other Scouts, other Patrols, and other Troops.

Participation in a real Scout Circus is an experience which your boys are not apt to forget quickly.

Other Events

The following events and others of a similar nature have been used in various Councils:

CAMPOREES. See page 214.

STATE AND COUNTY FAIRS AND EXPOSITIONS. These give an opportunity not only for Camporees and exhibits but also for valuable service to the public.

MOBILIZATION. An emergency service mobilization of all the Scouts within the community can be made into an exciting event for the boys and a demonstration to the public of the preparedness of Scouts.

PILGRIMAGES TO HISTORIC SHRINES. This may involve the location of an historic spot and the development of it into a shrine.

WINTER CARNIVAL. Winter sports and camping.

WATER SHOW. Swimming meets, life saving demonstrations and water pageantry.

COUNCIL CAMP FIRES. For the purpose of rallying the parents with the Scouts, for an evening's enjoyment.

COMMUNITY PROGRAMS. Scout participation in Memorial Day programs and similar activities.

REGIONAL, NATIONAL AND INTERNATIONAL ACTIVITIES

Looking even farther afield, there are Scouting events each year at which Scouts gather from different localities, different states, yes, different nations.

While it is seldom possible for a whole Troop to participate in these activities, it is often possible for a Troop to be represented by a couple of Scouts or by a Patrol.

Regional Activities

Regional activities may involve participation in State and Inter-State fairs, Scoutcraft displays at Regional Annual Meetings, Eagle Scout Trail Building within the Region, and Regional Explorer Expeditions.

National Activities

By participating in the Local Council celebration of Boy Scout Week, the Troop takes part in the greatest national activity of the year.

But, besides, there are Good Turns on a national scale, pilgrimages to national historic shrines, expeditions to Philmont Scout Ranch in New Mexico, and occasional National Jamborees for which Scouts gather from every state of our Union.

The World Jamboree is the greatest expression of the Scout Brotherhood. Scouts meet from around the world.

International Activities

And finally, we come to the activities of our great World Brotherhood. Scouts from one country often pay visits to others on International Good Will Tours.

Such activities are climaxed by the most inspiring event in all Scouting—a *World Jamboree*. Such Jamborees are normally held every four years, and Scouts from practically every country of the globe participate in them. As many as fifty thousand have taken part in some of these tremendous brotherhood gatherings.

Through these get-togethers of boys from around the world, Scouting is attempting to do its part — in the words of Baden-Powell—"to establish friendships among Scouts of all nations and to help to develop peace and happiness in the world and good will among men."

REMINGTON
SCHUYLER

Part II

THE SCOUTMASTER'S **SECOND** JOB: HELPING EACH INDIVIDUAL **BOY** TO GROW

CONTENTS OF PART TWO:

THE BOY

I

The Boy Becomes a Scout

The Boy Joins

CHAPTER 13

THE DOOR OF THE TROOP meeting room opens. There stands a new boy. He has been waiting weeks, maybe a year, for this moment.

He is ready to become a Scout. His hopes are high.

Right then and there you have him or you lose him!

First impressions are lasting. What the new boy sees and feels and does during the first meeting will have a great bearing upon his life as a Scout.

Good Scoutmasters have eyes in the backs of their

heads. So you notice the boy and walk over to him almost as soon as he enters.

"Oh, hello! Come right in. I'm Scoutmaster of this Troop—my name is Joe Brown. What's yours? Billy Jones? How are you, Billy? Have you come to join us?"

You raise your voice: "Fellows, we have a new boy with us tonight. His name is Billy Jones. Which Patrol wants to be his host for tonight? No, not all of you! Billy, do you know any of the fellows? You know Marshall Ford of the Eagle Patrol? All right, then, we'll let the Eagles take care of you tonight . . . they'll give you a good time. After the meeting, be sure to see me . . . we have to talk this Scouting business over together."

The boy is one big smile. He enters into everything. There is even a simple game for his benefit—one that requires no special training and has no complicated rules. During the meeting the Senior Patrol Leader comes around and says "hello!"

And afterwards, the boy sits down for a short, friendly chat with you. You tell him a bit about the Troop and what is in store for him. And you explain to him what will be expected of him, if he decides to become a member of the Troop.

With a cheerful, "See you next week!" you say, "So long." A Scout from the Eagle Patrol who lives in his neighborhood is hanging around waiting to walk home with him.

That boy feels that he is wanted. He sees that he will make a lot of friends in Scouting. He makes up his mind to become a Scout the gang can be proud of.

How Does He Come?

Boys come into Scouting in a number of different ways.

Cub Scouts logically move up into Scouting when they reach eleven (see page 292).

Some boys hear of Scouting and decide for themselves that they want to join. But the majority join because other boys have told them about fun in Scouting.

Sometimes a Troop sets out deliberately to get new boys by recruiting them through the church or the school. Recruit them at *eleven*. Don't let them drift in. Have Patrols *invite* them.

About two months before a boy's eleventh birthday, let a couple of Scouts from the Beaver or Owl Patrol drop in at his home and invite him to come to the Troop meeting. Greet him, make him feel at home, and invite him to come again. After a couple of meetings he is usually anxious to join.

BECOMING A SCOUT

There are four steps for a boy to become a Scout:

(1) He learns the Candidate Requirements: Repeats from memory the Scout Oath or Promise and the twelve points of the Scout Law, the Scout Motto, and the Scout Slogan, explaining each in his own words. He gives the Scout Sign, Salute and Hand-clasp.

(2) His Scoutmaster examines him in the Requirements.

(3) He presents his application and registration fee and is registered as a Scout.

(4) He is inducted into Scouting at a ceremony before his Troop and becomes a member of a Patrol.

Becoming a Tenderfoot Scout

Cub Scouts who have earned their Webelos badge and other boys who by the time they become eleven have learned all of the Tenderfoot requirements may qualify for Tenderfoot rank directly, without going through the step of being Candidate Scouts, and receive their badges at the time they are inducted.

Becoming a Candidate Scout

The moment a boy shows up at his Scout meeting, get him started on the Candidate Requirements.

In some Troops, the boy is helped along by receiving a copy of *Boy Scout Adventure*—a small and inexpensive pamphlet that contains much that a boy needs to know to become a Candidate Scout or a Tenderfoot Scout. Even better, encourage him to get the *Handbook for Boys*.

As soon as the boy has learned the Scout Oath and Law and the other things that are required of a Candidate Scout, sit down with him and review him. This is your first big chance to meet with the boy while you talk over what Scouting is going to mean to him.

Scout Badge and Uniform, Motto, Sign, Salute and Handclasp—Show the boy a Scout Badge and ask him to explain its significance as he points out each part of it. Have him tell you when and where to wear the Uniform and how to care for it. Then, "What is the Scout Motto? Tell me some of the things you think a Scout should 'Be Prepared' to do. Let's see you make the Scout Salute. And now the Scout Sign. What do the three fingers stand for? And now give me your hand in the Scout Handclasp—the left hand, the hand nearest your heart."

Scout Law and Oath—Talking over the ideals of Scouting is the most important part of your session with the new boy. It is possible that you will be closer to the boy during this early examination than at any other time in his whole Scouting career. So make the best possible use of the occasion, to help the boy understand the Scouting ideals and accept them as his code for the future. If you know boys, you will have no difficulty in finding the questions that will best draw out the boy who sits before you. The following can only suggest the lines you may follow: "Let me hear you say the twelve points of the Scout Law. What does 'loyal' mean to you? Can you give me some examples of Good Turns? Why is obedience necessary in the Troop, at home, and in school? What do you mean by 'clean in body' and 'clean of thought'? How can you show yourself 'faithful in your religious duties'? How would you set about to 'help other people at all times'? What do you mean by 'mentally awake' and 'morally straight'?"

When the review is over, let the boy know how glad you are that he is prepared to become a Scout. Try to make him realize that not only his Patrol but the whole Troop is behind him and wants to help him.

Then give him your left hand in a firm Scout Handclasp that will say "I trust you."

The National Registration

A boy is not a Scout and is not entitled to wear the Uniform and Badges of the Boy Scouts of America until he has qualified as a Candidate or Tenderfoot Scout and has been registered at the National Office through the Local Council. His membership does not start until his registration is completed.

That is why it is so important to have the boy registered right away. A boy's enthusiasm and faith in you and in Scouting will suffer if he has to wait for weeks for his registration card to come through.

Give the boy an Application for Membership (the national Form No. 4405, or the form used in your Council) to fill in and to return to you approved by his parents or guardian, with his registration fee. Then complete his registration as explained in Tool 2.

Upon completion of his registration, induct the boy into the Troop with a simple ceremony in which he receives his membership certificate and becomes a member of a Patrol. (See Induction Ceremonies in Tool 14.)

Becoming a Tenderfoot Scout

The boy is now ready for his next step in Scouting: becoming a Tenderfoot Scout.

Encourage him to take this step as quickly as possible so that he will get started learning the skills of Scouting.

The boy is helped in his Tenderfoot Scoutcraft skills

by the Scout who will be his Patrol Leader, or by some other Scout in his future Patrol. The boy and the Scout may get together over a copy of the *Handbook for Boys* or the *Scout Field Book*. A couple of Patrol meetings or a hike should be sufficient to do the job.

A boy who enters the Troop from a Cub Scout Pack may already have learned the Tenderfoot skills in earning his Webelos Badge, and simply needs to have them reviewed by his Scoutmaster.

When the Patrol Leader is satisfied that a new boy knows his stuff, he tells the Scoutmaster.

As Scoutmaster you are responsible for qualifying the boy in the Tenderfoot Requirements. No one else can do it for you. Try for these three things:

(1) Make it a friendly "talking-it-over," with both you and the boy completely at ease and enjoying it.

(2) Talk about a lot of things, so that you'll get an idea about what kind of youngster he is, and at the same time give him an opportunity to get to know you.

(3) Make sure he knows the Tenderfoot Requirements.

Most of the time, the boy will come to you knowing the requirements to the letter. Occasionally, a boy may not be completely prepared. If you find that a boy isn't quite ready, try to get him to suggest, by himself, that possibly he'd better do a little more work on the requirements.

In examining, start with the knot tying requirement, so that the boy has a chance to use his hands and forget himself. Then continue with wound care, The Flag, knowledge of Patrol and Troop, Scout Badge and Uniform, Sign, Salute and Handclasp, and wind up with a review of the Scout Law and Oath.

Knot Tying—Expect the boy to tie the required knots easily and quickly, and for actual use. A sheet bend, for instance, is used for tying two ropes together—so have the boy use two ropes in tying it. The clove hitch is for fastening a rope to a post or rail — so the boy fastens the rope that way.

Wound Care—Since the square knot is used in first aid, wound care logically follows knot tying. Have the boy show how to care for a simple wound on his leg, for example, finishing by winding neckerchief over a sterile dressing, or band-aid.

Emergency Knowledge—After the boy has shown how to handle a simple wound, it is natural to ask: "Now how would you get hold of a doctor or the hospital if the wound were serious?" And one emergency question leads to two more: "How would you report a fire, if we should have one around here?" and "How will you get hold of the nearest police or sheriff's office?"

The Flag of the United States—Get the boy to tell the history of The Flag in brief, or, better, hand him a pencil and ask him to sketch out roughly how The Flag looked when it was first made (thirteen stars, thirteen stripes), and what changes were made in it later. Ask him about the more important days on which to fly it, and the time of day to do it. Then have him demonstrate with an actual Flag how to put it up, how to salute it and how to fold it.

Patrol, Troop and the Outdoors—Listen to the boy as he tells you what he knows about the Patrol he is joining, of the Troop and its leaders, and the main things he needs to do to get on in Scouting—hiking for Second Class, camping for First Class. Here is the proper place to make the boy understand the precautions he must take before building a fire in the open, and the harm to a live tree that results from hacking it with an axe.

Scout Badge and Uniform, Motto, Sign, Salute and Handclasp—Quickly review with the boy this requirement in which you already examined him when he became a Candidate Scout (see page 309). Ask him how he is coming along earning money for his Uniform.

Scout Law and Oath—Follow up on the examination you gave the boy when he became a Candidate Scout (page 309). "Do you feel that you have done your best to live up to the Scout Law since you became a Candidate Scout? Do you try to do your Daily Good Turn?"

When the examination is over, congratulate the boy on the work he has done, and tell him that he is now ready to be invested.

The Tenderfoot Investiture

Finally, some evening at a Troop meeting, or maybe some night at a camp fire, the boy stands before you and the Troop for investiture as a Tenderfoot. The ceremony should not be elaborate. A simple, dignified ceremony is far more impressive!

Each Troop has its own traditions in this respect. Where a Troop is sponsored by a church, the Troop and the church together may have developed an investiture of a religious nature. The following ceremony is widely used and may appeal to you. Other suggestions are given in Tool 14 in back of book.

The Troop stands in horseshoe formation, with the Scoutmaster and the Senior Patrol Leader (or Assistant Scoutmaster) in the gap. The Tenderfoot with his Patrol Leader stands in front of his Patrol. The Senior Patrol Leader holds the Tenderfoot Badge and the neckerchief that will be presented to the boy.

The Scoutmaster gives a sign, and the Patrol Leader brings the Tenderfoot to the center. At the same time a flag bearer carries the Troop flag forward.

The boy and the Scoutmaster place their left hands on the staff of the Troop flag and raise their right hands in the Scout Sign. The whole Troop comes to attention with the Scout Sign. Looking at his Scoutmaster, the boy slowly, solemnly dedicates himself to the Scout Oath:

"On my honor I will do my best:
To do my duty to God and my Country, and to obey the Scout Law;
To help other people at all times;
To keep myself physically strong, mentally awake, and morally straight."

The Scoutmaster gives the boy his left hand in a firm grasp and says:

"I trust you, *Scout* Jones, on your honor, to keep this promise. You are now one of us, and to show that you belong, we present you with this Badge of our Scout World Brotherhood and with the neckerchief of our Troop."

The eleven-year-old becomes a Scout. Make the ceremony an occasion that will inspire him to do his best to be a REAL Scout.

The Scoutmaster puts the neckerchief over the boy's shoulders and the Senior Patrol Leader pins the Badge on his shirt. The Scout turns around and salutes the Troop. The Troop salutes him. The Patrol Leader takes the new Scout to his Patrol where he is received with the Patrol yell and where the Patrol medallion is presented to him.

The BOY has become a full-fledged SCOUT!

Starting Out

And now, as the new Scout starts out, keep in mind Baden-Powell's famous quotation:

"Remember that the boy, on joining, wants to begin 'Scouting' right away. So don't dull his keenness . . . meet his wants by games and Scouting practices, and instill elementary details bit by bit afterwards as you go along."

THE BOY

The Boy in Scouting

II

The Boy Stays

CHAPTER 14

TO CATCH THE BOY isn't difficult. But to hold him—"Ay, there's the rub," as Shakespeare would say.

The boy becomes a Scout because for some reason or other his interest has been awakened and must be satisfied. He stays in Scouting because his interest makes him. And when his interest dies—he drops out.

Most Local Councils regularly receive notices of dropped Scouts from their Troops. Many of these notices give as the boy's reason for dropping out: "Lost interest in Scouting." One Council decided to investigate these cases and discovered that the boys hadn't dropped out because they "lost interest in Scouting"—for the very simple reason that *they had never had any Scouting!* They dropped out because they lost interest in *the thing that had been dished up to them as being Scouting*— which is a different story.

The times that boys have dropped out because they lost interest in *real* Scouting in *good* Patrols in *strong* Troops under *able* Scoutmasters are so rare that you'll seldom hear of one. Even in cases where job and home-work and other obligations made it hard for a boy to continue, if he had the interest he found the way.

If you give the boys what they expect, they will stay on and on in Scouting. And it is by staying that they give you your chance to help them grow.

Now, how can you know that your boys are getting what they expect, that their experience in the Troop is so satisfactory that they want to stay?

Two things will tell you: their attendance record and the boys themselves.

CHECK THE ATTENDANCE

A boy's attendance at Troop and Patrol meetings and hikes shows his interest and his satisfaction. It is the old story of the satisfied customer who comes back again and again.

A great number of Troops send out a monthly calendar of events to their members. Some Troops use a single mimeographed or hectographed sheet; others mimeograph the calendar on a postcard. Still other Troops produce a simple "newspaper," telling of past events and of activities to come.

The Troop attendance record is like a barometer.

If it's high, you are pretty certain to have smooth sailing ahead.

If it drops, better watch your weather signs, take fresh soundings and rechart your course.

Naturally there are reasons besides loss of interest that make a boy miss Troop meetings. The boy may be sick or away with his family or have some other good excuse, and may fail to notify his Patrol Leader. You should know why a boy is absent. You should expect your Patrol Leaders to have their boys all present or to know why some boy isn't at the meeting.

Boys Need Reminders

Boys may occasionally forget about a meeting, but they should never be able to say: "Nobody told me."

Many Troops depend upon the Patrol Leaders to keep their boys informed. Other Troops tell their Scouts of dates and times by announcing them from one meeting to the next, with a follow-up to Scouts who are absent when the announcement was made. Still others send out a monthly calendar of activities (see page 318).

A combination of the three is used in a great many Troops.

Getting Parents Cooperation

Parents may need reminders too.

Secure their cooperation at a parents' meeting. Explain to them that their sons are expected to attend all regular gatherings of the Troop, and let them know the usual day of the Troop meeting and of the monthly outdoor activity.

You will find parents willing to support you and eager to encourage the boys in their attendance, provided they understand the routine and know of the activities of the Troop.

ASK THE BOYS

If you discover any flagging in the boys' interest, find out from them what is the matter.

Or, even better, find out *before* the interest is on the down grade.

This, of course, does not mean that you should stand up at a Troop meeting and say "You fellows don't seem to like what's going on here. What's the matter?" You wouldn't get much of a picture through that approach.

Here are three ways to go about it:

1. Tell the boys at a meeting that "We are all interested in having the best possible Troop. What do you think we can do to make our Troop better? Have a good talk about it in your Patrols, so that when the leaders get together next week for the Troop Leaders' meeting we'll be able to do some real planning to do the job right." Then give the Patrol Leaders a chance at the Leaders' meeting to put all their cards on the table for a free discussion of problems and best ways of solving them. That's the way that efficient Troops build their programs. (See Chapter 5.)

2. Talk over the Troop with as many individual boys as possible. Make these talks friendly, informal chats when opportunities present themselves on a hike, or after a Troop meeting, or when a boy drops in to see you some evening.

3. You may develop a sheet of questions that will have a bearing on the situation, have it mimeographed and use it some time at a Troop meeting as a quiz game. Each boy will check his sheet and turn it in unsigned. By tallying the answers you should be able to find the weak points of the Troop and set out to strengthen them.

It is impossible to say what you will find to be the strong or the weak points of your Troop. But it may be

Give the boy a warm welcome into Scouting. The boy who is made to feel that he belongs will want to stay on in the Troop.

of value to you to know what has been found in other Troops where boys who were staying on and boys who had dropped out were interviewed and questioned*

Let's see what the boys—the "consumers"—had to say about the situation:

Boys Want to Be with Their Friends

It was obvious that the boys liked to be together and do things in the gang, provided the gang was made up right and the boy leader was the right type.

Here is the positive side of the picture:

"We have lots of fun in the Patrol. We do a lot of things together."

"I like the Patrol meetings; they're sort of a club; you get a little loyalty in it."

* From study made by National Research Service and Chicago Council

"Jim is O.K. I think he's the best Patrol Leader in the Troop."

And here is the negative side:

"I like to be with a small gang of close friends and the Patrol didn't provide that."

"We had too few Patrol meetings."

"We met only once a month, and only a few would show up; the boys lived too far apart. They really were Patrols in name only—no activities except as groups in games at Troop meetings."

"Our Patrol Leader was too young—all he did was goof around."

"My Patrol Leader thought he was boss and gave no one a chance for fun."

Boys Want Plenty of Hiking and Camping

Here's why some boys stayed:

"The training for camping is one of the best things."

"Give me camp any day!"

"We go camping almost every month. Do we have fun!"

"I like the experience in the out-of-doors, hiking and camping."

"I like the overnight best of all."

Here's why some boys dropped out:

"We didn't do enough hiking. We always went to the same place; you get tired of the same place."

"We were always going but never did."

"We went out only twice or three times a year. We didn't go out far enough from the city to be really out-of-doors."

"Our Scoutmaster made many promises to us about going on hikes, but he never kept them."

Boys Want Interesting Meetings

The boys who stayed had many ideas on how Troop meetings might be improved:

"We play too much at Troop meetings. I think we should do more Scouting."

"I like games; most of the fellows do. I guess other things are more important, though — like learning things."

"I wish we'd have better games at meetings; I'm sick of Steal the Bacon."

"Our Committeemen talk too much and the kids get bored."

"There are some things that don't interest the boys. They don't like to sit still for long periods. They don't like drill and standing in ranks. Maybe it's necessary, but they don't think so."

And these are some of the reasons why boys stopped coming:

"Our meeting programs were *always the same old stuff.*"

"There was never any written program. They were always on the spur of the moment."

"There was too much fooling around and we didn't get much done."

"I joined another club I like better; there's more activity and more freedom there."

Boys Want to be in on the Planning

The boys feel strongly about getting a chance to plan their program. The ones who stayed had this to say:

"Boys like a Scoutmaster who listens to the fellows' suggestions when they offer them. Our Scoutmaster does."

"Our Scoutmaster lets the fellows run the Troop themselves. If he has a suggestion he puts it in and maybe he'll be carried by a popular vote."

"The ideal Scoutmaster would let the boys plan the meeting and let him approve it."

The boys who had dropped out said:

"The Scoutmaster did all the planning himself. Once he let the older boys run the meeting for a few weeks and then decided they didn't do a good enough job."

"The fellows like to be able to decide things more for themselves, not always be told what they should do and how they should do it. We never had a chance."

"There was always so much planning, but nothing ever came of it."

"The fellows don't like it when a Scoutmaster accepts things for the Troop to do without asking first if the Troop wants to do them."

Boys Want Leaders They Like

The boys like a Scoutmaster they can look up to, who is fair, who is neither too strict nor too easy, who has a sense of humor, who understands them and likes them:

> "The best possible Scoutmaster acts like an ordinary regular fellow. Our Scoutmaster is like that."

> "We haven't got a good Scoutmaster. He might at least crack a joke and laugh once in a while instead of keeping a mug on."

> "The leader played favorites; he wasn't fair."

> "You can't be stern and strict in the Scouts. Kids want somebody they can go and talk to. You only have to worry about discipline if you have a leaky program."

> "Our Scoutmaster was too easy; he let the kids get away with anything."

> "We don't like Scoutmasters who bawl us out every minute no matter what we are doing. They sit in back of a table and tell us to stand up straight. While we break our backs, they sit down."

> "The best kind of Scoutmaster would really know Scouting, and would go on hikes with the fellows in the Troop."

WHAT CAN BE DONE ABOUT IT?

The thing to do about it is, of course: Give the boy what he expects and wants in Scouting! That's the simple secret of making him stay, and it simmers down to this:

1. Give him a real *welcome* into the Troop. We said it before. But it is so important that we'd better say it again: Make his entry so memorable to him that he gets a strong feeling of belonging from the beginning. That means the personal touch of a warm greeting by the Scoutmaster, the friendly assistance of the Patrol Leader or the buddy who helps him with the Tenderfoot requirements and an impressive investiture ceremony.

2. Give him a chance to be in a *Patrol where he fits* — where he has friends, common interests with the other boys, a leader he will gladly follow, activities he

Good times with good friends, with lots of hiking and camping, will keep the boy, and make him advance in Scouting.

helps to plan and responsibilities he has to carry for the mutual welfare of the gang. A boy will not lightly break his relationship to a closely-knit gang. His whole impulse is to be loyal to the group and to want to stick with it.

3. *Get him outdoors, hiking and camping,* WITHIN A WEEK after he has joined—or, if not a week, certainly within a month—and make an outdoor experience a monthly event for him—or oftener whenever possible! Get him going quickly on Scouting skills—finding his way, taking care of himself, using an axe, building a fire and cooking his food, making himself comfortable in camp. Get him under the spell of a camp fire at the earliest possible moment!

4. Have *meetings that count.* There is a difference between "plain fun" and the "fun" of "doing something

important." Be sure the meeting program has both. Put yourself in the Scout's place: "What will I get out of being there?" "What would I miss if I failed to show up?"

5. Give the boy a chance to *have his say in planning the program,* through his elected boy leader at the sessions of the Patrol Leaders' Council, through suggestions he makes to you informally from time to time, and through an occasional quiz. Don't make any major decisions yourself about the program. Let the boys do it.

6. Be *the kind of leader* to your boys that you would like to have had yourself when you were a kid. That's a tough one! You must like them tremendously to be that kind of a leader. You must be patient, and friendly, yet firm. You must know your Scouting in and out and be enthusiastic about it. You must be "a good Scout" yourself to make your boys good Scouts.

How to go about all this? Simply follow the suggestions in the chapters of this book. They were written and designed to do the very things you have just been reading about.

MOVING ON IN EXPLORING

While the boy is a *boy,* give him real *Boy* Scouting. When he grows older, give him a chance to go in for more advanced Scouting.

When the boy eventually leaves the Troop, have him leave with a feeling of good will to the Movement and with a recognition of his Service in Scouting. Present the pocket Certificate of Service to him as a reminder of his Scouting days, at a short ceremony before the Troop, if possible.

While he is a boy, give him Boy Scouting. When he grows older, help him to stay in Scouting as an Explorer.

On his fourteenth birthday, a Scout automatically reaches Explorer status. He may—or he may *not*—jump right into the Explorer program. At first he may remain more of a Boy Scout than an Explorer in his attitude and associations.

Treat him as an individual. (No two boys are alike.) Have a chat with him. Tell him something about Exploring, and introduce him to the Explorer Advisor at the earliest opportunity. See that he is encouraged to take part in the special program of the other Explorers in the Troop. Gradually he will want to enter more and more into the activities of the older fellows' group. Don't push him, but give him every chance to grow.

If he would like to stay in his present Patrol for the time being, let him. If he is eligible for a junior leadership opening, recommend him for it. If he would like to join a separate Explorer Unit, help arrange for his transfer and his introduction to the Explorer Unit officers.

The Explorer has reached a new milestone in his growth and in Scouting. As soon as possible after his birthday, the Troop should hold a simple but impressive Troop ceremony recognizing his new status. Such a ceremony, which can be arranged by the other Explorers in the Troop and their Advisor, with your help and participation, is described in the *Explorer Manual*.

Transfers and Separations

When a Scout or Explorer moves away from the neighborhood of your Troop, everything necessary should be done to make it possible for him to join a Troop in his new community. For this purpose you should give him an Application for Registration Transfer (Form Cat. No. 6100), signed by you and your local Scout Executive, and giving his complete advancement record. The procedure for an Explorer who wishes to transfer into a separate Explorer Unit is the same.

Eventually, in spite of the holding power of your program, all of your Explorers, except the few who move up to Assistant Scoutmasterships, are going to leave the Troop for one reason or another. It is important that each one of them leaves with recognition of his service in Scouting, and a feeling of good will for the Movement that will go with him into adult life. Make him feel that he is still considered one of the "gang" and is welcome to visit the Troop whenever he likes. As a permanent reminder of his Scouting days he should be given a pocket Certificate of Service.

The Boy Grows

CHAPTER 15

THE DAY HE ENTERS SCOUTING, the boy promises to keep himself ". . . physically strong, mentally awake, and morally straight." Here is a simple three-fold guide you can use to determine the extent of his growth.

Human nature is so complex that the three cannot be separated into watertight compartments. It is only as they are considered together that they give the true picture of the boy. Yet within each of the categories there are certain points on which you can concentrate your efforts in helping the boy.

PHYSICALLY STRONG

"Physically strong" is another way of saying "physically fit." It does not mean that a Scout should aim to develop his body after the model of a professional strong-man with bulging biceps, but rather that he should do his best to keep his whole body in good working order at all times to meet the demands of life.

Any boy of Scout age understands that an airplane or a car requires proper handling, continuous care, regular check-ups and occasional repairs to give good performance. When he applies the same sort of thinking to himself he understands why it is important for him to follow the same general course.

A boy knows that he will have a better chance in life if he is healthy and fit when he reaches manhood. In his contacts with other people he will meet men who have been slowed down by physical defects—often some that could have been easily and inexpensively corrected in early youth—or stopped altogether by failing to heed the warnings that nature usually gives when something is wrong.

But the future is not the boy's main consideration. He wants to be fit *right now* to satisfy his ambition to excel in games or sports which require strength and skill, and where the winner is the fellow who is in best physical condition.

How to Help the Boy

There are many ways in which Scouting can help a boy to better physical fitness. Here are a few examples of actual cases:

A—— S—— was skinny, run-down. The physical examination showed that his tonsils were infected, his teeth poor. The Scoutmaster, after talking it over with the doctor went to the boy's parents. They had known about the condition from a previous examination in

Scouting uses no formal physical exercises. Instead, it gives the boys games, hiking and camping, sun and fresh air.

school, but it was the first time someone personally had suggested to them that they should do something about it. The Scoutmaster's advice was followed, and improvement in the boy's health was soon evident.

G—— P—— was sickly as a child and needed his mother's continual care. He became a Scout and went to his first summer camp. A rainy spell set in. The mother was in perpetual telephone contact with the Scoutmaster, asking him to check that her boy was wearing his rubbers, his raincoat, keeping dry, staying in shelter, wondering if she had better come and take him home. The Scoutmaster did not worry the boy with his mother's worries. He went to the boy: "I know that you had a tough time with your health when you were a kid, but your examination before camp shows that you are all right now. You and I are both interested in seeing that you stay that way, so I'll trust you to take care of yourself in camp so that you will be stronger when you go home than when you came." The boy accepted the challenge and for the first time in his life went through a summer without colds, without stomach upsets, without spending a number of days in bed.

S—— D—— had always been a quiet boy, keeping to himself, seldom getting into the play of other boys. Consequently he had never learned to swim in the way a boy usually does, with the gang. It took plenty of persuasion to get him to camp. A patient leader took him in hand and got him started in the water. Within a week, the boy had moved from non-swimmer to beginner. He became intensely interested in swimming. A week later he was in the swimmer's area. He returned home tanned, with improved posture and firmer muscles.

V—— B—— was small, timid, "a mouse." The Troop had a commando game. Each boy had a one-inch gauze bandage around his arm. One of the objects of the game was to get as many of these "lives" as possible. V—— ran away quickly when it looked as if trouble were coming his way. He was finally overtaken by a boy much larger than himself. He squirmed and wiggled like an eel in the grasp of the larger boy to protect his own "life" and to reach the "life" of the other. Finally, with a desperate effort he succeeded in tearing the bandage off the other boy's arm. He had won over someone much larger than himself! The new confidence caused by this had an astonishing effect on him. He realized that agility is just as important as strength.

The Health Examination

There are two important reasons why a boy should have a thorough health examination when he enters

When securing medical examinations for your boys, make use of the Scout's Medical Record, Form Cat. No. 4126. On one side, the parents give the health history of their son. On the other, the doctor writes his findings and recommendations. A yearly examination is recommended for every Scout.

Scouting and once a year thereafter—before each summer camp:

1. For his own protection—to determine whether or not he is suffering from any abnormal condition which might cause trouble when he takes part in such exercises as running, climbing or swimming. Many drowning accidents are actually the result of defective hearts overstrained by the exercise.

2. In order that a boy and his parents may do something about any minor or major defects that need correction.

In planning for health examinations, the Troop needs the cooperation of the parents. Unless the parents understand what the Troop aims to do, they may not see the reason for the examination, or may be unwilling to incur the expense.

The parents may want to have the examination made by the family doctor. However, in many instances Troop Committees get a physician to act as the Troop's doctor and conduct the examinations with the approval of the parents. A health history and medical examination form (see illustration page 332), is available from the Local Council Office. On this blank the parents give the health history of their son, and the doctor writes his findings and recommendations.

From the health record the Scoutmaster will get a good picture of the boy's physical condition and be able to protect him when on a Troop activity. He will also be able to help the weak boy build his strength, and help the boy with physical defects to set them right.

Exercise

Every growing creature needs exercise. Fortunately, nature has put in the growing boy an urge for action and fight, for running, tumbling, wrestling, jumping.

In Scouting we use no formal exercises. Instead we

give the boys rough and ready games, hiking. camping, exploring—things to do in the fresh air and in the sun. We encourage physical fitness skills, such as swimming, canoeing, rowing, skiing, and many others.

By taking part actively and whole-heartedly in all the activities of his Patrol and Troop, the boy can't help become more fit.

The adolescent boy has a special problem. His muscles crave exercise, the more the merrier. The boy is on the go all the time and is often on the verge of burning himself up. His heart, at the same time, demands rest to grow and to adjust itself to the larger body it has to serve.

You have to watch the boy. Let him become healthily tired on a Troop hike, but don't permit him to get exhausted.

Health Habits

In the Troop meeting room and on hikes the boy will pick up a number of safety skills. But it is in camp, where he is directly under your influence for twenty-four hours a day, that you can best help the boy establish proper health habits.

Many boys realize in camp, for the first time, what it means to have proper food, exercise, sun and fresh air, thorough cleanliness and sufficient rest and sleep. To have that effect on the boys, your camp must live up to the high standards that should be the tradition for camping in your Troop.

Your Example

Here again your own example will do much to establish good health habits in them. Do yourself what you want the boys to do. The Scoutmaster who urges his Scouts to keep clean but who doesn't do it himself, won't get far. The Scoutmaster who tells his boys to keep their

In camp, the boy is under your influence for 24 hours a day. Here you can help him establish proper health habits.

camp tidy but leaves his own stuff strewn about, can't expect to have much of an influence. Where *you* give the example, the boys will follow.

Similarly in other habits that involve health. Smoking by growing youngsters is admittedly undesirable. So is drinking. Even if it works a little hardship at times, most Scoutmasters are glad to abide by the policy of the Boy Scouts of America: "The National Council recommends that intoxicating liquors be not used in connection with Scout meetings, and that all Scoutmasters and other officials while on active duty refrain from the use of tobacco, and that those who are accustomed to the use of tobacco do not conceal the fact from the boys, but discuss frankly with them the desirability of refraining from its use until they have attained their full development."

MENTALLY AWAKE

It is impossible for a boy to be an active Scout without becoming "mentally awake" to a greater or lesser degree.

Preparing for hike and camp, learning new skills and playing new games, cause him to think, to judge, to decide. Observation, tracking, deduction, stalking, sharpen his capacity for noticing things and develop his memory. Leadership of Patrol or Troop or in special activities encourages initiative, ability to work with others, self-expression.

Here again, there are numerous direct and many subtle ways of helping boys grow.

Some Actual Cases

The Hawk Patrol had agreed to put on a knotting demonstration at the Troop meeting. On the evening of the event, the Patrol Leader, B—— J——, sadly informed the Scoutmaster that the Patrol had forgotten to bring rope. Instead of cancelling the event, the Scoutmaster smiled: "That shouldn't prevent you from giving your demonstration. Your Patrol goes on according to plan in ten minutes." And the Patrol did, after a huddle of strenuous mental exercise. The demonstration was better than if it had been made with rope, for it showed the emergency use of neckerchiefs, belts, stockings, shoe laces, electric cord.

G—— A—— was subnormal, clumsy. He was still in 5th grade at the age of 14. He was considered . . . well, just plain dumb. Everybody took for granted that he couldn't succeed in anything. His Scoutmaster's treatment of him as an equal with the other boys of the Troop inspired him with a dogged determination to become a First Class Scout. He mastered most of the requirements, but was stumped by signaling. One night he appeared before the Board of Review and went through everything, including signaling, with flying colors. The Scoutmaster later learned that G—— had persuaded his mother to work with him for three solid nights, the mother with the Handbook in her hands, until he was letter-perfect. G—— had tasted his first success in life; a keenness for getting ahead had been awakened in him as he discovered that he need not always fail.

The big family camp fire had been scheduled in camp for Saturday. Because of rain, it was postponed to Sunday. D—— R—— new Patrol Leader, 13 years old, of the Troop's Tenderfoot Patrol, was the leader of the Program Patrol for the day. For a fleeting moment the Scoutmaster considered shifting the responsibility for leading the camp fire to a more experienced boy. To his own later great satisfaction he didn't. He followed with amazement the manner in which D—— lined up the program for the evening and arranged for the other Patrols to put on stunts. When the camp fire started with an audience of about two hundred, a completely self-possessed youngster of thirteen carried through a highly successful program with the effectiveness of an old-timer.

On an early morning bird hike, the Scoutmaster noticed the complete absorption of W—— N——. He was full of questions that clamored for answers. The Scoutmaster gave him the answers he knew, then followed up by bringing the boy a good bird book. Bird study became an important hobby in W——'s life, eventually brought him a museum curatorship in bird lore.

This last case can be duplicated a hundred times over. There are numerous cases of boys taking up for a hobby or vocation a subject they first became interested in through Scouting. Many doctors can tell you how an interest in simple Scout first aid set them out on their careers. Swimming has turned many boys toward positions in physical education, besides being a great source of enjoyment to them. Nature exploration has caused others to take up teaching. Subjects ranging from camping and angling to astronomy and photography have become life-time hobbies.

Along this line, we have a definite measuring rod in Scouting of the boy's growth, in the way he advances in Scout Rank.

Advancement

Scout advancement provides a progressive series of requirements in various skills, sets standards for meeting them, and offers awards to the Scouts who master them, in the form of special badges.

Scout advancement has introduced a new principle in education. In most educational systems, boys are taught in classes, doing specified work in a specified time. In such classes the brighter boys are held back by those less bright, and the slower boys are forced ahead faster than they can grasp the subject. In Scout advancement each boy proceeds at his own speed. His rate of advancement depends upon his own ability and interest.

Also, Scout advancement is a new type of competition. Elsewhere, a boy is often urged to "lick" someone else in scholastic standing or in games. In Scout advancement the boy competes with himself against his own previous record. He can move as far as his own ambition carries him.

Scout advancement falls in three groups:

Basic Scout Rank advancement to Second Class and First Class Scout Ranks.

Merit Badge exploration in a large choice of subjects.

Star, Life and Eagle Scout Ranks for earning certain numbers of Merit Badges and demonstrating Scout service and leadership ability.

Basic Scout Rank Advancement

The requirements for Second Class and First Class Scout Ranks were developed in such a way that, when properly applied in Patrol and Troop, they will:

1. Promote SCOUT IDEALS—Assist a boy to become physically strong, mentally awake, and morally straight; help to make the boy self-reliant; encourage him to think of others and make it possible for him to

Tracking — observation and deduction — sharpens the boy's capacity for noticing things and makes him mentally alert.

help others by teaching him skills that might benefit other people.

2. Promote SCOUT PARTICIPATION — Encourage the boy to take active part in Patrol and Troop activities and service projects; provide for doing things together in the Patrol; give a boy a chance for advancement as a natural outcome of his life in Patrol and Troop.

3. Promote SCOUTCRAFT—Make the boy at home in the out-of-doors; encourage more than "just getting a badge" (the requirements add up to making the boy a good Scout hiker, a good Scout camper); stress *learning by doing—doing for a purpose* instead of just *knowing;* provide program material for Patrol and Troop.

The requirements are found in **Tool 20.** The subject matter is thoroughly covered in the *Handbook for Boys* and the *Scout Field Book* which are your boys' guides to advancement.

Encourage your boys to reach the rank of Second Class Scout as soon as possible after entering the Troop, and to aim for First Class as their minimum achievement in Scouting.

To reach a rank, four steps need to be taken. They are: *Preparation—Qualification—Review—Recognition.*

PREPARATION — The requirements for Second Class show a boy the way to become a good hiker; those for First Class give him a chance to become a good camper. By taking part in plenty of outdoor Patrol and Troop experiences, the boys can't help but learn these skills. They have to know how to use an axe, build a fire and cook, to make a meal in the open. They need to know how to use a compass and a map to go on a cross-country hike. They need to know some first aid to take care of themselves and to help others. They certainly want to swim to enjoy themselves in camp. And so on.

Rank advancement is therefore a *natural outcome* of the boys' participation in regular Scouting activities. Advancement takes place in the Patrol, and each Patrol Leader is responsible for encouraging and helping his boys to advance. To do this adequately your Patrol Leaders need the continued training you give them at the informal meetings and hikes of the Leaders' Patrol (see page 61).

To simplify the matter of keeping track of the Scoutcraft skills a boy masters, give him a SECOND CLASS or FIRST CLASS SCOUT RECORD card. These cards contain the requirements, with space for the leader's signature. The completed record is evidence to the Board of Review that all requirements are met.

QUALIFICATION—The examination of the Scout in the Rank Requirements may be made by the boy's own Patrol Leader—provided this leader already has the rank the Scout is aiming for. Otherwise, some other Troop leader will do the examining.

Qualification is really a checking-off process rather than a formal examination.

A Scout goes on several hikes and learns to cook a meal for himself. Some day, on a Patrol hike, he tells his Patrol Leader, "Well, I think I am ready now." The Patrol Leader then watches the boy as he prepares firewood, builds a suitable fire, and cooks his food. If the boy does everything smoothly and well, the Patrol Leader says, "You did fine!" and checks off the boy's advancement card to show that he has met the requirements.

An even more natural way is for the Patrol Leader to plan a Patrol hike that involves doing the things the requirements call for, without specifically telling the boy that it is advancement he is aiming for.

The method will have to fit the boys. Some boys will like the surprise of being told that they have met the requirements by doing the things in the normal process of hiking and camping. You'll get other boys who feel that this procedure cheats them of the feeling of achievement. A boy, for instance, who had proved himself a competent swimmer during two weeks in summer camp insisted upon being tested in the First Class swimming requirement according to the exact wording of the requirement.

The main thing is that qualification is an actual demonstration of the skill involved and conforms with the interpretation of the various requirements as given.

REVIEW—When a boy has finished all the requirements his record is reviewed by the Patrol Leaders'

Council and the Scoutmaster certifies on an official form that the Scout is ready to appear before the Board of Review.

A Board consists of members of the Troop Committee, supplemented by such other adults as the Committee may desire to ask to help it. The Neighborhood Commissioner or a member of the Advancement Committee may attend Troop Board of Review sessions. A Troop that has a good all-round record and an active, trained Troop Committee should conduct its own Boards of Review and Courts of Honor. If yours is not that kind of Troop yet, call on your Council or District Advancement Committee for advice and assistance. (For further information, read *Advancement in the Troop*.)

In a Troop where advancement goes on all the time, Boards of Review are planned at regular intervals during the year. In a new Troop, a Board of Review is called when a few boys are ready. The Board may meet in conjunction with a Troop meeting or on a separate night. Invite your Commissioner to attend.

Each boy is called in singly before the Board and asked enough questions to assure the members that he deserves the rank he seeks.

The members of the Board should keep in mind that the review is *not* a re-examination and does *not* require that the boy again demonstrate the skills in which he has been examined. The main purpose of the review is to make sure that the examination was up to standards. It is a checkup to see that *what should have been done was actually done*. It can be accomplished through a few simple questions, such as "What did you do to show that you can use an axe?" or "What did you cook for the First Class Requirement?" Answers to "Where? When? How?" and so on, will soon reveal whether the Scout has learned and demonstrated his skills under real-life conditions.

The review should be a friendly talking-it-over be-

The Scout has met the requirements for a higher rank. He receives his award before the Court of Honor.

tween a boy and some men who are interested in his welfare. It should be enjoyable for the boy as well as for the men. The nervous boy should be put at ease, the tongue-tied boy encouraged to talk. The review should strengthen the boy's confidence in the men behind the Troop. Trick questions, are, of course, out. They undermine the boy's confidence and serve no useful purpose.

If the review has been satisfactory, the boy is told so. If not, he is asked to prepare himself better in the subjects in which he is weak, and to come back before the Board when he has been examined in them again.

As soon as the Board of Review is over, the record of it and order for badges should be sent to the Local Council office so that the Scouts may promptly be credited with the advancement. A Scout's date of rank begins the day his application is approved by the Board of Review.

RECOGNITION—The badge is presented to the boy at a Troop Court of Honor before the whole Troop and, if possible, before an audience with the boy's parents present. Perhaps in your Council additional recognition may be given at a District or Council Court of Honor.

OUTLINE OF TROOP COURT OF HONOR PROGRAM

ENTRY OF SCOUTS with Troop and Patrol flags.

ENTRY OF COURT OF HONOR MEMBERS

ENTRY OF COLORS with Color Guard — Scouts and audience at attention.

PLEDGE OF ALLEGIANCE—parents and audience join.

OPENING of the Court of Honor with an appropriate ceremony, such as a candle lighting ceremony, Chairman announces Court of Honor in session.

INTRODUCTION OF SCOUTS—Senior Patrol Leader reads the names of the Scouts to receive Second Class Badges. They come forward and SPL introduces them to the Court.

PRESENTATION OF AWARDS — The Court of Honor Chairman calls on a member of the Court to make the presentations. Each Scout salutes as he receives his award and is congratulated by the Chairman and the Scoutmaster, using the Scout Handshake. (In many Troops the parents are called up with their boys, and the mothers are given miniature "mothers' pins" of their boys' new rank. When all Second Class badges have been presented, the SPL dismisses the group and reads the names of those to receive the next award, etc.

SPECIAL PROGRAM FEATURES — Scoutcraft demonstrations, brief address, singing, etc.

RETIRE COLORS

CLOSING—Court of Honor may close with the Troop's regular closing ceremony, which may include the Scoutmaster's Benediction and Taps.

Merit Badge Exploration

While Rank advancement is a natural outgrowth of the boy's Patrol and Troop experience, Merit Badge exploration is an individual pursuit.

A great variety of Merit Badges is available to the boy. In each case the subject has been broken into a series of requirements. These requirements are designed as a guide the boy can follow to get a fair knowledge of the subject. All Merit Badge requirements are found in the *Handbook for Boys*. To assist a boy in preparing for Merit Badges, there is a Merit Badge Library including over 100 pamphlets.

The Merit Badge subjects may be divided into these categories:

Animal Husbandry group: importance, care of animals.

Aquatics group: watercraft and aquatic skills.

Arts group: various related fields.

Building group: practical fields related to construction.

Campcraft group: Camping, Cooking; Pioneering; Surveying.

Citizenship group: Citizenship in home, community, nation; World Brotherhood.

Communication group: Fields related to communication.

Conservation group: Various areas of conservation.

Crafts and Collections group: Varied fields.

Nature group: Widespread areas of nature understanding.

Outdoor Sports group: Activities for outdoor fun.

Personal Development group: To expand practical skills.

Plant Cultivation group: Raising foods and crops.

Public Service group: In order to be more able to help.

Transportation group: Automobiling; Aviation; Railroading; Seamanship.

See page 503 in Tool 20 for a complete listing of Merit Badges under each group.

In Merit Badge advancement we have only three steps: *Preparation—Qualification—Recognition*.

PREPARATION—When a boy shows interest in earning a certain Merit Badge, get the Scout in touch with the Merit Badge Counselor on the subject.

Merit Badge Counselors are chosen by the Council from among the outstanding men in the community who are leaders in their particular field. They are men who believe in Scouting and are willing to give generously of their time to help boys. You can get their names and addresses from the Council office.

The boy and the Counselor meet first to get acquainted. The man gives the boy an idea of the importance of the subject and what is involved in preparing to meet the requirements. At other visits the Counselor checks with the boy on his progress.

QUALIFICATION—When the Scout is confident that he is ready for examination, he makes out a Merit Badge application, gets his Scoutmaster's approval on it, and contacts the Merit Badge Counselor. This time he brings with him the application and all materials that may be required. If he meets the requirements satisfactorily, the Counselor signs the application, certifying that the boy is entitled to the Merit Badge.

RECOGNITION—Finally, the Merit Badge is presented to the Scout at a Court of Honor.

When a boy has met the requirements for Star, Life or Eagle Rank, secure the proper application blank—Cat. No. 6112 for Star and Life, Cat. No. 6109 for Eagle. Fill it in, sign it, and submit it to the Local Council. The Council will secure further evidence of the boy's Scout Spirit from other people who know him.

Star, Life and Eagle Scout Ranks

One of the incentives that a boy has for Merit Badge advancement is the fact that by earning certain ones and proving himself a generally good Scout he becomes eligible for Star, Life and Eagle Scout Ranks.

To become a Star Scout, the boy must earn five Merit Badges; for Life Scout ten Merit Badges; for Eagle Scout twenty-one (for requirements, see *Handbook for Boys*).

The Merit Badges indicate the SCOUTCRAFT skills a boy has mastered. But in addition to these skills the boy must have proved himself a good Scout through his SCOUT SPIRIT and his SCOUT PARTICIPATION.

The requirements in those two areas are more intangible than the Merit Badge projects. The fact that they are harder to measure in specific terms adds to their importance, for they indicate growth in the things that really count in the development of a boy . . . initiative, sense of responsibility, leadership and the qualities implied in the Scout Oath, Law, Motto and Slogan.

When a Scout has earned the necessary Merit Badges and you are satisfied that he has met the Scout Spirit and Scout Participation requirements, give him the proper application blank to fill out, approve it and send it to the Local Council. The Scout is called before the Board of Review, and receives his award at a Court of Honor.

Explorer Advancement

Explorers have the privilege of continuing on the Scout advancement trail right up to Eagle. In addition, an Explorer may achieve recognition in the Explorer program itself. First he qualifies as an Explorer Apprentice by meeting certain requirements in the outdoor, vocational, social and service fields. Any Explorer who has reached Second Class Scout rank will have already met the outdoor requirements for Apprentice.

After he becomes an Apprentice, the Explorer may qualify for any of the Explorer Ratings—in Aviation, Craft Skills, Outdoor Skills, Seamanship, etc.—which lead to Bronze, Gold and Silver Awards. Requirements for these recognitions are given in the Explorer Manual.

The Explorer Leaders' Council, with at least one Troop Committeeman participating, sits as a Reviewing Board only for Explorer Ratings and Awards.

An Explorer who has not become a First Class Scout must earn either the Outdoor Skills Rating or the Bronze Award before he can qualify for Star, Life and Eagle, but an Apprentice may earn any Merit Badge.

MORALLY STRAIGHT

While the badges on your boys' sleeves will tell something of the kind of Scouts they have become, your success as a Scoutmaster, in the last analysis, will be written in terms of your ability to make the Scout Oath and Law vital in the lives of the boys.

What Does the Scout Law Mean to the Boy?

A—— G—— was well developed, strong, definitely the bully type. G—— F—— was a weak kid, considered "peculiar" by his school mates. The Scoutmaster had been dismayed over A——'s bullying of G—— and had been considering what could be done about it. One day, the Scoutmaster passed G——'s school just as it came out, and saw G—— surrounded by several boys who teased him, hit at him, pulled him, with G—— bewildered, unable to protect himself. At the next meeting, the Scoutmaster told A——, the bully, what he had seen, and said, "I wish you would take G—— under protection for awhile and teach him to defend himself." Two weeks later the two boys came to the Scoutmaster. G—— said: "Look what A—— taught me. All the kids in school get away from me when I do this," and he got himself into boxing position, with A—— standing by, proud of his pupil.

A Scoutmaster was told the following by a friend: "The other day when I passed the corner of Mountain

One of your greatest awards as a Scoutmaster comes the day you pin a well-earned Eagle Badge on one of your boys.

Road and East Main, a small kid skidded with his bicycle, fell and got his knee badly scraped. One of your boys was there. He picked up the bike and got the kid up on the sidewalk. He said, 'You stay right there,' and disappeared into a drug store. A moment later he had iodined and bandaged the kid's leg, and the kid was on his way again. 'That was a real Good Turn', I said to your boy. He only mumbled, 'Any fellow would do that to a kid.' "

The Good Turn of the Unknown London Scout who caused William D. Boyce to become interested in Scouting and start the Boy Scouts of America is a continuous inspiration to American boys.

The records of the National Court of Honor contain thousands of case reports of Scouts who have saved the lives of others at the risk of their own—some of them have died in their attempts. They represent the finest spirit of helpfulness and bravery.

Religious Awards

A Scoutmaster may help to strengthen a Scout or Explorer in his religious obligations by encouraging him to enroll in the program of religious instruction, experience and service which results in gaining for the Scout the RELIGIOUS AWARD of his faith. For the Protestant Scout there is the *God and Country Award;* for the Lutheran boy, the *Pro Deo et Patria;* for the Catholic boy, the *Ad Altare Dei;* for the Jewish boy, the *Ner Tamid;* for the boy belonging to the Church of the Latter-Day Saints, the *"Duty to God" Award.* The Scout is supervised in this program by his own minister, priest, rabbi, ward bishop or spiritual counselor.

Your Example

The old advice: "Do what I tell you to do and not what I do!" doesn't work in a Scout Troop any better than it does anywhere else. The Scoutmaster will lose a tremendous advantage if he tries to encourage boys to live up to standards which he does not practice.

Your Inspiration

There will be many occasions where you can inspire a boy to do what is right, by making him feel your trust and belief in him. A casual word—a glance, even—may do it. The Good Turn habit can best be sown in boys by creating a spirit of friendliness and helpfulness in the Troop that will carry over in their daily lives. Clean minds grow in a clean atmosphere.

By making your boys feel that you are their friend, that you respect them as equals and expect them to rise to the highest there is in them, you will help them grow.

A boy will not let down a leader who has shown him complete confidence and faith.

EPILOGUE

THE STORY IS TOLD. The panorama of Scouting has been unrolled before you, with its activities, its fellowship, its fun.

Has the multitude of details left you breathless? Have you felt that you will never be able to master the mass of them?

Don't worry!

The climb to the top need not be taken in one step. The rules of the Game you will learn as you play. The technical knowledge you will absorb with your boys as you hike the Scouting trail together.

Are you afraid that you will lose the way?

Never fear!

The hill may seem steep and the forest dark, and the road may be winding and long. But with strength of purpose and following the true course of your compass, you shall eventually succeed in leading your boys to the goal you have set.

And that goal is CITIZENSHIP—and that compass is the SCOUT OATH AND THE SCOUT LAW.

THE END

TOOL CHEST

SETTING OUT WITH THE TROOP

A. STARTING A NEW TROOP

OF COURSE you want a Troop with the kind of backing which will guarantee its permanence, and the kind of leadership which will produce a real Scout program.

To have such a Troop, three things must happen:

(1) The parent institution must understand the responsibilities of sponsorship, and sincerely want to have the Troop. This means the entire membership.

(2) Capable men must be selected by the institution to serve as its representatives on the Local Council, on the Troop Committee, and as Scoutmaster and Assistant Scoutmaster.

(3) All related adults, including the parents of boys, must understand the program's purpose and methods.

There are ten essential steps* to be followed:

I. AN INSTITUTION OR GROUP OF CITIZENS EXPRESSES A DESIRE TO ORGANIZE A SCOUT TROOP.

2. A COUNCIL SCOUTER INFORMS THE INSTITUTION HEAD ABOUT THE RESPONSIBILITIES OF SPONSORSHIP; EXPLAINS ORGANIZATION STEPS.

In describing local Council operation, he explains that Council and District work is planned to support the institution's program, not to replace or compete with it.

*For details, read *Ten Steps to Organize a Boy Scout Group* (B.S.A. Cat. No. 3084).

3. **AN ORGANIZATION COMMITTEE, SELECTED BY THE INSTITUTION, MEETS TO CONSIDER PROSPECTIVE TROOP LEADERSHIP AND PLANS A "GET ACQUAINTED WITH SCOUTING" MEETING FOR PARENTS AND POTENTIAL TROOP LEADERS.**

The institutional head usually serves as chairman of the organizing committee, which is composed of key men and women who are able and eager to enlist the support of others.

4. **COUNCIL SCOUTERS CONDUCT THE "GET ACQUAINTED WITH SCOUTING" MEETING.**

The responsibility for conducting this session is shared by Council and District Scouters.

5. **THE INSTITUTION TAKES FORMAL ACTION REQUESTING CHARTER FOR TROOP, APPOINTS AN INSTITUTIONAL REPRESENTATIVE ON THE LOCAL COUNCIL, AND A TROOP COMMITTEE.**

A special Form (Cat. No. 6186) is provided to help the Sponsoring Institution analyze its needs and indicate its desire for the Scouting Program and for specific Units.

6. **COUNCIL SCOUTERS INSTRUCT THE TROOP COMMITTEE IN ITS DUTIES; GIVE GUIDANCE IN THE SELECTION OF THE SCOUTMASTER.**

Before the Troop Committee starts performing its important duties it should be coached, started off in the right direction. This is especially true of its most important action—the selection of a Scoutmaster.

7. **THE TROOP COMMITTEE SELECTS AND RECRUITS A SCOUTMASTER AND ONE OR MORE ASSISTANTS.**

Where a prospective Scoutmaster has himself set the ball rolling, or where an old Troop is building a Troop around available leadership, the selection of a Scoutmaster should present no problem.

Where no such leadership is at hand, the Troop Committee must make a careful, personal investigation of the character and qualifications of possible candidates. The committee members must be convinced before appointment is made that the man picked is one to whose leadership and influence they would be willing to commit their own sons without reservation.

8. THE SCOUTMASTER, ASSISTANTS AND COMMITTEEMEN ARE TRAINED BY COUNCIL REPRESENTATIVES WITH VISITATION AND STUDY PROJECTS, COMPLETING BASIC TRAINING AT FIRST OPPORTUNITY.

The new Scoutmaster should make a general study of the *Handbook for Boys, Handbook for Scoutmasters,* and of the early chapters of the *Handbook for Patrol Leaders.*

He should, if possible, visit one or more successful Troops at their meetings and go on at least one of their hikes, in order to get a picture of the Scouting Program and to discuss with other leaders the running of a Troop.

He should, as soon as possible, discuss his job with the Scout Executive and the District or Neighborhood Commissioner, and begin basic training as described in Tool 19.

9. THE TROOP IS ORGANIZED: (a) THE TROOP COMMITTEE AND SCOUTMASTER ADOPT POLICIES AND DO INITIAL PLANNING; START CHARTER APPLICATION; (b) JUNIOR LEADERS ARE SELECTED AND GIVEN INTENSIVE TRAINING BY THE SCOUTMASTER; (c) PATROLS ARE FORMED AND BOYS ARE TRAINED IN TENDERFOOT WORK; (d) REGISTRATION AND CHARTER APPLICATIONS ARE COMPLETED AND SUBMITTED TO THE LOCAL COUNCIL.

The Troop Committee and Scoutmaster Meet

Such important policies as these will be determined:

1. Will a majority of boys come from families connected with the institution? What will be the recruiting plan?

2. What Troop meeting room facilities will be available?

Will they be set aside for the Troop's use on certain days?

3. What specific services will the Troop render to the Sponsoring Institution?

4. Will the Troop Committee render monthly or quarterly reports to the institution, covering membership, recruiting, advancement, service, finance, etc.

5. What Troop Budget will be adopted? How will a revolving fund be set up? It must be understood, of course, that the Scouts themselves should have a voice in adopting a budget. (See page 392.)

6. What will be the Troop Camping policy and hiking plans? How will religious values be safeguarded in camp?

7. Will applicants for membership be expected to have a medical examination?

Such a discussion of policies will occupy most of the meeting. In addition, the Scoutmaster will discuss the Troop program plans for the first few weeks.

TRAINING THE TROOP MEMBERS

The "Chosen Few"

There is one fundamental principle for organizing: START SMALL.

Eight to twelve boys, preferably eleven-year-olds, would be the most appropriate number for a formative group, since five is the national minimum for chartering a new Troop, and some of the first group may disappoint you. Only in case you have a nucleus of boys already Scouts, is it advisable to begin with a larger number.

Planning Ahead

Arrange with these boys for a definite time and place for the first meeting—then settle down to PLAN AHEAD.

Two important things enter into your planning:

1. To charter a Troop, each member must have met the Candidate Requirements.

2. To run a successful Troop, the Patrol Method should be used from the start.

This means that the main function of the first few meetings is to impart to the boys an elementary knowledge of Scoutcraft—as contained in the Tenderfoot Requirements—and to get Patrols formed. But also—and equally important—to instill in the boys the spirit of Scouting, to give them the joy of anticipation of great things ahead in their lives as Scouts.

Correctly planned and prepared for, it is possible to accomplish most of these objects in about four meetings, scheduled over a month's time, or possibly over six weeks or two months.

In the following pages you will find a set of suggested meetings. Each meeting is planned to occupy an hour and a half. It is obvious that they will have to be modified to suit your particular conditions.

Though this may be your first adventure in Scout leadership, approach it with confidence. Have a trained Scout or an Assistant on hand, if you will, but conduct the meeting, explain the Scout Requirements and make the announcements yourself.

It is important for the boys to realize your interest, and to recognize your leadership from the beginning.

Meeting I

OBJECTS

1. To explain the scheme and scope of the Scout Movement.
2. To suggest *indirectly* the reasons for entering Scouting.
3. To begin the Candidate and Tenderfoot instruction.
4. To establish a temporary organization.

EQUIPMENT

1. *Handbook for Boys.*
2. Membership application blanks.
3. Ropes for knot-tying, three-four feet long, ¼" thick.
4. Flag of the United States of America.

PROGRAM

Recreational Game—10 minutes. Explain that one part of the Scout Oath refers to keeping "mentally awake" and that you're going to test this right at the start with a game. Select something simple, such as Crows and Cranes (see index: Games). Oher suitable games are Jump the Shot, Swat 'Em and Do This—Do That. They all work well with ten or a dozen boys.

Talk on Scouting—10 minutes (boys seated). Say something like this, briefly, simply:

"Every boy who thinks of becoming a Scout ought to know just what he's getting into before he joins. So I'm going to tell you what Scouting is; what the three million Scouts of the world stand for:

"A Troop of Scouts is a bunch of fellows who are banded together for fun in outdoor adventure and in service to others. They train themselves in woodcraft and usefulness in emergencies so that they will 'Be Prepared,' as the Scout Motto says, to be stronger men and more valuable citizens to their country.

"We want the Troop we are organizing to be one of the finest and most active Troops in the whole country. Every Scout in it must be right on the job all of the time to be the best kind of a Scout he can.

"Now what will our Troop do? First we'll dig in and meet the Tenderfoot Requirements. We'll organize Patrols and select Patrol Leaders. At our meetings we'll go ahead and practice some of the advanced Requirements so that we'll move forward steadily. We'll have a lot of games and stunts. We'll try out what ' e know in special contests. We'll take hikes just as often as we can—overnight trips as soon as we're ready for them. We'll be having great adventures together that fellows who aren't Scouts couldn't have. At first we'll keep our numbers small; we'll pick our men.

"More important than anything else I have mentioned is the Scout Oath or Promise to which every member subscribes when he joins. It is this: (or who knows what it is?) 'On my honor I will do my best to do my duty to God and my country and to obey the Scout Law; to help other people at all times; to keep myself physically strong, mentally awake, and morally straight.' Unless you feel sure that you want to live up to this Oath the very best you can, you shouldn't become a Scout. The Oath and the twelve points of the Law are a tough lot of things for any fellow to live up to; only those with grit and nerve should tackle them. You had better think that part over pretty carefully before you make up your minds to be Scouts.

"Here's one more point—the real price of membership in this Troop will be unfailing regular attendance at its meetings, and steady progress in all the things that make a Scout 'Prepared.' If I put my own time into the activities of this Troop I shall certainly expect you to do your part with equal faithfulness. Is that plain—and fair?"

Knot-Tying—20 minutes. Practice two or three of the Tenderfoot knots. Begin with a rapid demonstration and explanation of the use of each one. Have all the boys provided with rope, and have them tie each knot as soon as it has been demonstrated. When they have learned several knots, have them try these in competition for speed. Have the boys hold the ropes above their heads until the signal to tie is given, each boy dropping his rope to the floor or holding it up and calling "Done!" when he has tied the knot called for.

Explanation of Candidate and Tenderfoot Requirements —20 minutes (Scouts seated).

a. Exhibit the *Handbook for Boys*—tell its importance and the necessity for securing it at once.

b. Explain the Candidate and Tenderfoot Requirements (from *Handbook for Boys.*)

c. Show the boys where to find the material on the Candidate and Tenderfoot Requirements in the *Handbook*.

d. Ask every boy to prepare to meet as many as possible of the Candidate Requirements by next meeting. Lay stress on learning the Scout Oath and Law thoroughly and promptly.

e. Mention the National Registration Fee of fifty cents, and the necessity for its prompt payment so that the Troop can be registered.

f. Distribute the application blanks and request their return by the following meeting, with registration fees.

Silent Scout Drill—15 minutes. (Have a visiting Scout or Scouter on hand for this instruction if necessary.) Use a few simple formations: Single line, relay, circle (see index: Scout Drill).

Closing ceremonies—15 minutes.

(a) Have each boy choose which Patrol he will join on a *temporary* basis (see Chapter 2).

Appoint an intelligent boy who appears to be suited for faithful detail work as Scribe. His duties at the beginning will be: make up a roll, receive applications and fees, and record the essential facts of each meeting. Later, the Simplified Troop Record Book will be found helpful for his work.

(b) Repeat request for return of application blanks and registration fees by the next meeting.

(c) Repeat request that Candidate Requirements be learned by the next meeting.

(d) Have a boy (or a visiting Scout) lead several Scout yells, such as: "A-M-E-R-I-C-A! BOY SCOUTS! BOY SCOUTS! U-S-A!"

(e) Close the meeting with the Pledge of Allegiance and the Scout Motto. (Boys do not formally repeat the Scout Oath until after they are installed as Candidate Scouts.)

Questions After the Meeting

Some boys will linger after the meeting to ask questions: *"When can we get Uniforms?"* "You are permitted to wear them as soon as you are Candidate Scouts and the Troop is registered." *"When do we get our badges?"* "About four weeks from now at the public installation meeting if you meet your Candidate Requirements promptly."

If you are unable to answer a question, frankly admit it by saying, "I don't know, but I'll find out and tell you next week." In the meantime consult your Handbook, or ask for help from the Local Council office.

Meeting 2

OBJECTS

1. Practice of Candidate and Tenderfoot Requirements.
2. Collection of application blanks and registration fees.
3. Building up further interest in Scouting.

EQUIPMENT

Same as for Meeting 1.

PROGRAM

Assembly—15 minutes.

a. Pledge of Allegiance.

b. Review of Scout Drill practiced previous week, with the addition of two or three new movements.

c. Roll Call—by the newly appointed Scribe. (Later on when Patrols are permanently organized, the Patrol Leaders will report the attendance.)

Knot-Tying—20 minutes.

a. Review all the knots learned the previous week, and teach additional Tenderfoot knots with a clear demonstration of their use.

b. Use competition, as before, using the temporary Patrols as teams.

c. Patrol Knot-Tying Relay (see index: Games).

Inter-Patrol Quiz on Scout Oath and Law. History and Respect Due The Flag. Simple First Aid. Meaning of Scout Badge and Uniform—20 minutes.

a. Separate the Patrols and see that each Patrol is provided with a Handbook. Give the Patrols ten minutes to study the Candidate Requirements.

b. Call the Patrols together (use Circle Formation) and have a snappy "spell-down" on the requirements they have been studying. In asking questions alternate between the Patrols and have the boys who miss fall out. Eliminate all who fail until only one Patrol has any left.

c. Announce that every boy will be expected to have his Candidate Requirements completed at the second following meeting. Arrange for Patrol meetings at the boys' homes or yours for study and practice during the week.

Games—20 minutes. Play several good action games, using the Patrol groups as teams, such as Steal the Bacon, Pull Him Over (see index: Games).

Closing Ceremonies—15 minutes.

(a) Assembly and repetition of announcements.

(b) Collection of membership applications and fees, if not already done.

The Scout Motto, and a Troop or Scout Yell.

The Personal Contact

During the following week, you will be talking with the boys, individually or in twos, probably at your own home, about the Scout Oath and Law. Deal thoroughly with the more difficult points and let the boys feel the seriousness of becoming Scouts. Make your talks all simple discussions. Try to learn the boys' own conception of the meaning of the Oath and Law. Tell them yours.

Work especially with Patrol Leaders and let them know you expect them to be responsible for the conduct of their own group and their understanding of the Oath and Law.

This is the time to find out intimate things about each boy—you will establish the beginnings of strong friendships based on mutual respect and confidence. These talks are vital, and you will enjoy them immensely. You will be surprised at the readiness with which most boys will discuss their problems of conduct, and a little patient friendliness will draw out the few who are reticent.

Meeting 3

OBJECTS

1. Further work on the Candidate and Tenderfoot Requirements.

2. Final steps in Troop organization.

EQUIPMENT

1. *Handbook for Boys.*

2. Ropes.

3. Adhesive bandages, Scout neckerchief, disinfectant, sterile pad.

4. Flag of the United States of America.

PROGRAM

Assembly—15 minutes.

a. Pledge of Allegiance to The Flag.

b. Practice Scout Drill, adding new formations.

c. Roll Call. Check up to see whether everyone has brought an application blank filled-out and paid the registration fee.

Simple First Aid—15 minutes. Demonstrate use of adhesive bandage ("Band-aid," "Handitape"), for care of simple wound. Show how Scout neckerchief may be used for bandage over dressing.

Patrol Period—20 minutes. Send the Patrols to their corners. Have them pick their leaders, then practice the Tenderfoot Requirements. You and your Assistants should lend a helping hand with the Patrols.

The Scout Law and Good Turn Idea—15 minutes.

a. Have the boys, in chorus, repeat the twelve points of the Scout Law.

b. Go through all or a part of the twelve points asking some boy to explain each in his own words, having the whole Troop vote which explanation is best.

c. Explain briefly but forcefully the Good Turn idea, asking each Scout to keep a record (for himself) of the Good Turns he does during the coming week.

Games—15 minutes. Repeat one of the games already played, and select one or two new ones from the game section of this *Handbook,* such as British Bulldog, Poison.

Closing Ceremonies—10 minutes.

a. Announce when you (or your Assistant) will be "at home" during the week for any boy who is prepared to meet his Candidate Requirements, and that all will be expected to complete them by the next meeting.

b. Close by singing one verse of "America the Beautiful."

Qualifying the Candidates

Be careful to make an exact serious inquiry of each Scout personally of his understanding of the meaning of the Oath and Law. Then examine in the other Candidate Requirements (see Chapter 14).

Meeting 4

OBJECTS
1. Final work on Candidate Requirements.
2. Preparation for Induction Ceremony.

EQUIPMENT

Same as for Meeting 3.

PROGRAM

Assembly—15 minutes.

a. Roll Call.

b. Scout Drill practice. Run through half a dozen signals snappily, followed by drill in the Do This — Do That manner.

Games—15 minutes. Use one or two lively games as suggested for previous meetings.

Knot-tying Review—15 minutes. Make a list of the boys' names, and see that each boy ties all Tenderfoot knots correctly. Your assistant or a visiting Scout can help with this check-up.

Final Check-Up on Candidate Requirements—30 minutes. With the rest of the Troop engaged in games already learned under the direction of one of the Patrol Leaders, take aside each boy who has not already fulfilled his Candidate Requirements and question him further upon any points on which he has seemed weak. Above all, be sure that he has a clear idea of the meaning of the Scout Oath and Law.

Announcements and Closing—15 minutes.

a. If any boys have failed to meet all the Candidate Requirements, ask them to see you immediately after the closing to iron out the difficulties which may prevent them from being inducted into the Troop at the next meeting.

b. Remind the boys to bring their parents and friends to the induction ceremony.

c. Close with the Scout Benediction: "May the Great Master of all Scouts be with us till we meet again."

Seeking Out the "Slower" Boys

In your closing announcements you have asked boys who have not completed their Candidate Requirements to see you. It is well to keep in mind that those very boys are probably the slower and more timid ones, who need Scouting, but who may become discouraged and "drop out." Bolster their morale by seeking them out yourself after the meeting and during the following week. Give them the extra encouragement—the extra help—that will mean so much to them.

Charter Application Completed

Membership applications should be distributed and explained at the first meeting and returned with registration fees at the earliest opportunity, so the Charter Application can be completed and forwarded to the Local Council office as soon as the boys have met the Candidate Requirements. Promptness in doing this will make it possible to have certificates and charter on hand for the formal installation.

The Troop's First Hike

The time between the mailing of the charter application and the induction meeting is an appropriate one for the Troop's first hike.

Make it a day trip to some nearby point of interest with the object of starting the practice of fire building, cooking, tracking and the like (see Chapter 10).

Preparation and *Program* are two essentials for the success of the hike. See to it that the boys know what to bring, how to carry it, what to wear, as well as the time for starting, meeting place, distance, carfare, and the time for arriving home.

Arrange for a couple of games on the out-trip. Then when you arrive at your destination, let this happen:

1. Assign cooking places by Patrols, and clear them.

2. Have boys gather and cut wood, by Patrols.

3. Demonstrate how to lay a fire and arrange cooking materials.

4. Let the boys "go to it" on their Patrol sites. Have them light their fires and cook their first Scout meal. There's a thrill for everyone!

The afternoon's program should consist of Scouting activities—games requiring skills which can be played only out-of-doors (see chapter on Troop Hiking for suggestions).

The possibilities of real Scouting while on a hike are great. Make the best use of your opportunity. Games such as Hare and Hounds, Flag Raiding, or stalking, study of nature, practice in use of knife and axe, are all good hike activities.

If possible, make part of your hike home cross-country for the adventure of exploration.

10. THE TROOP IS INSTALLED WITH PROPER CEREMONY, ATTENDED BY MEMBERSHIP OF THE CHARTERED INSTITUTION AND PARENTS. THE TROOP CHARTER AND SCOUTERS' COMMISSIONS ARE PRESENTED, AND BOY MEMBERS ARE INVESTED AS SCOUTS.

Make this occasion as impressive as possible. A public induction gives the Troop a solid start in the minds of the chartered institution, making it realize that the Scout Troop is a functioning body important in the community. It gives the new Unit the stamp of public approval. It gives the parents, the Troop Committee, and the boys, a realization that Scouting is a serious thing, a Movement with a definite purpose. It cements solidly the cooperation between Troop and Local Council.

Securing the Attendance

A strong personal invitation should be sent to the parents of every boy and to all others who should be present. This invitation should be extended jointly by the chartered institution, the Troop Committee and the Scoutmaster. It should make the importance of the occasion clear, and should be followed up by personal contacts. Either a District or Neighborhood Commissioner or other Scout official will, of course, be on hand to represent the Local Council and to conduct the induction ceremony. Arrangements for this should be made through the office of the Local Council.

The program may include the following features:

1. *Invocation.*

2. *Introductions,* by the head of the institution, of the Institutional Representative, then of the chairman of the Troop Committee, who in turn will introduce the Scoutmaster and Assistant Scoutmasters.

3. *The Installation.* The Council Scouters who have assisted with the organization of the Troop are introduced. One of them, representing the Council, presents the Troop Charter to the head of the chartered institution, with appropriate words on the responsibility involved, and installs the Troop Committee, Scoutmaster, and Assistant Scoutmasters, charging them with their responsibilities as set forth in the National By-Laws, and presenting them with their commissions.

4. The Scoutmaster proceeds with the *Induction Ceremony* for new Scouts. (Plans for simple and effective ceremonies are contained in Tool 14 of this handbook. If the sponsor is a religious body, there are available impressive Church ceremonies.) If desired, another Troop can be asked to stage this ceremony for the charter members of the new Troop. The Scout will receive his certificate or badge, or both, at this time.

5. The Scoutmaster then explains the duties of the Patrol Leaders, and presents to them their badges of office.

6. The Troop Organizer turns the Troop over to the Neighborhood Commissioner for service. This gives an opportunity to indicate the part the Local Council plays.

7. The Scouts may demonstrate a little of their new Scouting skill for the interest of the parents and members of the chartered institution.

8. The Scoutmaster should tell of the Troop's plans, and bespeak the cooperation of the parents and chartered institution in the Troop's work.

9. *Benediction.*

Finally, see to it that the organization and installation of the new Troop is properly reported to the local press, with names of all involved, including organizers, names of new Scouters and names of charter members.

There it is—the logical, orderly way to organize a Scout Troop which will have every chance of doing good Scouting, and of continuing in active existence year after year.

Such a Troop is a real satisfaction to the chartered institution and to the Local Council.

Such a Troop is the answer to the deep-felt, if un-expressed, desire of succeeding generations of boys, and to the prayers of their parents.

You will never do anything more significant in Scouting than the careful organization of a good Scout Troop!

B. TAKING OVER AN OLD TROOP

IT is one thing to start a new Troop, and another, quite different, to take over an old, established Troop.

What will happen depends on a number of different factors:

Are you new to Scouting or have you had previous experience as a Scout, a Patrol Leader or even as a Scouter?

Is the Troop you are to lead known as an exceptionally good Troop, a good Troop, an average Troop—or is there a doubt in someone's mind that it may even be classified as average?

What type of Scoutmaster was the previous leader? Was his leadership extraordinary, good, fair, or was he just tolerated by the boys? Did he make possible hiking and camping? Did he help his leadership by wearing the Scout Uniform? How are the Patrols functioning? How is the boy leadership?

As you see, there are many items to be considered and studied before you begin your leadership in the place left vacant by a retiring or transferring Scoutmaster.

Get Training First

If you are new to Scouting, by all means get a certain amount of training first. Study the official manuals to get a working basis. Then visit, with the advice of the Scout Executive and the District or Neighborhood Commissioner, a couple of *good* Troops that are run along the lines advocated as real Scouting. Talk over Scoutmastership with other Scoutmasters. Sit in at Patrol Leaders' Council meetings. Take part in a Troop hike if you can make it. Go through a Local Council training course if one is available at the time.

But what about the Troop in the meantime?

The Troop will not suffer, even if you have to postpone its meetings a couple of weeks. As long as the boys know that something will happen, they will be there when you call them.

Meet with the Troop Leaders

You have already, of course, met with the Troop Committee and discussed with it the Troop and its membership, and secured an estimate of the previous leadership. Now the time comes to have a conference with the Troop's boy leaders and Assistant Scoutmasters, if any.

Make it a friendly conclave. Get the Patrol Leaders at their ease. Show them your interest in their activities and let them feel your trust in them. Get them to tell of their activities, of their boys, of the grand experiences they have had in the Troop. Learn something about the Troop's traditions, its ways of doing things, its meetings and outdoor adventures. But don't attempt to "pump" the boys, or they may be less free with the information they volunteer.

Then settle down to discuss the glorious future of the Troop in general, and the next Troop meeting (your first with the boys) in particular. Plan it well, decide upon activities and assign leadership. Finally, dismiss the leaders wth a Scout Handclasp and a request for their cooperation: "I depend upon *you* to make *our* Troop the finest Troop possible."

Before Your First Meeting

In the interim, before the meeting, make a thorough study of the Troop records and the Troop roster. Study the attendance and the advancement, and try to memorize as many names as possible. You will find it effective to be able to say: "Oh, are *you* Bobby Jones? It certainly is wonderful that we have a Life Scout in the Troop!"

Then call the meeting, preferably by sending a personally signed postcard to each boy.

Your First Meeting

If well planned with the Patrol Leaders in advance, your first meeting should be a success. It will be well to have present a member of the Troop Committee, with whom the boys are familiar, or a Local Council representative to introduce you officially as the new Scoutmaster. If this is not feasible, you will have to introduce yourself. In any event, you should use a part of the program to tell your boys of your enthusiasm and interest in the Troop, of all the good things you have been told about them, and of your hopes for a great future for the Troop, which will be assured through the combined efforts of everyone.

After the meeting, make a special attempt to meet the boys separately for short friendly chats.

Study the Troop

As you become familiar with the boys and with the leaders, you will be able to chart the future course of the Troop. You will discover the efficiency—or lack of it—of the leadership, and will learn to what extent the Patrol Method has been used. If the Troop organization is strong, you will naturally make every effort to further strengthen it. If, on the other hand, the Patrols are only "sham" Patrols with figurehead leaders, you will set about to reorganize the Troop.

But go slow, so as not to antagonize the present leaders or the boys. Take up the matter of reorganization at a Patrol Leaders' Council, and either secure the Patrol Leaders' promise to improve their Patrols and their own leadership, or their cooperation in undertaking the reorganization (see Chapter 2).

The Program of the Troop

The program of the Troop should be made a special consideration at Patrol Leaders' Council discussions. There may be many remarks such as "That's how we do it in Troop 1" that should be heeded. On the other hand, do not follow slavishly the previous procedure of the Troop. Certain features may be a success under one type of leader, but not under another. Anyway, the boys will expect new things from a new leader. Set up objectives to reach and decide upon a long-span program for the Troop.

"A Scout Is Loyal"

As you gain the confidence of the boys they may start to speak unguardedly to you of their old Scoutmaster. This will become the greatest test of your tact and diplomacy.

The previous Scoutmaster may have been good, yet may have had human frailties or certain peculiar characteristics which the boys may like to recall and elaborate upon for your edification. Make them realize from the start that you do not stand for gossip. Make them understand the unfairness of attempting to ridicule a man who gave of his time and his efforts to serve them. Make them see that they owe loyalty to their old leader.

On the other hand, the previous leader may have been exceptional and beloved by every boy in the Troop. You may feel humbled at times—maybe even a bit jealous—because of their frequent mention of their old Scoutmaster, and their continued tendency to idolize him. This is perfectly natural. But by all means, do not let the boys sense this. Turn their hero-worship into an asset to the Troop. There may be many instances in the beginning when a tense situation may be straightened out with a soft spoken: "Do you really think Mr. So-and-So would have been proud of you for having done this and that?" Eventually, as you grow in your boys' estimation there will be fewer and fewer references to their old leader.

Then it may be *you* who may bring up his name from time to time, and thus add his remote influence for character-building and citizen-training to your own, and make both vital in the lives of your Scouts.

CHARTER AND REGISTRATION

UNTIL A TROOP is duly chartered and its leaders commissioned by the Boy Scouts of America, it is not a Scout Troop. Similarly, a boy is not a Scout until he is registered (through the Local Council) with the National Council.

Importance of Registration

In the earliest days of Scouting in the United States, no registration system was in effect. Reports of the Movement's progress were based on estimates. Any boy in anything that looked like a Scout uniform could claim himself a Scout and set out on exploits which were often damaging to the good repute of Scouting.

It was soon found that if Scouting were to prosper as a character-building Movement, it had to talk *facts* and not estimates; it had to safeguard itself against interlopers.

The registration system came into being. This has made possible business-like administration by establishing definitely who is a member, and how many are members of the Boy Scouts of America. It has made possible the protection of the Scout Uniform by making certain that only registered members can secure it. It has put into practice one of the principles of Scouting—that a Scout is self-reliant—by giving each member an opportunity to share in the operation and extension costs of his own Movement.

CHARTERING A NEW TROOP

The chartering of a new Troop involves
1. Individual application of each adult member.
2. Individual application of each boy member.
3. Application for Troop Charter.
4. Payment of the registration fees of men and boys.

Adult Applications

Each adult member of the Troop—members of the Troop Committee, Scoutmaster, Explorer Advisor and Assistant Scoutmasters—must submit an *Application for Adult Registration* (Form No. 6115) at the time the application for Charter is submitted.

On this application, the new member gives certain vital details about himself, accepts the Scout Oath and Law, and agrees to be guided by the Constitution and By-Laws of both the National and Local Councils. He further subscribes to the Declaration of Religious Principle of the Boy Scouts of America:

> "The Boy Scouts of America maintains that no boy can grow into the best kind of citizenship without recognizing his obligation to God. In the first part of the Boy Scout's Oath or Promise, the boy declares 'On my honor I will do my best to do my duty to God and my country, and to obey the Scout Law.' The recognition of God as the ruling and leading power in the universe, and the grateful acknowledgment of His favors and blessings, are necessary to the best type of citizenship, and are wholesome things in the education of the growing boy. No matter what the boy may be—Catholic or Protestant or Jew—this fundamental need of good citizenship should be kept before him. The Boy Scouts of America therefore recognizes the religious element in the training of the boy, but it is absolutely nonsectarian in its attitude toward that religious training. Its policy is that the organization or institution with which the Boy Scout is connected shall give definite attention to his religious life.
>
> "Only persons willing to subscribe to this declaration of principle shall be entitled to certificates of leadership in carrying out the Boy Scout Program." (National Constitution, Article IV, Section 1)

Boy Applications

Each boy fills out an *Application to Become a Boy Scout* (Form No. 4405) if he is 11, 12 or 13, or an *Application for Explorer Membership* (No. 4203) if he is 14, 15, 16 or 17. Some Councils use different forms.

The application must contain the signature of parent or guardian, indicating his or her willingness and desire that the boy become a member of the Boy Scouts of America, and agreeing to assist him in observing the rules of Scouting. The parent or guardian also waives any claim against the Boy Scouts of America or its leaders for "any and all causes which may arise in connection with the activities of the above organization."

Troop Charter Application

The application for the establishment of a Troop is made on *Application for Troop Charter* (Form No.

6184). The front of it is designed for adult membership, the back for the boy members. It is important for the quick chartering of the Troop and registration of its members that all information requested be *complete* and *legible:*

APPLICATION OF SPONSORING INSTITUTION — This section gives the name and address of the sponsoring institution, and is signed by an officer authorized by the institution.

ACTION OF THE TROOP COMMITTEE—This is signed by the Chairman of the Troop Committee, indicating that the Committee has approved all applications submitted and recommends the men named as Scoutmaster and Assistants.

INDIVIDUAL APPLICATION OF TROOP OFFICIALS—The personal signatures are required here of all Troop officials. Space is provided for the signatures of the Chairman of the Troop Committee, the Institutional Representative, members of the Troop Committee, Scoutmaster, Assistant Scoutmasters and Explorer Advisor. Each man must be 21 years of age or older (Assistant Scoutmaster 18 years or older) and be American citizens or have first papers. Names should be written plainly so that Certificates can be issued with *names spelled correctly.* Under Status column on the form, indicate new men by "N" and former Scouters returning as "SR."

ROSTERS OF BOY SCOUT AND EXPLORER MEMBERSHIP — The Scoutmaster completes the Roster side of the application, providing all information asked on each boy—name, address, age, rank, etc. A minimum of five boys is required to register a Troop.

Registration Fees

The share which each boy and man pays toward the administration and growth of our Movement through the registration system amounts to 50 cents yearly for a Scout, $1.00 yearly for a Scouter, such as Scoutmaster, Assistant Scoutmaster or Troop Committeeman. These FEES *MUST* ACCOMPANY THE APPLICATION, and checks for fees be made payable to the Local Council.

BOYS' LIFE Subscriptions

If the Troop desires to make BOYS' LIFE available to its member, the best time to do it is at the time of the Charter application. In that case, the subscription order blank attached to the application form should be filled out.

Submitting the Application

When the Charter application has been filled out, it is forwarded to the Local Council Office with the fees.

If the application is filled out *correctly*, it will promptly be submitted to the National Office, and the Charter and the registration cards can be prepared immediately.

Additional Boy Registrations

New boys are registered when they have met their Tenderfoot requirements. Each boy fills out the *Application to Become a Boy Scout* or an *Application for Explorer Membership*, secures the signature to the application of his parent or guardian, and pays his registration fee.

The individual application is sent to the Local Council Office, accompanied by the application form for *Additional Enrollment* (Cat. No. 6102) and the required fee.

The fee to be paid for the boy depends upon the number of months left until the Troop Charter expires, according to the schedule printed on the form.

It is strongly recommended that a new boy on joining pay the complete fee of 50c. The proportionate fee only will be sent to the Local Council Office with his registration, while the remainder will be placed in the Troop's revolving fund, as suggested in Tool 5.

Transfer Boy Scout to Explorer within Troop

When a Boy Scout becomes fourteen—after the Troop is registered, he is automatically recognized as an Explorer in the Troop. This change of status should be reported immediately to the Local Council on a special transfer form (Cat. No. 6196) so that a registration certificate as an Explorer may be issued. No additional registration fee is required.

Transfer to Another Unit

If a Scout leaves your Troop by reason of moving to another town, or to join a separate Explorer Unit, you should provide him with an *Application for Registration Transfer* (Form Cat. No. 6100) properly filled out, to make it easy for him to join his new Unit.

Similarly, when a Scout comes to your Troop from another Troop, or when a Cub Scout graduates into your Troop, he should bring with him his transfer blank, so that he can quickly get credit for his previous experiences in Scouting.

The transfer blank is sent to the Local Council Office with the *Additional Enrollment* blank, and with the necessary proportionate fee. See schedule on preceding page.

Dropped Scouts Reregistering

A former Scout who wants to get back into a Troop will fill in a new application (Boy Scout or Explorer) and pay his registration fee. He is registered on the *Additional Enrollment* form with the notation SR (Separated-Reregistered).

His proportionate fee to be sent to the Local Council is figured on the same basis as for a transferred Scout.

Additional Adult Registrations

The same procedure holds true for adults as described for boys—whether new Scouters joining, or old Scouters transferring or reregistering—with the exception that the adult form, *Application for Adult Registration,* is used, and the pro-rated fee is twice that for boys.

RE-CHARTERING AN OLD TROOP

A successful Troop will want to go on serving boys year in and year out. To do this, it needs to extend its Charter for another year each time its previous Charter expires.

This re-chartering should never be permitted to be simply a matter of getting signatures on an application blank and paying the fees—it should be an important event in the Troop's yearly life. To accomplish this, there should be a Charter Review Meeting between Troop Committee, Troop leaders, representatives of the Institution and the Local Council. At this meeting past operation will be reviewed, on the basis of the *Annual Report of Troop Committee* (Form Cat. No. 6135) made up in advance, and presented by the Chairman. Future plans for the Troop will be discussed, and the *Application for A Troop Charter* will be filled in as described previously.

A dignified Charter Presentation should follow.

PATROL LEADERS' TRAINING

THE MONTHLY PLANNING MEETING of your Patrol Leaders' Council can serve as the start for getting the Patrol Leaders' training under way. Initiate it here, then follow through at such times and places as are determined by the group. Make reading assignments ahead of time. Give the Senior Patrol Leader or a Junior Assistant Scoutmaster the job of gathering needed equipment.

Start with the subject of greatest importance to your leaders. Perhaps it's meetings—or maybe it's hiking—then pick up the other subjects as you go along. It is not necessary to follow the order laid out here.

Adopt as your guide in these training experiences the slogan KISMIF—*Keep It Simple, Make It Fun.* The big thing is to make these experiences enjoyable for your Junior Leaders—with lots of ACTION, and plenty of LEARNING BY DOING.

PATROL SPIRIT AND PATROL ORGANIZATION

PRELIMINARY READING ASSIGNMENTS:

For Scoutmaster and adult leaders: *Handbook for Scoutmasters,* Chapters 1, 2 and 4.

For Patrol Leaders: *Handbook for Patrol Leaders,* Chapters II and IV (chapter and page references are for 1950 edition and later printings).

NEEDED MATERIAL:

Paper and pencils. Copy of *Patrol Record Book.* One three-foot length of rope for each participant. Several short lengths of rope. String.

PROGRAM:

(a) *Simple Opening Ceremony.* Recitation of the Second Point of the Scout Law in full. Reading by Senior

Patrol Leader of "A Patrol Leader's Creed" (HPL, Chapter I, p. 7).

(b) *Purpose of Training and Establishing Patrol.* Tell briefly what you expect to accomplish. Declare the Patrol officially formed with you as its Patrol Leader, the Senior Patrol Leader as Assistant Patrol Leader, Assistant Scoutmasters and Junior Assistants as special instructors, judges in contest, leaders of games and handicraft activities, and the boy leaders as the members of the Patrol.

(c) *Make Notebooks.* Fold letter-head sized sheets in half, or use a cheap composition book for each member in which he can take notes. Insist that a sufficient amount of notes be taken by all boy leaders.

(d) *Discussion of Patrol Name.* The why and how of selecting a name that will have a definite significance to the Patrol. Talk over various names. Make a preliminary selection of a few, then put them to popular vote. Decide upon the Patrol Cry and Call to fit the name.

(e) *Call and Yell Contest.* Have each pair of buddies get up a rousing Patrol call and develop a short yell, incorporating the Patrol name. Vote for best yell.

(f) *Patrol Flag Contest.* Using the same buddies, have teams prepare a rough sketch of a flag for the Patrol. The idea counts more than artistic execution. Hold short Art Gallery session, and vote for best design to be made into permanent flag.

(g) *Instruction Games,* such as Signal Winks, Buddy Knotting, Buddy Slings, Scout Law Acting. Use buddy teams throughout. Winners give Patrol Call.

(h) *Election* of members to fill the jobs of Patrol Treasurer, Scribe, Quartermaster, Hikemaster, Grubmaster, Cheermaster (HPL, Chapter IV). In case of a large group, turn a single job over to a buddy team to handle. Rotate these jobs monthly to give each boy a chance.

(i) *Work Session.* With the "job-holders" chosen, get them busy right away. Have a short session to get them started on their responsibilities—the Treasurer developing a budget, the Scribe filling in pages of the *Patrol Record Book;* the Hikemaster working out a route to a camp site; the Grubmaster making up a Patrol menu; the Cheermaster producing a list of songs popular with the Patrol members.

(j) *Handicraft Project.* Have each boy draw from a hat the name of a Tenderfoot knot and provide him with the necessary pieces of rope to produce the knot for a knot-board. Main project is to whip rope ends, and the finished knots to be turned over to volunteering buddy team for mounting.

(k) *Recreational Games.* Two or three, chosen from HPL, Chapter X, such as Peanut Race, Oratory, Laughing Handkerchief, or Do This—Do That. If time is short, run game only until the Scouts have caught on to the rules, then shift to another. The object should always be to give the boy leaders a variety of program material for their Patrol meetings, rather than to play each game to its completion.

(l) *Simple Closing Ceremony.* Singing of Taps.

AFTER MEETING:

Before dismissing the Training Patrol, give a short resumé of the ground covered. Tell the leaders to make use of the material in their next Patrol meetings, and ask each Patrol Leader to make a short talk on how the material worked out at next training meeting.

Follow this procedure after all future training meetings.

PATROL MEETINGS

PRELIMINARY READING ASSIGNMENTS:

For Scoutmaster and adult Leaders: *Handbook for Scoutmasters,* Chapters 6 and 7.

For Patrol Leaders: *Handbook for Patrol Leaders,* Chapter V.

NEEDED MATERIAL:

Paper and pencils.
Copy of *Patrol Record Book.*
Materials for neckerchief slides.
Material as required for games selected.

PROGRAM:

(a) *Opening Ceremony.* Divide Patrol up into buddies. Have four teams in turn put on one of the opening ceremonies from HPL, Chapter V. Take a quick vote for most effective ceremony, the best to be used at future meetings.

(b) *Business Period.* Treasurer collects "dues," Scribe makes attendance notations in his *Patrol Record Book,* then reads the minutes of previous meeting from Patrol

Log Book. Corrections are made if necessary, a motion is made and seconded to have minutes adopted, and proper vote is taken. (This procedure should be followed at all Training Meetings.) Following this, the different Patrol jobs are rotated to next boys in line, as decided at First Training Meeting (h). Brief report from each Patrol Leader of his use of items learned at last training meeting in his Patrol.

(c) *Scoutcraft Instruction* in the form of PROJECTS. Have Assistant Scoutmasters and Junior Assistants in turn stage the four first aid projects: 1. Arterial Bleeding of forearm, 2. Sprained ankle, 3. Broken arm, 4. Carbon monoxide suffocation. In each instance, make use of a buddy team while the rest watch. After each project discuss first aid method used.

(d) *Work Period.* Brief discussion of work projects that may be undertaken by a Patrol during its meetings such as making of camping equipment, decorating Den, various handicraft items, repairing toys as Good Turn, and so on (HPL, Chapter IX). Have each member list the items discussed in his notebook. As a specific project, each boy makes a neckerchief slide (have a variety of materials on hand: leather scrap, bone, horn, thin rope, etc.).

(e) *Scoutcraft Games.* Use a couple of games from HSM, Game Section, such as Object Hunt, Kim's Game, The Peddler, Compass Facing with each member of the Training Patrol on his own, or divide the Patrol into two teams, and try Knot Hoop Relay, Newspaper Study, Height Judging (of objects in the room).

(f) *Planning.* Make a quick analysis of the features of a Patrol Meeting as described in the HPL, Chapter V, indicating at the same time how closely the Training Meeting covers the suggestions given there (although rearranged) for Ceremony, Checking, Coaching, Projects, Plans, Play. Then go through the details of an effective Planning Period: Making plans for future meetings, hikes, camps, equipment making, money earning, Good Turns, special stunts for Troop get-togethers.

(g) *Recreation.* 1. *Games,* chosen from HSM: Indian Hand Wrestling, Indian Leg Wrestling, Hand Slap, Slap Jack. If time is short, run game, as indicated in First Training Meeting, only until the Scouts have learned its features, then shift to another. 2. *Tall Story Contest.*

3. *A couple of yells* from HPL, Chapter X.

(h) *Closing Ceremony.* Try a couple of the closing ceremonies from HPL, then vote for one to be used at future sessions.

PATROL HIKES I

PRELIMINARY READING ASSIGNMENTS:

For Scoutmaster and adult leaders: *Handbook for Scoutmasters,* Chapters 7 and 9.

For Patrol Leaders: *Handbook for Patrol Leaders,* Chapter VI.

NEEDED MATERIAL:

Paper and Pencils.

Patrol Record Book.

Tin cans, pieces of wire, hammer, large nail, copper rivets.

Map.

If possible: Hiking equipment for demonstration.

PROGRAM:

(a) *Opening Ceremony.* Senior Patrol Leader stages ceremony which was chosen favorite at the Second Training Meeting.

(b) *Business Period* — short, but sweet (see Second Training Meeting).

(c) *Hike Instruction.* Short discussion on "Patrol Hikes," including leadership requirements, hiking technique, based upon HPL, Chapter VI. Explain difference between "Sandwich Hikes" and "Chop Hikes," and announce that forthcoming Leaders' Hike will be a Chop Hike. If possible, have a demonstration of hiking equipment.

(d) *Hike Planning.* Divide the Patrol up into four groups, and give each group the responsibility for developing the details of one of the following items in preparation for the hike.

1. *Route*—(Hikemaster in charge). Plan an appropriate route on a map of the local territory. 2. *Equipment* (Quartermaster in charge). Prepare list of essential equipment to take along. 3. *Commissary* (Grubmaster in charge). Suggest menu and food list. 4. *Activities* (Assistant Patrol Leader in charge). Kind of hike, activities

on out-trip, at the hike destination and on the return journey. After the plans have been completed, they are discussed by the whole Patrol, until final adoption. Distribute leadership, decide upon meeting place and time, and equipment and grub to be brought by each Scout.

(e) *Instruction Game.* "Uncle Quizzie." Have an Assistant Scoutmaster develop about thirty questions on outdoor Scouting, such as fire-building, cooking, knife and axe, compass, mapping, signaling. Divide group into two teams, and run game like a radio quizz, with alternating boys of alternating teams answering questions put to them. Each correct answer means 100 for the team, partly correct answer a proportionate amount of points. Team with most points at end of game is winner.

(f) *Work Period.* Making of simple cooking pots from No. 10 tin cans. Have such a pot ready to show how it is to be done.

(g) *Recreation.* 1. *Games* — one or two chosen from HPL, such as Animal Hunt, Hand Wrestling, Cock Fight. (If games planned for previous meetings have not all been used, make use of them now.) 2. *Singing*—Go through the Song Book, *Camp Songs 'n' Things,* pick out and rehearse a couple of songs suitable for the open road.

(h) *Closing Ceremony.* Use closing ceremony voted most popular at previous Training Meeting.

PATROL HIKES II: GREEN BAR TRAINING HIKE

NEEDED MATERIAL:

As decided on at Patrol Hikes I Session.

PROGRAM:

(a) *Assembly.* Quartermaster and Grubmaster check equipment and grub to insure that everything is in readiness.

(b) *Outbound Journey.* 1. *Hiking Technique:* Follow suggestions in the HPL and HSM in regard to proper methods of hiking, and correct Patrol hike formation on highways. 2. *Activities.* Start activities as soon as possible —whether observation games, nature study or whatever was decided at Training Meeting. Give the different boys a chance to lead the Patrol from time to time.

(c) *At Destination.* Have an Assistant Scoutmaster or a Junior Assistant put on a quick demonstration of the subject of the hike, then get the boys to work on axemanship, fire-building, cooking—or mapping or signaling—according to the program for the day. Cooking should be done on a Patrol basis. Also run a couple of *Instruction Games,* such as Signal Relay, the Leaking Packsack, String Burning, Height Judging, Leaf Matching (HSM, see Games Index). *Rest Period Recreation Games:* One or two of the following: Capture the Flag, Skin the Snake, Antelope Race, Border Scouting (HSM). Clean-up.

(d) *Return Journey* — Do not attempt any specially planned activity during this, although a game such as Far and Near (HSM) may be tried. Make use of the hike songs rehearsed during training meeting. Dismiss at appropriate spot.

PATROL ADVANCEMENT

PRELIMINARY READING ASSIGNMENTS:

For Scoutmaster and adult leaders: *Handbook for Scoutmasters,* Chapters 7, 15 and Tool 20.

For Patrol Leaders: *Handbook for Patrol Leaders,* Chapter VIII.

NEEDED MATERIAL:

Paper and pencils.
Patrol Record Book.
Buzzers or flashlights.
Knives and sticks. Carborundum stone.
Game material as required.

PROGRAM:

(a) *Opening Ceremony.* Senior Patrol Leader stages ceremony which he considers his favorite of those tried at the Second Training Meeting.

(b) *Business Period* — as usual: short! (see Second Training Meeting).

(c) *Discussion. "Scoutcraft Advancement in the Patrol"* —led by Assistant Patrol Leader based upon HPL, Chapter VIII (specifically the opening pages), and HSM, Chapter XV. Why advancement? What constitutes normal advancement? Why is it important that the Patrol Leader is ahead of the fellows in his Patrol? How does hiking and camping make advancement possible?

(d) *Scoutcraft Instruction. Signaling.* Divide group into

four teams. Place one team in each corner of room. Teams diagonally opposed work together, sending and receiving complete messages, using flashlights or buzzers. The messages should have been developed in advance by an Assistant or Junior Assistant Scoutmaster.

(e) *Work Period.* Knife-craft project: paper knife. Each Scout uses his own knife (or one he has borrowed). Have a short demonstration of the proper way of sharpening a knife, staged by the Quartermaster, then have each boy sharpen his own. Sticks are distributed (¾ to 1 inch in diameter and 8-10 inches long) and paper knives are carved. Time limit: 10 minutes.

(f) *Instruction Games.* Use a couple of games from HSM. For further practice in signaling and knot-tying, try Knot Signals, for compass work, Compass Facing; for safety, Safety First; for observation, Haunted House or Kim's Game. (See Games index)

(g) *Planning.* Make a quick review of the meeting up to this point, pointing out how many different Scout Requirements it has been possible to introduce through games and projects. Discuss an effective plan for advancement in the Patrol, making use of buddy teams.

(h) *Recreation.* 1. *Dramatics.* In charge of Cheermaster. Cut out suitable jokes from *Think and Grin,* Boy's Life, and distribute them to buddy teams for snappy dramatization. 2. *Singing.* Each buddy team to introduce a solo-and-chorus song, the buddies to sing the solo part, then lead the whole Patrol in the chorus. For suggestions, study *Songs Scouts Sing.* 3. *Story* told by the leader of the Training Patrol, that is, the Scoutmaster.

(i) *Closing Ceremony.* Senior Patrol Leader puts on one of the ceremonies, already tried, or a new one especially developed for the occasion.

PATROL FEATURES

PRELIMINARY READING ASSIGNMENTS:

For Scoutmasters and adult leaders: *Handbook for Scoutmasters,* Chapters 2, 7 and Tools 4, 14, 15, 16 and 17.

For Patrol Leaders: *Handbook for Patrol Leaders,* Chapters II, IX and X.

NEEDED MATERIAL:

Paper and pencils.

Patrol Record Book.

Loose-leaf "log book" from 5-&-10.

Tree leaves, a few candles, white paper.

Game material as required.

PROGRAM:

(a) *Opening Ceremony.* Senior Patrol Leader leads the Patrol's favorite among those attempted previously.

(b) *Business Period.* Usual procedure (see Second Training Meeting).

(c) *Informal Instruction Game. Observation.* Have a visitor drop in for a moment and interrupt business proceedings, then disappear. When business is finished, divide into buddy teams and ask for report of appearance of visitor. Have visitor re-enter for check. Or, instead, try Object Hunt (HSM).

(d) *Discussion.* "*Patrol Features That Build Patrol Spirit,*" based upon HPL, Chapter II. What place do special features and activities have in the life of the Patrol? How can they be worked into the Patrol program? How can the boys be interested in them? Which to choose first? What about flag, den, log book, handicraft, yells, songs, Patrol signatures, camping outfit?

(e) *Work Period.* 1. Demonstrate how to make smoke prints of leaves (HPL). Have each boy make smoke print. 2. Distribute paper to buddy teams, each team to fill a sheet or two with *illustrated* report of the Training Hike. Best report wins prize of the evening: two candy bars.

(f) *Fun Games.* 1. *Buzz-Buzz* or *Tractor* from *Handbook for Boys.* 2. *Indian Hand Wrestling* or *Hand Slap* from HSM. If time is short, run game only until the boy leaders have learned it, then shift to another.

(g) *Recreation:* 1. *Yells* from HPL. each buddy team to pick its own and modify it to suit it. 2. *Patrol Song.* Decide upon appropriate, popular tune and give the buddy teams five minutes to make simple words for it, then sing it. Best team becomes the Patrol's "Official Warblers." 3. *Scoutmaster's Minute,* based upon one point of the Scout Law.

(h) *Closing.* Form circle, all arms lifted high. Lower arms slowly while singing Taps. Scoutmaster then says: "Be Prepared!" And the rest answer in unison: "We are prepared!"

PATROL CAMPING
AND PATROL LIVING

PRELIMINARY READING ASSIGNMENTS:

For Scoutmasters and adult leaders: *Handbook for Scoutmasters*, Chapters 7 and 10.

For Patrol Leaders: *Handbook for Patrol Leaders*, Chapter VII; also Chapters I, III, XI and XII.

NEEDED MATERIAL:

Paper and pencils.
Patrol Record Book.
Camp equipment and pack.
Material as required for games selected.

PROGRAM:

(a) *Opening Ceremony.* Senior Patrol Leader stages the Patrol's favorite ceremony, or one not previously used, developed by him in cooperation with an Assistant Scoutmaster.

(b) *Business Period.* Usual short session (see Second Training Meeting). Review of notebooks kept by boys participating in training, with special comment on the best by the Scoutmaster.

(c) *Instruction Game.* "Pete Tenderfoot's Pack." Assistant Scoutmaster shows pack filled to the brim, empties it on the floor, then repacks it, describing quickly the various items he puts in. Each Scout makes list from memory under these three headings: 1. What necessary equipment did Pete have in his Pack? 2. What unnecessary equipment had Pete included? 3. Which important camp equipment had he forgotten to pack? When lists are completed, make rapid check and decide on winner of this memory game?

(d) *Discussion. Start discussion of "Patrol Camping"* by going over lists just produced, agree upon necessary equipment, then continue, covering such items as: Why is Patrol camping important? How much hike training is necessary before first Patrol camp is undertaken? What about the program of the Patrol Camp? Cooking? Health and safety? Leadership responsibility?

(e) *Camp Planning.* Divide Patrol into two groups, to fit organization described in HPL, for work prior to overnight camp and work in camp. Then get to work planning for training camp.

1. *Consents and Program* (Patrol Leader, Scribe): Develop suitable form for getting parents' consent for boys' participation in Patrol camp. Make outline program for camp. 2. *Equipment* (Quartermaster, Cheermaster): Break down the equipment list already developed into two divisions, covering Tenting and Cooking, then decide upon items for which various Patrol members will be responsible. 3. *Site, Travel, Collecting of Camp Fees* (Treasurer, Hikemaster): Decide upon camp site, method of getting there, and after consultation with Grubmaster, work out amount to be paid by each participant. 4. *Food* (Grubmaster, Assistant Patrol Leader): Make menu for camp, based upon samples in HPL. Develop food list and estimate cost. After all plans have been completed they are presented to the whole Patrol for discussion, correction (if necessary) and adoption.

(f) *Fun Games.* Two or three from HPL, such as Peanut Race, Leg Wrestling, Oratory and Dog Collar Tug-O-War. Rather than playing one only in its entirety, try several games. When one has been learned by the boy leaders shift to the next.

(g) *Recreation.* 1. *Singing* of a couple of appropriate camp fire songs. 2. *Round Robin Story.* One boy starts a dramatic adventure story introducing hero and villain, after one minute, he is interrupted, and the next boy takes over, starting where former boy left off, even if in middle of sentence and so on, until every boy has taken part. 3. *Scoutmaster's Minute,* based upon one point of the Scout Law.

(h) *Closing Ceremony.* Under leadership of Senior Patrol Leader, group comes to salute and recites Scout Law. This is followed immediately by usual closing ceremony.

PATROL CAMPING II:
THE GREEN BAR TRAINING CAMP

NEEDED MATERIAL:

As decided at Patrol Camping I Session.

PROGRAM:

First Day:

(a) *Assembly.* Quartermaster and Grubmaster distribute equipment and food stuff to be carried, and make a quick check of the items which boys were to bring.

(b) *Outbound Journey.* Trip to camp site, as arranged for by Treasurer and Hikemaster.

(c) *Camp Making.* Upon arrival, form "duffel line." Look over site for best location of tents, kitchen, latrine, etc., then make camp, following plan described in HPL, using Tenting and Cooking crews. When camp is completed, make thorough inspection, covering points in HSM, page 207.

(d) *Evening Activities.* 1. *Supper*, eaten in family style. 2. *Game Period.* Use Tag, Spud or Capture the Flag (HSM, See Games Index). Following the games, the 3. *Camp Fire* is lighted, and an appropriate program put on (see page 275), under the leadership of the Cheermaster or the Senior Patrol Leader, with each Patrol Leader contributing a song, a stunt or a game. At the end of the program, the Scoutmaster takes over for a short talk on "Patrol Living," covering the highlights of Chapters I, III, XI and XII of HPL, especially emphasizing the Patrol Leader's loyalty to his Patrol members, and the Patrol's loyalty and helpfulness to the Troop and the community. The Scoutmaster finishes by asking the Patrol Leaders if they are ready to reaffirm their Leader's Promise now that they have received the leader's training. The Troop flag is brought into the camp fire circle, and the boy leaders pledge themselves to the *Patrol Leader's Promise*, reciting it after the Senior Patrol Leader. This is followed immediately by Taps. *It is of greatest importance to the success of this whole leaders' training that this last period be of great dignity and sincerity.* It is the challenge to the Patrol Leaders and the keynote of the Troop's future work.

Second Day:

(e) *Morning and Noon Activities:* 1. *Breakfast*, prepared by a group different from the one that cooked the evening meal. Here again, the meal is cooked as a Patrol meal and served family style. Clean-up of camp is followed by 2. *Scoutcraft Activities*, such as Signal Relay, Robbed Camp, Bombing the Camp, Water Boiling, Nature "Scavenger" Hunt, or a Treasure Hunt. 3. *Noon Meal* is prepared on Patrol basis, with responsibilities for cooking again shifted. After clean-up, a 4. short *Rest Period* is decreed.

(f) *Breaking Camp* follows closely the procedure described in the HPL, the Cooking Crew of the previous day now doing the work of the Tenting Crew and vice versa, to give the participants the opportunity to handle all of the equipment. After the packing is done, and the packs have been arranged in the familiar duffel-line, a thorough inspection of the campsite is made—one group inspecting kitchen site, the other tent site, then changing over to discover during a second inspection what was overlooked during the first.

(g) *Return Journey*. As arranged for by Hikemaster and Treasurer working together. Discussion on way home of good and weak points of experience. Back in town, the Quartermaster checks in the camping equipment. Then general dismissal.

The End and the Beginning

And thus, this series of training experiences comes to an end, with your boy leaders more than ever realizing their responsibilities and more than ever capable of carrying them through.

Remember that the real reason for this training is to give the Junior Leaders ideas and skills to use in their Patrols and in their Troop jobs. Think in terms of the Patrol at all stages of the game.

But with these training experiences completed, the training of the Troop's boy leaders is not yet finished. On the contrary! This is *a continuous job, never completed.*

Other Junior Leader Training Events

In addition to the type of training presented above, which is carried on within the Troop, encourage all of your junior leaders to take part in special training events conducted for them by the Local Council. Many Councils offer Junior Leaders' Conferences and Scoutcraft Events which will greatly strengthen their leadership ability and their interest in Scouting. Find out, through your Commissioner, if your District or Council has scheduled any such inter-Troop training activities.

NOTE: There are excellent filmstrips aimed at assisting you in training your Junior Leaders. Your Council Office will be able to give you the information regarding them and their use.

PATROL RECOGNITION

SO MANY SCOUTMASTERS have found continuous friendly competition between the Patrols valuable, that it might be considered an essential feature of a successful Troop. The only justification for the use of a recognition plan, however, is to stimulate and unify each Patrol through the recognition of Patrol achievements in which the boys work together for *its* glory, while advancing *themselves* in Scoutcraft and Scout Spirit.

Point System

The principle of a point system of recognition is that points are awarded to the Patrols on the basis of a predetermined scale, for such items as attendance, advancement, games and contests, and special features. The points should be developed in such a way that *every* Patrol has a chance.

The duration of a point system should not be too long. If it is permitted to drag, the Patrols which fall behind are apt to feel themselves hopelessly outdistanced and become discouraged. The interest in such competitions should be renewed by finishing one and starting another. This may be done at the end of a definite length of time (three months, for example) or when one Patrol has earned a certain number of points.

Working Out the Points

Since the success of any point system depends upon the whole-hearted acceptance of it by the Patrols, it is obvious that the set-up must be discussed at a meeting of the Patrol Leaders' Council. To save time, have some schedule prepared ahead by a Junior leader, but leave it up to the Patrol Leaders to make the decisions and accept the scheme.

No one system of points would be equally well adapted to all Troops. Each Troop should consider its own needs in working out its schedule. The arrangement of points given below is simply a sample to serve as a guide:

ATTENDANCE AT TROOP ACTIVITIES

Troop Meeting—Entire Patrol Present in correct Uniform.... 100 Points
(When less than 100% of the Patrol is present in Uniform, award a proportionate number of points. When a Scout who owns a Uniform is present but not in Uniform, count him as only ½-Scout present. When a Scout is absent but has reported, before the meeting opens, a satisfactory reason for his absence, count him as ½-Scout present.)

Troop Hike (same scale as above)........................ 200 Points

ATTENDANCE AT PATROL ACTIVITIES

Patrol Meeting—(It is not considered a Patrol Meeting unless at least 2/3 of the Scouts are present.) Entire Patrol present in Scout Uniform...... .... 100 Points
(Same rules as above)

Patrol Hike (same scale as above)...................... 200 Points

DUES

Paid in full on time................................. .... 50 Points

ADVANCEMENT—Count advancement in rank only, not the meeting of the individual Requirements.

Second Class .... 100 Points
First Class .... 150 Points
Each Merit Badge .... 50 Points

PATROL GAMES AND SPECIAL COMPETITIONS

Patrol placing first .... 50 or 100 Points
Patrol placing second .... 30 or 60 Points
Patrol placing third .... 10 or 30 Points

SPECIAL FEATURES

For especially interesting features, periodically staged stunts at Troop meetings or on hikes, or outstanding Patrol projects, the Scoutmaster may award at his discretion. up to 100 Points

Experience has shown that it is unwise to include any penalties in a point contest of this kind. A positive stimulus is much better than a negative threat or punishment.

Progress Charts

The Patrol progress under the point system should be recorded on a chart so that the boys may follow their achievements—or lack of them.

The following methods have proved successful:

Climbing the Ladder—Four ladders, one for each Patrol, are painted on a large piece of cardboard. On each ladder is placed a little pasteboard Scout, representing the Scouts of that Patrol. Each rung counts 100 points. The height of each pasteboard Scout on the ladder indicates the progress of that Patrol. Or change the ladder into Mount Everest, or the Washington Monument. Or turn the pasteboard Scout into a stratosphere plane, or an elevator "going up."

Canoe Race—A similar idea is to have a frieze painted at the top of the meeting room's wall. The frieze should picture a river, with a tree, a boulder, a shrub, etc., painted on the bank at regular intervals. Each landmark represents 100 points, and each Patrol is shown by a pasteboard canoe paddling toward the goal. Or make it airplanes on a trans-Atlantic hop, or automobiles on a racetrack, or pirate ships on the way to Treasure Island.

Trophies

There may be some outward, visible trophy of achievement for recognition of Patrols that reach the "top of the ladder" or the "end of the river"—in other words, the established Troop standard. Let it be something simple, like a streamer with an inscription in indelible ink for the Patrol flag staff, or a leather skin stretched on a rustic wooden frame, with the names of the Patrol members and details of the competition.

As recognition, a Patrol may be given the privilege of carrying the Troop colors. Or the winning Patrol may be taken on a special camping trip arranged by the Troop Committee.

Expensive prizes should *never* be used. They may encourage the mere winning of a prize rather than the gaining of an honor for the Patrol.

In all Patrol recognition the spirit of fair play must be constantly kept in the foreground. Winning must never become more important than the fun of playing the game.

Becoming a National STANDARD PATROL

After having used an easy Point System for awhile in the Troop to check the effectiveness of the Patrols, you will eventually arrive at the point where you may want to have them measure themselves against a more exact standard. It was to make this measuring possible that the National STANDARD PATROL Plan was developed.

This STANDARD PATROL Plan is described in detail in the *Handbook for Patrol Leaders* (pages 360-366), with methods of scoring and suggestions for reaching STANDARD PATROL Honors.

FINANCING THE TROOP

A TROOP, like any other going concern, must have money with which to conduct its activities. The sooner a Troop gets on a sound working basis financially, the longer it is likely to function.

The Troop Budget Plan

In business, the budget system has been accepted as the most successful and logical means of forecasting and meeting financial obligations. The experiences of Troops using a Troop budget show conclusively the values inherent in it, among them the following:

It insures the *prompt reregistration* of the Troop. When a boy first joins the Troop, he is required to pay his registration fee. The following year his reregistration fee will be provided for through the budget—

It develops in the Scouts a sense of real *responsibility* to the life of the Troop, thus providing an incentive to engage in systematic *saving* and stimulating *regular payment of dues*—

It provides for the *upkeep of Troop equipment,* resulting in pride of ownership on the part of each Scout—

It makes available to each Scout *Badges* and *Insignia* of advancement and office, to be presented to him on behalf of the Troop—

It makes Boys' LIFE available to every Scout, in this way putting this "Silent Assistant" to work in your Troop, training your boys.

Through the provision in the Budget for community service and social welfare work, there is developed in each Scout an appreciation of his responsibility and obligation to society. It encourages in him *the spirit of sharing.*

Establishing the Troop Budget Plan

The Troop Budget Plan involves three distinct steps:

1. The adoption of a definite budget—
2. The establishment of a Revolving Fund to meet immediate financial needs—
3. The regular weekly payment of a small sum—usually a nickel or a dime—by each member of the Troop.

Planning the Budget

Discuss the Troop budget in the Patrol Leaders' Council. There are two important decisions to be made by the Patrol Leaders:

First: How much can we expect each Scout to pay each week—a dime, or a nickle? How much can he save weekly? How much can he earn? Determine upon weekly dues that will not be too much of a burden and yet will make each Scout feel that he contributes a real share. The Scouts should be definitely urged to *earn* the money for their weekly dues.

Second: What should be included in the budget? Among the items should be reregistration fees, subscriptions to BOYS' LIFE, badges for new and advancing Scouts, upkeep of Troop property. A majority of Troop Budgets provide for welfare work or charity. Usually, the budget should *not* include provisions for such things as tents, or other Troop equipment. Finances for such expenditures should be raised from other sources.

After the Troop Leaders have discussed the budget, it should be reviewed and approved by the Troop Committee; and the Treasurer (a member of the Troop Committee) should make himself responsible for its operation with the aid of the Troop Scribe.

The budget is then presented to the entire Troop for adoption, together with a full explanation of what the Budget Plan is. Emphasis should be placed on each boy's personal responsibility for making a success of the plan by prompt payment of his own share of the necessary Troop funds. Parents should likewise be taken into confidence at the first possible occasion so that they may understand that the plan is not just a matter of collecting funds, but also a real thrift measure with business training possibilities for their sons.

The budget as finally developed may look like this:

On the basis of weekly dues of 10 cents—

INCOME (One Year)	EXPENSES (One Year)	
10c weekly,	Reregistration Fee.............	$ .50
50 weeks.............. $5.00	Insignia (Tenderfoot, Second Class, First Class), Troop Numerals, Patrol Emblems, Community Strips, etc.	.50
	Good Turn Fund (service to Chartered Institution, community, individuals, etc.)...........	.50
	Troop supplies — to be used as Troop needs are apparent...................	1.75
	Boys' LIFE (Concession Offer to Scouts).............	1.50
	Troop Reserve Fund........	.25
$5.00		$5.00

The Revolving Fund

The Revolving Fund enables a Troop to finance certain items of its budget prior to the collection of dues which cover these items. This fund is simply a sum of money secured for use only in spending for budget items, with the understanding that the money will be replaced after the income from dues and other sources is secured by the Troop. The amount needed for the Revolving Fund depends on the Troop expenditures planned prior to the receipt of income to cover the items.

The Troop Committee and the Chartered Institution should together develop plans, and assume the responsibility for securing this fund. One of the following methods may be used:

1. Perhaps the most desirable method is to have this Fund established by the Institution itself, if it is financially in a position to do so. The matter should be presented to the governing board by the Troop Committee as an opportunity to participate in the thrift training of the Troop.

2. If the institution cannot make this fund available, possibly some organization — such as the Men's Bible Class or the like—within the Institution may be able to do so.

3. In some cases members of the Troop Committee may themselves establish this fund.

4. The Troop itself may earn the necessary amount through special Troop money-raising projects.

Collecting Dues and Keeping Records

When the Budget Plan is put in operation, every effort should be made to have dues paid with absolute regularity.

Make it the definite responsibility of each Patrol to collect the dues from its own members on time, and the responsibility of the Troop Scribe to follow through on this. Dues paid on time may be credited toward the Patrol's standing or efficiency.

The Patrol Dues Envelope (Cat. No. 3160) is a method of collecting dues—by Patrols. Here is a suggested plan:

1. The Troop Scribe should give each Patrol Scribe or P.L. an envelope each week.

2. Records are marked on the outside of the envelope and dues placed inside and sealed.

3. These envelopes should be turned over to the Troop Scribe. He should give the Patrol a receipt, as provided for on pages 18-19 of the *Patrol Record* (Cat. No. 3276).

4. The Troop Scribe should then make appropriate entries in the *Simplified Troop Record Book*.

5. These sealed envelopes are turned over to the Troop Treasurer as soon as possible after being received from the Patrols. He opens them in the presence of the Troop Scribe and gives him a receipt.

6. Troop Treasurer makes appropriate entries in the *Troop Financial Record Book* (Cat. No. 3817).

7. Troop Treasurer deposits the money in a bank.

8. It is suggested that a petty cash account in the amount of $5.00 or so be established for the Scribe, this money to be used for making small cash purchases such as badges, insignia, etc. When the Scribe has spent the amount and returns to the Treasurer receipted bills for his expenditures, another $5.00 is issued so that he may carry on. Larger bills are paid by the Treasurer upon Scoutmaster's recommendation, approved by the Troop Committee.

The complete financial records of income and disbursements are kept by the Treasurer, who furnishes a brief report to the Troop Committee and to the Troop on the status of the Troop Treasury.

It is recommended that a new Scout, on joining the

Troop, pay the full fifty cents registration fee, regardless of Troop Charter duration at the time of his entry. The Troop sends to the Local Council office only the required *pro rata* fee, putting the balance in the Revolving Fund for use at reregistration time. It should be explained carefully to the new Scout that he is expected to pay weekly dues. Also he should be told how the money is spent so that he will realize that he has a definite responsibility to keep his dues paid up and that he will benefit thereby.

The Scoutmaster of a Troop operating on the Budget Plan has complete control of the Troop's BOYS' LIFE subscriptions at all times. If a Scout transfers or drops out of the Troop, his subscription can be transferred to a new incoming Scout or stopped altogether. In the latter case a cash refund of the unused balance of the subscription price will be made by BOYS' LIFE to the Troop.

Money Earning Projects

As mentioned before, finances for the purchase of Troop flags, tents or other equipment are not provided by the Troop Budget. The Troop Budget is to take care of the *running expenses. Capital expenses* must be procured in some other way, preferably earned by the Troop.

Before deciding on a money earning project, the Troop and its Committee should have clear understanding of the policies of the Boy Scouts of America in these matters, as presented in the By-Laws of our Movement:

COMMERCIALISM

No member of the Boy Scouts of America, Scout Unit, chartered Council, or any officer or representative of the Boy Scouts of America shall have the right to enter into a contract or relationship of a commercial character involving the Boy Scouts of America unless duly authorized by the National Executive Board, and then only in connection with the carrying out of the purposes of the Boy Scout Movement.

Nor shall any Local Council or Scout Unit enter into a contract or business relationship with a business or commercial agency or corporation, or individual which may be construed as using the Boy Scout Movement for commercial purposes, such as an effort to capitalize public interest in the Boy Scout Movement rather than depending upon the merits of the business proposition. This shall not be interpreted, however, as interfering with any Scout earning money for his own Scout equipment or for his Unit, provided the money is earned through services actually rendered, and is not dependent upon capitalizing interest in the Boy Scouts of America. (By-Laws, Art. XVII, Sect. 1.)

SOLICITATION OF MONEY, OR SALE OF TAGS AND TICKET SALES

Boy Scouts, collectively or individually, shall not be used in the solicitation of money for the sale of tags, or other similar methods of solici-

tation of money in connection with efforts to raise money incidental to the expenses of Scouting, provided, however, this shall not prohibit Local Councils from sanctioning the sale of tickets for the public display of Scout activities such as Merit Badge Shows, Rallies, Demonstrations, etc., when the nature of the program or function offers a value commensurate with the purchase price of tickets offered for sale, and the sale of tickets is not used as an indirect method of defeating the purpose of this By-Law; and provided further that Scouts' participation in the sale of tickets for such affairs shall be confined to their parents and immediate friends, and not involve methods similar to those used in the sale of tags or other general solicitation. The Scout Uniform must not be capitalized in such sale of tickets, but this shall not be construed to forbid Scouts in Uniform selling tickets to Scout Circuses, Rallies and similar Scout events. (By-Laws, Art. XVII, Sect. 2, Cl. 1.)

Setting Out to Earn Money

The decision to undertake a money earning project should be taken by the Patrol Leaders' Council and the Troop Committee. When the project has been decided upon, set out to create a real interest for it in the Troop, so that everyone will pitch in with enthusiasm.

Whatever project you choose, be certain that *it does not take work from someone who needs it.*

And *check with your Local Council in advance* to make positive that the method you intend to use is in accordance with the policies of the Boy Scouts of America, and has the approval of the Council.

Money earning projects that are best handled by the Troop Committee and the Parents' Auxiliary of your Troop, are described in Chapter 4. Here are a few the Troop itself may undertake:

1. *Dramatic Performance*—Scout circus, minstrel show, play, camp fire type display.

2. *Exhibit*—Merit Badge show, hobby show, handicraft booths, possibly arranged in gymnasium or vacant store.

3. *Handicraft Articles*—Sale of Scout-made objects: carpentry items, birdhouses, handmade kitchen gadgets, etc.

4. *Greeting Cards*—There's good business in Christmas Cards. Watch for advertising offers in Boy's Life. Or make your own from linoleum blocks, or have them printed from an original design and colored by the boys.

5. *Waste Paper* is another good money-maker. Before collecting, make contact with local paper mill, or buyer, to make sure of your market.

TROOP EQUIPMENT

YOUR TROOP will need certain equipment for games and projects at Troop meeting, or hiking and camping.

What is required depends upon the Troop. If your Troop specializes in first aid, you will need plenty of first aid equipment. If you go in for map making, you need compasses, plane tables, and drawing equipment. If pioneering is your specialty, you need axes and lashing ropes.

The list of equipment which follows will suggest to you some of the things you may want to have.

A Troop Is Thrifty

The equipment should, as far as possible, be purchased with money earned by the boys themselves.

Then, as you get the equipment, adopt a businesslike way of taking care of it and checking it in and out, so that it will be in good condition and losses at a minimum:

1. Make a Troop Quartermaster responsible for the equipment, possibly with the help of an Assistant Scoutmaster.

2. Have a chest or cabinet in the Troop meeting room in which equipment can be kept.

3. Get a book and mark it "Troop Property." Keep in this a list of the Troop equipment, and a check of equipment going out and its return.

Main Items of Troop Equipment

SCOUTCRAFT EQUIPMENT

    32—4 ft. pieces of ¼″ rope or sash cord (for knot games)
    12—Triangular bandages (for first aid practice)
    12—Rolls 2″ bandage
    6—Rolls 1″ bandage
    4—Compasses (for hiking)
    4—Rulers (for mapping)

```
 4—Topographic maps of your locality
 4—Signal kits
 1—Ball Binder twine
32—15 foot lengths of ¼″ rope (for lashings)
 4—Felling axes (for pioneering)
 2—Fire-by-friction sets
 1—Model homemade pack
 1—Model homemade tin can cook kit
 1—Troop first aid pouch
```

CAMPING EQUIPMENT

See Camping chapters

FLAGS

```
1—Flag of the United States, parade size, on staff
1—Troop flag, parade size, on staff
2—Flag belts
2—Floor stands for flags
```

RECORDS AND LITERATURE

```
1—Troop log book (for the Troop history)
1—Troop file book (for clippings, pictures, letters)
1—Troop record book (complete with forms)
4—Patrol record books              4—Handbook for Boys
1—Advancement chart                4—Scout Field Books
1—Attendance chart                 4—Handbooks for Patrol Leaders
1—Bulletin board                   1—Handbook for Scoutmasters
1—Game book, such as Smith's Games and Recreational Methods
1—Book of nature and conservation activities, such as Hillcourt's Field
     Book of Nature Activities, or Pettit's Book of Nature Hobbies
1—Set of the more common Merit Badge pamphlets
```

INSIGNIA

```
12—Community strips            6—Troop neckerchiefs
12—Troop numerals                Patrol Medallions
```

4. Have every piece of equipment marked with Troop number. Paint it on canvas. Ink it on flags and books. Carve it into wooden articles. Scratch and etch it into metal.

5. Make it a rule to return flags, ropes and other things to the equipment chest immediately after their use at the Troop meeting. Check in hike and camp equipment as soon as the boys get home. Keep a record of equipment lent to Patrols and individual boys, and rely on the record rather than on memory to keep track of them.

6. Take an inventory around October 1, January 1 and May 1, just as any business concern does. This will help to teach system and thrift to the Scouts.

TROOP MEETING ROOM

FINDING a suitable Troop meeting room is one of the duties of the Troop Committee. If the Troop is sponsored by a church, school, or other institution that has a building of its own, an adequate meeting room should be found there. If the Troop is sponsored by some group of citizens that does not have a house of its own, the Troop Committee will have to locate a room in some existing building.

Forget any idea you may have of building a Troop house. Based upon the sad experiences of Troops who have tried it, the policy of the Boy Scouts of America is opposed to the erection of Troop buildings.

What to Look for

The Troop meeting room should be large enough for simple games and for the construction of Patrol corners—yet not so large that the Troop gets "lost" in it.

It should be attractive enough to make the boys feel at home—yet simple enough to make them want to improve it.

It should be well lighted, heated, ventilated, and not too far away from where the boys live.

It should be located in a safe building, preferably on the ground floor. It should have, besides a door opening outward, at least one other fire exit. *Fire traps, damp, dark, unsanitary, ill-ventilated rooms, or rooms that can't be properly heated are, of course, unusable.* Toilet facilities should be present. Drinking water is desirable.

Making the Arrangements

When a suitable room has been found, a definite understanding regarding its use should be arrived at with the landlord before it is occupied.

If rent is to be paid, the amount should be decided on, and the Troop Committee should take the responsibility for getting it paid when due. The Troop must know whether it can consider the room its own and can decorate it accordingly, or must share it with other groups, in which case decorations must be removable. Also, it should be clearly understood on what evenings and at what hours the room may be used, so that the noise from the games and singing will not interfere with activities elsewhere in the building. Finally, the Troop must know how the heating will be taken care of during the winter.

Developing the Meeting Room

The development of the meeting room should be the joint responsibility of the Troop Committee and the boys. There will be certain things in the carpentry, plumbing and painting lines that need to be handled by experienced men. Most other things can be done by the boys.

It may be a good idea to place the decoration of the room in the hands of a boy committee, consisting of the Troop Quartermaster (if you have one), and a boy from each Patrol, with the Senior Patrol Leader or Explorer as chairman.

The responsibilities of this committee would be something like this:

1. Gather ideas for decorating the room from all possible sources—the boys and leaders of the Troop, available literature, even architects and artists of the community. You will be surprised at the amount of help you will receive from such people, if *boys* ask them.

2. Decide upon the style of decoration of the room and make detailed plans.

3. Secure money for lumber and paint, and borrow tools.

4. Get volunteers from the Patrols to help do the decorating.

TROOP RECORDS

WHAT DID WE DO last Columbus Day? How many
Scouts were present at the Troop hike last month?
Who were they? How far has Bill Jones advanced? When
did Jack Strong join the Troop?

Those are some of the facts the Troop needs to have.
Without records it is hard to know where you stand and
plan where you are going.

The Troop Log Book

The Troop Log, or "Book of Traditions," contains the
history of the Troop.

It is not a collection of dry meeting and hike outlines,
but a vivid report of the doings of the Troop, the Patrols
and individuals in it, written with humor, tact, and good
judgment. It is proudly shown to new Scouts to give them
an idea of the wonderful Troop they are joining. And it is
a continual source of delight to the old boys. When you
hear some quiet chuckles in the Troop room, you should
be fairly certain that someone has casually picked up the
Log Book and read a few pages.

Usually the Troop Scribe is also the Keeper of the Log.
He became a Scribe because of the very qualities that
make him a good recorder of the Troop's history.

It is not his job to do all the work—on the contrary. It
is his responsibility to get every body to help in creating
a worthy history of the Troop.

The Keeper of the Log encourages each Patrol to submit
reports of special events, the Troop "wit" to write the
Troop doings from a humorous angle, the journalist of the
clan to make up the news accounts, and the Troop "poet"
to write verses and jingles and ballads of the heroic adventures of the Troop. He gets the artists to make car-

toons and sketches, and lines up the photographers to contribute their best shots.

After the material is gathered—weekly or every two weeks—it becomes the Keeper's job to edit it and put it in shape for posterity, by copying out the literary efforts and pasting in photographs and art work.

To hold the pages, a loose-leaf binder, letterhead size, is ideal. It may be secured in any stationery or five-and-ten-cent store. Decorate the cover to suit, or get the Troop's leathercraft expert to tool a special cover.

Records

While the log tells more or less romantically of the doings of the Troop, Records tell of the same doings statistically. To be effective they should be simple, complete, and up-to-date.

BOOK RECORDS—Adequate Troop records consist of:

a. The Troop's copy of its Charter Application.
b. The Troop Roster, with space for each Scout's name, address, phone number, age, records of tenure, Troop offices held, transfer and separation.
c. Advancement record for all Scouts.
d. Full records of Scouts' attendance (at meetings, on hikes and other events) and of dues paid.

The *Simplified Troop Record* (Cat. No. 3521) book provides space for keeping all of these necessary records in one place. Order your copy from your Local Council.

CHART RECORDS—*Attendance Chart*—Hangs on the wall of the Troop meeting room where every boy can see it as a continual reminder.

Advancement Chart—Shows graphically the advancement record of each boy. Available from National Supply Service.

Patrol Contest Chart—Indicates standing of Patrols.

In a Troop where the Troop Scribe is not a member of a Patrol, it should be possible for him to keep the Log Book and all the records, with the help of an Assistant Scoutmaster on the advancement, and of the Senior Patrol Leader on the attendance. On the other hand, if he is a member of a Patrol, it would be better to arrange for him to be the keeper of the Log and appoint someone else, a Junior Assistant for example, as Keeper of the Records.

UNIFORMING THE TROOP

IF YOU ASK a group of Scouts why they became Scouts, you will probably discover that the desire to wear the Scout Uniform was one of their reasons. Why? Because the Uniform is part of the romance of Scouting. It suggests adventure.

A boy gets into the uniform, and immeditely it does something to him. To be dressed like a Scout makes him want to act like one, makes him want to do the things that Scouts do! Besides, it gives a boy pride in his appearance. helps him toward self-confidence, gives him a standing in the eyes of the public. With boys dressed alike, rich and poor, a real brotherhood can be established.

The values of the Scout Uniform have long been recognized, even by the Congress of the United States. When Congress granted a Federal Charter to the Boy Scouts of America in 1916, it established a permanent protection of the Scout Uniform, Badges and Insignia.

There is only ONE Official Boy Scout Uniform and the Insignia of our Movement appears on every piece of it. Look for it and accept no Uniform that does not bear the Official Seal. The Uniform is made by the Official National Outfitter, and is sold only by the National Supply Service, and only to Scouts and Scouters who show an unexpired membership certificate at time of purchase. No other person is permitted to purchase or wear the Scout Uniform.

Getting the Troop Into Uniform

There is one simple key to the problem of getting your Troop uniformed. Your own attitude and example. You have to make up your mind to get a Uniform for yourself and wear it at *all* Troop undertakings. With that one point taken care of, your boys will realize that you mean business and will quickly want to get into Uniform themselves.

You may find that the boys cannot afford the Scout Uniform. Possibly they can't—this very minute. But if they set out with determination to get it, it will not be long before they have the necessary amount earned and saved. And earning and saving, by the way, is the method recommended for every Scout, whether he be poor or well-off. Money earned by the boys individually may be matched with money earned through Troop and Patrol projects in which the boy participates. These joint money-earning projects have a value beyond the securing of Uniforms—the value of giving each boy an increased feeling of belonging, of being part of the "team."

Suggestions on Uniforming

Sell your Patrol Leaders on getting their Patrols completely uniformed, and discuss in the Patrol Leaders' Council how it may be done. Here are a few ideas that have worked in other Troops and may work in yours:

1. At the time of his Tenderfoot Investiture, give the boy a part of the Uniform, purchased by the Troop Budget Fund. In many Troops the boy gets his Tenderfoot Badge on this occasion. Fine! But make it the embroidered badge rather than the metal one. Why? Because he will pin the metal badge on anything from a sweater to a skull cap, while the embroidered, on the other hand, belongs on one spot only: on the pocket of the Scout shirt you want to encourage him to get. Some Troops present the new boy with the Troop neckerchief. Others provide him with the Troop numeral, community strip, and Patrol medallion, soon after he has joined.

2. Suggest methods of earning money to the boys, such as: Make and sell handicraft articles; handle a paper route; weed gardens; take care of furnace and remove ashes; wash automobiles; cut and pile wood; caddy for golfers; help janitor in church, school or other building shovel snow; clean windows; pick fruits and berries; beat rugs and carpets; deliver packages and run errands; mow lawns and rake leaves; take care of children.

3. It is a responsibility of the Troop Committee to "cooperate with the Scoutmaster in developing opportunities whereby members of the Troop may earn money to secure the Uniform." The members of the Troop Committee may

FIGURE 1   FIGURE 2

BOY SCOUTS wear either of the uniforms in Figs. 1 and 2, with neckerchief, official web belt and tan shoes. Such items as the jacket, winter cap and leggings, as well as the broad-brimmed hat, sweater and poncho or raincoat, are optional. The Troop should choose the combination best suited to locality and season, and all Scouts should be uniformed alike in every activity.

EXPLORERS may continue to wear the khaki Scout uniform with the "Explorer BSA" strip over the right pocket, a maroon tie

FIGURE 3   FIGURE 4

and the Explorer emblem on the right sleeve; or they may adopt the green Explorer uniform (Fig. 3). The Explorer fatigue uniform is optional.

SCOUTERS have a wide choice of uniform combinations. Many leaders favor the uniform in Fig. 4, but wear one of the Scout uniforms as a field uniform. A wool serge or tropical worsted dress uniform (including a coat worn with white shirt) is also available through official distributors of Scout uniforms and equipment. The Scouter necktie is green.

investigate the community and dig up small jobs for the boys.

4. At parents' meetings remind fathers and mothers of the Uniform. Boys have birthdays, and Christmas comes around once a year. Uniform parts make excellent gifts.

5. Start a Troop Uniform Saving Bank in which the boys deposit dimes and quarters, as earned. A responsible person—Assistant Scoutmaster or Troop Committee member — must be available to handle the accounts.

6. Many Troops secure continued uniforming through a Uniform Exchange. Whenever a boy outgrows his Uniform or ceases to be a Scout his Uniform is appraised. If it is in sufficiently good condition, it is purchased by the Troop for resale to one of the boys.

7. And finally, keep the boys Uniform-conscious at all times, through regular inspections at Troop meetings and by insisting that the boys wear all the Badges and Insignia to which they are entitled, and wear them correctly. The proper way of wearing them is shown in the *Scout Field Book* and the *Handbook for Boys*.

SCOUTMASTER'S BADGE
Silver and Green

ASST. SCOUTMASTER
Gold and Green

Tool 10

PROGRAM THEMES

THEME: General Suggestions for Development of Theme

LEADERS

Leaders' Council

Laying out the program, scheduling the details of the theme over the time decided upon—usually one month, but possibly two.

Determining responsibilities for leadership of all phases and for securing necessary material.

Patrols volunteering for demonstrations, display or equipment projects.

Leaders' Patrol

Training in technical details, given by Scoutmaster, experienced Explorer, or outside expert.

Method of putting the subject over in the Patrol.

PATROLS

Training in technical details, under Patrol Leader or expert brought in by him.

Rehearsal of demonstrations.

Making of display or equipment project.

Preparation for Theme CLIMAX.

TROOP

Demonstrations by Patrols.

Inter-Patrol games on subject.

Scoutcraft projects on subject.

Movie on subject, if available.

CLIMAX: Realistic outdoor experience in the subject.

NOTE: In the following pages, page and chapter numbers and abbreviated titles refer to these books:

Handbook for Scoutmasters—HSM.

Handbook for Patrol Leaders—HPL.

Handbook for Boys—HB.   *Scout Field Book*—SFB.

Scouting for Boys, World Brotherhood Edition—SB.

The majority of names of games and projects are of items included in this *Handbook for Scoutmasters*—see index under Games and Projects.

THEME: Hikecraft I (General Hiking)

LEADERS

Leaders' Council

Laying out program; determining leadership responsibilities; Patrols volunteering for domonstrations.

Leaders' Patrol

How to organize the Patrol for hiking, HPL VII.

Use of map for laying out routes.

How to get variety in hikes.

Technical training in

How to hike, at day, at night, with pack, SFB 30; hike clothing and equipment, SFB 29; hike menus, HLP VII; care of feet, SFB 29; safety on the road, SFB 32; safe water supply, SFB 32; resting, SFB 31; personal first aid for hike emergencies: blister, sunburn, insect bite, snake bite, sprain, SFB, Pow-Wow 36; waste disposal. Judging distances, heights, time, numbers, SFB Pow-Wow 5; measuring distances, heights, SFB 48; using staff for scale; Scout's Pace for measuring time and distance, SFB 34.

PATROLS

Training in technical details, under the Patrol Leader.

Organize Patrol for Patrol hiking, HPL VII.

Carry through on hike organization; Hikemaster suggesting hike spots; Grubmaster, menus; Treasurer handling expenses, etc., HPL VII.

Get topographical maps of favorite hike territory; mount map for folding.

Get first aid kit.

Train in hike cookery, SFB Pow-Wow 17.

Make log book of Patrol hikes, HPL IV.

Draw hike routes on mounted map in den, HPL VI.

Cut Scout staves, with permission; turn them into measuring devices.

TROOP

Patrol Demonstrations:

Hike clothing and equipment; hike first aid; mounting of maps; using staff for measuring distances, etc.

Games:

Compass Readings; Where Am I?; How High?; How Long?; Minute Judging; Scout's Pace Relay (HSM).

Projects:

Blindfolded Compass Course; Height Measuring; Crossing the Gap; String Burning; Tree Hunt (HSM).

CLIMAX

Sealed Orders Hike (HSM Tool Chest: Hikes).
Scoutcraft Field Day, HSM 270.

THEME: Hikecraft II (Orientation)

LEADERS

Leaders' Council
Laying out program; determining leadership responsibilities; Patrols volunteering for demonstrations.
Leaders' Patrol
Demonstration of compass, map making equipment (plane table, alidade).
Lay out step course and determine length of step, SFB 49.
Technical training in
Use of compass in the field, Scouts taking turns in leading, SFB 39; finding North with watch, SFB 43, and with North Star, SFB 45.
Map signs, SFB 59; orienting and use of map in field, Scouts taking turns, SFB 56; map making, SFB 60.

PATROLS

Training in technical details under the Patrol Leader.
Make crude compass with magnetized needle; compass chart, HPL VI.
Make plane table and alidade, SFB 63.
Lay out step course and have each Scout determine length of his step, SFB 49.
Make map of campsite by buddies, HPL VI.
Make map sketches from memory.
Make contour model, SFB 61.
Take Night Hike, using North Star for orientation, HPL VII.
Take Compass Hike, HPL VII.
Take Map Hike, map reading and making, HPL VII.
Secure a topographical map of main hike routes, mount it on cloth.

TROOP

Patrol Demonstrations:
Home-made compasses; Maps of camp sites; Mounted maps; Contour model.

Games:
Compass Facing; Compass Change; Compass Readings; What's the Sign?; Where Am I? (HSM Games).

Projects:
Blindfolded Compass Course; Lay Out Squares; Map Reading Race (HSM Projects).

CLIMAX:
Wide Game: The Idol of Bulalonga (HSM Tool Chest: Wide Games).

THEME: **Campcraft (Camp and Camporee Preparation)**

LEADERS

Leaders' Council
Laying out Program.
Determining leadership responsibilities.
Patrols volunteering for demonstrations.

Leaders' Patrol
Discuss and develop list of necessary personal and Patrol equipment.
Demonstration of cooking equipment, preferably home-made, HPL VIII.
Demonstration of tent making, waterproofing, SFB 133 and HPL IX.
Demonstration of pack making, HPL, and proper technique in packing, SFB 140 and HPL.
Develop menus for overnight camp, HPL VIII.
How to organize for Patrol camping, HPL; and Patrol cooking, HPL VIII.
Technical training in
Tent pitching, ditching, SFB 145; construction of latrine, beds, fire place, camp gadgets, SFB Pow-Wow 14; food protection; garbage and waste disposal; fire prevention; Patrol cooking, HPL VIII; camp fire leadership, HSM.

PATROLS

Training in technical details, under the Patrol Leader.
Organize the Patrol for Patrol camping and cooking, HPL VIII.

Develop menus for overnight camp, HPL VIII.
Make individual camping equipment: Packs, bags, sleeping bags, HPL IX.
Make tents; waterproof them, HPL IX.
Make cooking pots and other tin can equipment.
Train in packing, SFB 140.
Rehearse in camp-making on hike and on camping trip.
Prepare Patrol meals.
Make final preparations for CLIMAX, HPL VIII.

TROOP

Patrol Demonstrations:
Tenting equipment; Cooking equipment; Improvised and complete sleeping bags; Pack and packing.

Games:
Campsite Finding; Lay Out the Camp; Tenderfoot Jim's Pack; Pack Relay; Chopper's Relay (HSM Games).

Projects:
Tent Pitching; Blanket Rolling; Tent Peg Making; Wood Chopping Relay; The Robbed Camp (HSM Projects).

CLIMAX

Troop Camporee, HSM X.
Troop Summer Camp, HSM XI.

THEME: Campcraft II (Fire Building and Camp Cookery)

LEADERS

Leaders' Council
Laying out program.
Determining leadership responsibilities.
Patrols volunteering for demonstration.
Leaders' Patrol
How to organize for Patrol cooking, HPL VIII.
Building of Patrol menus, buying, transporting, protecting in camp, HPL VIII.
Sanitation: Water, refrigeration, dish washing, disposal of garbage and greasy water, HSM XI.
Technical training in
Selection and cutting of fire wood, SFB 151 and 161; fire building and fire safety, SFB 163; fire places, SFB 167.

Technical training in

Cooking without utensils of kabob, eggs, twist, potatoes, SFB 171; cooking with utensils of menu planned for Leaders' Patrol hike or camp.

PATROLS

Training in technical details, under the Patrol Leader.
Organize Patrol for Patrol cooking, HPL VIII.
Develop favorite Patrol menus, HPL VIII.
Training in fire making in the rain.
Make models of fires and fire places, HPL VI.
Make Patrol cooking pots from No. 10 tin cans.
Make reflector oven.
Make other tin can equipment: Cups, individual pan, griddle, oven, broiler.
Plan and train in Patrol specialty for CLIMAX, SFB 184.

TROOP

Patrol Demonstrations:
Model of fires and fire places; Reflector oven; Pot making; Tin can equipment.
Games:
Choppers' Relay; Fuzz Stick Relay; Fire by Friction Relay; The Grocer (HSM Games).
Projects:
Fire Building and Water Boiling; String Burning; Fire by Flint-and-Steel and Water Boiling; Flapjack Baking (HSM Projects).

CLIMAX

Troop Feast, each Patrol making dish for whole Troop: Planked fish, barbecue, imu, baked beans, SFB 184-189.

THEME: Woodcraft (Nature, Knife and Hatchet)

LEADERS

Leaders' Council
Laying out program.
Determining leadership responsibilities.
Patrols volunteering for demonstrations.
Leaders' Patrol
Study up on useful local wild plants; make list of them preparatory to looking for them in the field.
Technical training in
Sharpening and proper use of knife for whittling fuzz sticks, pot hooks, fork and spoon, SFB 159; sharpening

and proper use of hatchet, for cutting dead brush, kindling wood, tent pegs, SFB 151.

Technical training in
Locating edible plants, preparing them into Patrol meal, SFB 316; cooking without utensils, SFB 171; finding wood, fiber and tinder suitable for fire making, SFB 161; make fish line from natural fiber; improvise shelter, make beds, SFB 144.

PATROLS

Training in technical details, under the Patrol Leader.
Sharpen Patrol hatchets and knives.
Hike to collect material for fire-by-friction sets; looking for flint for flint-and-steel fire making, SFB 168.
Make fire-by-friction sets, SFB 168.
Make fish line and improvised hooks; catch fish, plank them, SFB 175.
Collect and press edible wild plants for nature display, HPL VI.
On hike, make use of wild plants, SFB 316.
Make final preparations for CLIMAX.

TROOP

Patrol Demonstrations:
Fire-by-friction sets; Flint-and-steel sets; Fish lines and hooks; Mounted specimens of plants and usable plant parts.
Games:
Fire by Friction Relay; Fire by Flint-and-Steel Relay; What Is It?; Tree Spotting; Nature Scavenger Hunt (HSM Games).
Projects:
Fire by Friction and Water Boiling; Fire by Flint-and-Steel and Water Boiling; Nature Hunt; Tree Lore (HSM Projects).
CLIMAX:
Survival Hike (or Camp) (HSM Tool Chest: Hikes).

THEME: Observation (Tracking, Use of Senses)

LEADERS

Leaders' Council
Laying out program.
Determining leadership responsibilities.
Patrols volunteering for demonstrations.

Leaders' Patrol

How to stage "detective" problems.

How to solve "detective" problems: What to look for; making details add up.

Seeing, hearing, feeling, smelling, tasting games.

Technical training in
Laying trail with Scout trail marks, SFB 97; using whiffle-poof, SFB 98; making and using tracking "irons."

Technical training in
Finding and following tracks, and deducing their meaning. SFB 99; making plaster casts of tracks, SFB 104.

PATROLS

Training in technical details, under the Patrol Leader.

Observation games at meetings, HPL X.

Stage "detective dramas" in den, SB 166.

Dig tracking ground, study human tracks, SFB 100, SB 155.

Trailing hike, laying and following trail made with Scout trail marks, HPL VII.

Make whiffle-poof, SFB 98; and tracking "irons."

Take track prints of Patrol members.

Make models of trail signs.

Take Tracking Hike, finding and following animal tracks, making plaster cast of the clearest imprints, HPL VII.

Hare and Hounds hike, HPL VI.

TROOP

Patrol Demonstrations:
Track casts; whiffle-poofs and tracking "irons"; models of trail signs; human track print.

Games:

Object Hunt; Kim's Game; Haunted House; The Peddler; The Leaking Packsack (HSM Games); Far and Near, SB 142; Track Memory, SB 156.

Projects:
What Did You See?; The Robbed Camp (HSM Projects).

CLIMAX:

Treasure Hunt (HSM Tool Chest: Hikes).

THEME: **Concealment (Stalking and Camouflage)**

LEADERS

Leaders' Council
Laying out program.
Determining leadership responsibilities.
Patrols volunteering for demonstrations.
Leaders' Patrol
Demonstrations of sketches and photos of concealment
and types of camouflage, and simple stalker suit.
Technical training in
Practice of personal concealment, SFB 111; concealed
motion, including silent walking, crouching, creeping,
crawling, SFB 113; "freezing," SFB 112; use of back-
ground, SFB 112.
Technical training in
Personal camouflage, use of natural material, making
simple camouflage suit, SFB 117; camouflage of camp.

PATROLS

Training in technical details, under the Patrol Leader.
Make model of concealed camp.
Make simple stalker suits, SFB 117.
Conceal camp; break it, leaving no trace.
Learn to make smoke-free fire, using proper wood.
Take Dispatch Bearer Hike, each Scout getting chance to
practise concealment, SB 171.
Take Night Patrolling Hike, with listening posts, SB 65.
Use Patrol stalking games, SB Yarn 14.

TROOP

Patrol Demonstrations:
Disguise with simple means; model of camouflaged
camp; stalker suits; concealment motions.
Games:
Sleeping Indian; Walking Statues; Submarines and
Mine Field; Deer Stalking (HSM Games); Ambush-
ing, SB 173; Stalking and Reporting, SB 173.
Projects:
Infiltration; Crossing the Gap (HSM Projects).

CLIMAX:
Wide Game, involving camouflaged Patrol camps, use
of stalker suits: Trip to Mars (HSM Tool Chest: Wide
Games).

THEME: Pioneering (Rope and Axe)

LEADERS

Leaders' Council

Laying out program.

Determining leadership responsibilities.

Patrols volunteering for demonstrations.

Leaders' Patrol

Demonstration of sketches, photos and models of bridges, rafts, shelters, towers.

Technical training in
Sharpening of axe, SFB 152; handling axe, SFB 153; cutting of saplings and larger trees, lopping and logging, SFB 156.

Technical training in
Types of ropes, SFB 191; whipping, SFB 193; review of Tenderfoot knots, with special emphasis on clove and timber hitches, SFB 196; square, diagonal and shear lashings, SFB 200.

Make trestles by half-Patrol teams, put them together to form bridge, SB 95.

PATROLS

Training in technical details, under the Patrol Leader.

Sharpen Patrol axes.

Secure lashing rope for each Scout, ¼″ thick, 15′ long; whip both ends.

Training in speed knot tying; blindfold or blackout tying, HPL VI.

Make knot board.

Hike to collect material for model making; and Scout staves for trestle poles, SB 95.

Design bridge or tower; make model, HPL VI.

Make raft model that will float, SB 102.

Make "camp fire" for Patrol den.

Train in trestle making, SB 95.

On hike or in camp, build shelter, raft or bridge, SB Yarn 8.

Make final preparations for CLIMAX.

TROOP

Patrol Demonstrations:
Model bridges; Model signal towers; Model rafts; Knot boards.

Games:
Knot Hoop Relay; Chain Gang Race; Knot Champ-Nit; Roman Chariot Race; Choppers' Relay (HSM Games).

Projects:
Knot Tying Relay; Flag Pole Raising; Bridge Trestle Lashing; Wood Chopping Relay (HSM Projects).

CLIMAX:
Radio Tower Commando Raid (HSM Wide Game: Commandoes).
River Crossing—raft or bridge, SB Yarn 8.

THEME: Communication (Messages and Signaling)

LEADERS

Leaders' Council
Laying out program.
Determining leadership responsibilities.
Patrols volunteering for demonstrations.

Leaders' Patrol
How to organize Patrol for messenger service.
How to stage relay signaling.
Demonstration of signaling devices.
Technical training in
Use of telephone; making up a message, SFB 477; practice in hiding message on person.
Technical training in
Signal Code and simplest way to learn it, SFB 72; signaling indoors and out, SFB 74 and 80.

PATROLS
Training in technical details, under the Patrol Leader.
Train in making up messages, then in remembering them.
Make buzzer, SFB 73; heliograph, SFB 81; blinker or light sender, SFB 81; or set of signal flags.
Learn code and practise it at meetings.
Make up secret code, SFB 84.
On hike, distance signaling using flags or heliograph.
Make curtain set-up for fire signaling for CLIMAX.

TROOP
Patrol Demonstrations:
Buzzer; Heliograph; Blinker; Signal flags.
Games:
Message Relay; Silent Fun; Morse Relay; Signal Touch (HSM Games). Dispatch Running, SB 82.

Projects:
Message Signaling; Long Distance Signal Relay (HSM Projects). Code Treasure Hunt; Message Obstacle Race.
CLIMAX:
Night Fire Signaling (HSM Tool Chest: Hikes).

THEME: Emergencies (First Aid, Rescues)

LEADERS

Leaders' Council
Laying out program.
Responsibilities (Emergency Service Explorers).
Patrols volunteering for demonstrations.
Leaders' Patrol
How to organize Patrol for quick mobilization.
How to stage "accidents"—samples.
Technical training in
Shock, SFB 409; wounds and bleeding, SFB 411; sprains and fractures, SFB 436; transportation, SFB 442; artificial respiration, SFB 428; fire rescue, SFB 396; ice rescue, if seasonal, SFB 402.

PATROLS

Training in technical details, under the Patrol Leader.
Rehearsal in Patrol first aid demonstration, as agreed upon in Leaders' Council, with necessary equipment.
Make Patrol first aid kit, SFB 435.
Develop Patrol mobilization plan.
Train in use of neckerchief for bandage, SFB 418.
Develop suggestion for Troop fire drill.
Staged accidents at Patrol meetings or on hike.
Make final preparations for CLIMAX.

TROOP

Patrol Demonstrations:
Shock, wounds, bleedings; Sprains and fractures; Transportation; Artificial respiration.
Games:
Tourniquet Relay; Save My Child; Live Wire Accident (HSM Games).
Projects:
Accidents; Bandage Demonstration (HSM Projects).
CLIMAX:
First Aid Meet, HSM 274.
Lost Child Hike (HSM Tool Chest: Hikes).

Tool 11

GAMES AND PROJECTS

BADEN-POWELL gave us a simple formula for the activities of Scouting: "The training of Boy Scouts is done mainly by means of games, practices and competitions such as interest them . . ." "Games"—for the purpose of picking up elementary knowledge about Scoutcraft, and for fun; "practices"—on hikes and in camp to master the skills; "competitions"—in the form of projects to determine to what extent the skills have been learned, and for further practice.

GAMES and PROJECTS suitable for competitions are covered in the following pages. Suggestions for practices are found in chapters throughout this Handbook.

Hints on Games

It is impossible to suggest which games may meet with success in your Troop. Like cake recipes, the same game ingredients will give different "cooks" different results.

Your games must fit your Troop. They will have to be chosen over a period of trying and testing. A popular game may be used repeatedly — yet, don't overwork any one game. Make a change while it is still good. Try out new games from month to month.

Everybody should be active. Boys who are only "looking on" get bored and will start getting into mischief.

Game teams should be the Patrols. Make it an extremely rare exception to break up Patrols to form teams.

Let boy leaders lead. Games may appropriately be the responsibility of a Junior Assistant Scoutmaster, possibly alternating with the Senior Patrol Leader. Give each Patrol Leader a chance regularly to introduce and lead a new game.

Introduce the game properly. A game will not be a success unless the rules for playing it are understood by all the players. This is done effectively in this manner:

1. *Name the game*—the boys will remember the name and will know which is meant the next time it is to be played.
2. *Get the Patrols in formation to play it*—whether line, relay, etc.
3. *Explain the rules*—make it short and clear!
4. *Demonstrate the game*—if a relay, have the first boys of each team run up and back; if a line game, go through the motions.
5. *"Any questions?"*—give the boys a chance to get the explanation to points which may not be clear to them.
6. *Run the game*—with the necessary equipment and judges ready.

Hints on Projects

As mentioned in the chapter "Troop Meeting Tonight!," the distinction between a Scoutcraft game and a project is this: "A Scoutcraft game may be considered *playing at it* for further practice, while a project is *doing the real thing,* or a reasonable facsimile, for the sake of determining the Patrol's ability." Projects, therefore, are more formal than games, require more specific rules, and generally more preparation.

As in games, *project teams should be the Patrols or Patrol representatives.* The scores are credited to the Patrol, not to any individual.

The steps for running successful projects are these:

1. *Discuss the project in the Patrol Leaders' Council* and include it in the Troop's program.
2. *Announce the project in advance* to give the Patrols an opportunity to train in it. If possible, have written instructions available for the Patrol Leaders.
3. *Explain exactly what is involved,* or better, demonstrate the project before the whole Troop at the time of the announcement.
4. *Announce the method of scoring.*
5. *Answer all questions through the Patrol Leader.*
6. *Run the project on the date decided upon* — with equipment and judges on hand.

Classification of Games and Projects

The games and projects in the following pages have been classified as:

A. SCOUTCRAFT GAMES — which may be used for elementary practice in various Scout skills. SCOUTCRAFT PROJECTS—for testing Scoutcraft skills.

B. RECREATIONAL GAMES—for fun, recreation and physical action, and to add variety to the game "menu."

C. WIDE GAMES—over wide territory, providing practice in numerous Scout skills and physical exercise (Tool 13).

Each game has been further classified to help the game leader decide whether the game is suitable for his purpose.

This classification includes:

1. Games suited for *Indoor* uses are marked I, for *Outdoor* uses O. I-O indicates that the game may be played indoors as well as outdoors.
2. The *space* required, such as *Small* (Patrol corner, small meeting room, camp fire circle), *Medium* (the average Troop meeting room), *Large* (very large meeting room, gymnasium or playground), and *Wide* (cross-country).
3. The type of *activity* inherent in the game. The games are identified as being *Quiet, Lively, Vigorous* or *Strenuous*.
4. The *teams* participating, such as *Whole Troop, Troop against "It," Patrols,* and so on.
5. The *equipment* needed.

A. SCOUTCRAFT GAMES AND PROJECTS

Scout Law

GAMES

Scout Law Relay   I

    Space—Medium   *Type*—Lively
    Teams—Patrols   *Formation*—Parallel File
    Equipment—One hat for each Patrol with slips of papers numbered
    from 1 to 12. Pencils.

Hat with slips placed about 20 feet in front of each Patrol. On signal Scout No. 1 runs to hat, draws slip, reads number, writes on paper the point of the Scout Law of that number, drops paper beside the hat, runs back and tags next Scout, who repeats performance, etc., until all slips are answered. First Patrol finished with most correct answers wins.

Scout Law Story   I

    Space—Small   *Type*—Quiet
    Teams—Whole Troop   *Formation*—Troop Circle
    Equipment—Written story, paper and pencil per Scout.

Scouts seated. Leader tells story illustrating Scout Law, such as:

"Bobby Jones was a Scout. One summer day another boy from his Patrol came to take him swimming. 'Sorry I can't go yet. I first want to cut our lawn, because a Scout is .... It is a shame, but I suppose a Scout is .... After I have finished, I'll need a bath, for a Scout is ...., etc.' "

The Scouts write down points of Law represented. Answers are collected. Patrol with most correct answers wins.

Newspaper Study   I

    Space—Small   *Type*—Quiet
    Teams—Patrols   *Formation*—Patrol
                                     Corners
    Equipment—One current newspaper per Patrol.

Patrols in Patrol corners, each win the same day's issue of a newspaper. On signal Patrols start a search for news items which definitely illustrate the Scout Law. Items are cut out and numbered according to number of Law. Patrol with most clippings in given time wins. (Smart Patrol Leader distributes pages between his Patrol members).

Orientation (Compass and Map)

GAMES

Compass Facing   I

Space—Medium   *Type*—Lively
Teams—Whole Troop   *Formation*—Informal
Equipment—None.

The walls of the meeting room are called North, South, East, West (or 000, 180, 090, 270 degrees). All boys stand, or move around in room. Leader calls out various compass directions (or degrees), whereupon all Scouts face the direction called. Scouts making mistakes drop out. Continue until only one is left or for a certain number of minutes.

Compass Change   I

Space—Medium   *Type*—Lively
Teams—9, 17 or 33 Scouts preferably   *Formation*—Circle
Equipment—None.

Scouts facing inward, each Scout representing a compass point, except the "It" who stands in the center. "It" calls out two compass points. The Scouts representing the points mentioned attempt to change position, while "It" tries to take the place of one of them. Scout left without place in ring becomes next "It," the other two change name to fit their new place.

Compass Readings   I-O

Space—Medium   *Type*—Lively
Teams—Patrols   *Formation*—Parallel File
Equipment—For each Patrol: Compass, pencil and list of 8 features
   of room (such as flag, doorknob, etc), or of 8 landmarks, if outdoors (large tree, rock. etc). Chalk for drawing circles, or stick
   for scratching them.

Patrols in relay formation. Opposite to each Patrol, in other end of room, is circle, just big enough for boy to stand in. Here lie compass, pencil, list of objects. Player No. 1 runs up, stands in circle, takes reading to first object, writes it down. Runs back, touches off next player, and so on, until all readings are made. Give 10 points for readings within 10 degrees, 5 points for readings with error from 10 to 20 degrees.

What's the Sign?

Space—Medium
Teams—Patrols
Type—Lively
Formation—Parallel File
Equipment—For each Patrol a pencil and a large sheet of paper with the names of twenty conventional map signs.

Patrols in relay formation, facing lists tacked to opposite wall. On signal, Scout No. 1 runs up, draws a conventional sign next to its name. Boy runs back, touches off next player, who runs up, and so on, until all signs are drawn in. Score two points for each correct sign, plus ten points for Patrol finishing first.

Camp Site Finding

Space—Small ....*Type*—Quiet
Teams—Patrols
Formation—Informal
Equipment—One topographic map for each Patrol. Paper, pencil.

Patrols in Patrol huddles pore over map for purpose of finding best possible location for camp. Draws map sketch of spot, lay-out of tents and camp features, lists distances to water, hospital, etc. Best report wins.

Where Am I?

Space—Small
Teams—Patrols
Type—Quiet
Formation—Circle
Equipment—Description of route, paper, pencil.

Troop is seated in circle around game leader. Leader tells his hiking experience:

"I started from road sign at Main and Mountain Streets, walked 200 feet north, turned left at oak tree, walked 450 feet north-west to white cottage, turned left again, hiked 300 feet to crossroads marked with red signpost . . ." and so on, according to about ten local landmarks familiar to the Scouts.

Leader finishes by asking, "Where am I?" Patrols go into huddle, bring in their answers in writing.

Lay Out the Camp

Space—Small
Teams—Patrols
Type—Quiet
Formation—Informal
Equipment—Sand table, made from sheet of wallboard with a one inch wood edge; miniature trees, tents; powdered colors (blue for laying out streams, black for roads). Paper and pencil for each Patrol.

Sand table is made up in advance, with miniature camp in position. On signal Scouts gather around. They have three minutes for studying camp. When time is up, they retire to their Patrol corners to make sketches from memory. Best map sketch wins for the Patrol submitting it.

PROJECTS

Blindfolded Compass Course

One boy represents the Patrol. He takes an azimuth reading to a numbered stake 100 feet away. A large paper sack is then placed over his head, which just enables him to see the ground and the compass held close to his waist. He is turned around on the spot three times, then takes a compass reading and proceeds toward the stake, on the way taking as many more readings as desired. When he figures that he is within 5 feet of his goal, he halts and calls the judge.

Equipment—Brought by contestant: Compass. Furnished by judges: Large paper sack, marked stake.
Scoring—Contestant within 5 feet of stake   60 points
         Contestant within 10 feet of stake   40 points
         Patrol participating at all   20 points

Lay Out Square

Patrol is the team. It starts out at a point where a stake is driven down with its top almost flush with the ground, barely visible. Patrol takes compass readings and walks off distances. It proceeds 200 feet at 090 degrees, then 200 feet at 180 degrees, 200 feet at 270 degrees, finally 200 feet at 360 degrees. At finishing point Patrol places a stake. Patrol should not be able to see starting stake from place where last reading is made.

Equipment—Starting stake. Compass, finishing stake.
Scoring—Patrol within 20 feet of starting stake   60 points
        Patrol within 50 feet of starting stake   40 points
        Patrol participating at all   20 points

Map Reading Race

Four-man team (or entire Patrol). Each team is given a sketch map showing magnetic North, scale, and two objectives, not too far from starting point. Team orients map, plots the azimuth to the first objective, goes to it, finds what it is (low stake with a colored card for each competing team attached to it), takes a card as evidence of having found spot; plots azimuth to second objective, finds similar card here, returns to starting point with both cards. Judge should set reasonable time for course.

Equipment—Brought by team: Compass. Supplied by judges: Sketch map with two objectives, stakes with identification cards.
Scoring—Team finishing within time set by judge   60 points
        Team using 1½ times the time set   40 points
        Patrol participating at all   20 points

Measuring

GAMES

How High? How Long?　　　　　　　　　　1·0

Space—Medium　　　　　　　　*Type*—Quiet
Teams—Patrols　　　　　　　　*Formation*—Patrol
Equipment—Paper and pencils.

The members of each Patrol judge the height of tree (or flag pole, wall, window, etc.), lengths of distances to land-marks (or lengths of chalk lines), and write findings on paper. Patrol Leaders collect papers, add up results, divide by number of boys and turn in the result. Patrol closest to correct height or distance wins.

Minute Judging　　　　　　　　　　　　　|

Space—Small　　　　　　　　　*Type*—Quiet
Teams—Individuals　　　　　　*Formation*—Informal
Equipment—Watch.

Scouts are seated on the floor. Leader looks at watch, says "Go." All the boys try to judge when a minute is over. When a boy thinks the time is up, he rises. Scout to rise closest to exact minute wins for his Patrol. Repeat, using other lengths of time.

Scout's Pace Relay　　　　　　　　　　　O

Space—Large　　　　　　　　　*Type*—Lively
Teams—Patrols　　　　　　　　*Formation*—Spaced
Equipment—None

The Scouts of the various Patrols are scattered along a measured mile of a road, with approximately equal dis-tance apart. On signal Scout No. 1 proceeds in Scout's Pace. He tags the second Scout who continues and tags No. 3. When last Scout passes mile mark, time is checked. Patrol closest to 12 minutes wins.

Bombing the Camp　　　　　　　　　　　O

Space—Large　　　　　　　　　*Type*—Lively
Teams—Patrols　　　　　　　　*Formation*—Patrol
Equipment—One "bomb" (of newspapers) for each Patrol and one
　　　pail of water.

Returning from a hike, Troop is stopped one mile from camp by a scared messenger, who tells a fantastic story of having overheard a couple of bandits talking of blowing up the camp in exactly 12 minutes. "Rescue the camp! If you get there 15 seconds too late, it will already have been blown up. If you get there more than 15 seconds too early, the bandits will not yet have placed the bomb and will be able to blow up the camp at some other time." The judge places "bombs" in position at the camp exactly 11 minutes and 45 seconds after start of Patrols and removes them 30 seconds later. Each Patrol arriving while "bombs" are placed wins by throwing one "bomb" in the water.

PROJECTS

Height Measuring

Each Patrol member separately to estimate height of flag pole (or tree). There is to be no guessing; some type of measuring must be used, either pencil, stick, shadow, dirty water method, etc. Patrol Leader adds total of estimate of every member of Patrol, divides by number of members to get Patrol average, and gives result to Observer.

> *Equipment*—As desired.
> *Scoring*—Patrol average within 12 inches   60 points
>   Patrol average within 24 inches   40 points
>   Patrol participating at all   20 points

Communication

GAMES

Message Relay   I

> *Space*—Medium   *Type*—Lively
> *Teams*—Patrols   *Formation*—Parallel File
> *Equipment*—For each Patrol message of twenty words, written on paper, then each word cut out separately, and pieces mixed together. Paper, pencil

Patrols line up in relay formation, opposite to hat containing cut-up message. On signal, one boy at a time runs up, takes one word from hat and brings it back to Patrol Leader who is in charge of arranging words into what he thinks is the original message. When finished, he writes out message, delivers it to the judge. Even better: The message orders something done—first Patrol to do it wins.

Silent Fun   I-O

> *Space*—Medium   *Type*—Lively
> *Teams*—Patrols   *Formation*—Various
> *Equipment*—None.

Senior Patrol Leader gives twelve to fifteen silent signals for formations and field work, one after the other: Parallel file formation, open columns, spread out, dismissal, down, attention, etc. Object is for each Patrol to follow each signal as quickly as possible. First Patrol to get into a formation or to obey a field signal scores 10 points. Patrol talking, or moving with unnecessary noise loses 5 points.

Morse Relay

Space—Medium   *Type*—Lively
Teams—Patrols   *Formation*—Parallel File
Equipment—One signal flag for each Patrol, or one flashlight or blinker.

Patrols line up in relay formation. On word "Go," first player from each Patrol runs up to flag or blinker and sends Morse letter "A." Races back to touch off next player, who runs up, sends "B," returns, and so on, until all letters of the alphabet have been sent. First Patrol to finish with correct letters wins.

Signal Touch   O

Space—Medium   *Type*—Lively
Teams—Whole Troop   *Formation*—Single Rank
Equipment—One signal flag.

Leader, standing at a suitable distance in front of the Troop, sends word naming an available object. When word is finished, each boy who has read it runs and touches object mentioned. Build words of letters which all the boys master—for example: Shoe, Me, Teeth, etc.

Signal Do-This-Do-That   O

Space—Medium   *Type*—Lively
Teams—Whole Troop   *Formation*—Single Rank
Equipment—One signal flag.

Similar to Signal Touch, except that words are sent expressing actions which may be executed—for example: Sit, Hit Tom, Hoot, etc., depending upon number of letters learned.

PROJECTS

Message Signaling

Patrol to have one signaler, rest to be receivers. Starter gives signaler a message of 20 letters. Using flags, he sends message (by any code preferred) to receivers, 100 yards away. Each receiver writes message on paper. No repeats by signaler, but he must be slow enough to be understood by all his Patrol members. When message is completed, Patrol Leader collects slips and checks with signaler on the correct letters with Observer present. Total correct letters received by Patrol are added, then divided by number of receivers to give the Patrol average.

Equipment—One flag. Pencil and paper for each receiver.
Scoring—Patrol average 15 correct letters   60 points
          Patrol average 10 correct letters   40 points
          Patrol competing at all   25 points

Long Distance Signal Relay

Three buddy teams from each Patrol. Team 3 is sent 200 yards away from starting point, Team 2 100 yards. Judge gives Team 1 sealed envelope with message of 20 letters. Team 1 sends message to Team 2. Team 2 sends it to Team 3. Team 3 writes it down, then races it to starting point.

> *Equipment*—Signal flag for each buddy team.
> *Scoring*—Team finishing in 10 minutes   60 points
>   Team finishing in 15 minutes   40 points
>   Patrol participating at all   20 points
>   NOTE: Add one minute for each incorrect letter.

Observation and Memory

GAMES

Kim's Game

> *Space*—Small   *Type*—Quiet
> *Teams*—Patrols   *Formation*—Informal
> *Equipment*—Miscellaneous small articles, paper and pencils.

Patrols gather before a tray covered with cloth. Cloth is lifted for one minute, and the Scouts are permitted to study the twenty to thirty small articles which are revealed: Button, pocket-knife, clip, nut, coin, pencil, Scout badge, string, etc. Patrols retire, go into a huddle and make lists of items. One point for each article remembered, two points subtracted for articles mentioned which were not on the tray.

The Peddler

> *Space*—Small   *Type*—Quiet
> *Teams*—Patrols   *Formation*—Informal
> *Equipment*—As needed. Paper, pencils.

An Assistant Scoutmaster or a Troop Committee member, dressed up as a peddler, enters Troop meeting room with a suitcase. From this he drags out ten or fifteen different articles with a steady stream of sales talk, then retires. The Patrols go into huddle and try to make a list of articles in their proper order.

Object Hunt

> *Space*—Medium   *Type*—Quiet
> *Teams*—Whole Troop   *Formation*—Informal
> *Equipment*—As needed.

ANIMAL HUNT—Stand a small toy animal somewhere in the room, tell the Scouts to start looking for it, but that each one, as soon as he sees it, is to sit down quietly without giving it away. The fun comes in watching the last ones.

Hunt the Stamp—Played in the same way. Stick a two-cent stamp on the Troop numeral of some Scout.

Hunt the Candy—Hide candy, preferably paper wrapped, all over the room. Each Scout upon spying a piece must point his nose at it and give his Patrol call, whereupon his Patrol Leader comes and collects it. Patrols finally eat the candy collected.

The Leaking Packsack   O
Space—Large   *Type*—Quiet
Teams—Patrols   *Formation*—Single File
Equipment—As needed. Also paper and pencils.

Game leader arranges various articles not too conspicuously along one side of a path. They may include: Flashlight, toothbrush, soap, toothpaste, stocking, matchbox, spoon, comb, etc. The whole Troop passes slowly along the road in single file. No one is permitted to walk back when he has passed a certain article. Afterwards Patrols go into huddles and prepare list of articles seen, in right order.

Haunted House   I
Space—Small   *Type*—Quiet
Teams—Patrols   *Formation*—Horseshoe
Equipment—As needed.

Horseshoe formation, with center the corner of meeting room where a blanket is hung up, behind which certain sound effects are produced, such as: Pull cork out of bottle, drop key on floor, turn pages of book, turn pages of newspaper, unwrap cellophane wrapper, strike match, etc. After having listened, Patrols retire to their corners and make list of noises identified in order of appearance.

PROJECTS

What Did You See?
The whole Patrol is the team. Thirty different items are shown to the Patrol for two minutes, in the same fashion as in Kim's Game or The Peddler. Patrol makes up a list of items seen and remembered.

Equipment—30 items (axe, knife, button, pencil, etc). Paper and pencil.
Scoring—Patrol listing 25 items   60 points
   Patrol listing 20 items   40 points
   Patrol participating at all   20 points

The Robbed Camp
A Patrol camp (or camp kitchen) is set up with utensils,

packs, other equipment in certain positions. The whole set-up is roped off. A whole Patrol forms the team. Competing teams are permitted to move around the set-up to study it for two minutes. They are then taken away from the scene while twenty changes are made (items moved from one position to the other, or removed altogether). Teams are brought back for another two-minute study of the layout, then retire to make list of the changes they have observed.

> *Equipment*—Items necessary for the camp set-up. Paper and pencils.
> *Scoring*—Patrol correctly reporting 16 changes   60 points
>   Patrol correctly reporting 12 changes   40 points
>   Patrol participating at all   20 points

Stalking

GAMES

Walking Statues   I-O

> *Space*—Medium   *Type*—Lively
> *Teams*—Troop against "It"   *Formation*—Two Lines
> *Equipment*—None.

Two half-Troop (or Patrol) teams start from opposite ends of a room, or field, advancing on a leader who stands halfway between them. A team can only advance while the leader is facing the opposite way. He turns around at will whereupon everyone he faces must be motionless. If he detects the least movement, the guilty party is sent back to the starting line to begin again. This continues until some player reaches the center and touches the leader, thus winning for his team and becoming the next leader.

Sleeping Indian   I-O

> *Space*—Medium   *Type*—Quiet
> *Teams*—Troop against "It"   *Formation*—Circle
> *Equipment*—Seat for Indian, item to be guarded.

"Indian," blindfolded, sits in center of large circle of boys. In front of him lies an axe (in its sheath) or other item of similar size. Object is for Scouts to stalk up and remove the axe without being noticed by the Indian. If the Indian hears the oncoming stalker, he quickly points at him. If he points correctly, unlucky stalker must return to starting position for another try. Scout getting the axe, unnoticed by Indian, scores for his Patrol.

Submarines and Minefield   I-O

> *Space*—Medium   *Type*—Quiet
> *Teams*—Patrols   *Formation*—Patrol lines
> *Equipment*—Neckerchiefs for blindfolding.

Blindfold the Scouts of one Patrol and line them up across room, feet wide-spread, outer sides of feet touching next fellow's, hands to the sides. Other Patrols form lines, one behind the other across one end of room. On signal from game leader first Patrol in line attempts to go under or between the blindfolded "mines" without being heard. If a "mine" hears a "sub," he tries to blow him up by touching him. A blown-up sub is out of the game. A sub safely through scores a point for his Patrol. When one Patrol is through, signal is given to next Patrol, and so on. When all Patrols are through, another Patrol becomes the mine field.

Deer Stalking O

Space—Large
Teams—Troop against "It"
Equipment—None.

Type—Quiet
Formation—Circle

The "deer" takes up position in field or wood. The Scouts are sent out from him about 200 feet in different directions, where they fall down. On signal, they start to stalk toward the deer, using whatever cover is available. When the deer sees a Scout, he yells to him to stand. The Scout who comes closest without being seen wins for his Patrol.

Spies in the Woods O

Space—Large
Teams—Patrols
Equipment—Pieces of paper. Pencil for each player.

Type—Active
Formation—Scattered

Place on different trees and shrubs, blank pieces of paper two to three feet above the ground. Two or three of the leaders become spies and roam about a given area where papers have been placed (number of spies depends on size of territory to be covered). The idea is for a player to locate the papers and write his name on each of them without being seen. If player is seen by a spy within 15 feet of a paper, the spy puts his name in "black book." For scoring, names in the spies' books are subtracted from the number of signatures on the papers. Patrol with most successful stalkers wins.

PROJECTS

Infiltration (Night project)

Project is laid out as follows: Two blindfolded listeners are placed in the center of a 75-foot circle. The perimeter is marked with a number of small white stakes. A circle is made of a number of small white cards (3″ x 5″ filing cards) at a distance of 8 feet around the listeners. Each listener has a flashlight.

One (or two) contestant(s) from each Patrol. Contestant starts from the perimeter when signal is given. His object is to walk or crawl silently toward the men in the center, pick up a white card and return to the perimeter with it, without being heard by listeners. If his motion is detected by a listener, the listener will try to hit the stalker squarely with the beam of his flashlight. If hit, the stalker must return to the perimeter silently and begin again. A card brought back safely is proof of a mission successfully completed. Time limit: 10 minutes.

> Equipment—Marking stakes, 3″ x 5″ filing cards, 2 flashlights.
> Scoring—Team bringing in 8 cards 60 points
> Team bringing in 4 cards 40 points
> Patrol participating at all 20 points

Crossing the Gap

In broken terrain or underbrush, a course is laid out, about 500 long, with starting and finishing points indicated. Two or more observers move along a line parallel to the course but about 200 feet removed from it, to look for anyone moving along the course. A whole Patrol forms the team. On a signal, the Scouts "hit the dirt" at the starting point, then attempt to creep or crawl, using all natural cover, to the finishing point without being seen by the observers. Set an appropriate time limit for the course. Any boy seen is called to stand up, and remains standing until time is up.

> Equipment—Marker for start and finish.
> Scoring—Patrol getting 75% safely through 60 points
> Patrol getting 40% safely through 40 points
> Patrol participating at all 20 points

Camp Equipment

GAMES

Tenderfoot Jim's Pack

> Space—Small Type—Quiet
> Teams—Patrols Formation—Informal
> Equipment—Packsack with a variety of items, for camp as well as general articles.

Similar to *The Peddler*. Leader drags articles out of pack, with steady stream of gab, then throws them all back in. Patrols retire to their corners, makes list of items shown, then checks off those that are useful for camping, those that are useless, and adds important items that Tenderfoot Jim has forgotten.

Pack Relay

Space—Medium   *Type*—Active
Teams—Patrols   *Formation*—Relay
Equipment—For each Patrol a pack and all the articles required
for a successful overnight camp.

Patrols line up in relay formation opposite to empty pack and camping articles. Scout No. 1 runs up, packs first item, runs back, touches off next Scout, who runs up and packs an item, and so on. Patrol with best-packed pack, with items packed in best order, wins.

PROJECTS

Tent Pitching

Patrol lines up with 4 tents neatly rolled in front of it, poles and pegs enclosed inside of tents. Patrol at attention. A command "Go," Patrol sets up its tents. Tents must be neat and tight. When tents are erected, Patrol lines up in front of them at attention. NOTE: Instead of a Patrol putting up 4 tents, have a team of 2 Scouts put up 1 tent.

Equipment—4 tents with poles and pegs; axes.
Scoring—Satisfactory job in 5 minutes   60 points
Satisfactory job in 10 minutes   40 points
Patrol participating at all   20 points

Blanket Rolling

Patrol lines up in relay formation with 8 blankets in front of it. On word "Go," No. 1 takes a blanket and rolls it up into a tight roll, finishing with "ears" tucked in the roll. No straps or strings can be used. Blanket must be secure enough to be picked up and transported without loosening. When No. 1 has completed, No. 2 rolls a blanket, and so on, until all 8 blankets are rolled. (NOTE: In case of a small Patrol, one or more Scouts may roll two bankets, until all 8 are rolled.)

Equipment—8 blankets.
Scoring—Patrol completing in 10 minutes   60 points
Patrol completing in 15 minutes   40 points
Patrol participating at all   20 points

Axemanship

GAMES

Choppers' Relay

Space—Small   *Type*—Lively
Teams—Patrols   *Formation*—Parallel File
Equipment—For each Patrol: One hatchet, one board 12" long and
at least 6" wide, one chopping block.

Patrols in relay formation, opposite equipment. On signal, No. 1 runs up and splits one piece off board, runs back and touches off next player, and so on. The idea is to find out which Patrol can split the greatest number of pieces from the board in three minutes.

PROJECTS
Tent Peg Making
Patrol lines up in relay formation. No. 1 runs 50 feet, takes axe and makes regular tent peg, pointed at one end and with notch at the other. He runs back and No. 2 goes. Continue until 8 pegs are made. Pegs to be neat, usable and uniform.

> *Equipment*—8 pieces of wood, 9 inches long. Axe, chopping block.
> *Scoring*—Patrol completing in 10 minutes   60 points
>   Patrol completing in 15 minutes   40 points
>   Patrol participating at all   20 points

Wood Chopping Relay
Patrol lines up, in relay formation, about ten feet from spot where a log lies on the ground, kept firmly in position by four stakes. At the signal Scout No. 1 runs up to log, takes axe stuck in log, and takes six strokes, in an effort to chop the log in half. He sticks axe in log, runs back to touch off No. 2, who runs up, takes six strokes, runs back, and so on. Judge should set a reasonable time for cutting the log in half, depending upon the type of wood.

> *Equipment*—One log, 8″ to 12″ in diameter, 2′ to 3′ long, 4 stakes for holding it in position, 1 three-quarter axe.
> *Scoring*—Patrol finishing within time set by judge   60 points
>   Patrol using 1½ times the time set   40 points
>   Patrol participating at all   20 points

Cookery (Fires and Cooking)

GAMES
Fuzz Stick Relay   I-O
> *Space*—Medium   *Type*—Lively
> *Teams*—Patrols   *Formation*—Parallel File
> *Equipment*—For each Patrol, one piece of wood, ½″ x 1″ x 8″, and a sharp knife.

Patrols in relay formation opposite to pile of wood pieces. Scout No. 1 runs up, makes one cut, forming long sliver still attached to stick. He runs back, touches off next boy, who runs up, and so on. Score half for speed, half for quality of fuzz sticks.

Fire by Friction Relay   I-O
> *Space*—Medium   *Type*—Lively
> *Teams*—Patrols   *Formation*—Parallel File
> *Equipment*—Friction set per Patrol.

Friction set placed about 30 feet in front of each Patrol.

Scout No. 1 runs up to set, makes fire (must burst into flame), puts it out, runs back and tags second Scout who repeats performance. And so on until eight runs have been made.

Fire by Flint-and-Steel Relay
I-O

Space—Medium
Teams—Patrols
Equipment—Flint-and-Steel set per Patrol.

Type—Lively
Formation—Parallel File

Flint-and-steel set placed about 30 feet in front of each Patrol. Scout No. 1 runs up to set, makes fire (must burst into flame), puts it out, runs back and tags second Scout who repeats performance. And so on until eight runs have been made.

The Grocer

Space—Small
Teams—Patrols
Equipment—A number of grocery items according to recipes picked.

Type—Quiet
Formation—Informal

Pick out from a camp cook book the recipes for a complete meal. Write out the items needed, then make up packages to represent them and place them in a large bag. With the Scouts gathered around him, the game leader brings out the items, telling what they are. When all items have been shown, Patrols go into huddle, list the articles from memory, then *determine what the meal is.*

PROJECTS

String Burning

Two Scouts form the team. Two strings are stretched tightly between two vertical sticks—one string 18 inches above the ground, the other 24 inches. The team gathers wood, prepares it and makes a fire-lay under the strings. Top of fire-lay must be at least 4 inches below the 18 inch string. Only natural tinder and wood may be used. On signal, fire is lighted. Two matches only. *After lighting, fire must not be touched, nor extra wood added.*

Equipment—Stakes, string. Wood, axe, knife. 2 matches
Scoring—Team burning through both strings   60 points
             Team burning through 18 inch string   40 points
             Patrol participating at all   20 points

Fire Building and Water Boiling

Two Scouts make up the team. On "Go," Scouts place pot on suitable support (stones or on edges of small ditch), cut wood, strike match, light fire, keep it going until water boils over edge of pot. Axes must remain in sheath and knives in pocket until signal is given. No preliminary preparation of wood permitted. Kindling must be made from wood provided; no newspapers, leaves, pine needles or similar material may be used. No windbreak except hat or body; no bellows except lungs. Only two matches are issued; additional matches may be had by running to a point designated by the judge and returning, getting only one match each trip. Spilling water disqualifies.

Equipment—Brought by team: 2 axes, 2 Scout knives. Supplies to each team: Two pieces of wood, 2"x4"x12"; 2 large matches; quart can, without handles, filled to within 1" of top with water, with 1 teaspoon of soap flakes added.
Scoring—Team causing water to boil over in 10 min.   60 points
         Team causing water to boil over in 15 min.   40 points
         Patrol participating at all   20 points

Fire by Flint-and-Steel and Water Boiling

Two Scouts make up the team. On signal Scouts prepare fire wood, lay fire, suspend pot on simple crane, light the fire using flint and steel, charred cloth and tinder, keep fire going until water boils over. Only bark tinder and wood supplied by judge may be used for the fire — no paper, grass or leaves. Spilling of water disqualifies team.

Equipment—Brought by team: Flint, steel, charred cloth punk, cedar bark tinder (not chemically treated), 2 axes, 2 Scout knives, sticks for crane. Provided to team: Two pieces of wood, 2"x4"x12"; quart can with wire bail handle, filled to within 1" of top with water, with 1 teaspoonful soap flakes added.
Scoring—Team causing water to boil over in 10 min.   60 points
         Team causing water to boil over in 15 min.   40 points
         Patrol participating at all   20 points

Fire by Friction and Water Boiling

Same as Fire by Flint-and-Steel and Water Boiling with the exception that team brings friction set and tinder instead of flint, steel, punk and tinder.

Flapjack Baking

Two-man team. At starting signal, team builds fire, prepares batter, cooks a flapjack, at least four inches in diameter, and presents it to the judge. (To add fun, a string may be stretched horizontally seven feet high, with cook required to flip flapjack over the string, using the frying pan as flipper, catch it in pan, return to fire and finish frying on the other side).

Equipment—Team brings its own wood, axes, pancake flour, liquid, bowl for mixing, grease and frying pan.
Scoring—Team making satisfactory flapjack in 15 min.   60 points
         Team making satisfactory flapjack in 20 min.   40 points
         Patrol participating at all   20 points

Ropework

GAMES

Knot "Champ-Nit"   I

Space—Small
Teams—Patrol Representatives
Equipment—As needed.

Type—Quiet
Formation—Informal

Patrols in corners in charge of Patrol Leaders. Under his direction members race to tie a square knot, for instance, and drop it to the floor. Winner steps out and rest of Patrol repeats contest. Winner steps out each time, so that the last one is the "Champ-nit" of the Patrol. Troop assembles, and Patrol Champ-nits compete to find Troop Champ-nit. This method may be used for numerous Scout subjects. The merit of it is that the Scout most in need of practice gets most of it.

Knotting Circle (Knot Run)   I

Space—Medium
Teams—Whole Troop against "It"
Equipment—One knotting rope.

Type—Lively
Formation—Circle

Scouts facing inward, hands behind their backs. "It" walks around outside circle, places rope in someone's hands, yells name of a knot and starts speedy run around circle. If recipient succeeds in tying knot correctly before "It" comes back, "It" must proceed again. Otherwise recipient becomes "It" and previous "It" takes his place in the circle.

Chain Gang Race   I-O

Space—Medium
Teams—Patrols
Equipment—One rope per boy.

Type—Lively
Formation—Parallel File

On signal, boy No. 1 ties rope around his ankle with a bowline and hands end to second boy. Second boy ties his rope on to first boy's with a square knot, then ties rope to his own ankle with a clove hitch and hands loose end to third boy, who treats himself likewise. When all are tied together Patrol races to a finishing line.

Knot Hoop Relay   I

Space—Medium
Teams—Patrols
Equipment—One rope per Patrol.

Type—Lively
Formation—Parallel File

On signal, first Scout ties rope into a loop with a square knot (or sheet-bend, fisherman's knot, etc.) and passes it over his head and down around his body. He steps out of the hoop, unties knot and passes rope to next Scout, who repeats procedure, and so on down the line.

One Hand Knotting

Space—Small
Teams—Two Scouts per Patrol
Equipment—One rope per boy.

Type—Quiet
Formation—Facing Lines

Boys of each pair stand facing each other, each boy with rope in right hand, left hand in pocket. On signal they attempt to tie their ropes together using knot called. First pair successful wins.

Save My Child   I-O

Space—Medium
Teams—Patrols
Equipment—One burlap bag per Patrol, one rope per boy.

Type—Lively
Formation—Parallel File

"Child" (one boy of the Patrol) sits on burlap bag about thirty feet in front of first boy of each Patrol. On signal the last boy in each Patrol file ties his rope with sheet bend to rope of boy in front of him, who in turn ties it on to the next, etc. Front Scout in each Patrol ties bowline around himself, "swims" to "child," sits down next to him on bag, holds on to him, is pulled back by rest of Patrol. First Patrol finished wins.

Roman Chariot Race

Space—Medium
Teams—Patrols
Equipment—For each Patrol: Five Scout staffs or poles 4-5′ long, six pieces of twine for lashings.

Type—Lively
Formation—Informal

Equipment is placed in a pile opposite to Patrols. On signal, Patrols run and lash "chariot." This is done by making a "trestle" frame as in building a bridge (four staffs form square, fifth staff is lashed diagonally to two opposite sides). When frame is finished, two Scouts pull "chariot" and a rider to finishing line.

PROJECTS

Knot Tying Relay

Patrol team of 8 boys (in case of a small Patrol, one or more Scouts must each tie two knots) line up in relay formation, about 10 feet from a staff, held horizontally 30 inches off the ground. Eight ropes are laid out below the staff. On signal, Scout No. 1 runs up, ties knot, runs back, tags off No. 2, who runs up, ties knot, and so on, in the following order: 1. Square Knot; 2. Sheetbend; 3. Fisherman's Knot (for these, join ends of rope with tight knot, staff running through loop); 4. Clove Hitch; 5. Two Half Hitches; 6. Timber Hitch (for these, tie rope to staff, pull knot tight); 7. Taut-Line Hitch; 8. Bowline (for these, tie knots so that staff runs through loop).

Equipment—Staff; 8 ropes, about 4 feet long.
Scoring—Patrol completing in 4 minutes .... 60 points
Patrol completing in 8 minutes .... 40 points
Patrol participating at all .... 20 points
NOTE: For each incorrect knot, add 1 minute.

Flag Pole Raising

Patrol lines up with four Scout staffs (or equivalent) and the Patrol flag attached to a fifth staff. On signal, Scouts lash the five staffs together (Patrol flag staff at top) to form pole, approximately 20 feet long. They then attach three guy lines about two-thirds of the way to the top, raise pole, and stake down the guy lines so that pole stands vertically. When finished, Patrol forms single line at base of pole, comes to attention.

Equipment—5 staffs, about 6′ long, 1″ in diameter, one of them with Patrol flag attached; 8 pieces of heavy cord for four double lashings; 3 guy ropes, about 17 feet long; 3 wooden stakes. Axe or hammer for driving stakes.
Scoring—Patrol finishing in 10 minutes .... 60 points
Patrol finishing in 15 minutes .... 40 points
Patrol participating at all .... 20 points

Bridge Trestle Lashing

Patrol is the team. Object is to lash together a trestle for a rustic bridge. Trestle consists of two uprights, top crosspiece, bottom crosspiece, and two diagonals. Lashings are to be firmly made, using ¼″ rope. All lashings are square lashings with the exception of one: The diagonal lashing that springs the two diagonal pieces together in the middle.

Equipment—Logs, 2″ to 2½″ diameter as follows: 2 8-foot uprights, 1 5-foot top crosspiece, 1 5½-foot bottom crosspiece, 2 6½-foot diagonals. 9 15-foot lengths of ¼″ rope, whipped at both ends.
Scoring—Patrol finishing in 5 minutes .... 60 points
Patrol finishing in 10 minutes .... 40 points
Patrol participating at all .... 20 points
NOTE: For each incorrect or poor lashing, add 1 minute.

Nature

GAMES

What Is It?   1-O

Space—Small   *Type*—Quiet
Teams—Patrols   *Formation*—Informal
Equipment—As needed, also paper and pencils

The Troop's nature expert collects specimens of things every Scout should know, such as a puff ball, milkweed pod, cat-tail, pine cone, wasp nest, leaves, insects, etc. About fifteen of them are attached to cardboard, numbered consecutively, and placed before Troop. Each boy makes list of the items he recognizes. These are turned over to judge, who gives one point to each correct answer. Total points divided with number of boys in the Patrol give each Patrol's standing.

Tree Hunt ○

Space—Large   *Type*—Quiet
Teams—Patrols   *Formation*—Informal
Equipment—Paper, pencils.

Patrols are given ten minutes (on hike or in camp) to gather *one* leaf only from each of as many different trees as they can locate. When brought in they are arranged on the ground or a blanket, and slips of paper with names arranged next to them. Most leaves correctly identified wins.

Tree Spotting ○

Space—Medium   *Type*—Quiet
Teams—Patrols   *Formation*—Informal
Equipment—Paper and pencils.

During rest on hike or while in camp the Troop's nature expert paces a circle with a radius of about 200 feet, identifies and makes a list of trees found within circle. On signal the Patrols investigate the section and finally bring in their findings. Best report wins.

Nature Scavenger Hunt ○

Space—Large   *Type*—Active
Teams—Patrols   *Formation*—Informal
Equipment—Sheet of instructions for each Patrol.

On a hike, each Patrol is given sealed letter, containing the following instructions:

"Greetings and Salutations:—Believe it or not, your Senior Patrol Leader has fallen desperately in love, but—the fair lady does not return his love. He will pine away unless he drinks a dose of my patent falling-out-of-love potion. For this I shall need the following items within an hour from the moment you read this:

Four White Oak Acorns   Eighteen Pine Needles
Twenty Dandelion Seeds   Bit of Rabbit Fluff
Six Inches of Sassafras Branch   Four Dead Flies
. . . .

Good luck and good hunting!   (Signed)   Hoo-Doo, Witch Doctor."

Make list of about twelve to twenty items, fitting your locality and the season. Patrol bringing in largest number of items within one hour wins.

PROJECTS

Tree Lore
Twenty leaves of local trees are placed before the Patrol.

Patrol has five minutes in which to write down the names of the trees.

> *Equipment*—Leaves of 20 trees
> *Scoring*—Patrol correctly naming 18 leaves   60 points
>   Patrol correctly naming 10 leaves   40 points
>   Patrol participating at all   20 points

Bird Recognition

Twenty pictures of local birds are placed before the Patrol. Patrol has five minutes in which to write down the names of the birds.

> *Equipment*—20 colored pictures of birds (National Audubon Society series)
> *Scoring*—Patrol correctly naming 18 birds   60 points
>   Patrol correctly naming 10 birds   40 points
>   Patrol participating at all   20 points

Nature Hunt

The Patrol is shown an exhibit of thirty labeled nature specimens—leaves, flowers, twigs, rocks, and so on. On signal, Scouts set out to collect specimens corresponding to those on exhibit. When brought in, they are labeled or provided with tags. Time limit: 30 minutes (or more, depending upon locality).

> *Equipment*—Collection of 30 labeled specimens. Material for labeling or tagging; pencils.
> *Scoring*—25 specimens collected and labeled   60 points
>   15 specimens collected and labeled   40 points
>   Patrol participating at all   20 points

First Aid

GAMES

Tourniquet Relay   I-O

> *Space*—Medium   *Type*—Lively
> *Teams*—Patrols   *Formation*—Parallel File
> *Equipment*—Each Scout using his own neckerchief.

One boy from each Patrol lies about 30 feet in front of it with arterial "bleeding" of left wrist. One judge for each victim. On signal, first Scout runs up, applies tourniquet. When correct, judge yells "Off," Scout removes tourniquet, runs back to Patrol, tags off next Scout, who repeats operation.

Live Wire Accident   I-O

> *Space*—Medium   *Type*—Quiet
> *Teams*—Patrols   *Formation*—Patrol Groups
> *Equipment*—Long rope.

Patrols in groups on starting line. Across meeting room or field is laid a long rope to indicate a dropped high power electric wire. One member of each Patrol places himself under the "wire." On signal, the Patrols run to "wire" and start to rescue their friend. They must devise their own way of doing it safely with material at hand. If the judge decides that rescuer has contacted the "wire" he, too, is to fall "unconscious" and be rescued. Patrol bringing victim first to starting point wins.

PROJECTS

Accidents
Each of the accidents suggested for First Aid Field Day in camp (page 274) may be used as a separate project, with the Patrol the team.

Equipment—As required
Scoring—Patrol doing excellent job   60 points
          Patrol doing acceptable job   40 points
          Patrol participating at all   20 points

Bandage Demonstration
One member of Patrol to be patient, the rest first aider. On "Go," No. 1 goes to patient and ties head bandage and goes back. Then No. 2 ties cross chest, No. 3 thigh, No. 4 ankle bandage, No. 5 sling for arm, then No. 6 and No. 7 go up and by chair-carry transport patient to starting point. NO TIME ELEMENT. (NOTE: In case of a small Patrol, one or more Scouts may go up twice, until project is completed.)

Equipment—As needed.
Scoring—Patrol with 5 bandages completely acceptable   60 points
          Patrol with 3 bandages completely acceptable   40 points
          Patrol competing at all   20 points

B. RECREATIONAL GAMES
Whole Troop

Jump the Shot   I-O
Space—Medium   *Type*—Lively
Teams—Whole Troop   *Formation*—Troop Circle
Equipment—Long rope with soft weight (sandbag) in end

Troop circle formation, with one boy in center who swings rope around circle below knees of others, who must jump it. If hit by rope or bag, they drop out. Game continues until only one is left.

Poison   I-O
Space—Medium   *Type*—Vigorous
Teams—Whole Troop   *Formation*—Troop Circle
Equipment—None.

Troop circle formation, but with Scouts of the various

Patrols alternating. Mark a circle on the ground, five-six feet in diameter. All Scouts join hands and move rapidly around the circle, while each Scout tries to force the opponent next to him on either side to step into the inside circle. Any Scout stepping into circle is "poisoned" and drops out of game. Game is continued until only one is left. The Patrol to which he belongs is the winner.

Do This—Do That   I-O

Space—Medium   *Type*—Quiet
Teams—Whole Troop   *Formation*—Line
Equipment—None.

Leader, in front of Troop, performs certain movements, preceding each with "Do this!" or "Do that!" All movements following the order "Do this!" must immediately be executed by all players, while movements following "Do that!" must be ignored. Players making mistakes drop out. Continue until all are out or a certain length of time.

Whole Troop Against "It"

British Bull Dog   I-O

Space—Medium   *Type*—Strenuous
Teams—Troop against "It"   *Formation*—Troop line
Equipment—None.

One or two older Scouts take position in center of room —or area—facing Troop. At "Go," the entire Troop charges from one end of room and tries to reach the other end, without being caught. To catch someone, "bulldogs" in the center must lift player off floor long enough to yell "1-2-3 British Bull Dog." When a player is caught, he, too, becomes a "bulldog" for the next charge. Not more than 3 men can tackle a player. If a struggling player is not lifted completely off the floor while Troop slowly counts to ten, he is decared free for another charge. Game is run until everyone has been caught. Last man left is winner.

Swat 'Em   I-O

Space—Medium   *Type*—Lively
Teams—Whole Troop against "It" *Formation*—Troop Circle
Equipment—A wrapped newspaper or cloth sausage.

Each Scout with his hands held cup-shape behind him. "It" carries wrapped newspaper or cloth sausage to use as swatter. He leaves it in the hands of some one of the players in the circle, who from that moment on has the privilege of swatting the boy at his right on the back, below the neck, as long as that boy is on the journey around the circle and back to his own place in the circle again. When this chase is completed the new holder of the swatter circles mysteriously about the ring, leaving the swatter in the hands of another boy, and taking a place in the circle.

Tags   O

Space—Large
Teams—Whole Troop against "It"
Equipment—None.

Type—Vigorous
Formation—Informal

CROSS TAG—"It" must continue chasing same Scout until he catches him, or until another Scout crosses between them, in which case "It" must catch the Scout who crossed.

ANKLE TAG—To escape being tagged one must grasp another Scout by the ankle. The Scout whose ankle is grasped, however, is liable to be tagged unless he has hold of someone else's ankle. The playing area must be small enough to make the game feasible.

CHAIN TAG—The first man tagged joins hands with the man who is "It," and later as each man is tagged he is added to the chain. The playing area must be limited so all can be caught finally.

SKUNK TAG—Each player holds his nose with one hand, holds up one foot with the other. Player can only be tagged if he lets go with either hand.

Half Troop Teams

Take the Mat   I-O

Space—Medium
Teams—Half Troop
Equipment—Mat or chalk.

Type—Vigorous
Formation—Informal

Two opposing teams line up the same distance from a mat or space about 25 square feet chalked off on the ground. At the leader's signal they rush for the mat and try to place as many men on it as possible. At the end of one minute a whistle is blown and the team having the most men on the mat wins. Opponents can be pulled, pushed or thrown, but clothing must not be grasped.

Crows and Cranes   I-O

Space—Medium
Teams—Half Troop
Equipment—None.

Type—Vigorous
Formation—Facing lines

Divide the boys into two teams lined up facing each other, one side called the "Cranes," the other the "Crows." When the leader calls out "Cranes!" or "Crows!" all on the team named must turn and run to the wall in back of them. If a boy is tagged by an opponent before reaching the wall, he is captured and becomes a member of the other team. This can be kept up until one team has captured all those on the other side. The leader can add fun by dragging out the words and by giving occasional false alarms—for example: "Cr-r-r-rows" or "Cr-r-r-ranes" or "Cr-r-r-rash."

Steal the Bacon · 1-O

Space—Medium
Teams—Half Troop
Equipment—One neckerchief.
Type—Lively
Formation—Facing lines

Troop, in two teams, lines up with thirty feet between the lines. Teams face each other and number through, thus there are two Scouts for each number—one in each line. Two "ones," two "fives," etc. The "bacon"—neckerchief—lies on the ground in the center. The leader calls "sixes," and the two "sixes" dash out, each trying to seize the "bacon" and get "home" before the other "six" tags him. Score: one point for getting safely home, or for tagging Scout trying to carry "bacon" home.

Capture the Flag (Flag Raiding) O

Space—Large
Teams—Half Troop
Equipment—Two signal flags.
Type—Strenuous
Formation—Informal

Each team has its own territory in which its Scouts are free to move as they please, but on which opponents enter at their peril. The territories are separated by a boundary line such as a brook or a trail, etc. Any Scout crossing this line may be captured by the enemy.

The teams assemble close together at a starting point near the center of the line, each team in its own territory. On a signal the teams proceed to set up their flags at any point within 200 steps of the starting point. The flags must be visible, although it is permissible to place them as inconspicuously as possible.

After three minutes another signal is given for start of game. The object now is to enter the enemy's territory, capture the flag, and carry it across the line into home territory without being caught. Scouts may be posted to guard the flag, but must not get nearer than 50 feet to it, unless an enemy Scout goes within the 50-foot circle. They may then follow him.

Any Scout found in the enemy's territory may be captured by grasping him and holding him long enough for the captor to say "Caught!" three times. When a Scout is captured he must go with captor to the "guard house"—a tree or rock 50 feet from the boundary line.

A prisoner may be released by a friend touching him, provided the prisoner at that time is touching the guard house with a hand or a foot, whereupon both return to their own territory. If the rescuer is caught by the guards before he touches the prisoner, he, too, must go to the guard house. A rescuer can rescue only one prisoner at a time.

If the flag is successfully captured, it must be carried across the line into home territory. If the raider is caught before he reaches home, the flag is set up again at the point where it was rescued and the game goes on as before. If neither side captures the enemy's flag within the time agreed upon (say, ½ hour) the game is won by the team having most prisoners.

Patrol Teams

Skin the Snake   I-O

Space—Medium   *Type*—Lively
Teams—Patrols   *Formation*—Parallel File
Equipment—None.

Each player stoops over, putting his right hand between his legs and grasping the left hand of the player behind him. At a given signal the last man in line lies down on his back, putting his feet first between the legs of the player in front of him. The line walks backward, striding the bodies of those behind, boys immediately lying down upon having no more to stride. When finished, all are lying on their backs. The last man to lie down rises to his feet and strides forward up the line, the rest following as fast as their turn comes. Team which breaks grasp is disqualified.

Antelope Race   O

Space—Large   *Type*—Vigorous
Teams—Patrols   *Formation*—Parallel File
Equipment—None.

On signal, Scouts run in single file with one hand on the belt of the Scout ahead to a point fifty yards away, make left turn and run back to starting point. Falling down or breaking apart throws out the team.

Under and Over Relay

Space—Large
Teams—Patrols
Equipment—Ball.

Type—Lively
Formation—Parallel File

Front player has a ball—or other large object—which he passes over his head, using both hands, to the player behind him, and so on down the line. When the last player gets the ball he runs to the front and passes it between his legs back down the line. Next time over the head, and so on. Ball must be passed, not thrown. First team to regain its original order wins. Variation: Front player always passes over and the next under, and so on alternately.

Patrol Representatives

I-O

Duel Contests

Space—Small
Teams—Patrol Representatives
Equipment—None, or as needed.

Type—Quiet
Formation—Informal

To be most effective, duel contests should be preceded by more or less formal challenges, a boy from one Patrol challenging: "I, Scout So-and-so, challenge anyone in Indian Hand Wrestling." It is accepted by someone else saying: "I, Scout This-and-that, accept the challenge." The two go at it, the winner is decided and is promptly challenged by someone else, until a certain time has elapsed, a certain number of rounds have been played, or one Scout has been the winner three times in succession.

INDIAN HAND WRESTLING—One contestant places the outside of his right foot against the outside of the other's. Both brace themselves by placing their left feet a long step to the rear. They grasp right hands and attempt to throw each other. The one who first succeeds in making the other move his feet or lose his balance is the winner.

ONE-LEGGED HAND WRESTLING—Each contestant holds his left leg behind him in his left hand, grasps the other's right hand. Then each proceeds to try to throw the other.

COCK FIGHTING—Same position as for One-Legged Hand Wrestling, with the exception that the hands are held on the back. Players charge each other, push with shoulders and upper arms only, attempt to upset each other.

INDIAN LEG WRESTLING—The two contestants lie down with their backs flat on the ground, side by side, but with their legs in opposite direction. On a signal each lifts his inside leg to vertical position, then on the next signal tries to lock leg with the opponent and twist him over.

TROOP HIKE IDEAS

Historical Hike

Have the Patrols consult the library, their school teachers, their pastor, and the local Chamber of Commerce, for historical facts of your locality. Decide on a hike route which will include the greatest possible number of interesting spots.

Send out the Patrols to investigate as many places as possible. At the hike destination each Patrol reports on its findings.

Nature Hike

This may involve a hike to a certain habitat — marsh, lake, field, woods, and so on—to make an investigation of all types of wild life here. Or it may be a specific quest for one certain type of wild life: Trees, flowers, birds, animals. Each Patrol brings a notebook to list its discoveries.

Various nature games may be played, such as a Patrol *Nature "Scavenger" Hunt* for about a dozen items—a piece of bark from shagbark hickory, a dried acorn, a wild rose thorn, a three-lobed sassafras leaf—these items to be found within a certain length of time. Or have a *Tree Identification Game* in which numbered tags are placed on several trees by the leader, after which the Patrols try to find tags and make a list of the names of the trees to which they were attached.

Nature specimens may be collected: Pressed flowers and tree leaves, smoke prints, plaster casts of tracks.

Star Hike

Make this a part of a late afternoon and evening hike. For beginners, a night lighted by a moon in its first or last quarter is best. At such time all smaller stars and the milky way disappear, thus emphasizing the stars which make up the constellations.

Focus flashlight into a strong, narrow beam and use this for a pointer. Starting with the Big Dipper and the Polar Star, point out the main constellations in a natural, progressive manner. Have a contest to see which Patrol can point out the greatest number of constellations. Which constellation is most helpful? Then plot directions by the stars.

Explorers

An envelope is prepared for each Patrol with a small map sketch and a letter with the following contents:

"You are a group of explorers sent out from the American Museum of Natural History. You have landed in a far-off spot of the globe, and it is your job to make a survey of the territory from here to the spot marked **X** on the map. We want to know its (1) birds, (2) animals, (3) trees, (4) general type of country, (5) roads and paths, (6) lakes and rivers, (7) inhabitants, and (8) its history. In order to get as much information as possible, divide your Patrol into buddy teams, each pair of buddies to specialize in two of the subjects. The buddy teams will start out independently as soon as they are instructed. Your whole group of explorers must come together again at the point X on the map at ...... o'clock, ready to make a report of your findings and submit drawings and map sketches made along the way."

Make the hike about five miles and allow the Patrols three hours in which to cover the distance and make their observations.

On a signal, the Patrols open their envelopes. They proceed as soon as they have noted their contents. Upon arrival at the hike destination, they are judged on precision and the quality of their reports.

Treasure Hunt

Numerous variations of Treasure Hunts are possible. The clues are most easily laid in the opposite order from that in which they are to be followed. The following description of a Treasure Hunt suggests some of the possibilities:

Each Patrol Leader gets a sealed envelope. On the front of it is a small sketch map with a cross. Under it is: "Proceed to spot marked X, then open envelope." The spot is easily located. The Patrol Leader breaks the seal. Inside is a message in Morse code: "Go to the tallest oak you can see from this point. Then follow the direction of its biggest branch two hundred feet." The Patrol goes and finds—nothing. That is, until one of the boys yells: "Here's a stone that has just been moved." Under it someone discovers the next clue: "SW to tree with unnatural fruit." The tree proves to be a hickory with several pine cones tied to its limbs. At the foot of it starts a trail of Scout trail marks that leads to the foot of another tree.

No clue around! What to do next? Someone finally looks up and sees a tag hanging on a branch high above. A Scout is sent up to investigate it. It only says: "Look west!" "Well, look west then. What do you see?" "Looks like a red neckerchief in a tree about four hundred feet away!" The Patrol gets to the tree and finds the next clue attached to the neckerchief: "WSW 200 feet," and two hundred feet west-south-west it locates a pile of stones. Diving into it, a Scout finds the last clue: "Dig under the dead chestnut!" The tree is quickly found, the Patrol digs where the earth has recently been turned over and finds . . . well, maybe not a chest of pieces-of-eight but certainly at least a box of salted peanuts to be divided among the lucky treasure hunters.

Industrial or Institutional Hike

Arrange with some manufacturing company to allow your Scouts to tour its plant and have the processes explained to them. Be sure the company knows exactly when you will arrive and how many Scouts will be with you. At the last meeting preceding the Industrial Hike devote part of the program to telling the Scouts about the products manufactured in the plant they are to visit.

Or make arrangemens to visit an institution such as a museum of natural history, a science museum, a college, or an historical society.

Encourage each Scout to bring pencil and notebook with him to record his most interesting observations.

Industrial and Institutional Hikes are of particular interest, often, to rural Scouts because they give them an opportunity to become familiar with things beyond their immediate environment.

Long Distance Hike

After some shorter hikes, take a Ten-mile Hike. Get the Patrols and the individual boys interested in taking Ten-mile Hikes of their own toward earning the Hiking Merit Badge.

Swimming Hike

To lake or swimming pool where swimming may be practiced under safe conditions. See Chapter 11.

Mountain Climb

May be undertaken, if adequate leadership can be secured. Obviously a stunt only for physically fit older boys.

Primitive Cookery Hike

Study suggestions in *Scout Field Book,* Pow-Wow 16, for cooking without utensils. Train in certain of the methods until each Scout can prepare a complete menu of primitive dishes.

Survival (Robinson Crusoe) Hike

For a Primitive Cookery Hike you bring foodstuffs but no utensils. For a Survival Hike it is the other way round. Here you bring utensils but gather the food-stuff in its wild state. Preliminary nature study is required of local edible plants, roots, berries and fruits. See *Scout Field Book,* Pow-Wow 28.

Rovering Knights

Lay out on a map a route for each Patrol to follow, and decide on a gathering point for the whole Troop, and a definite time for Patrols to get there.

Scouts set out to see how many Good Turns they can find to do. A blind man stops at a street corner, a Scout goes to his aid . . . a broken milk bottle is lying in the gutter where someone might park a car . . . a child tries vainly to fix the seat of his bicycle . . . the mooring of a boat has come loose . . . a fence post needs fixing to keep the cattle in.

At the time decided upon the Patrols come together and the Patrol Leaders submit unsigned reports. Read reports, then simply say: "Amazing how many Good Turns you can find to do if you only keep your eyes open for them!"

Conservation Hike

Decide upon most appropriate places for feeding stations, with the cooperation of local bird and game experts. Assign definite jobs to the various Patrols. Earn money and buy feed.

Tree planting, tree repair, clearing of brush, cutting of trails, erection of birdhouses, are in this class.

"Lost Child" Hike

"A child is lost. A search has been going on all night. The only place that has not been scoured is a stretch of woodland, indicated on map sketch. Our help has been requested." Combine this with a Troop mobilization (see Tool 18).

Warn boys at previous Troop meeting that they may be called out a certain day between certain hours, but do not disclose reason. The "child" is a life-size doll, made up of pillows and child's clothing, placed in a spot not too conspicuous.

Following the mobilization, as soon as a Patrol is complete, instructions are given and the Patrol proceeds with orders to meet at a given spot at a given time when search will end, whether or not the "child" has been found. Patrol locating "child" or otherwise showing most intelligent procedure, is the winner.

Commando Hike (Wide Game)

Commando Hikes are thrilling to every Scout. They provide practice in numerous Scout skills. For suggestions see games index.

North Pole Race

For snow country. At previous meeting tell story of conquest of North Pole (or South Pole). Announce race, each Patrol to bring a sled loaded with "provisions" and "instruments." Decide in Patrol Leaders' Council the weight of the load. Hike may be combined with Beeline Hike (see below).

Start off Patrols, giving them a definite destination indicated on a map sketch, or a compass direction and a certain number of miles to travel, there to place the Patrol flag and to report to an established "station" within a given time.

Bee-Line (Columbus) Hike

Locate on a map a suitable destination and as many starting points as there are Patrols. Determine the compass direction each Patrol will follow (remember difference between magnetic and true North) and the number of miles each Patrol will travel.

The hike itself is similar to the North Pole Race. After each Patrol has reported the distance between spot where Patrol flag is planted and the actual destination is measured (or judged), Patrol coming closest is winner. A Patrol may pass an insurmountable obstacle by going around it in 90-degree angles.

Map Hike

Follow a cross-country route marked on a topographic map. Report to be made later, including interesting items observed on the hike. Or make map sketch or tracing for the Patrols to use, of a winding road, at least three miles long.

Signal Hike

Select hilly territory where several signal stations may be established. Each Patrol is equipped with signal flags and a map to be followed according to directions received by Morse or Semaphore.

The Patrols at the starting point are simply told: "Use your eyes!" On looking around they see a Scout, some distance away, signaling a message of directions. As soon as a Patrol has received the message, it proceeds according to instructions. As it reaches its first destination, it sends its call letters, until another signal station acknowledges it, and sends further directions. And so on for as many stops as desired. The messages may involve the doing of certain things besides giving the route to follow.

First Aid ("S.O.S.") Hike (Ammunition Explosion)

On a hike, an "explosion" (fire cracker) is heard from the distance. All Patrols proceed on the run and find lying on the ground as many "victims" as there are

Patrols. On each is a label giving the "injury" and the "addresses" of the "doctor" and "policeman" (Assistant Scoutmasters or other helpers at a prearranged, nearby spot). The Patrols carry on as they think fit.

Any messengers to the "doctor" are told to convey the "victim" on some suitable stretcher to the "hospital" (the destination of the Troop hike), while messengers to the "police" are asked to make a report of anything that may have a bearing on the case, and to go to the "hospital" where there will be a consultation with the "doctor."

The Scoutmaster notes how each Patrol acts, and after consultation with the "doctor" and the "police," can make appropriate comments.

Scoutcraft Obstacle Hike

Several Explorers or Troop Committee members are required for judges at the various obstacles. The obstacles cover Scout Requirements and opportunities for application of the Scout Oath and Law. The Patrols are instructed in advance about what equipment to bring.

The Patrols start off with ten or fifteen-minute intervals. Obstacles may include: (1) Signaled instructions; (2) boy bitten by rattlesnake; (3) boy's bicycle broken down; (4) small river to be crossed (boat at other shore with one oar. Solution: Have one boy swim over for boat, then row the others over); (5) "Susie was frightened by a bear and climbed up in that tree. She must be hoisted down with a rope" ("Susie" is a life-size doll made of pillows, draped over a high branch); (6) an unfinished bridge to be completed to permit Patrol to cross an imaginary impassable marsh; and so on. Let your imagination run rampant.

Sealed Orders (Mystery) Hike

Each Patrol Leader receives a series of numbered envelopes. Each envelope contains specific instructions covering a stage of the hike. The first may order the Patrol to proceed to a certain crossroad by a certain route. The second, which is to be opened when the hikers reach the end of the first stage of the journey, gives the second part of the route, and so on. Each order should include specific instructions for observation, Scoutcraft, etc.

This method of giving instructions keeps the interest and anticipation at a high pitch, especially as the final destination is not disclosed until the last sealed envelope is opened.

Advancement Hike

From time to time you will find that the Scouts are almost ready to advance in rank, and only need a final push to get finished.

Plan an Advancement Hike, with each boy bringing whatever equipment he needs. Each Patrol works at its own site, with the Patrol Leader examining his boys in Requirements he himself has already met.

Visiting Troop Hike

Many of the above mentioned hikes are suitable for entertaining a visiting Troop from your own or some other town. Such occasional visits will prove of mutual benefit, and spur the boys on to further accomplishments.

Father-and-Son Hike

The fathers are invited to the Troop's favorite camp site, where special games and contests may be held, ranging from horse-shoe pitching to relay races, and where a hike meal is served.

Reunion (Old-timers') Hike

Many Troops have established the tradition of an Old-timers' Hike on the last Saturday or Sunday of the year, when old members are home for the Christmas holidays. An adequate attendance promotion and a suitable program are required. Old-timers and Explorers of the Troop take part.

The hike may be an automobile trip to a suitable starting point, a short hike to a country inn where refreshments have been arranged for, and where a couple of hours may be spent discussing the old glory of the Troop, and singing the old songs. Then a return hike to the automobiles, and back to town again.

Or the hike may be to the Troop's favorite camp site, where a roaring fire is going, and where a meal of baked beans are "doing" underground.

WIDE GAMES

A GAME of a more ambitious kind than those described in Tool 11 is the so-called Wide Game (Field Game or Cross-Country Game).

The Wide Game takes in a considerable amount of territory and occupies from one to several hours. It requires thorough planning in advance, by the Patrol Leaders' Council. The wide game provides romance and adventure, helps to develop initiative and leadership, and increases the boys' Scoutcraft knowledge and physical fitness.

Planning the Wide Games

In its simplest form the wide game is a refinement on the old boyhood games of "Cops and Robbers" or "Cowboys and Indians," made a little more exciting.

To plan the game the following steps are necessary:

(1) Decide upon the *theme* of the game. Get your ideas from national or local history, from books of fiction, from stories, or even from the daily newspapers. But no matter from what source you secure your theme, make sure of its romantic appeal.

(2) Study a map of your favorite *territory* and decide the positions from which the teams are to start and where they are to move.

(3) Be sure that the comparative *strength* of the various teams is correct.

(4) Develop the *rules* of the game. Each game should contain attack and defense in equal measure for each team. Be certain that no team is given advantages over the other.

(5) Decide upon *method* of capture, i.e., how to put opponents out of commission. The simplest method is a piece of one-inch gauze bandage tied around the upper arm, left or right to indicate team. The capture of bandage constitutes the loss of "life." Provide a central place to which Scouts may come to secure extra "lives" and thus continue in the game.

(6) Have the necessary *equipment* available or placed before the game starts.

(7) Decide upon the *time* for the start of the game, the finish of the game and when the Scouts are to gather at a specified spot after the game to hear the result of it.

(8) Prepare a sealed *message* to the leader of each team to be opened at the start of the game. This message should describe the theme, the objects the team is to accomplish, scoring and special rules. It should also contain a map sketch of the territory (or refer to map brought by each team leader).

Types of Wide Games

Most wide games may be divided into the following types (although many other classifications are possible):

TREASURE TYPE—Each of two or more teams attempts to obtain a treasure and bring it to safety against the opposition of the other teams.

SEIZURE TYPE—Each of two teams attempts to bring a treasure from one spot to the other, at the same time trying to seize the treasure of the other team which is moving in the opposite direction.

CONQUEST TYPE—Each of two teams attempts to conquer a specified spot of ground defended by the opponents, at the same time keeping the opponents from conquering its own piece of ground.

Sample of Treasure Type

THE MAYAN TREASURE: A sealed envelope is given to each Patrol Leader. On the outside is written: "To be opened at (time) o'clock at (start position) and read before your Patrol." At the appointed time the Patrol Leader tears open the envelope, which contains a marked map sketch and the following message:

> *Story*—"I am the well-known explorer (name). It has come to my knowledge that an aviator flying over Yucatan has spied a large ruin never before discovered. I have the suspicion that the ruin is that of a Mayan palace and contains the lost treasure of the Mayas. I have therefore called you together so that we may set out and find the treasure. I have already secured provision and weapons for the dangerous expedition. But I have learned that our deadly enemies (names) are planning similar expeditions. They shall not succeed!
>
> *Objects*—"We will proceed to the Mayan palace (marked treasure on map) where the treasure (a packsack with stones) is buried, dig this up and transport it to our goal, Numa, where we shall be able to convert it into real money. We will do everything in our power to prevent our opponents from getting the treasure and bringing it to Numa.
>
> *Score*—"Treasure found ....10 points
> Treasure possessed at the end of game ....20 points
> Each opponent captured .... 2 points
> *Special Rules*—"(Method of capture). Game starts at (time), stops at (time). Troop gathers at (place) at (time)."

Variations of Treasure Type

THE INHERITANCE: Each Patrol Leader is the son of a man who died ten years ago. On the tenth anniversary of his death each son receives from a lawyer a letter describing where the father buried his treasure, hoping that after ten years the old animosity between the sons would have disappeared. But it is worse than ever. Each son sets out with his own gang to find the treasure and prevent his brothers from getting it. The treasure must be brought to a bank for safety.

THE POLAR EXPEDITION: Each Patrol is a group of polar explorers racing to the North Pole in competition with the other Patrols. On the North Pole they will find The Flag which Admiral Byrd threw down from his airplane when crossing the top of the world. This flag (signal flag) must be brought back to the office of the Geographical Society, before the explorers' claim can be acknowledged.

THE IDOL OF BULALONGA: Each Patrol is a tribe of Zulus in the wilds of Africa. Through their medicine men they are informed that the tribe which finds the image of the heathen god Bulalonga and brings it back to the spot from which it was stolen by the pygmies, will forever after be in Bulalonga's favor. The image may be a staff decorated with a couple of neckerchiefs.

The treasure type wide game may be combined with the features of a regular *Treasure Hunt* (see Hike section).

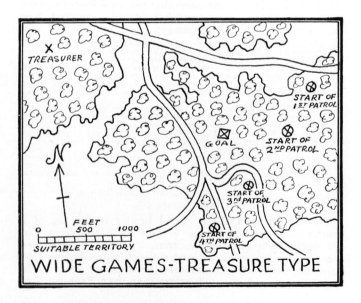

WIDE GAMES-TREASURE TYPE

Sample of Seizure Type

The Gems of Mustapha: A sealed envelope is given to each of the two team leaders to be opened at a specified spot at a specified time. Each envelope contains a marked map sketch, and one only of the following two messages:

Message for *TEAM I* (to be opened at I on map).

Story—"We are the Luxor Desert Police. The rich Arabian Merchant, Mustapha, has come to us and has asked for an escort to take him through the desert. He carries with him a treasure of gems (a packsack filled with leaves) and has learned that the notorious bandit Ali Baba is on the rampage. Our spies have discovered that Ali Baba's righthand man (with turban) still carries with him the loot from the bandits' last robbery (also a packsack with leaves).

Object—"We shall escort Mustapha with his treasure safely from Aswan (I on map) to Kharga (II on map). And while we are out in the desert we shall also use the opportunity to destroy the robbers and recover their loot.

Score—"Mustapha brought to Kharga ....10 points
Mustapha's treasure brought to Kharga ....20 points
Ali Baba's righthand man caught ....10 points
Ali Baba's loot brought to Kharga ....20 points
Each opponent captured .... 2 points

Special Rules—"(Method of capture). Mustapha wears a neckerchief turban. He must carry his treasure throughout. If treasure is captured it may be recaptured. Game starts at (time). Stops at (time). Troop gathers at (place) at (time)."

Message for *TEAM II* (to be opened at II on map).

Story—"I am Ali Baba, and you are my gang of desert bandits. have learned that Mustapha, the rich merchant who always wears turban, is going to travel through the desert. He carries with him a treasure of gems (a packsack filled with leaves) and has therefore asked the Luxor Desert Police for an escort. But that does not scare us. We have another important job before us. The loot from our last robbery (also a packsack with leaves) which is carried by Ben, my righthand man, must be brought to safety.

Objects—"We shall steal Mustapha's treasure and destroy the police. And also, we shall bring Ben and our loot from here (II on map) to our secret hide-out right in the town of Aswan (I on map).

Score—"Ben brought to Aswan ....10 points
Ben's loot brought to Aswan ....20 points
Mustapha captured ....10 points
Mustapha's treasure brought to Aswan ....20 points
Each policeman captured .... 2 points

Special Rules—"(Method of capture). Ben wears a neckerchief turban. He must carry the loot throughout. If it is captured it may be recaptured. Game starts at (time). Stops at (time). Troop gathers at (place) at (time)."

Variations of Seizure Type

The Opium Smugglers: One team is smugglers, the other border police. The smugglers attempt to carry their "opium" to a certain spot, and at the same time take away from the policemen much needed weapons and ammunition. The policemen try to get the "opium" and keep the smugglers from taking their weapons. "Opium" and "weapons" are carried in one or two packsacks.

THE THREE MUSKETEERS: One team is the three Musketeers and their helpers, the other Cardinal Richelieu and his men. The Musketeers are on their way to Buckingham in England with a code message from the Queen in Paris when they learn that the Cardinal's men have stolen the secret code from Buckingham and are proceeding toward Paris with it. The Cardinal's men in turn have discovered that the Musketeers have a message which decoded would help Richelieu gain his aims. The Musketeers attempt to get the code and the code message both to Buckingham, while the other team tries to get them to Paris. Count extra if the team brings in the decoded message. Code and message are written on large pieces of heavy paper and enclosed in cardboard mailing tubes, to be carried in full view.

THE SACRIFICE TO BALA: The teams are two tribes of Australian bushmen. Each has an idol to whom must be sacrificed a human offering of a child of the enemy tribe. The braves of each tribe have successfully stolen a child from the village of the enemy and are bringing it home when they are informed that the enemy has a child from

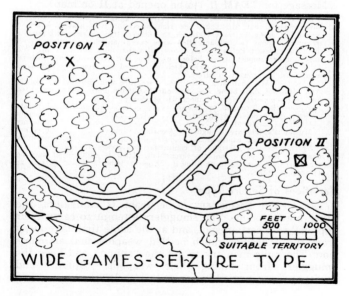

their village. Each team of braves, of course, wants to rescue the stolen child of its own tribe and also bring home for its idol the enemy child. The "child" is a dummy (a stuffed sack) which must be carried on a stretcher.

Sample of Conquest Type

THE TRIP TO MARS: A sealed envelope is given to each of the two team leaders to be opened at a specified spot at a specified time. Each envelope contains a marked map sketch, and one only of the following two messages:

Message for *TEAM I* (to be opened at I on map).

Story—"I am the famous aviator, Colonel Bud Stoop. With you, my brave fellow airmen, I have just completed a flight to Mars where we have landed our stratoplane (indicate by placing four signal flags on 5-foot poles at the corners of a fifteen-foot square). Unfortunately, in landing we smashed our water tank, and since there are no rivers on Mars we are in a dangerous position. We have seen from the air NE from here one of the portable tanks in which the Mars people store their artificial water, but it will be dangerous to reach it since the Mars men are violent enemies of the Earth people.

Objects—"We must capture the water tank (marked by four five-foot poles to which are tied signal flags which must all be pulled out) and bring it to our stratoplane. At the same time we must defend our plane. If the Mars people take it we shall forever be prevented from returning to earth again.

Score—"Water tank captured (all four poles) ....20 points
Stratoplane held intact ....20 points
Each Mars man captured .... 2 points
Special Rules—"(Method of capture). If stratoplane is captured it may be recaptured. Game starts at (time). Stops at (time). Troop gathers at (place) at (time)."

Message for *TEAM II* (to be opened at II on map).

Story—"I am the king of Mars. Some of the vicious earthmen have just landed on our globe SW from here. They came in one of their great metal birds that rumbles like a volcano. My spies have just told me that they are looking for water and that they may try to get one of the tanks in which we store our artificial water (indicate by placing in the ground four five-foot poles to which signal flags are tied. These poles are placed at the corners of a fifteen-foot square).

Objects—"We must prevent them from capturing our water tank. With its water they will live and kill us all. But they shall not succeed. We shall take their metal bird (marked by four signal flags which must all be pulled up and brought into the water tank square) and we shall destroy every one of the ghastly earthmen.

Score—"Metal bird captured (all four poles) ....20 points
Water tank held intact ....20 points
Each Earthman captured .... 2 points
Special Rules—"(Method of capture). If water tank is captured it may be recaptured. Game starts at (time). Stops at (time). Troop gathers at (place) at (time)."

Variations of Conquest Type

COMMANDOES: Two tiny countries are trying to get into the good graces of one of the big countries. To do this, each of them establishes a radio tower (three twenty-foot poles, lashed together in tripod style, with a streamer at the top), and begins a barrage of propaganda, praising itself and defaming the other country. Each government decides to stop the propaganda of the rival country by sending into it a team of men on a commando raid, for the purpose of destroying its radio tower (team to bring home evidence of its destruction in the form of the streamer from its top).

THE FIGHT AT THE STOCKADE: One team is Indians, the other settlers. The Indians attack the stockade and defend the Indian village, the settlers the opposite. To make it more exciting, two settlers may have been left in the stockade. The Indians are then to prevent them from getting out and joining their friends, while the settlers are to bring them aid. Stockade and Indian Village are indicated with four poles.

Scouts take to wide games readily and will soon start clamoring for more. And, fortunately, more are always available. All that is needed to create them is imagination with which to clothe the simple skeletons suggested above —and to design others.

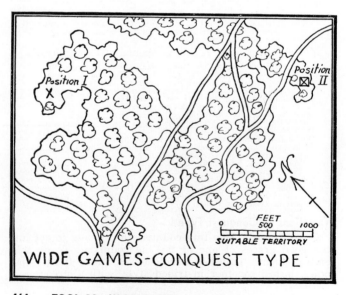

WIDE GAMES-CONQUEST TYPE

CEREMONIES

CEREMONIES are used in Scouting to inspire the boy with the high purpose of the Scout ideals, to make him realize the serious aspects of the game of Scouting. To be effective, Scout ceremonies should be *dignified—simple—short.*

Horse-play initiations are taboo in Scouting. Investitures are to fill the heart of the boy with determination to become a good Scout—not with mistrust and apprehension.

Types of Ceremonies

Particular activities which lend themselves to the use of ceremonies are:

1. *Induction*—Admitting the new boy to membership in the Troop and the World Brotherhood of Scouting.

2. *Advancement Courts of Honor*—Awarding the Scout with the ranks in Scouting.

3. *Installation of Individuals*—Elevating boys and adults to offices within the Patrol and the Troop.

4. *Explorer Investiture*—See *Explorer Manual.*

5. *Installation of Patrol or Troop*—Officially establishing the new unit.

6. *Troop Meeting Ceremonies* — Opening and closing ceremonies. (See Chapter 8.)

7. *Camp Ceremonies* — Flag-raising ceremonies, camp fire ceremonies, etc. (See Chapter 11.)

The ceremonies of the Troop should be worked out in the Patrol Leaders' Council, or at least approved there. From time to time, various Patrols should be encouraged to attempt to develop a new ceremony for the Troop. A suggestion or two should be enough to get the Patrol started. When completed and approved, have the Patrol itself stage the new ceremony.

INDUCTION CEREMONIES

In addition to ceremonies suggested here, see also chapter 13, The Boy Joins.

The Circle of the Square Knot

Scouts form a circle, each boy with a three-foot length of rope. Tie all ropes together with a square knot, but leave one open. Bring Candidate into the center, then tie final knot. Tell Candidate he is standing in the "circle of the square knot." If he is worthy and willing to make the Scout Oath and Law the law of his life he may join the circle. He recites the Oath, and is given a piece of rope. The leader of the Patrol to which he is to belong takes him to the circle. This is broken and enlarged, and the boy is admitted the moment he joins his rope to the rest.—Salt Lake City Council, Utah.

The Four-Square Ceremony

The Troop is lined up in a square. At each corner is a Scout holding a scroll. On one of the scrolls are inscribed the three promises of the Oath. Four points of the Law are inscribed on each of the others. The Candidate is escorted to each corner where the scroll is unrolled and the Keeper of the Scroll explains the meaning of his part. At the conclusion of this instruction the Candidate pledges himself to the Oath. After this, the boy is introduced to all members and shakes hands around.

The Light of Scouting

This ceremony requires fifteen Scouts and fifteen flashlights. The Candidate stands in the center of a circle formed by the Troop and the flashlight-bearers. The room is darkened. Starting with the Scout Oath and continuing through the twelve points of the Law, each Scout, one at a time, lights his light, points it to the ceiling and recites his portion of the Oath or Law. At a given signal, all lights are pointed at the Candidate. The Scoutmaster tells him that he is now bathed in the light of Scouting. If he intends to follow its gleam he must take the pledge. The Candidate makes the Scout Sign and recites the Oath, after which lights are turned on and the boy joins his Patrol.—Ogden Area Council, Ogden, Utah.

TENDERFOOT INVESTITURE

Circle Tenderfoot Investiture

Senior Patrol Leader takes the Candidate into an anteroom and blindfolds him. The Flag of the United States and the Troop flag are placed in the center of the meeting room. The Troop falls in with hands joined, using the Scout handclasp, facing out, with their backs to the flags. The Troop Leaders are inside the circle.

Scoutmaster says: "Be Prepared!" The *Scouts* answer in chorus: "We are prepared!" This is the signal for the Senior Patrol Leader to lead in the Candidate, halting him outside the circle, opposite the Scoutmaster.

Scoutmaster: "Senior Patrol Leader, who is with you?"

Senior Patrol Leader: "He is Candidate ....
(name), who wishes to join our Troop and become a Scout. He has met the requirements and is duly qualified."

Scoutmaster: "Remove his blindfold. (To Candidate) Candidate, you come from the darkness into the light of Scouting, and you see before you the Scouts of Troop ...., in an unbroken circle of comradeship, guarding the flags of their country and their Troop. How will you, an outsider, secure a place in this circle?"

Patrol Leader of the Patrol which the Candidate is joining speaks from his position in the circle: "Sir, the ....
.... (name) Patrol will open the circle and admit the Candidate."

Scoutmaster: "Good. In doing so, remember you vouch for him."

Senior Patrol Leader conducts the Candidate to the opening which the Patrol Leader has made by dropping his right hand, and leads him into the center of the circle in front of the Scoutmaster.

Scoutmaster (to Troop): "Unclasp hands. About face. (Circle now faces in.) (To Candidate): You have been admitted into our Troop circle to be made a member of the greatest boys' movement in the world. Place your left hand upon the flag of your Troop and raise your right hand in the Scout Sign. (The color bearer inclines the Troop flag toward the Candidate.) Dedicate yourself to the Scout Oath. (Candidate recites the Scout Oath, then drops his hand.) Now, where will I get a Badge for this Candidate?"

At this point some Scout who has been designated beforehand, steps forward, salutes and says: "Sir, I offer my Tenderfoot Badge for this Candidate." (This Scout may be a personal friend of the Candidate or some Scout whom the Candidate respects. If possible, he should be a Second or First Class Scout actually passing on his own Badge.)

Scoutmaster nods to the Scout who steps to the Candidate and pins the Tenderfoot Badge on him.

Scoutmaster: "Candidate, you have been given a Badge which has been worn with honor and distinction by a Scout who has gone before you. This shows our friendship for you and the trust we place in you. By the authority vested in me by the National Council, Boy Scouts of America, I make you a Tenderfoot Scout." (Here the Scoutmaster brings his right hand down sharply on the Candidate's left shoulder.)

The Troop cheer leader leads a Troop cheer for the Candidate. The Scoutmaster commands, "Fall Out." The Scouts shake hands with the new Scout. His Patrol Leader then takes him in tow and puts him in his place in the Patrol.—J. Harold Williams, Providence, R. I.

ADVANCEMENT COURT OF HONOR CEREMONIES

The following ceremony may be used for the opening of Courts of Honor, and as a general ceremony for many other functions.

Candle Lighting Ceremony

The materials required include a small table covered with a dark cloth, a simple candelabrum with twelve candles to represent the twelve points of the Scout Law, and three larger candles to represent the three parts of the Scout Oath, and a small taper representing the "Spirit of Scouting."

The ceremony proceeds as follows:

Twelve Scouts are detailed to take part. They line up, six at either side of the candelabrum table facing the audience, odd numbers on the right, even numbers on the left. The Senior Patrol Leader stands directly behind the candelabrum table.

When all is in readiness, all lights are extinguished and the Senior Patrol Leader lights the small taper representing the "Spirit of Scouting." He hands this to the Scout designated to give the first point of the Scout Law. This Scout takes the taper in his left hand, lights the first candle on the right-hand side, makes the Scout Sign and recites the first point of the Scout Law. He then hands the taper to the Scout who is to recite the second point (the first candle on the left side) and steps back to his previous position. This is continued until all points have been recited.

The Senior Patrol Leader calls the entire Troop to attention and lights the three top candles representing the three parts of the Scout Oath. The entire Troop recites in unison each promise of the Oath as the candles are lighted.

This ceremony, though simple, is extremely effective when well done.

Other Advancement Ceremonies

1. The Troop Court of Honor is in session. The Scout's Patrol Leader escorts him and his mother (if mother cannot be present, the boy alone) before the Court, and presents them. The Chairman says appropriate words of commendation, then pins the badge on the pocket of the boy's shirt. They exchange Scout Handclasp and Salute. The Scout faces his mother and pins a Mother's pin on her.

2. Camp fire investiture ceremony. The fire is allowed to die down to embers. The Troop Court of Honor lines up on one side of the fire, the Scout who is to be awarded on the other side. Other Scouts are in the background. The Scoutmaster tells the group of the accomplishments of the Scout. As he makes a point, the Scouts in the backgroud shout "How! How!" (Indian exclamation of approval). The Chairman says: "All has been dark, but the Scoutmaster speaks good words. Let the light shine on the face of this Scout. (At this point a handful of oil-soaked waste is thrown on the fire, which immediately blazes up.) By the light of this friendly fire we see that Scout.......................... is worthy. He may step forward and receive the badge."
—Ogden Area Council, Ogden, Utah.

3. The Troop has a book or a scroll in which are recorded the names of Scouts who have won honors. This "Book of Honor" has a page for each rank. Before a boy is invested, the roll of those who have reached the same rank before is read. Then the Chairman proposes that the name of the Scout should also be entered. He asks if there is anyone who objects to the honoring of the Scout. There

usually is no objection. The name is entered. The Scout is then called forward, is met by one of the Court who says: "I am happy to present Scout.................................to this group as a ....Class Scout." The Scoutmaster or the Chairman steps forward and pins on the badge, salutes, shakes hands and the Scout returns to his place.

INSTALLATION OF LEADERS

Installation of Junior and Senior Leaders

A general ceremony for the installation of junior or senior leaders in the Troop may be run along the following lines:

1. The Troop is formed in a circle or semi-circle.
2. The Scoutmaster (or Chairman of Troop Committee if Scoutmaster is being installed) explains in a few words the importance of the office and announces the appointment of a Scout (or Scouter) for the position.
3. The new officer is called forward. He places his left hand on the pole of the Troop flag, above that of the Scoutmaster (or the Chairman), salutes and gives the *Troop Leader's Promise* (Scouter's Promise): "I promise to do my best to be worthy of my office as.............................. for the sake of my fellow Scouts, my Troop and the World Brotherhood of Scouting."

Or the *Patrol Leader's Promise*: "I promise to do my best to be worthy of my office as Patrol Leader (or Assistant Patrol Leader), for the sake of my fellow Scouts, my Patrol and my Troop."

4. The Scoutmaster (or Chairman) says: "I trust you to keep your promise and herewith present to you the insignia of your new office." He then pins the insignia on the sleeve of the new leader, salutes and shakes his left hand.
5. The Troop is led in a cheer for the new leader.

For an adaption of this ceremony as used at the time of a Patrol Leader's appointment, see Chapter 2.

Installation of Den Chief

The installation of a new Den Chief is a Troop function which, appropriately, may take place at a Troop meeting, a Parents' Night, or at a Troop Court of Honor. Invite the Cubmaster.

For the ceremony below, the following equipment is required: Den Chief's Cord, Troop Leader's Warrant, *Den Chief's Denbook,* one blue cord and one yellow cord.

The Troop is formed in a semi-circle, with an artificial camp fire (or, better, a real one) in the center. The new Den Chief faces the Scoutmaster, who is assisted by two Scouts—one holding the blue cord, the Den Chief's Cord and the warrant, the other holding the book and the yellow cord.

Scoutmaster: "We shall now do honor to a new Den Chief. Scout.., you have been selected to serve your Troop in this important position of leadership. (Takes blue cord from Scout). This blue cord represents your Scout Troop, the Scout Oath and the Scout Law. It also stands for leadership and Good Turns. (Takes yellow cord from Scout.) This yellow cord represents the Pack with all its Cub Scouts, leaders and parents. It also stands for the Cub Scout Promise, the Law of the Pack, and for Good Will. As you will notice, these cords are made up of many strands the way the Pack and Troop are made up of many boys. Now let us bind together these cords to show that the Pack and Troop are bound together in a bond of friendship."

Scoutmaster and *Den Chief* each grasp an end of the cords and twist in opposite directions for three or four turns. The Scoutmaster then holds up the combined cords before the Den Chief.

Scoutmaster: "So, you see, the symbol of the bond of friendship between Pack and Troop becomes the totem of your office as Den Chief. It is known as the Den Chief's Cord. (Hands twisted cords to one of the Scouts.) Because you are a good Scout and because we believe that you can lead so that the others will follow, you have been chosen a Den Chief in Pack.........................This means that you are being given the responsibility of leading boys who will some day become Scouts like yourself. You are given the opportunity to live the third point of the Scout Law—A Scout Is Helpful. Will you accept these responsibilities?"

Den Chief: "I will."

Scoutmaster: "Will you do your best as a Scout and as a Den Chief to give the Cub Scout Program to the boys of your Den?"

Den Chief: "I will."

Scoutmaster: "Scout..........................., in recognition of the office you are about to assume and the importance of the services you will be rendering your Troop, I award you this Den Chief's Cord and the Troop Leader's Warrant." (Receives Cord from Scout, encircles right sleeve of Den Chief with it, and pins it to shoulder. Then gives him Warrant, and shakes his hand in the Scout Handclasp).

Troop gives a cheer for the new Den Chief.

If the Cubmaster is present for the ceremony, he may add the following:

Cubmaster: "Welcome to leadership in Pack...................... The Cub Scouts in your Den, the parents and I are counting on you to do your best in your office as Den Chief. We know that you will help the Cub Scouts get the most of their Cub Scout experience and you will serve as their example, of what a real Boy Scout should be. The better your example, the more anxious they will be to follow in your footsteps and become Boy Scouts. I'm happy to present you with your *Den Chief's Denbook* to help you in your work. Count on me as Cubmaster to assist you in every way possible." (Gives him *Den Chief's Denbook,* and shakes hands with him using Cub Scout Handclasp.)

INSTALLATION OF PATROL

The Troop is lined up in a semicircle, the Scoutmaster, Assistants and Troop Committee facing it.

Senior Patrol Leader (speaking to Scoutmaster): "Sir, a new Patrol has been formed in Troop.................................. Scout.. has been chosen Patrol Leader and Scouts.., etc., are the other members. (Facing the Troop he says): Old and new Patrol Leaders of Troop..........................., front and center."

The Patrol Leaders form a line in front of the semicircle, with the new Patrol Leader facing the other Patrol Leaders. The old Patrol Leaders line up in order of speaking. All Patrol Leaders carry unlighted candles.

Patrol Leader of Tiger Patrol (to new Patrol Leader): "Do your men know and understand the Scout Law?"

New Patrol Leader: "Yes, to the best of my knowledge and belief, they do."

Patrol Leader of Beaver Patrol: "Do they believe in the Scout Oath, believe it in their hearts?"

New Patrol Leader: "I feel sure that they do."

Patrol Leader of Stag Patrol: "Are they doing their best to 'Be Prepared?' "

New Patrol Leader: "They are."

Patrol Leader of Flaming Arrow Patrol: "Are they aware of their obligation to 'Do a Good Turn Daily?' "

New Patrol Leader: "They are."

Senior Patrol Leader (to Scoutmaster): "I am willing to vouch for this new Patrol Sir, and believe it to be worthy of having a part in the life of Troop............................ (Turning to new Patrol Leader): What name has been chosen for this new Patrol?"

New Patrol Leader: "The Bears, Sir!"

Scoutmaster (to old Patrol Leaders): "Old Patrol Leaders light your candles to light the way of our new Patrol. (All candles are lighted, except Patrol Leader's of Bears. Announcement to electrician, lights out.) May the Scout Oath and the Scout Law guide and aid this new Patrol in Troop.................................. May their quest for adventure in the Troop room and the Patrol den, and in the out-of-doors always be governed by the golden rule of playing the game squarely. May the light of these candles flickering here and the one shortly to be lighted, ever stand as a beacon for all that is good in Scouting. (To new Patrol Leader): Knowing your previous record in Troop............ it gives me a great deal of satisfaction to place the flag of this new Patrol in your hands. Remember, you are a leader, and a leader does not stand still."

New Patrol Leader makes the Patrol Leader's Promise, the Scouts of the new Patrol stand at attention.

Scoutmaster (to the boys of the new Patrol): "The second point of the Scout Law is, 'A Scout is Loyal'—he is loyal to his Patrol Leader, his Troop, his home and his country. We are expecting great things from the Bear Patrol. Do not disappoint us. Light the unlit candle and may the light of your Patrol ever shine with the others in Troop.. (Candle is lighted by new Patrol Leader.

Scoutmaster (to electrician): "Lights! Patrol Leaders, take your posts!"   *H. F. Price.*

INSTALLATION OF TROOP

(See Tool 1)

S C O U T   D R I L L

A CERTAIN AMOUNT of drill is necessary for getting the Troop and Patrols into position for various activities and for moving the Troop with a semblance of order and smartness.

For this Scouting does not resort to military drill, but has developed its own technique, easily learned and considered by the boys as a game rather than a drill.

Main Features of Scout Drill

The main features of Scout drill are:

1. *Alert Signal*—In the out-of-doors: The Troop's special bird or animal call. In the Troop meeting room the leader raises his right hand in the Scout Sign high above his head, indicating "Attention," "Silence," "I have an announcement to make." If a formation is to follow, the leader takes a position, before making alert signal, facing the center of the formation he is going to call.

2. *"Freezing,"* that is, becoming instantly immovable, or "frozen," on the alert signal. As soon as a Scout notices the sign, he stops what he is doing and puts up his hand in the same way. When everybody is making the sign, the leader lowers his hand. So do the boys and wait for the signal to follow.

3. *Arm signal* by the leader indicating formation to be taken. This signal is held until all have fallen in.

4. The Troop falls into position *on the run,* its center opposite the leader. The Patrol Leaders must be first in place since they are the key men of their Patrols' positions. The flanks of the formation should pick up their dressing automatically from the center. The Scouts stand at ease. It is necessary to establish a definite arrangement of the Patrols, so that each of them knows where to fall in.

5. The only word-of-mouth commands necessary are

"Troop Atten . . . tion!" "Troop at . . . ease!" "Scout
Sign!" or "Scout Sa . . . lute!" and "Hands . . . down!"
and even these may be substituted by silent signals invented by the Troop.

Formations

IN FORMAL ASSEMBLY ("Come here") Leader swings his
extended right arm in a small circle over his. Scouts rush
toward him.

SINGLE RANK FORMATION (TROOP LINE)—*Signal:* Leader
extends both arms horizontally, parallel to the line he
wishes Troop to take (with his palm turned front if he
wants Patrols in front of him; with palm turned back if
he wants Patrols behind him). *Execution:* Patrol Leaders
take up position in front of the center of their Patrols.
Patrols fall in line two paces behind their leaders, with a
two-pace interval between Patrols. Assistant Patrol Leader
is on right of Patrol, the other members on his left in
order of sequence established by the Patrol. The line
dresses right without command. *Uses:* For general line-up.
For inspection in meeting room.

COUNCIL OR "U" FORMATION (HORSESHOE)—*Signal:* Leader
raises arms from the sides, sideways about 45 degrees,
palms toward the body. *Execution:* Scouts fall in, in a
single line semi-circle around leader. Patrols observe same
order of sequence as in Troop Line, though Patrol Leaders
fall in on the right of their Patrols. *Uses:* For demonstrations, announcements or special ceremonies.

TROOP CIRCLE FORMATION—*Signal:* Leader raises arms
sideways 45 degrees, then swings them from front to rear
and back several times. *Execution:* Patrols form a complete circle around the leader in same order as in Troop
line. *Uses:* For ceremonies and circle games.

OPEN COLUMN OF PATROLS—*Signal:* Leader extends arms
forward, but bent at right angles at elbows, with fingers
toward the sky. *Execution:* Patrols fall in, one behind the
other, dressing immediately on the front Patrol and on
the right. A distance equal to the length of each Patrol
should be left between it and the Patrol in front of it.
Patrol Leader two paces in front of the center of his Patrol.
Uses: For inspection and parade formation:

CLOSE COLUMN OF PATROLS—*Signal:* Same as for Open
Column of Patrols, except that *clenched fists* are extended

toward the sky. *Execution:* Similar to Open Column of Patrols, except that each Patrol falls in *two paces behind* the one in front of it, with the Patrol Leader on the right of his Patrol. *Uses:* For assembly in small room and crowded parade formation.

PARALLEL FILE FORMATION (PATROL FILES)—*Signal:* Arms extended forward at shoulder height, palms together.

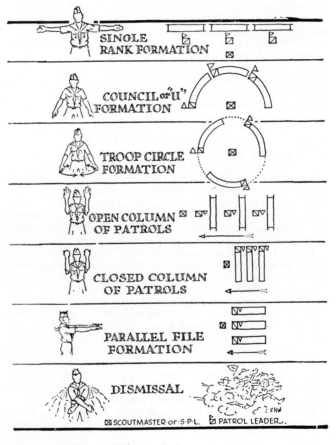

Execution: Patrol Leaders take positions two paces apart, their Scouts fall in behind them. *Uses:* For relays and other games.

DISMISSAL—*Signal:* Swinging arms from a crossed-front position, repeated several times.

Movements

Movements of the Troop are usually made from the Column formations. The leader turns around, and precedes the Patrols throughout the movements.

MOVE FORWARD (FORWARD MARCH!)—*Signal:* Right arm raised vertically, then moved forward into horizontal position.

TURN RIGHT OR LEFT (COLUMN RIGHT OR LEFT)—*Signal:* Right (or left) arm extended right (or left) at shoulder height.

HALT—*Signal:* Hand, palm front, thrust upward from shoulder height to full extent of arm.

Tool 16

S I N G I N G

BOYS like to sing! Singing in the Patrol or in the Troop makes them feel of and with the group. The right songs at the right time can tone them down if they are too exhuberant, or pep them up if they are feeling low. Singing is a great builder of morale, of unity, of tradition even, and only a singing Troop is a truly "complete" Troop.

So sing! Sing at the Troop meeting—at least ten minutes during each camp fire period—sing on the hike, sing at special get-togethers with parents and friends.

Who Should Lead?

The boys!

There are Scoutmasters of non-singing Troops who give for their alibi: "I can't carry a tune to the corner!" They don't have to. In most cases there are boys right within their Troops who can. Get the boys to lead the Troop in singing. Call on the Patrol Leaders and the Patrol Cheermasters and see what they can do. You are apt to get the surprise of your life.

The technique of song leadership is described in the opening pages of *Camp Songs 'n' Things*.

Choosing the Songs

The vigor and sprightliness associated with youth and Scouting should characterize Scout singing. Try to develop a reputation for your Troop as singers of worth-while songs, who can always be counted upon to know and if necessary to lead in the singing of any of the old standard songs—not merely for the first verse and chorus, but all the way through.

Select your songs and adopt some good standard song as

your special Troop song, one that can mean something to the Troop, one that can be used for closing a camp fire, for greeting a new boy, or for bidding good-bye to a Scout who is leaving.

Set out to create for the Troop a treasury of songs from which may be drawn fun and laughter, fellowship and great memories.

Suggestions for Your Repertoire

The following titles are worth considering for your repertoire:

Patriotic Songs

"The Star-Spangled Banner"
"America"

"America the Beautiful"
"God Bless America"

Songs for Inspiration

"Hail! Hail! Scouting Spirit"
"Trail the Eagle"
"Forever True Scouts"

"The Torch of Scouting"
"A Scout Leader's Prayer"
"Leader's Song"

Songs for Hiking

"Trek Cart Song"
"Hi Ho for Scouting, Oh!"
"The Far Northland"
"Alouette"
"Good Old Open Trail"
"There's a Long, Long Trail Awinding"
"Three Good Turns"

"Scout Marching Song"
"Sling Your Pack Across Your Back"
"Pack Up Your Duffle"
"As We Swing Down the Trail"
"Scouts of the U. S. Hiking"
"Swinging Along"

Songs for Fun

"Climbing up the Ladder"
"Old MacDonald Had a Farm"
"The Tree in the Wood"
"Jamboree"
"Indian Love Song"
"There Were Three Jolly Fishermen"

"Yon Yonsen"
"John Brown's Body"
"Three Wood Pigeons"
"Under the Spreading Chestnut Tree"
"The More We Camp Together"
"Johnny Schmoker"

Songs for Soft Moods

"When You Come to the End of a Boy Scout Day"
"Scout Vesper"
"Camp Fire Song"

"By the Blazing Council Fire's Light"
"Home on the Range"
"Taps"

S T O R Y   T E L L I N G

STORY-TELLING is the Scoutmaster's opportunity to get close to his Scouts by capturing and holding their imaginations, to extend their horizons, to influence their characters by holding before them deeds of courage, and sacrifice and valor.

The Story is the Thing

Many factors enter into successful story-telling—seating of the audience, meeting the mood, dramatic presentation. But first of all: THE STORY IS THE THING.

The question then is: What kind of yarns do boys like? Where do I get them?

Boys like all kinds of yarns, provided they contain action, have sustained suspense, and end in a conclusive, definite manner.

In your own reading, it will happen time and again that you say: "That would make a fine story for the gang." Make a brief notation of the title, the author, where you ran across the story and a sketch map of the plot.

Another place to get stories is out of your own experience. Every man has, at some time in his experience, had a personal adventure which can be retold—a trip into the back country, an ocean voyage, a great fire witnessed.

The field of exploration offers another rich opportunity for the garnering of stories: Byrd's expedition to the South Pole, Roy Chapman Andrew's explorations in the Gobi, Lawrence's adventures in Arabia.

The history of the United States in peace and war is a treasure mine of stories to tell the boys.

When you have found a story which you feel is suited for retelling, read it through until you have its sequence of events firmly fixed in your mind. Then tell it before a mirror to coordinate gestures, timing it at the same time.

If you are to tell a story dealing with your own experiences, guard against the too frequent use of "I"—"I did this," "I did that," "I said," "I acted," "It was due to MY." Tell the story in the second person or by generous use of the editorial "WE."

Getting Ready for Telling

Before starting, be sure your audience is comfortable. Don't let attention be divided between the story and a cramped leg or an uncomfortable seat. Allow a couple of minutes during which everyone may find a comfortable position. Start when the crowd is silent, not until then.

Deal with minor disturbances as they occur. If low talking is heard in the outskirts of the circle, pause until quiet is restored.

Telling the Story

The start is important. The attention of the listeners must be caught in the very opening statement. Starting with a long description of the circumstances leading up to the predicament of the hero, of his attire and what he had for breakfast, dispels attention. You are likely to hear an impatient whisper: "Why doesn't he come to the point?" Jump right into your story: "Our boat was overloaded and we were quickly drifting into trouble. Ahead of us the tide was going out through the narrow inlet with high waves ripping every which way. It seemed inevitable that we would be caught. 'Hold her off!' Jack shouted. 'Look out—watch that oar'—but before he had finished we were in the midst of what seemed a gigantic whirlpool. . . ." You get the idea?

Then there must be an ending and there must be no question about the ending. All threads must be gathered together. All business disposed of. All obscure points made clear so that there is no doubt in the listeners' minds as to what happened to every character presented.

"But I can't tell a story. . . ." Try it. You'll be surprised to find how quickly you can make yourself into an accomplished story-teller.

TROOP MOBILIZATION

EVERY YEAR Scouts, somewhere, have rendered excellent emergency service in time of disaster. The most efficient service can be done when the Scouts can be mobilized quickly and with little confusion. The way to assure this is to develop a Troop Mobilization System and practice it from time to time.

Preparing the Troop Mobilization System

Inform the parents of every Scout that the Troop may be called upon to assist in handling local emergencies and secure their cooperation. Provide blanks for them to sign, granting their permission.

Arrange detailed plan for reaching every available Scout in the shortest possible time. For example: Scoutmaster phones two Assistants; each Assistant phones two Patrol Leaders and the Senior Patrol Leader or Junior Assistant Scoutmaster respectively; each Patrol Leader phones his Assistant Patrol Leader and three Scouts, the Assistant Patrol Leader taking care of the rest.

For every man, have an alternate—along this line: If Assistant Scoutmaster cannot be reached, an older Scout is called and does the Assistant's work.

Community-Wide Mobilization

Arrange an alternate plan for reaching the Scouts in case the telephone system is not working—or where Scouts do not have telephones. Use foot, bicycle or automobile.

Supply each Scout or Scouter who is responsible for calling others with a list of names, addresses, telephone numbers and any additional instructions needed. Let him understand that persons difficult to reach are to be left till the last. The idea is to get the greatest possible number in motion in the shortest possible time.

A community-wide call will originate with the Scout Executive or the Local Council Office, which will call District Commissioners, who in turn will contact the Scoutmasters.

A quick and effective method for communities of moderate size is to display a mobilization flag (or a light if the call is issued at night) on the city hall or other designated place. Instantly a Scout sees it he spreads the word.

Another method is to secure the cooperation of the local fire department and arrange with them for a special call to be sounded on the fire alarm system. A list of persons authorized to give orders to have this call sounded should be on file at the fire department headquarters.

Another very effective method is to get the help of the local radio station, if any, to send the call over the air.

If arrangements are made with the school authorities, parents and employers of the Scouts, a call may be issued at any time of the day.

A definite place should be designated in advance for all mobilizations.

Types of Mobilization

There are two types of orders for mobilization: "General Emergency Mobilization" and "Immediate Emergency." The former allows time for each Scout to be equipped with uniform, packsack, rope, signal flags, one day's prepared rations, first aid kit, trolley tickets or carfare. The latter calls for immediate response by Scouts without equipment other than that regularly carried on their person: Pocket first aid kit and carfare—and, of course, Scout identification, consisting of Scout registration card and Scout pin.

SCOUTMASTER GROWTH

SCOUTMASTER TRAINING

Basic Training Experience

Basic training aims at the Scoutmaster's two main jobs—helping boys to grow, and training and guiding boy leaders. This training covers seven subjects—Boy Scouting Fundamentals; Patrol and Troop Organization and Leadership; Program Planning; Meetings; Hiking; Camping, and Helping the Individual Boy to Grow. Certain threads—the boy, the Patrol, junior leader training, Scoutcraft training, ideals of Scouting, advancement, and health and safety—run all through the training.

A Scoutmaster or Assistant Scoutmaster may meet the requirements for a basic training certificate (as listed in the Scoutmaster Basic Training *Notebook for Scouters,* B.S.A. Cat. No. 4177) by one of three methods.

1. *Group Training*—participation in a series of training sessions with a group of other Scouters, providing an opportunity to exchange ideas and successful experiences. This is by far the preferred method. Find out from your Commissioner when your District or Local Council Training Committee has scheduled such training events.

2. *Personal Coaching*—for the man who cannot attend scheduled training sessions. A Commissioner, training Committeeman or other experienced Scouter guides the Scoutmaster through the training projects.

3. *Home Study*—when neither of the first two methods is available. This method gives the leader no opportunity to discuss or get guidance in subjects he does not understand, but it may be the only way he can fulfill the training requirements.

Arrowhead Honor

By making his basic training effective in the lives of Scouts through a series of practical projects, a Scoutmaster (or Assistant) will earn the Arrowhead Honor. The Honor is a cloth Arrowhead worn on the left sleeve just below the badge of office.

Arrowhead Honor projects cover the following subjects:

1. Patrol and Troop Organization and Leadership
2. Program Planning
3. Troop Meetings
4. Troop Administration
5. Hiking
6. Camping
7. Helping the Boy Grow

When a Scouter completes a project, he requests that a coach be designated by the District Training Committee or the Council to inspect his work and appraise the results. If the Scouter feels the need for additional help before he launches his projects, specially designated coaches should be able to give it.

The *Notebook for Scouters* contains a list of Arrowhead Honor projects and a form on which a coach may give his approval for satisfactory completion.

Scouter's Key and Scouter's Award

The *Scouter's Key* is awarded to a Scoutmaster who, over a period of at least three years, has met prescribed requirements in four areas: training, performance, service and tenure. The *Scouter's Award* is a recognition for Assistant Scoutmasters and Troop Committeemen who meet similar requirements, including three years' tenure. Individual record cards are available for checking off the requirements as they are met.

Arrowhead Honor   **Scouter's Key**   **Scouter's Award**

LITERATURE HELPS

The following bibliography is kept down, by design, to bare essentials. It contains books and pamphlets that have proved of definite help to Scoutmasters in starting and handling Troops. For bibliographies of technical books relative to camping, nature, first aid, and so one, we refer you to the *Scout Field Book* and the *Handbook for Boys*.

All the books and pamphlets described below are available through the National Supply Service.

Manuals and Pamphlets

Handbook for Scoutmasters
The Scoutmaster's main tool.

Handbook for Boys
The boy's book of Scouting and guide to advancement.

Handbook for Patrol Leaders
The official handbook for boy leaders.

Explorer Manual
The Explorer program handbook for young men.

Scout Field Book
Scoutcraft activities for boys and leaders alike.

10 Steps to Organize a Troop
Details of the steps in organizing a new Troop.

The Active Troop Committee
Its duties and functions.

Advancement in the Troop
The steps in Scout advancement.

Notebook for Scouters
Basic training guide for Scoutmaster and Assistants.

Boy Scout Leader's Program Notebook
One of the planning tools available through Local Councils for each program year.

The Book of Games, by G. S. Ripley.

Boy Scout Games, by Charles F. Smith.
Two collections of Scoutcraft and recreational games.

Field Book of Nature Activities, by William Hillcourt.
Activities in many phases of nature, including numerous conservation projects.

The Book of Nature Hobbies, by Ted Pettit.
Nature ideas for Patrols and Troop.

Cub Scouting Guide Book
   Highlights of the Cub Scout program.

Hints on Explorer Leadership.
   Functions of the Explorer Advisor and young men leaders in conducting the Explorer program.

Junior Leader Training Events
   Details of inter-group conferences and events.

Fun Around the Campfire
   Campfire leadership, program planning and activities.

Open House Guide Book
   Planning and putting on Parents' Nights, etc.

Merit Badge Library—100 subjects.

Troop and Patrol Stunts

Periodicals

SCOUTING *Magazine*
   The official leaders' magazine for all registered Scouters.

THE BOY SCOUT PROGRAM QUARTERLY
   This quarterly brings to all Troop Scouters a wealth of program suggestions.

BOYS' LIFE *Magazine*
   The official Boy Scout magazine.

VISUAL AIDS

The Visual Education Service makes available a number of films and filmstrips which will be useful to a Troop for training and other purposes. Among these are the program and activities motion pictures, *Scout in the Forest, Philmont Adventure, A Rock Climb, A Canoe Expedition, Colorado River Expedition, World Jamboree* and *Jamboree 1950 Is History;* skill and craft motion pictures, *Ice Rescue, Winter Camping, Axemanship, Making a Pack Basket, Making Indian Moccasins, Knifecraft, Tin Can Craft, Dutch Oven, Save This Life* and *Making An Indian Tipi;* and training filmstrips, "So Now You're a Patrol Leader," "Hiking with Your Patrol," "Meeting with Your Patrol," "So You're Going Camping," "Learnin' By Doin' in Your Patrol," "YOUR Patrol Leaders' Council In Action," "Boy Scout Advancement," "Troop Budget Plan" and "Using Games in Scouting."

You may obtain complete information on the availability and use of these visual aids from your Council office.

Tool 20

SCOUT REQUIREMENTS

WHEN PROPERLY APPLIED in Patrol and Troop, the basic Boy Scout requirements should:

Promote SCOUT SPIRIT

Assist a boy to become physically strong, mentally awake and morally straight.

Help to make the boy self-reliant.

Encourage him to think of others and make it possible for him to help others by teaching him skills that might benefit other people.

Promote SCOUT PARTICIPATION

Encourage the boy to take active part in Patrol and Troop activities and service projects.

Provide for doing things together in the Patrol.

Give a boy a chance for advancement as a natural outcome of his life in Patrol and Troop.

Promote SCOUTCRAFT

Make the boy at home in the out-of-doors.

Encourage more than "just getting a Badge"—they add up to making the boy a good Scout hiker, a good Scout camper.

Stress learning by *doing*—*doing* for a purpose instead of just *knowing*.

Provide program material for Patrol and Troop.

TENDERFOOT SCOUT

To become a TENDERFOOT SCOUT, you must be at least eleven years of age and do the following:

I. Scout Spirit — Learning about the ideals and traditions of Scouting:

1. Repeat from memory the Scout Oath or Promise and the twelve points of the Scout Law, the Scout Motto and the Scout Slogan, and explain the meaning of each in your own words.

   By "points of the Scout Law" is meant the point itself (such as "A Scout Is Loyal"), and not the point plus its explanatory text. The boy should study the *Handbook for Boys'* explanation of each point so that he can tell the meaning of it in his own words. The Scout Slogan is "Do a Good Turn Daily."

2. Describe the Scout Badge and explain its meaning. Tell when to wear the Scout Uniform and how to use and care for it.

   Retell in general the section in the *Handbook for Boys* entitled "What Does the Badge Mean?" and the sections "When to Wear the Uniform" and "Care of the Uniform."

3. Give the Scout Sign, Salute and Handclasp.

   As explained in the *Handbook for Boys* and *Scout Field Book.*

II. Scout Participation — Knowing about the Patrol and Troop, the community and the county of which you are a part:

1. Explain the name of the Patrol you will join and give its call or yell. Tell who your Scout leaders are and what they do in the Troop. Explain, in a general way, what you have to do to become Second Class and a First Class Scout.

   By Scout leaders are meant those with whom the boy comes in direct contact, such as Patrol Leader, Senior Patrol Leader, Junior Assistant Scoutmaster, Assistant Scoutmaster, Scoutmaster. The general idea of advancement involves the three important features: Scout Ideals, Scout Participation and Scoutcraft. The Scoutcraft for Second Class is intended to make a Scout a good hiker; for First Class, a good camper.

2. Tell how, in an emergency, you would get in contact with the doctor or hospital, and the police or sheriff's office nearest to your home. Explain how, in your community you would report a fire.

> This involves knowing the addresses, in case the boy will have to take a personal message, and the method of making the contact through the telephone. In a small town, it may also mean familiarity with a local method of making a fire alarm.

3. Describe The Flag of the United States of America and tell its history in brief. Tell when to fly it. Show how to hoist, lower, display and fold The Flag, and how to salute it.

> *Description:* Stripes, union, stars; number and arrangement. *History:* Colonial Flag (Queen Anne); Cambridge Flag; first flag with 13 stripes; the Flag of 15 stars and 15 stripes; change back to 13 stripes; The Flag of today. *When:* Time of day; important days of year; special method for Memorial Day. *Hoist and Lower:* When flag pole is used. *Display:* On wall, on stage, in audience. *Fold:* Into triangle. *Salute:* In Scout Uniform, as civilian.

III. Scoutcraft — Setting out to learn a few simple things that all Scouts should know:

1. Tell why it is important to care for a cut or a scratch and show on yourself how to do it. Tie a bandage with a square knot.

> The general idea of danger of infection in untended wound. Adhesive compresses ("Bandaids," "Handi-Tapes") may be used to show care. Bandage may be gauze or folded neckerchief, laid over dressing on boy himself or someone else.

2. Explain what care should be taken before building a fire in the open. Describe the harm to a live tree that results from hacking with an axe, or other sharp tool.

> The main intention here is CONSERVATION—to instill in the boy the idea that Scouts are careful not to start forest fires, that Scouts protect trees instead of marring them and maybe killing them.

3. Whip the ends of a rope at least one-quarter inch in diameter. Join two ropes with a sheetbend. Attach a rope to a post or rail with a clove hitch, then untie and fasten it again with two half hitches. Fasten one end of a rope around your waist with a bowline.

> Self-explanatory.

When you have met the Tenderfoot Requirements before your Scoutmaster (or have been reviewed in the Cub Scout Webelos Requirements by your Scoutmaster) and have proved to him that you thoroughly understand the Scout

Oath or Promise and Law, he registers you as a Scout (unless he has already registered you as a Candidate Scout). You take the Scout Oath or Promise at a ceremony in front of your Patrol and Troop and are then entitled to wear the Tenderfoot Badge and the Official Uniform of the Boy Scouts of America.

This explains the Tenderfoot procedure: Examination by the Scoutmaster and registration with the National Council through the Local Council Office. It makes it a definite obligation on the part of the Troop to receive the boy into Scouting at a simple and dignified Investiture Ceremony.

SECOND CLASS SCOUT

To become a Second Class Scout, you do the following:

I. Scout Spirit

While a Tenderfoot Scout, satisfy your Scout leaders that you do your best, in your everyday life, to live up to:

1. The Scout Oath or Promise
2. The Scout Law
3. The Scout Motto
4. The Scout Slogan

The boy's term as a Tenderfoot Scout is best reviewed at a meeting of the Patrol Leaders' Council, where each leader who has had contact with the boy may have a chance to express himself as to his Scout Spirit. Decision may be taken by the Scoutmaster or left by him to the vote of the Leaders' Council. If the boy's performance has been unsatisfactory, he will be given a chance to improve until the leaders again take up his case. The Scoutmaster may also want to talk *informally* with the boy's parents, teachers, and others.

II. Scout Participation

While a Tenderfoot Scout, show to the satisfaction of your Scout leaders that you:

1. Work actively in Patrol and Troop meetings, outdoor activities and service projects.

   The Troop and Patrol records will show the boy's attendance. The testimony of the leaders involved, preferably given at a meeting of the Patrol Leaders' Council, will indicate how "actively" the boy participated. The Troop will set its own standards for "active participation." **The absolute minimum of time for showing such participation is thirty days from the day the boy became a Tenderfoot Scout.**

2. Do your share in helping in your home, your school, your church and your community.

   The Scoutmaster will check *informally* with home, school and church to learn if the boy is helpful — in the spirit of the daily Good Turn. No written or signed statements should be called for.

3. Take care of things that belong to you, the property of others, and your country's natural resources.

Emphasis here is CONSERVATION—proper care of personal belongings, protecting instead of destroying other people's property (window panes in empty building, for example), safe-guarding wild life (living up to game laws, careful fire building in the open, refraining from hacking trees, etc.).

4. Maintain a personal savings plan (such as regular payments into a savings account or into a savings project sponsored by your family or Troop).

The *regular practice* of thrift is what counts—not the amount. The account may be in the form of a savings book, bonds, or insurance policy. Savings project by the Troop may be toward camp fees, uniform, equipment.

III. Scoutcraft

1. PREPARE FOR SCOUT HIKING

a. Clothing and Equipment — Present yourself for inspection suitably clothed for the locality, season and weather, and equipped for a five-mile hike.

If the boy is ready in the summertime, his clothing will be that for a summer hike; if in the winter, suitable for a winter hike. Equipment depends upon the hike planned—it may involve compass, map, cooking kit, and so on.

b. Hiking Methods — Tell the safety precautions to take on the highway and cross-country for day and night hiking. Show correct way of walking and proper care of feet. Demonstrate at least six Silent Scout Signals for formations and field work. Demonstrate how to purify water for drinking. Explain how to make a one-man latrine. Identify local plants that may cause skin poisoning. Tell what to do if lost.

Safety, walking methods, what to do when lost, as described in *Handbook for Boys* and *Scout Field Book*. *Silent Signals* are for such formations as Single Rank, Parallel File, Circle, etc.; and for such field movements as Forward, Assemble, Hurry, Halt, and so on. *Water purification:* Water purification tablets (such as "Halazone" and others), or boiling. *One-man latrine:* Simple cat-hole, earth scooped up, about 6" diameter, 8" deep. *Poison plants:* Poisonivy, poisonoak, poisonsumac, depending upon locality.

c. First Aid — Demonstrate artificial respiration. Demonstrate first aid for shock and fainting and, on yourself, for the following: arterial bleeding of arm and leg, common cuts and scratches, bites of insects and chiggers and ticks, burns and scalds, sunburn, blister on heel, skin poisoning from poison plants, object in eye, sprained ankle.

Techniques are found in *Handbook for Boys* and *Scout Field Book*. An *actual demonstration* of each item is required, using proper first aid materials where necessary. Note the emphasis on *personal* first aid.

2. FIND YOUR WAY

   a. *Compass*—Explain how a compass works and give its eight principal points. Set a compass and take a degree reading with it.

   Know that earth's magnetism attracts needle. Points: N, NE, E, SE, S, SW, W, NW. Degree reading: Find the direction to a landmark in degrees.

   b. *Measuring*—Determine the length of your step. Walk a course for which you must take three compass degree readings and measure three distances with your step. OR lay out, in this manner, and stake a four-acre tract of land.

   Step length: Walk a measured step course (for instance 400 feet); divide number of steps into length of course to find length of individual step. *Course:* From starting point, walk proper lengths in correct directions (for instance: 300 ft. 280°, 240 ft. 35°, 280 ft. 110°). OR four-acre tract: Place stake at starting point. Measure and stake three sides, as shown in *Handbook for Boys* (fourth side, of course, is from last stake placed to stake at starting point).

   c. *Map Reading*—In the field, orient a map (preferably a topographic map) and follow a route far enough to prove that you know how to use the map. Read at least ten different conventional signs on a map, including contour lines.

   Technique is described in the *Handbook for Boys* and in *Scout Field Book*. "Far enough to prove that you know how to use the map" depends upon locality—in flat territory where roads have few windings and where there are few landmarks, distance may have to be comparatively long; in mountainous country, a short distance may show the boy's ability. The leader will be the judge of "far enough."

3. COOK A MEAL IN THE OPEN

   The intention of this whole Requirement 3 (consisting of the four parts a, b, c and d) is to make preparing a meal a complete process, from getting fire wood, making a fire, cooking to the clean-up, rather than isolated Requirements of using an axe on one hike, building a fire on another, and so on.

   a. *Preparing Fire Wood*—Sharpen a knife and an axe, and use these sharpened tools to prepare kindling and fuel.

   Sharpening: Sharpening stone for knife and file and stone for axe. To show use of knife, fuzz-sticks are suitable. Enough wood is to be prepared for cooking a Second Class meal (Requirement 3c).

   b. *Fire Building*—Locate and prepare a suitable fire site. Lay and light a fire (this should normally take not more than two matches). Keep the fire going for cooking a meal.

   Fire site to be cleared of inflammable material for radius of 5 feet from spot where fire is to be built. When dry wood is used, two matches should be sufficient. The important thing is the locating, and laying of a good fire for cooking.

c. *Hike Cooking*—Cook a meal from raw meat (or fish or poultry) and at least one raw vegetable.

The Scout has the choice between cooking the meal without utensils (as kabob, on broiler, in the ground) and using utensils (stewing, frying, baking).

d. *Clean-up*—Dispose of garbage in proper manner. Clean utensils. Put out fire. Clean up the site thoroughly.

Garbage should be burned. If utensils are used, they should be cleaned with hot water. Put out fire by sprinkling water on it. Clean site so that it is almost impossible to see that anyone has had a fire there.

4. BE OBSERVANT

a. *Observation*—Do ONE of the following:

TRACKING. Follow the track of a person or an animal in soft ground or snow for ¼ mile, reading the main meaning of the track. OR

TRAILING. Follow a track made with trail signs for ½ mile. OR

STALKING. Follow another Scout, who knows that you are stalking him, for a distance of ½ mile, without being seen by him.

The techniques involved are found in the *Handbook for Boys* and *Scout Field Book*.

b. *Wild Life*—Find evidence, in natural surroundings, of at least six different kinds of wild mammals, birds, reptiles or fish. Identify them.

The simplest "evidence" is, of course, the discovery of the animal itself. Other evidence: In case of mammals, tracks, dens, or burrows; in case of birds nests, dropped feathers, owl "pellets," etc.; shed skin of snake, turtle eggs; egg masses of certain fish—and so on. Scout must identify the animal from the evidence discovered.

5. TAKE A HIKE

The Second Class Hike[1]—After you have done the above, prove yourself a *Scout Hiker* by taking a hike,

---

[1] NOTE on the SECOND CLASS HIKE
If a physician certifies that the Scout's physical condition for an indeterminable time does not permit the Second Class Hike, the Advancement Committee of the Local Council may authorize the following substitution for the hike: The requirements for any one "outdoor" Merit Badge (such as camping, pioneering, nature subjects, etc.) which the Scout is capable of meeting. *In EACH individual case, application for a substitution must be made in advance by the Scoutmaster to the Advancement Committee and the specific substitution must be approved in writing by the Committee, after thorough review.*

This provision is to take care of boys seriously handicapped physically (cripples, heart cases) and will be applied in extreme hardship cases only. In case the Committee authorizes the Requirements for an "outdoor" Merit Badge that is restricted to First Class Scouts, the boy will meet the Requirements, but will not be eligible for the badge itself until he reaches First Class.

properly clothed and equipped, with your Patrol (or, if this is impossible, with at least one companion approved by your Scoutmaster). On this hike, cover a route of a total distance of not less than five miles indicated on a map or map sketch; show correct hike style and highway safety, cook a meal, clean up, and return in good condition.

This is a "climax" experience, to wind up the boy's work for Second Class. It is a separate hike, taken after the boy has had a satisfactory experience in Scoutcraft on previous hikes. The "one companion approved by your Scoutmaster" may be a junior leader, a responsible boy already at least Second Class, or even the boy's own father. The hike is to cover all the activities of a real hike as listed.

FIRST CLASS SCOUT

To become a FIRST CLASS SCOUT, you do the following:

I. Scout Spirit

While a Second Class Scout, satisfy your Scout leaders that you do your best, in your everyday life, to live up to:

1. The Scout Oath or Promise
2. The Scout Law
3. The Scout Motto
4. The Scout Slogan

The boy's term as a Second Class Scout is best reviewed at a meeting of the Patrol Leaders' Council, where each leader who has had contact with the boy may have a chance to express himself as to his Scout Spirit. Decision may be taken by the Scoutmaster or left by him to the vote of the Leaders' Council. If the boy's performance has been unsatisfactory, he will be given a chance to improve until the leaders again take up his case. The Scoutmaster may also want to talk informally with the boy's parents, teachers, and others.

II. Scout Participation

While a Second Class Scout, show to the satisfaction of your Scout leaders that you:

1. Work actively in Patrol and Troop meetings, outdoor activities and service projects.

The Troop and Patrol records will show the boy's attendance. The testimony of the leaders involved, preferably given at a meeting of the Patrol Leaders' Council, will indicate how "actively" the boy participated. The Troop will set its own standards for "active participation." **The absolute minimum of time for showing such participation is thirty days from the day the boy became a Second Class Scout.**

2. Do your share in helping in your home, your school, your church and your community.

The Scoutmaster will check *informally* with home, school and church to learn if the boy is helpful — in the spirit of the daily Good Turn. No written or signed statements should be called for.

3. Take care of things that belong to you, the property of others, and your country's natural resources.

The emphasis here is CONSERVATION—proper care of personal belongings, protection of other people's property, safeguarding wild life (see Second Class Requirement).

4. Maintain a personal savings plan (such as regular payments into a savings account or into a savings project sponsored by your family or Troop).

The *regular practice* of thrift is what counts. (See Second Class Requirement.)

III. Scoutcraft

1. PREPARE FOR SCOUT CAMPING

a. Clothing and Equipment—Present yourself for inspection suitably clothed for the locality, season and weather, and equipped and packed for an overnight camp.

If the boy is ready in the summer, his clothing will be that for summer camping; if in the winter, suitable for winter camping. Equipment may be packed in a regular pack, pack basket or pack frame, or in an improvised pack carried on the back.

b. Health Protection—Explain methods used in camp for care of food and drinking water, fire protection and waste disposal.

The boy must show that he knows what is involved so that he will be able to use these methods when he goes camping.

c. First Aid—Give artificial respiration for three minutes. Explain danger of taking laxative for pain in stomach. Improvise a sterile dressing. Use triangular bandage for arm sling and as binder for wounds on head, hand, knee and foot. Demonstrate first aid for one problem from each of the following groups (problems to be chosen by your leader after you have trained for all of them):

Arterial bleeding from face, throat, arm, leg.
Shock, heat exhaustion, sunstroke, frostbite, internal poisoning.
Puncture wounds from splinter, nail, fishhook, dog bite, poisonous snake bite.
Fracture of collarbone, upper arm, forearm, lower leg.

Explain under what circumstances a person should or should not be moved. Improvise a stretcher and, with helpers, under your direction, transport a presumably unconscious person.

Techniques are found in *Handbook for Boys* and in *Scout Field Book*. *Sterilize dressing:* By scorching gauze, dry baking or boiling. Triangular bandage to be applied over dressing. Specific problems for testing to be unknown to boy until he is called upon to demonstrate them. *Improvised stretcher:* Poles with shirts, blankets, rope. The problems may be "staged" and thus become an interesting part of outdoor activities.

2. GET THE LAY OF THE LAND

a. Directions—Lay out on the ground a true north-south line with the help of the sun by day *and* the North Star by night, and a magnetic north-south line using a compass.

The "line" may be scratched in the ground, or may be a pole laid in the proper direction. The boy should have a general idea of the difference between *true* north-south and *magnetic* north-south.

b. Measuring—With simple means and using your own personal measurements, determine a height you cannot reach (such as a tree) and a width you cannot walk (such as a river or a canyon).

"Simple means" involve small sticks (as in the pencil method for measuring height of tree), rustic poles (as in the inch-to-foot method of measuring heights), stakes (in triangle method of measuring width of river). "Personal measurements" needed may be length of step, span of hand, width of thumb, and so on. Techniques are found in the *Handbook for Boys* and in *Scout Field Book*.

c. Map Sketching—Select a site suitable for a Patrol camp and make a map sketch for laying it out. Make a map sketch by which someone unfamiliar with your camp location can find his way to it over a distance of at least two miles.

Map sketch of camp should use proper conventional signs for natural features, with tents, fireplace, and other camp features indicated by simple signs. *Two-mile map sketch* may be made from memory, after boy has been over route. It is not a map, but a rough sketch not concerned with specific distances and compass degrees. The main features of this sketch will be landmarks that indicate where turns are to be made, types of roads designated by proper signs (path, dirt road, highway), north arrow to show general lay of land.

3. LIVE IN CAMP

a. Camp Making—Sharpen an axe and use it for cutting light wood into tent pegs. Locate a tent site and pitch a tent, fastening the guy line with a taut-line hitch. Prepare a comfortable ground bed. Improvise a piece of camp equipment requiring lashings.

Generally self-explanatory. "Comfortable ground bed" may be made of grass, leaves, boughs or may simply be ground cleared and smoothed, hip and shoulder holes scooped out, use of waterproof ground sheet and sufficient blankets. Camp equipment requiring lashings: Camp broom or rake, fire crane, kitchen rack, wash stand, latrine seat, and so on.

b. Wood Lore—Find and identify ten different trees or shrubs. Tell their uses.

"Uses" may be suitability for fuel, poles for pioneering, wood for tool handles, edible parts. In the identification, the Scout may identify ten *trees* only, or ten *shrubs* only, or a combination of trees and shrubs to the number of *ten in all*.

4. COOK YOUR MEALS

a. Camp Cookery—Prepare in the open, for yourself and a companion from raw ingredients, a complete breakfast of fruit, hot cereal and bacon-and-eggs (or griddle cakes); and a complete dinner of meat (or fish or poultry), vegetable, dessert and bread (or biscuits, or twist baked on a stick).

While Second Class cooking provided for an individual meal, First Class introduces "buddy cooking" as the next step toward cooking for the Patrol. Breakfast may be prepared on one camping trip, dinner on another. The dishes are to be served as a complete meal, in their proper order. Breakfast fruit may be raw fruit (citrus, banana, etc.). Dessert for dinner must be a cooked dessert, such as stewed fruit, pudding. Bread (or biscuits) may be baked in reflector pan, Dutch oven, etc. For recipes, see *Handbook* and *Field Book*.

b. Edible Wild Plants—Find and identify four different edible wild greens, roots or fruits.

Greens range from watercress to dandelion leaves; roots from cattail to Indian cucumber; fruits from wild grape and numerous berries, to crabapple and a great variety of nuts. Even in winter snow-country, a Scout will have little trouble finding four wild "edibles": Certain lichens and tree buds can be eaten, black birch and sassafras which provide materials for teas are acceptable. It is not necessary to collect and cook the edible plants found.

5. GO SWIMMING

Swimming[2]—Tell what precautions must be taken for a safe swim. Jump feet first into water over your head

---

[2] NOTE on the FIRST CLASS SWIMMING REQUIREMENT
Under certain very exceptional conditions, where the climate keeps the water cold the year round, and/or where there are no suitable and accessible places within a reasonable traveling distance to swim at any time during the year, or in cases where a physician certifies that the Scout's physical condition for an indeterminable time does not permit swimming, the Advancement Committee of the Local Council may authorize a substitution for the First Class Swim (as indicated on the "Application For Substitution for Swimming Requirement for First Class Rank" Cat. No. 4418).
In EACH individual case, application for a substitution must be made in advance by the Scoutmaster to the Advancement Committee on the special standard form provided for this purpose, and the specific substitution must be approved in writing by the Committee, after thorough review.

As stated, this provision is to take care of cases where "very exceptional conditions" keep a boy from becoming a First Class Scout by preventing him from learning how to swim. The procedure for approval of a substitution is deliberately kept involved to discourage anyone from attempting to evade the swim in cases where a bit of ingenuity might overcome the obstacle. Complete interpretation is found on the Application Form Cat. No. 4418.

in depth. Swim fifty yards. During the swim, stop, make a sharp turn, level off and resume swimming.

By precautions are meant: 1. Have Medical Examination and follow doctor's orders; 2. Know your swimming ability and stick to the swimming place that fits your skill; 3. Always swim with a buddy; 4. Wait two hours after meal; 5. Follow all rules and orders given by waterfront men; 6. NEVER dive into unknown water, NEVER take a dare to show off in the water, NEVER swim long distances unless someone goes along with a boat. The 50-yard swim itself is self-explanatory.

6. GET A MESSAGE THROUGH

Morse Signaling—Know the International Morse Code, including necessary procedure signals. Using this code, send and receive, by any suitable means, a message of 20 words (100 letters) over a distance of at least 100 yards.

"Suitable means" are flags, blinker, loud sound device, and similar arrangements. No speed is involved. Not more than 5 errors permitted and none that garble the meaning of the message. Procedure signals included: For sending, Attention, Error, End of Word, End of Sentence, End of Message; for receiving, Go Ahead, Repeat, Word Received, Message Received.

7. GO CAMPING

The First Class Camp—After you have done the above, prove yourself a *Scout Camper* by camping, properly clothed and equipped, on a suitable camp site for not less than twenty-four hours with your Patrol (or, if this is impossible, with at least one companion approved by your Scoutmaster). During this camp, cook at least one hot meal, sleep in a tent or improvised shelter or under the stars, keep camp clean and safe, and leave camp site in good condition.

This is a "climax" experience, to wind up the boy's work for First Class. It is a separate camp, taken after the boy has had the preliminary Scoutcraft experiences on previous hikes and camps. The "one companion approved by your Scoutmaster" may be a junior leader, a responsible boy already First Class, or even the boy's own father. The camp is to cover all the activities of a real camp, as listed.

STAR SCOUT

To become a Star Scout you must be a First Class Scout or the Explorer equivalent* and:

I. Scout Spirit

Satisfy your Scout or Explorer leaders that you do your best in your everyday life, to live up to:

---

*Explorer equivalent of First Class is any of the following: Bronze Award; Outdoor Skills Rating; Ordinary Sea Explorer; Observer Air Explorer.

1. The Scout Oath or Promise
2. The Scout Law
3. The Scout Motto
4. The Scout Slogan

> The purpose of the Scout Spirit requirements is to help the boy carry out the obligations of the Scout Oath and Law; to help him become self reliant; and to make it possible for him to help others by teaching him skills that might benefit other people.
>
> Before receiving the award for Star Rank, satisfactory evidence that he has fulfilled the requirements in Scout Spirit will be required. This evidence will be obtained from his parents, school teacher, employer, pastor, Sunday school teacher, or others who know of his behavior and activities.

II. Scout Participation

1. While a First Class Scout or the Explorer equivalent for a period of at least three months, show to the satisfaction of your leaders that you:

   a. Are active in meetings, outdoor activities and service projects of your Unit and dependable in your Unit obligations.

   b. Do your best to help in your home, school, church and community.

   c. Take care of things that belong to you and respect the property of others.

   d. Understand how to use wisely and conserve our natural resources (soil, water, forests, grasslands, wild life) and have taken part in a conservation project.

   > The boy must present definite evidence from those who know him that he understands how to use wisely our natural resources and that he has taken part in a conservation project.

2. Have earned *one* Merit Badge from the CITIZENSHIP or PUBLIC SERVICE groups. (See pages 9-10 for Merit Badge groups.)

   > The purpose of the Scout Participation requirements is to encourage a boy to take part in the activities and service projects of his Unit. Emphasis is placed on service obligations to home, school, church, community and nation; also evidence of developing leadership ability.
   >
   > Satisfactory evidence will be secured of participation in Unit activities and service projects, as well as in obligations to home, school, church, community and nation.

III. Scoutcraft and Life Interests

1. Have earned *one* Merit Badge from any of following groups: CAMPCRAFT, AQUATICS, OUTDOOR SPORTS, NATURE, CONSERVATION.

2. Have earned any *three* additional Merit Badges.*

   The purpose of the Scoutcraft and Life Interests requirements is to help further develop skill as an outdoorsman and to provide opportunities for explorations into fields of personal interest including hobbies and life work.

LIFE SCOUT

To become a Life Scout you must be a Star Scout and:

I. Scout Spirit

Satisfy your Scout or Explorer leaders that you do your best, in your everyday life, to live up to:

1. The Scout Oath or Promise
2. The Scout Law
3. The Scout Motto
4. The Scout Slogan

   Before receiving the award for Life Rank, satisfactory evidence that the boy has fulfilled the requirement in Scout Spirit on a higher level than for Star Scout rank will be secured. This evidence will come from his parents, school teacher, employer, pastor, Sunday school teacher, or others who know of his behavior and activities.

II. Scout Participation

1. While a Star Scout for a period of at least three months, show to the satisfaction of your leaders that you:

   a. Accept and carry out responsibilities in meetings, outdoor activities and service projects of your Unit.

   b. Do your best to help in your home, school, church and community.

   c. Take care of things that belong to you and respect the property of others.

   d. Have completed a conservation project approved in advance by your Unit leader.

   Satisfactory evidence of participation in Unit activities and service projects, as well as in obligations to home, church, school, community and nation, and of developing leadership ability will be obtained. Such evidence will come from those who know of your activities and ability. This conservation project should be of a more ambitious nature than that for Star Scout Rank. You must approve of the project ahead of time and help the boy decide what to do and where to get help in completing the project.

2. Have earned the First Aid Merit Badge.

*This makes a total of *five* Merit Badges required for the rank (including one from the CITIZENSHIP or PUBLIC SERVICE groups).

3. Have earned *two* Merit Badges from the CITIZENSHIP group.*

III. Scoutcraft and Life Interests

1. Have earned the following Merit Badges: *

   One from CAMPCRAFT group;
   One from OUTDOOR SPORTS or AQUATICS group;
   One from NATURE or CONSERVATION group;
   One from PERSONAL DEVELOPMENT group;
   One from any of the following groups: ANIMAL HUS-
     BANDRY, PLANT CULTIVATION, COMMUNICA-
     TION, TRANSPORTATION, BUILDING.

2. Have earned any *two* other Merit Badges.**

   The Merit Badges earned will be evidence of meeting the requirements in Scoutcraft and Life Interests.

EAGLE SCOUT

To become an Eagle Scout you must be a Life Scout and:

I. Scout Spirit

Satisfy your Scout or Explorer leaders that you do your best, in your everyday life, to live up to:

1. The Scout Oath or Promise
2. The Scout Law
3. The Scout Motto
4. The Scout Slogan

   Since the boy is working for the highest rank in Scouting, satisfactory evidence must show beyond any doubt that he lives up to the ideals of Scouting in every phase of his everyday life. Those who know him and his activities will be asked regarding his character and everyday actions.

II. Scout Participation

1. While a Life Scout for a period of at least six months show to the satisfaction of your leaders that you:

   a. Work actively as a leader in meetings, outdoor activities and service projects of your Unit.

   b. Do your best to help in your home, school, church and community.

---

*Merit Badges previously earned may be included.

**This makes a total of *ten* Merit Badges required for the rank (including First Aid and two from the CITIZENSHIP group).

c. Take care of things that belong to you and respect the property of others.

2. Have earned *one* Merit Badge from the CONSERVATION group.*

3. Have earned *three* Merit Badges from the CITIZENSHIP group.

> By this time the Scout or Explorer should have developed as a leader in his Unit and there should be no doubt as to his ability to lead in meetings, outdoor activities and service projects. You and others who know his leadership ability should be able to present evidence in his behalf. Also, there must be evidence that he has met his obligations to home, school, church and community willingly and ably.

III. Scoutcraft and Life Interests

1. Have earned the following Merit Badges:

Camping	Personal Fitness
Cooking	Public Health
Swimming	Safety
Life Saving	Firemanship
Nature	First Aid

One from OUTDOOR SPORTS group;

One from any of the following groups: ANIMAL HUS-BANDRY, PLANT CULTIVATION, COMMUNICA-TION, TRANSPORTATION, BUILDING.

Have earned any *five* other Merit Badges.**

> The Merit Badges earned will be evidence of meeting the requirements in Scoutcraft and Life Interests.

---

*Merit Badges previously earned may be included.
**This makes a total of 21 Merit Badges required for the rank.

MERIT BADGE GROUPS

1. ANIMAL HUSBANDRY

Animal Industry
Beekeeping
Beef Production
Dairying
Dog Care
First Aid to Animals
Hog & Pork Production
Pigeon Raising
Poultry Keeping
Rabbit Raising
Sheep Farming

2. AQUATICS

Canoeing
Life Saving
Rowing
Swimming

3. ARTS

Architecture
Art
Dramatics
Indian Lore

3. ARTS — *Cont.*

Mechanical Drawing
Music
Photography
Pottery
Sculpture
Woodcarving

4. BUILDING

Electricity
Farm Home & its Planning
Farm Layout & Building
Arrangement
Farm Mechanics
Home Repairs
Machinery
Masonry
Metalwork
Painting
Plumbing
Woodworking

5. CAMPCRAFT

Camping
Cooking
Pioneering
Surveying

6. CITIZENSHIP

Citizenship in the Home
Citizenship in the
Community
Citizenship in the Nation
World Brotherhood

7. COMMUNICATION

Bugling
Journalism
Printing
Radio
Signaling

8. CONSERVATION

Forestry
Soil & Water Conservation
Wildlife Management

9. CRAFTS & COLLECTIONS

Basketry
Bookbinding
Coin Collecting
Leatherwork
Stamp Collecting
Textiles

10. NATURE

Astronomy
Bird Study
Botany
Chemistry
Geology
Insect Life
Nature
Reptile Study
Weather
Zoology

11. OUTDOOR SPORTS

Archery
Athletics
Cycling
Fishing
Hiking
Horsemanship
Marksmanship
Skiing

12. PERSONAL DEVELOPMENT

Business
Farm Records &
Bookkeeping
Personal Fitness
Public Speaking
Reading
Salesmanship
Scholarship

13. PLANT CULTIVATION

Agriculture
Corn Farming
Cotton Farming
Fruit & Nut Growing
Gardening
Grasses,
Legumes & Forage
Crops
Landscape Gardening
Small Grains & Cereal
Foods

14. PUBLIC SERVICE

Fingerprinting
Firemanship
First Aid
Public Health
Safety

15. TRANSPORTATION

Automobiling
Aviation
Railroading
Seamanship

INDEX

Games indicated thus: (G). Projects indicated thus: (P)